18 TIMES AND THAT'S A FACT

A RED-EYED VIEW OF MANCHESTER UNITED'S RECORD BREAKING SEASON

JUSTIN BLUNDELL

EMPIRE PUBLICATIONS

EMPIRE PUBLICATIONS
1 Newton Street, Manchester M1 1HW
© Justin Blundell 2009

ISBN 1 901 746 59 3

Cover design and layout: Ashley Shaw

Printed in Great Britain by:
Digital Book Print Ltd, Milton Keynes, UK.

CONTENTS

INTRODUCTION

It's 2 o'clock in the morning of 22nd May 2008...

As the Red Army celebrated their third European Cup, the rain thumps down and John Terry sobs, ITV's pitchside reporter Gabriel Clark makes a beeline for Ronaldo. There's only one question he needs to ask.

"Cristiano, this must mean you're staying, it must mean you're staying".

Ronaldo nods "I'm staying put".

It was exactly what every United fan wanted to hear. Unfortunately it wasn't what Ronaldo really wanted. As soon as he left for the Euros the rumours about Madrid began. At first it sounded like the mischievous work of the slippery Ramon Calderon and his mouthpiece, *Marca*. But as Ronaldo first flirted with Madrid – saying 'I love to play in white' – and then ludicrously branded himself a slave (a £120,000 a week one at that), it was clear he was desperate to get his 'dream' move to the Bernabeu. For Reds it was hard to take in. Only one player in recent memory has wanted to leave the club while still at his peak. And with all due respect to Andrei Kanchelskis he was no Ronaldo.

Hard-liners, disgusted by his disloyalty (and the sight of him holidaying in his micro-shorts), were all for taking the £75 million Real were meant to be offering. His legacy was tainted, he was going to go sometime anyway, so why not now? Optimists hoped that it was just another of Ronaldo's summer flings and that somehow everything would be OK. Most Reds just wanted to hang on to him because it seemed absolutely vital that United – European champions remember – showed that no club, especially Madrid, could boss them around.

Unsurprisingly, Fergie agreed with the majority, flying out for a peace summit and talking Ronaldo round, just as he had done with Eric back in 1995. A fortnight before the season started, Ronaldo, now recovering from an ankle operation that would rule him out until mid-September, finally announced he'd be staying at the plantation. It was a victory. But it was a victory that had come at a major cost, both to Ronaldo's reputation and his legacy. A couple more years like he'd just given us and he could have gone to Spain with our thanks and blessings ringing in his ears. Now everything he's ever achieved in a Red shirt will be accompanied by a great big ugly 'but'...

The Ronaldo saga tainted the summer. But even if he'd spent it declaring his undying love for us it would hardly have been one to remember. The council followed through on their pledge not to have a victory parade, and in the process cost Manchester the best free advert it would ever have. United chased Berbatov but couldn't get Spurs to sell, not in time for the new season anyway. Queiroz, who just won't accept that he's a great coach but a bad manager, couldn't resist the lure of the Portugal job and became the first man to leave Old Trafford with Fergie's blessing twice. Tevez remained curiously unsigned. Mark Hughes did his own legacy no good by 'doing a Schmeichel' and taking the City job. And a day with Gary Neville (who stood in for Fergie as tour guide) convinced Cardiff 'wonderkid' Aaron Ramsey to sign for Arsenal rather than us.

On the flip side, United retained the Charity Shield with another penalties win, this time against Portsmouth. Wayne and Coleen managed to get hitched without any of their relatives kicking off and Rio was amusingly crowned Chief Fiwagbaloo by the King of Nigeria. But there can't have been many Reds who weren't mightily relieved when the first game, against Newcastle, finally came around. Unlike in 1999, when we wanted the summer to last forever so we could bask in the memories of Barcelona, this season couldn't get started quickly enough...

FAPL 17/08/2008

UNITED 1 NEWCASTLE 1
Martins 22, Fletcher 24.

YOU CAN PICTURE the scene down at Carrington as Fergie greeted his players after the summer break. "Youse all did well last year," he'd say whilst fixing anyone who dared to nod with an icy stare. "Now the challenge is to do the exact same thing again this time around." As we've shown time and time again in the Premiership years, the great thing about United is that they're well capable of taking that sort of challenge head on.

Mind you, if the players really were told to play last season again, they didn't have to be so literal about it. A year ago the season started with a drab penalty win in the Community Shield against Chelsea, an injury crisis and a 0-0 draw against Reading, a team we were fancied to steamroller. This time around it started with a drab penalty win in the Community Shield against Portsmouth, an injury crisis and, now this, a 1-1 draw against another team we were fancied to steamroller. Worst of all, thanks to a quirk of the fixture list and the not so Super Cup game in Monaco, United wouldn't get the chance to make it up to Old Trafford regulars for another 41 days...

GOAL ACTION

0-1 (22): United don't tend to fall behind when they're playing at home on the opening day. In fact it's only happened twice in 24 years (against Fulham in 2001 and Leicester in 1998). But it appears Obafemi Martins is no respecter of history as he capitalises on a lapse of concentration from his marker Fletcher to head a corner past Van der Sar...

1-1 (24): Fortunately Fletch wastes no time making up for his error, making a smart near-post dart to poke Giggs's low centre past Given.

WHAT WAS GOOD?

NOT A LOT. But then again, look at that team (the midfield that ended the game consisted of O'Shea, Scholes, Possebon and Rafael).

NEWCASTLE'S PACY ARGENTINE WINGER GUTIERREZ: who looked like a star in the making on his debut… before disappearing, like his new team, into a season of despair.

WHAT WAS SURPRISING?

THE OPEN-AIR URINALS that had popped up in the summer at the side of the Development Office. Whatever next…

WHAT WAS BAD?

JUST LOOK WHO WE WERE MISSING BY THE END OF THE GAME: ROONEY – knackered, TÉVEZ – bereavement, GIGGS – off with hamstring, CARRICK – off with damaged ankle, HARGREAVES – out with his dodgy knees, NANI – suspended, MANUCHO – metatarsal, ANDERSON – Olympics, SAHA – take your pick, FOSTER – likewise, RONALDO – on crutches after his operation, PARK – no one seems to be sure.

VIEWS FROM THE PRESSBOX

"For the second Sunday in a row Manchester United showed why they need to recruit a 'top striker', as their manager Sir Alex Ferguson put it in his programme notes, but, unlike last weekend, they didn't get away with it.

"They defeated Portsmouth in the meaningless Community Shield but, this time, when it really mattered, there were no penalties. United had to rely on open play and, worryingly for them, were found lacking. It's a problem Ferguson said needed to be addressed last week. Now it's even more urgent." – *The Indie bemoans United's latest striker shortage…*

"The longer Manchester United battered against Newcastle United's well-blockaded backdoor yesterday, the higher Dimitar Berbatov's value rose. With Chelsea finding their stride so quickly, the Double-winners know they may have to stump up £30 million to bring the striker from Tottenham Hotspur. On this evidence, they cannot wait." – *So does the Telegraph.*

"The elation of Newcastle United's supporters [at the end] was in stark contrast to the mood among the home fans, who may have been wondering what kind of deficit their team will face when they return to Old Trafford in late September. By a quirk of the fixture list, complicated by their participation in the Uefa Super Cup against Zenit St Petersburg on August 29, in Monaco, United do not have another home game in the Barclays Premier League until the visit of Bolton Wanderers on September 27, by which time they will have been to Portsmouth, Liverpool and Chelsea without the injured Cristiano Ronaldo. This was not the game in which they would have expected to drop points in a tough start to the season, but, with Ronaldo sidelined, Carlos Tévez absent because of a family bereavement and Dimitar Berbatov yet to complete his protracted move from Tottenham Hotspur, they lacked the wit and the penetration to break down a surprisingly spirited Newcastle." – *The Times paints the same depressing picture.*

NEWCASTLE – THE VERBALS

"I did not expect to lose a goal at a set-piece to a header from a guy who is 5ft 8in. Once we got the equaliser, I thought we would kick on. But while we were the better team, they were always a threat on the counter-attack - and we have to take into account the personnel we have missing." – *Fergie's phlegmatic...*

"The attitude was spot-on and I've told them in the dressing-room that if they can come here and do that, they can go anywhere and do it." – *Keegan's delighted.*

"We have been handicapped by the fixture list but there are 37 games to go, so we have plenty of time." – *Fergie starts the mind games early.*

MATCH FACTS

UNITED: VAN DER SAR, BROWN, VIDIC, *CHIEF FIWAGBALOO*, EVRA, FLETCHER, CARRICK (O'SHEA 25), SCHOLES, GIGGS (POSSEBON 63), CAMPBELL (RAFAEL DA SILVA 80), ROONEY
BOOKED: CAMPBELL, BROWN, ROONEY
NEWCASTLE: GIVEN, BEYE, TAYLOR, COLOCCINI, N'ZOGBIA, MILNER, BUTT, GUTHRIE, GUTIERREZ, DUFF, MARTINS [KEEGAN]
ATT: 75,512 **REF:** MIKE RILEY **H-T:** 1-1

OTHER SCORES

ARSENAL 1 WEST BROM 0, CHELSEA 4 PORTSMOUTH 0, SUNDERLAND 0 LIVERPOOL 1

"Ronaldo's ripped body, slicked-back hair, shiny white teeth and jewellery swung the votes his way. He looks like any gay man or woman's dream."

NEWS PART I

JOHN TERRY IS chosen as England captain. Presumably Fabio Capello couldn't handle the thought of all that sobbing if he'd chosen Rio or Gerrard instead. Tubby Scouser Brian Barwick gets dumped from his job as FA Chief Executive. Does that mean we'll get some easier cup draws this year? David Gill denies he's going to replace him. Anderson has to settle for a bronze medal at the Olympics as Brazil get thumped 3-0 by Argentina in the semi-finals, and then beat Belgium 3-0 in the third place play-off. Thaksin Shinawatra slinks back to London after deciding that facing those pesky corruption charges in Thailand might not be such a good idea after all. And just months after Fergie is spotted with a sympathetic arm around Arsene Wenger (after Arsenal lost at Old Trafford) comes another disturbing sign that the two mortal enemies are starting to get on. Or was there a more devious motive behind his willingness to sanction Mickey Silvestre's cut-price move to Arsenal?

TAKING THE MICKEY

After 9 years, 361 games, 10 goals, 5 Premier League titles, 1 FA Cup and 1 League Cup and countless pub arguments on whether he's a liability or not, Silvestre moves to Arsenal for £750,000.

"He's a really nice lad and a great professional. We have no complaints, we got the price we wanted and we wish him well. We could have been selfish and said 'you're going to be a reserve for the rest of your contract'. We recognise the service he's given us." – *Mickey leaves with Fergie's blessing.*

"See, I can surprise sometimes, because he was one signing who people didn't suspect. I wanted to take him a few years ago when they extended his contract with Manchester United. He has a great team attitude and we're a bit light experience-wise in the dressing-room." – *Wenger's pleased with himself after beating City and Sunderland to the signing of Silvestre. But should he be? As Reds know all too well, Mickey can look like a Rolls Royce of a defender. He can also look like a dozy clown. Was Fergie effectively selling Wenger the football version of a Trojan horse?*

PUB QUIZ QUESTION OF THE WEEK★

Who was the last player to move from United to Arsenal?

NEWS PART II

The papers go to town on the idea that Fergie will coach the GB Olympic team in the London Olympics. Don't they know how old he'll be in 2012? Lee Martin's off to Forest on loan. Former United kid Ben Collett, 23, is awarded more than £4.5m in compensation for the broken leg he suffered against Boro reserves in 2003 that ended his career. And Ronaldo beats off competition from Judy Garland, Elton John and Liza Minnelli to win the 'gay icon of the year award'. Was it the silver micro-shorts that swung it?

INTERNATIONAL FRIENDLY REDS

Wes Brown grabs his first ever international goal as England draw 2-2 at home with the Czech Republic. Ferdinand and Rooney also feature. John O'Shea helps the Republic to a 1-1 draw in Norway. Evans and Fletcher are in opposition as ten-man Northern Ireland draw 0-0 at Hampden Park. Nani scores the first in Portugal's 5-0 battering of the Faroe Islands. Tévez plays for Argentina in their 0-0 draw in Belarus. Evra's France beat Sweden 3-2... and Tottenham's Berbatov scores both Bulgaria's goals in their 2-1 win over Bosnia Herzegovina.

CRY ME A RIVER

"It means the world to me. It is a great achievement for me. I am very proud. I think I am a role model on and off the field [*ARF!*]. I do a lot, I wear my heart on my sleeve and do everything I can do." – *New England captain – and former club brawler – John Terry.*

SCHPEAK OF THE DEVIL
(youtube clip of the month)

Forget the gorilla on the drums, that fat kid singing Backstreet Boys or any other youtube hit. Steve McClaren, the new manager of FC Twente, makes one of the best youtube appearances of the year, suddenly adopting a comical Dutch accent in his interviews with the press.

BLUE LOON

The opening salvo of the season from City chief executive Garry Cook, the latest in a long line of amusing City 'characters' who just don't know when to speak… and when to shut up:

"Is Dr Thaksin a nice guy? Yes. Is he a great guy to play golf with? Yes. Has he got the finances to run a club? Yes. I really care about those three things. I need a left-back who can win tackles, get the crosses in and Jo can bang them in. Whether he's guilty of something over there, I can't worry too much about." – *Cook on the man Amnesty International called a 'human rights abuser of the worst kind'*.

"He has not skipped bail. He's not gone back to face the charges." - *Er, that must be OK then.*

"I worked at a company – Nike – where we were accused of child labour rights issues. I managed to have a career there for 15 years and I believed we were innocent of most of the issues. Morally, I felt confident in that environment. Morally, I feel comfortable in this environment." – *What a credit to our national game Cook is.*

"It is very loose [the fit and proper person test]. It's almost a tongue-in-cheek term that you would use for Premier League football over the last 10 years. There are plenty of unfit and improper individuals." – *In fairness, he's got a point here. There are plenty of them just in Manchester.*

RUMOUR OF THE WEEK

The Sunday Mirror *reckons Rooney might have been deliberately poisoned in close season break in Nigeria.*

"The Man Utd stars think there has been foul play because they all ate and drank the same things, yet only Rooney and Michael Carrick - who made a swift recovery - fell ill. One United player said: "Wayne does eat and drink more than any of the other lads [which could explain the belly he brought back with him from his summer honeymoon] - and some say that might be why he was the only one who was ill."

And a club insider added: "There has been a lot of speculation as to what could have happened. It could have simply been a joke or something more sinister - such as part of a betting scam."

QUOTES OF THE WEEK

"My wife and I will stay in England where democracy is more important." – *Thaksin Shinawatra, Amnesty's favourite former PM, changes his tune now he finds himself on the other side of the law.*

"We'll be as big as Manchester United. If I didn't have that goal,

I wouldn't be here. Can we win the Premier League? Yes. Will we? It might take a bit longer. Can we win the Champions League? Growing up at Nike, you don't sit around saying, 'Can we?' You say, 'We will'." – *Garry Cook again. Ribs hurting yet?*

"Ronaldinho was up for it but he got a call from AC Milan. One day we're going to be a club that players say, 'Manchester City just called me, I had no choice'." – *And again. Hahahahaha.*

NON-FOOTBALL QUOTE OF THE WEEK

"We felt it was something appropriate and that it would be interpreted as an affectionate gesture." - *Spanish basketball player Jose Manuel Calderon defends his team-mates for posing for a 'slitty eyed' photo during the Beijing Olympics. And they wonder why Spain's got a reputation for racism...*

QUOTE OF THE WEEK

"It's just the way it is here. It's so [that] Dutch people can understand." - *Schteve McClaren explains that accent.*

RUNNER-UP

"Ronaldo's ripped body, slicked-back hair, shiny white teeth and jewellery swung the votes his way. He looks like any gay man or woman's dream." - *A spokesman for gaygolddiggers explains why Ronaldo is Canal Street's favourite guy.*

★ Brian Kidd in 1974 (for £100,000)

FAPL 25/08/2008

PORTSMOUTH 0 UNITED 1
Fletcher 32

IT SOUNDS CRAZY now. It was crazy then. But at the time this really did feel like a game United had to win. The new-look Chelsea, armed with an extra weapon in Deco and liberated by the arrival of a manager who seemed to know how to entertain as well as win, were looking worryingly strong. Liverpool had started with a bang too. A defeat or draw at our bogey ground tonight and injury-hit United, who had a pointless date with Zenit St Petersburg at the weekend, could have entered September a hefty eight points behind all their rivals.

In the circumstances this has to go down as one of the season's great, unsung performances, and results. United didn't create massive amounts – though only a dozy linesman stopped Rooney scoring a deserved second – but the passing and movement, harassing and tackling were outstanding. The polish and fluidity of Scholes, Fletcher, Rooney and Evra in particular was exceptional. But it was Anderson who deserved a special mention. He'd spent most of pre-season playing almost every other day for the bronze-medal winning Brazilian Olympic team. He'd spent most of the week on a plane home. He hadn't even had time to braid his hair which made him look like he'd just peed on a pylon. But jetlag or no jetlag, he was outstanding. If only he could stop himself turning into a nervous wreck near the opposition goal, what a player he would be...

GOAL!

1-0 (32): Up and running... Scholes wins a free-kick deep in United's half. 11 passes later Tévez is slipping a perfect eye-of-the-needle ball inside Glen Johnson for the galloping Evra. His low cross to the near post was always going to be tough for Campbell. Fletcher's late run makes it fatal, the ball ricocheting off both men and beating James and Distin's desperate goal-line lunge.

VIEW FROM THE PRESSBOX

"This is still very much a patched-up side for Sir Alex Ferguson, considering the high proportion of absentees in midfield, and the substitutes' bench looked like a Carling Cup tie come early. Even so, there is an ethos at the club that extends beyond the celebrity names and even a second-string United are capable of putting together passing movements of exquisite beauty, verve and ambition, such as the one that brought the goal." – *The Times*

FRATTON PARK – THE VERBALS

"We played some excellent football tonight. This is a difficult place to come, so it is a bonus to come here and win. We tried to play a system where the players would be comfortable. We wanted to have Anderson playing centrally, close to Carlos Tévez. We let Paul Scholes control the game, and used Darren Fetcher's energy." – *Fergie the tactician.*

"His barnet is shocking at the minute! His extensions have come out and he's been in China where he's had nobody with the capability to braid him up. Hopefully now he's back in Manchester he can get hold of the person who normally does it for him!" – *Rio voices concerns about Anderson's grooming...*

"Anderson did well... until he got to 60 minutes and started blowing! No, we have a little joke with him about that kind of thing. But he's a fantastic footballer with great abilities and we've not seen the best of him yet, I'm sure." – *And his fitness.*

MATCH FACTS

PORTSMOUTH: JAMES, KABOUL, CAMPBELL, DISTIN, JOHNSON, DIOP, DAVIS (UTAKA 66), DIARRA, ARMAND TRAORE (THOMAS 56), CROUCH, DEFOE [REDKNAPP]
BOOKED: DIOP, DEFOE
UNITED: VAN DER SAR, BROWN, FERDINAND, VIDIC, O'SHEA, FLETCHER, ANDERSON (POSSEBON 76), SCHOLES, EVRA, ROONEY, TÉVEZ
BOOKED: BROWN, FLETCHER.
FRATTON PARK ATT: 20,540 REF: CHRIS FOY H-T: 1-0

OTHER SCORES

LIVERPOOL 2 BORO 1; FULHAM 1 ARSENAL 0; WIGAN 0 CHELSEA 1

"Manchester's main attraction is considered to be the timetable at the railway station, where trains leave for other, less rainy cities"

NEWS

SIT DOWN AND take a drink, this one's gonna hurt. After 4½ years and 3 appearances, the contract of Dong Fangzhou – many Reds' idea of the worst centre-forward ever to wear the shirt – is terminated by mutual consent.

More sadly Louis Saha, who could have been an excellent United player, is packed off to Everton on a pay-as-you-play deal. Somehow he manages to pass his medical – which begs the question whether Everton used the same quack who gave the thumbs up to Hargreaves's busted knees. Manucho gets a work permit and a metatarsal injury – both of which seem to be basic requirements for United forwards these days. Dimitar Berbatov moves a step forward to sulking his way out of White Hart Lane – and into Old Trafford? - as he gets himself dropped from the Spurs squad for the Sunderland game...

...And Vidic gets himself stitched up by Russian magazine *Football Weekly*. Made up or not, though, you have to say it's a wonderful rant...

'RANT' OF THE WEEK (THE POTTED HIGHLIGHTS)

"In Russia and Serbia the people's way of life is similar. In England it's totally different. Here they just don't have time to feel the joy of life. Throughout the week they work so hard. They only talk to people at lunch. Then in the evening they watch TV so they can get up early for work the next day." – *Love the idea that Muscovites radiate the 'joy of life'. Anyone see a smile in Moscow in May?*

"I will never stay to live in England, that's for sure. You get only a brief glimpse of sunlight before it's all cloudy again. The winters are mild, but in summer the temperatures seldom go higher than 20C. And it rains, rains, rains." – *Do you know what Moscow's average monthly maximum temperature is between October and March? 9, 2, -5, -9, -6 & 0...*

"In future, I would like to test myself in another top league. I'm thinking of Spain. At least there will be no reason to complain about the weather. In England, they say that Manchester is the city of rain. Its main attraction is considered to be the timetable at the railway station, where trains leave for other, less rainy cities." – *Priceless.*

DENIAL OF THE WEEK

"I'd like to clarify that I did not make these particular remarks. I spoke about the difficulty I had settling in to life in Manchester, but that does not reflect how I feel now. I enjoy my life very much as a footballer at Manchester United and I'm very happy to be a part of this great club. I think I show that in the way I play every week. I also have far too much respect for the people of Manchester, and England, to criticise them in this way." – *Welcome words from Vidic.*

THE NEW MICHAEL FISH
(Good spot from football365):

According to Nemanja Vidic, the people of Manchester only catch "a brief glimpse of sunlight before it's all cloudy again. The winters are mild, but in summer the temperatures seldom go higher than 20C. And it rains, rains, rains".

Today's forecast for Manchester from the BBC: 'A high of 20 degrees with rain to follow in the afternoon.'

CHAMPIONS LEAGUE NEWS

We've only just got rid of the smell of one set of drunk Glaswegians. Now we've got to ready ourselves for another Scottish invasion after being paired with Celtic in Group E of the Champions League. Giuseppe Rossi's Villarreal and Bruce Rioch's Aalborg make up the rest of the group. Chelsea, Arsenal and Liverpool (who somehow survived a battering by Standard Liege in the qualifiers) all get straightforward draws too, with 'Big Cup' B-listers Atletico Madrid, Roma and Porto providing their only serious opposition.

QUOTES OF THE WEEK

"So it's Man United? Here we go again! Oh well, if you're going to play in the Champions League you might as well come up against the Champions League champions. It doesn't get any easier does it?" – *Celtic boss Gordon Strachan after being drawn with the reigning Euro champions for the 3rd year on the row.*

"I did not select him because I do not feel he is focused and I do not feel he would be good for the dressing room or team effort. It doesn't matter how good a player is if he is not in the right frame of mind - then he will not perform well" - *Juande Ramos explains why he dumped Berbatov.*

"I'm now in Tottenham but no one can disagree with me wanting to follow my dream. I'm not angry about the decision of Juande Ramos to name me as a substitute. I'm not crying. But if I was laughing when I was on the bench, people would say I was an idiot. I noticed that Eric Cantona never smiled but I don't know if anyone ever asked him why he didn't look happier." – *Berbatov's riposte. Nice Cantona reference too.*

SLINKING BACK HOME
More nice work from football365:

Having had his dreams - and possibly career - torn to shreds by Sir Alex's admirable obstinacy over Cristiano Ronaldo, Spanish daily *AS*'s man in Manchester has just one more thing to say before possibly being handed his marching orders after writing his expense-account funded rubbish for the past two months.

In Sunday's edition, the hapless hack returned to his favourite haunt – lurking outside Ronaldo's mock tudor mansion – to try and fail to get a promise from the Portuguese pouter that one day, even in a parallel universe, he will wear the white shirt of Madrid.

"He's back to work," sighed the *AS* correspondent getting in one last dig before having his pen and dictaphone taken away from him. "In the constant rain that inundates Manchester, even in August where the thermometer doesn't go over 15 degrees".

POT, KETTLE, REAL

Anti-Madridistas will like this too. Real quiver with 'shock' and 'outrage' as Chelsea – prematurely as it turned out – announce the signing of Robinho:

"Real Madrid profoundly regret the conduct of the Chelsea directors, who despite knowing perfectly well the decision not to transfer the player, have continued making declarations and have gone as far as to sell shirts of the player through their official website." *Reads a statement from the club. Hmmm.*

As a quick reminder, here are a few random statements taken from another transfer saga of the summer:

"Manchester United is not a club that sells its main assets. In order to service our debts we need a very successful team on the pitch, and you don't achieve that by selling Cristiano Ronaldo" - *David Gill, May 20.*

'Further to Friday's press speculation about where Cristiano Ronaldo's future lies, the club has moved to reiterate its stance on the matter: United are not listening to offers' - *Man Utd Official Website, June 20.*

"We made it clear to them [Real Madrid] from day one we wouldn't welcome a bid, it wouldn't be accepted and therefore I don't think there is not much point in putting one in" - *David Gill, July 23. Take breath*

QUOTE OF THE WEEK

"Its main attraction is considered to be the timetable at the railway station, where trains leave for other, less rainy cities" - The highlight of the Football Weekly's naughty – but brilliant – Vidic 'rant'.

29/08/2008
EUROPEAN SUPER CUP FINAL
UNITED 1 ZENIT ST PETERSBURG 2
Pogrebnyak 45, Danny 59, Vidic 73

THE COMMUNITY SHIELD is a trumped up friendly that only Scousers count as a proper trophy but it does at least whet your appetite for the new season. The Club World Cup makes itself look ridiculous by finding room for more teams from Oceania and Japan than anywhere else... but it does at least give us the chance to sort out who's the best club side in the world. But the European Super Cup? Try finding a single saving grace there. It's a pointless game on a crap pitch in a soulless stadium played at a time when all you want to do is watch United get stuck into the league. And if that sounds like sour grapes because United lost to Zenit (deservedly), it really isn't. Even if we'd battered the Russians this would still have felt like a massive waste of time.

PS: And as for you Scholesy, what the **** were you thinking of son?

MATCH ACTION

0-1 (45): The last time we made the Super Cup final, back in '99, we saved half the team for a league game against Newcastle a couple of days later. And went down tamely to Lazio. This time Fergie could choose as many big names as he wanted. But it doesn't matter who you pick if the opposition have got their heads right – and you haven't. Zenit were far more turned on by the idea of beating United than the other way round and were well worth the lead they grabbed in first-half injury time. Denisov gets a flick on to a near post corner, the ball loops across goal and bowl-headed centre-forward Pogrebynak applies the crucial touch at the far post.

0-2 (59): Zenit were so convinced that Andrei Arshavin, the man behind the summer's third most tedious transfer saga (after Ronaldo and Berbatov) was off to Spurs that they splashed a cool £24 million on a replacement playmaker, Danny. On this evidence it looked like money well spent. The floppy haired Portuguese was the most dangerous player on the pitch and his goal – a weaving dribble into the area and a low shot inside Van der Sar's near post - was a cracker. The watching Abramovich certainly enjoyed it. By the way, how many teams does that man support? He's as bad as Zoe Ball.

1-2 (73): At 2-0 down United finally realise that the evening could be about to turn embarrassing and they spark to life. Their first sustained spell of pressure culminates in Rooney collecting a short corner and picking out United's best player Tévez at the back post. He cuts it back to Vidic who half-scuffs the ball past a thicket of defenders from close range.

OFF! (77): But almost as soon as Vidic gives us a sniff, Scholes gets himself sent off for needlessly punching the ball into the net. And with that pointless gesture – and it's hard to think of a more gormless way to get a red – the cup was effectively won... and lost.

WHAT WAS GOOD?

ZENIT - OK, United didn't play well or look that fussed. But the Russians, who had lifted the UEFA Cup on that night in Manchester were undeniably useful. And with Gazprom's financial muscle behind them you wouldn't rule them out for being the first Russians ever to seriously challenge for the Big Cup (though funnily enough they went on to fluff their lines in this season's Champions League, winning just 5 points in an admittedly tough group featuring both Juve and Real).

TÉVEZ – Wouldn't know how to play at any less than 100% - which is why we all love him. Was just about the only Red to turn up.

WHAT WAS BAD?

THE RED ARMY – First there was talk of Moscow not selling out (though it was pretty hard to spot a gap in the United end) and now Reds are massively outnumbered by Zenit fans in Monaco. Strange...

HISTORY REPEATING - In 5 games in August last year none of the forwards managed a single goal. In 4 goals in August this year none of the forwards managed a single goal. Hmmm.

SCHOLESY – can you think of a more pointless red card? It means he'll miss the Champions League opener against Villarreal.

UNITED'S RECORD AGAINST RUSSIAN TEAMS:
P 5 W 0 D 4 L 1 F 3 A 4

HARGREAVES'S WITHDRAWAL WITH ANOTHER CASE OF DODGY KNEES - Will he ever be fully fit?

MONACO – THE VERBALS

"I cannot deny that Zenit deserved to win the game. I think that they probably just shaded it a little from us. We played better when we were 2-0 down and made some good chances and when we scored with something like 17 minutes to go, we still found time to recover and get back into the game. But the game was running away from us a little bit." – *Fergie, who was bidding to be the first ever manager to win the Super Cup three times, takes defeat on the chin.*

"I thought Tévez was outstanding – probably the best player on the park." - *So why haven't we signed him up yet? I thought David Gill said he'd be on the case in the summer.*

VIEWS FROM THE PRESSBOX

"In the end it was a thoroughly disappointing evening for Manchester United although it is difficult to imagine that, even if their name had been engraved on the Uefa Super Cup, we would have seen a giddy Wayne Rooney pretending to slurp champagne from the trophy or Sir Alex Ferguson doing that uncoordinated little hop, skip and jump that he reserves for the genuinely important occasions.

"All week United have been insisting that they would treat this game with deadly seriousness but they did not look too distraught at the final whistle, just faintly irritated after a night in which the European Cup and Premier League winners got going only after falling two goals behind and suddenly realising that they were in danger of being outplayed." – *The Guardian going through the motions with United.*

"Scholes has scored a few opportunistic goals in his time but none quite as sly as the one he punched into the net in the closing minutes as United chased an equaliser in the European Super Cup final. It was the hand-of-God treatment from the Maradona of Middleton and he was never likely to get away with it." - *The Independent on 'sly' Scholes.*

"The night had begun badly for Ferguson when he tripped over one of the television wires on his way to the dugout and, for one horrible moment, seemed set to take out his embarrassment on the unsuspecting chap who was reeling it in. Some of his players seemed unsure of their step too, in particular Gary Neville, who was frequently caught out of position until he was replaced with 15 minutes to go. The evening of extravagant, attacking football that Ferguson had predicted certainly never materialised and there were long spells when United were slow to the ball and short of ideas in attack." – *The Guardian with the image of the night.*

ONE OUT OF THREE
United's record in previous Super Cup games:

19/11/91 – United 1 (McClair) Red Star Belgrade 0 (at Old Trafford – attendance: 22,110!)
Schmeichel, Martin, Bruce, Pallister, Irwin, Kanchelskis, Webb, Ince, Blackmore, McClair (1), Hughes (sub: Giggs)
27/08/99 – United 0 Lazio 1 (Salas)
Van der Gouw, G.Neville, Berg, Stam, P.Neville, Beckham, Keane, Scholes, Solskjaer, Cole, Sheringham (subs: Cruyff, Curtis, Greening)

MATCH FACTS
United: Van der Sar, Neville (Brown 76), Ferdinand, Vidic, Evra, Anderson (O'Shea 60), Nani, Scholes, Fletcher (Park 60), Rooney, Tévez
Zenit St Petersburg: Malafeev, Anyukov, Krizanac (Radimov 71), Puygrenier (Shirokov 62), Sirl, Denisov, Tymoschuk, Zyrianov, Dominguez (Arshavin 46), Pogrebnyak, Danny [Advocaat]
Stade Louis II Ref: Claus Bo Larsen (Denmark) h-t: 0-1

OTHER SCORES
Arsenal 3 Newcastle 0, Aston Villa 0 Liverpool 0,
Chelsea 1 Spurs 1

LEAGUE TABLE
1. Chelsea 7 (3) 2. Liverpool 7 (3) 3. City 6 (3) 4. Arsenal 6 (3)...
9. United 4 (2)

"I don't play for the money. If I wanted to play for the money, I would accept Manchester City's offer or Chelsea's. I want to play for the biggest club in the world."

NEWS

Mickey Phelan gets Carlos Queiroz's old job full-time. Rene Meulensteen is installed as full-time coach. United are drawn against Middlesbrough in the Carling Cup. Alan Curbishley is put out of his misery at West Ham. Keegan quits/ is forced out of Newcastle. Mike Ashley embarrasses himself at the Emirates. And Manchester has a deadline day it'll never forget…

DEADLINE DAY
(the condensed United version)

Where do you start? City get taken over by mega-rich Arabs and make bids for every player they can think of, including Berbatov. Spurs take the bait. Berbatov flies to Manchester, apparently to meet up with City. Fergie hijacks Berbatov at the airport. Berbatov makes it clear he's only interested in United. United rush him off for a medical. Spurs protest they haven't given us permission to speak to him. It gets to the midnight deadline. Have we left it too late? Sky Sports News beam pictures of Berbatov shaking hands inside Old Trafford. At 12.30am the deal is official. United get their man, Spurs get £30.75m and Fraizer Campbell (who seemed Wigan-bound at the start of the evening) on loan. James Cooper – the excitable little guy Sky pinched from Granada – explodes.

DEADLINE DAY
(the condensed City version)

Where do you start? City get taken over by mega-rich Arabs and excitable Blues rush around with teatowels on their heads. City make bids for every player they can think of, including Berbatov. Spurs take the bait. Berbatov flies to Manchester. City prepare a welcoming party. Fergie beats them to it. Berbatov isn't interested. Midnight passes. The Arab money has come too late? No. They've got Robinho. For £32 million. Sparky celebrates. Mums and wives across Stockport search for missing tea towels. Abramovich fumes.

DEADLINE DAY
(the leftovers)

Everton buy Fellaini for £15 million. Everyone says 'who?'. Liverpool miss out on Barry but buy City reject Riera and a few more foreign kids. Arsenal, who desperately need a stronger spine, commit season suicide by not buying anyone. Chelsea wonder how Robinho got away.

'DEADLINE DAY' QUOTE OF THE DAY

"I don't play for the money. If I wanted to play for the money, I would accept Manchester City's offer or Chelsea's. I want to play for the biggest club in the world and that's why I'm here. I'm thankful for everybody, for the help they have given me and for the work they did." – *Dimitar Berbatov, United's new No. 9.*

RUNNERS-UP

"Robinho told Calderon: 'I do not want to stay. I would rather be a travelling salesman, sell cakes in the fair, than remain at the club'" - *Robinho's agent Wagner Ribeiro spills the beans.*

"With the Americans who own Man U, all their wealth is built on credit. But with the people who bought us, it's all built on oil. It's nice to know every gallon of petrol a Man U fan buys will be going into our transfer kitty" – *A giddy Noel Gallagher.*

DIG OF THE WEEK

"The big surprise was Liverpool paying £20million for Keane." – *Fergie reviews the summer's transfer business.*

WEAK COMEBACK OF THE WEEK

"I am very surprised that John O'Shea doesn't play [for United] every week" – *Robbie Keane doesn't really mean that about Sheasy does he?*

DEADLINE DAY WINNERS

BERBATOV: Has been crying out for a move to Old Trafford for over a year. Now he gets his wish. And at 27 – a year older than Eric when he moved to his rightful stage – he's the perfect age to meet the challenge.

CITY: After chasing the pink pound in 2006 and a pile of tainted bahts a year ago, they've finally struck gold, in a stroke being transformed from a massive club with massive problems to the richest club on the planet.

GARRY COOK: Laughed out of the room by journalists just a few days ago when he boasted that City were going to take over the world. But no one's laughing at him now (don't worry, it won't last).

SPARKY: Seemed to be taking a gamble when he joined City despite the massive question marks over Shinawatra and the club's financial future. Now he's got the biggest war-chest the game has ever seen.

MANCHESTER: Remember when Elmer Fudd (former City chairman David Bernstein) predicted that Manchester would be the capital of the football world again? For the wrong reasons he may be proved right.

UNITED: OK, Berbatov cost more than he perhaps should have done (and £20 m more than he would have cost 2 years ago) but what a signing. And what a squad we've got ourselves. Tévez, Manucho, Giggs, Park, Scholes, Hargreaves. That could be our front 6 in the reserves!

MANCHESTER'S WANNABE WAGS: The big guns keep on coming.

LOSERS

CITY: I know they're desperate for a saviour but it's still unsavoury how few problems they have just giving their history away (though, having said that, with a history like theirs...).

ROBINHO: We all knew he was desperate to leave Madrid. But surely he wasn't this desperate? Did his agent tell him he was coming here to sign for Manchester (the name United are known by around the world)?

TEL BEN HAIM: I wonder how City's new centre-back will react to the news that his club's new owners come from a country that doesn't allow Jews in.

THE BIG FOUR: could City be about to muscle in on their Champions League places?

MADRID: After all Calderon's talk and manoeuvrings which superstars did they sign? Rafael Van der Vaart. Precisely...

TÉVEZ: A great season last year but the man most in danger now Berbatov is here.

ARSENAL: Lost two defensive midfielders plus Hleb and replaced them with United target Ramsey and Nasri. No signings on deadline day either.

SPURS: Managed to squeeze a few quid more out of the Berbatov deal by playing hardball but at the same time left themselves with no time to spend the money.

SPURS CHAIRMAN DANIEL LEVY: Had the cheek to moan about United's tactics in pursuit of Berbatov. What about what he did to Seville when he wanted Juande Ramos last year? Still to recognise that you're always vulnerable to clubs higher up the food chain.

CHELSEA: Had it all their way for years. Now got even richer kids on the block – though that London postcode still gives them an advantage.

CHELSEA (AGAIN): Used to have piles of wingers. After missing out on Robinho they only have the ordinary Malouda and Cole. Perhaps they should have bid for SWP?

PETER KENYON. How is he still in work? As brilliant as ever at signing up Brazilians. Kaka? No. Ronaldinho? No. Robinho? No.

FRAIZER CAMPBELL: The pawn in the Berbatov deal. Will he get the game time he needs at White Hart Lane?

'HEAR HEAR' COMMENT OF THE WEEK

"The way that Ramos flew the coop and abandoned his team en route to London last year totally disrupted our season and now I'm pleased that Spurs are being paid back in kind over the Berbatov transfer. Their complaints are hypocrisy personified" - *Sevilla president Jose Maria Del Nido has little sympathy with Spurs over Berbatov.*

BIG MOVERS

A rundown of every club's most expensive summer signing:

Arsenal (Nasri £15.8m), Aston Villa (Milner £12m), Blackburn (Robinson £3.5), Bolton (Elmander £11m), Chelsea (Bosingwa £16.2m), Everton (Fellaini £15m), Fulham (Johnson £10.5m), Hull (Anthony Gardner £2.5m), Liverpool (Keane, arf, £20.3m), City (£32.5m), United (Berbatov, £30.75), Boro (Digard £4m), Newcastle (Coloccini £10m), Portsmouth (Crouch £11m), Stoke (Kitson £5.5m), Sunderland (Anton Ferdinand £8m), Spurs (Modric £16m), West Brom (Valero £4.7), West Ham (Behrami £5m), Wigan (Kapo/Cattermole £3.5m).

INTERNATIONAL REDS

Rooney scores one and makes two of Walcott's three goals as England batter Croatia 4-1 in Croatia. Fletcher's Scotland beat Iceland 2-1, Evans's Northern Ireland draw 0-0 at home against the Czechs and O'Shea's Republic side draw 0-0 in Montenegro. Vidic loses with Serbia against France. Evra is an unused sub. Nani scores again as Portugal go down to a shock 3-2 home defeat against Denmark.

LEAST SURPRISING QUOTE OF THE WEEK

"Fabio Capello has never spoken to me" - *David Nugent.*

MOST SURPRISING QUOTE OF THE WEEK

"Sometimes I lie in the bed with my players. I go to the room of (Vedran) Corluka and (Luka) Modric when I see they have a problem and I lie in bed with them and we talk for 10 minutes. You have to do it. Sometimes football managers think 'If you do that you're losing the distance and the authority'. No, you're gaining" - *Slaven Bilic, the only international manager I know of to look like a sheep, reveals some unorthodox management techniques*

THIN EXCUSE OF THE WEEK
From the Mike Ashley camp as the buffoon was spotted downing a pint in the stands at Arsenal, something that we all know is a big no-no in football grounds these days:

"Mike was offered a drink which he thought was non-alcoholic so he took it in good faith."

UNIMPORTANT STAT OF THE WEEK

13.05 seconds – the time it took Ashley to down his 'Kaliber'.

FAPL 13/09/2008

LIVERPOOL 2 UNITED 1
Tévez 3, Brown og 27, Babel 77

"WE NEVER WON a tackle. When you have bad days, the big thing is to get something from them but we conceded two goals that were absolute shockers. People will say that it is some Conference team defending when they see us on television. It was shocking stuff. The first was a really scabby goal to lose and the second was a shocker." - *Fergie.*

I guess it had to come sometime. We've been playing mediocre football at Anfield ever since Benitez brought his own special brand of weirdness to the Premier League. And somehow we've managed to win almost every time. This time we played mediocre, nay crap, football and got exactly what we deserved.

But as the hack pack flagellated themselves with the 'Liverpool are back' line they've been dying to use since the Spice Boys, one pesky truth got forgotten. If Van der Sar hadn't played like a retarded daddy long legs... If, as a puce Fergie raged afterwards, we hadn't defended like Conference idiots... If United players hadn't made all of Liverpool's best chances... Tévez's classy opener would have been enough to win us all three points. And Liverpool's best season for years would have been badly derailed before the title race had even really begun.

MATCH ACTION

1-0 (3): Fergie goes for broke with his team selection, pushing Rooney to the right to allow Berbatov to make his debut next to Tévez. For a little under 3 minutes it looks like an inspired move as Berbatov walks his way past Carragher and pulls the ball back for Tévez to score with a swaggering curler...

1-1 (27): But United never seem to recover from the shock of scoring so early. Tévez and Berbatov play like the strangers they are. Rooney tries and fails to come to terms with his new role on the right. Carrick has to hobble off with a broken foot, Anderson and Scholes get harried out of it by Liverpool's non-stop sniping. And Van der Sar goes AWOL in the head, flapping at everything, crashing into his defenders and eventually gifting Liverpool an equaliser. Alonso's ultra-optimistic long ranger shouldn't have posed a problem as it looped up off Evra but Van der Sar gets lost in no man's land, panics and palms the ball against Brown's knee. The ball could have trickled harmlessly wide. It doesn't.

1-2 (77): And finally, after close on 800 minutes, a Liverpool player scores a league goal against United. It's another defensive shambles, a genuine park pitch shocker. Giggs refuses an obvious opportunity to clear his lines, Mascherano picks his pocket and Kuyt rolls over a cross which Babel miskicks into the ground and high into the net.

RED: And just to make the day even better, Vidic gets a harsh second yellow for a stray but accidental elbow on Alonso. Which means he'll miss the next game, against Big Phil Scolari's new, improved Chelsea at Stamford Bridge. Great.

WHAT WAS GOOD?

RONALDO'S BACK NEXT WEEK.

WHAT WAS BAD?

DON'T GET ME STARTED.

WEIRD STATS OF THE DAY

1 – the number of goals Liverpool players have scored for Benitez against United.

2 – the number of goals United players have scored for Benitez.

VIEW FROM THE PRESSBOX

"Manchester United never recovered from the shock of an early goal. The fact that it was they who had scored it did not save them from falling into a daze. They looked befuddled by the thought that beating Liverpool might be even easier than usual. Whatever the reasons, the inert visitors could come up with no response to the equaliser or to the goal with which Rafael Benítez's team went ahead." – *The Guardian*

MATCH FACTS

LIVERPOOL: REINA, ARBELOA, SKRTEL, CARRAGHER, AURELIO, BENAYOUN (GERRARD 68), ALONSO, MASCHERANO (HYYPIA 87), RIERA (BABEL 71), KUYT, KEANE [BENITEZ]
UNITED: VAN DER SAR, BROWN, FERDINAND, VIDIC, EVRA, ROONEY, SCHOLES (HARGREAVES 66), CARRICK (GIGGS 46), ANDERSON (NANI 78), TÉVEZ, BERBATOV.
SENT OFF: VIDIC (90) - BOOKED: TÉVEZ, VIDIC, NANI.
ANFIELD ATT: 44,192 REF: H. WEBB H-T: 1-1

OTHER SCORES

BLACKBURN 0 ARSENAL 4, CITY 1 CHELSEA 3.

LEAGUE TABLE

1. CHELSEA 10 (4) 2. LIVERPOOL 10 (4) 3. ARSENAL 9 (4) 4. HULL 7 (4)...
14. UNITED 4 (3)

*"I'm already in the history of the club.
When I play the fans will love me again."*

NEWS

UNITED SPONSORS AIG become the latest high-profile victims of the financial crisis and have to be bailed out by the US government.

Which means that United aren't just owned by Americans, they're sponsored by the Federal Bank. And Mo Watkins is appointed chairman of greyhound racing's governing body which is terrible news for any mutts accused of missing doping tests. They'll be on a plane to Korea within hours...

JOURNALIST OF THE WEEK
Martin Samuel, the hairy bloke from The Times*:*

"Come on, be honest, there is a part, even within the most optimistic Manchester City supporter, that thinks we are all going to wake up tomorrow and it will turn out to be that bloke from the *News of the World* again.

"There is no Abu Dhabi United Group for Development and Investment, no al-Nahyan royal family and Dr Sulaiman al-Fahim turns out to be an undercover reporter with a tin of cherry blossom, two white sheets, a JCloth and an accent borrowed straight from *It Ain't Half Hot Mum.*

"He has taped Thaksin Shinawatra coughing the lot on corruption in Thailand, plus a few idiotic asides from Garry Cook, the City executive chairman, about how this new partnership with the Middle East is going to help the club to maximise the central entity and buy Cristiano Ronaldo in the January transfer window before winning the World Series of Soccerball. At which point City return to their traditional state as the butt of a million wisecracks and the world goes back to work, sniggering."

MR MODESTY

"I'm already in the history of the club. When I play the fans will love me again." – *Ronaldo doesn't even try to butter us up prior to his comeback against Villarreal.*

AIMING HIGH

"Ronaldo has said he wants to play for the biggest club in the world, so we will see in January if he is serious." – *New City owner Sulaiman Al-Fahim immediately comes down with the giddiness disease.*

ALL SAINT

"I am religious and I take The Bible everywhere with me. There are many good pieces of advice for those like me in The Bible. This is a matter of good upbringing. I don't swear in my daily life. I try to do everything with style - not only in football. And if I manage to give any positive examples then that is great" – *Dimi Berbatov... intriguing us already.*

5 MORE THINGS YOU DIDN'T KNOW ABOUT BERBATOV
From The Mirror:

1. Mum Margarita was a professional handball player and dad Ivan a professional footballer with CSKA Sofia.
2. He always pretended to be Marco Van Basten as a kid. But he became obsessed with Shearer after Euro 96 and even used to sleep in a Shearer Newcastle shirt. *That's forgivable, right?*
3. He's only won 2 trophies as a pro, the Bulgarian National Cup with CSKA Sofia and the Carling Cup with Spurs.
4. In his first season at Tottenham he wore an armband with the slogan "You are not alone", campaigning for the release of five Bulgarian nurses sentenced to death in Libya on charges of injecting hundreds of children with HIV in the 1990s. Berbatov is a also goodwill ambassador for Unicef.
5. He learnt English by watching the Godfather films – which explains why he joined Manchester United. He models his hair on Andy Garcia. And just like Rooney he likes the odd tab.

MUCK RAKERS OF THE WEEK
The Sun adds a sixth Berbatov fact:

"MANCHESTER United striker Dimitar Berbatov has a dark family secret – his dad was convicted over a gang rape. Former player Ivan Berbatov spent two years in jail for his part in a football team "roasting" of a Norwegian girl." *I wonder how long The Sun waited to make this story public. Just long enough for Berbatov to sign for United do you think?*

LAUGH. OUT. LOUD.
The boys back home, er, wish Robinho well in his career at his new club:

"Chelsea are lucky. This boy needs some serious counselling. In my view he has been badly advised." – *Pele.*

"This is one of the most disgraceful episodes in Brazilian football. He is a player who is an idol to children, an example. But he has not acted like one." - *Santos President, Marcelo Teixeira.*

"We are ashamed at having produced such a player." - *Santos general manager, Jose Fernandos.*

AND THEY JUST KEEP ON COMING

"We have to understand that his dream is to be a good player in a mediocre English team and we have to respect him" – *Real coach, Bernd Schuster, on City's £32m new boy.*

"It would be suicidal for my career at my 21 years of age to move to City. It would make no sense" – *Cesc Fabregas.*

17/09/2008
CL GROUP E

UNITED 0 VILLARREAL 0

It was the question all Reds were asking themselves throughout that long depressing summer. What would we all do when we saw Ronaldo again? Would there be boos and venom? Or stony silence? Or cheers? If Ronaldo had been fit for the start of the season, when his post-Moscow betrayal (and memories of those ridiculous micro-shorts) was still so fresh, when many of us would have gladly sold him and Roman Calderon into gay slavery, things could have got heated. But a month on, with United struggling for any semblance of form, it had become clear that, whatever you think of Ronaldo the man, we desperately needed Ronaldo the player. So when he rose from the bench with an hour gone in this dirgy match against dirgy Villarreal there were no jeers, no Judas salutes, only cheers. But if Ronaldo really did think we'd instantly fall back in love with him just for pulling on our shirt again, he had another thing coming. Us football fans might be fickle Ronnie, but we're not daft...

MATCH HIGHLIGHTS

Are you kidding? It's United-Villarreal we're talking about here. Apart from Franco's flick against the post, Evans's late header against another post and Ronaldo's return this was the sort of game that makes you wonder how on earth United manage to shift so many tickets. Even the opportunity to boo Robert Pires didn't make this non-event worth 40-odd quid.

VIEWS FROM THE PRESSBOX

"More bad news for Uncle Sam's beleaguered financial system. The stock of the soccer team now effectively sponsored by the US government fell slightly after the Champions League holders failed to begin their defence with a win. Manchester United, whose sponsors, AIG, are now 80 per cent owned by the US Federal Reserve bank following yesterday's $85bn (£47bn) bail-out, were held at home by an organised but under-strength Villarreal team. United hit the post late on, through Jonny Evans but only after Villarreal, who deserved their point, had done the same." – *Like most of the papers,* The Independent *can't resist talking about United's unplanned new sponsors.*

"In other news Manchester United fans still love Cristiano Ronaldo. The 'want-away star' was cheered to the rafters when he rose from the bench with an hour gone. It was immediately easy to see why Sir Alex Ferguson had insisted on keeping him, and why he and the faithful had put Ronaldo's summer dalliance with Real Madrid to the backs of their minds. He failed to turn the game last night, but with him on the pitch United looked far more threatening." - *The Indie again.*

"Manchester United fans keep reminding the world that they are "champions of England, champions of Europe" but the players need to start living up to such a distinguished billing. One victory in five this season, including the Uefa Super Cup, represents a truly disappointing start, although the welcome return of the talismanic Cristiano Ronaldo promises brighter times ahead." – *The Telegraph aren't the only ones to be getting nervous about our DDWLLD start.*

VILLARREAL – THE VERBALS

"Cristiano Ronaldo has had a turbulent summer and a lot has been said about it, but when I had my meeting in June in Portugal with him that was over. The crowd's reception was important for Cristiano. I think he realises what a great club he is at and how loyal the fans are. He will take great encouragement from that." – *Fergie's pleased the fans kept their views about Ronaldo's behaviour to themselves.*

DEJA VU

Did you know the last two times United won a European trophy, we were also held 0-0 in our first defence – by Athinaikos in 1991 and Ossie Ardiles's Croatia Zagreb in 1999? For the record Denis Law scored a hat-trick as United beat Waterford 3-1 away in the first

European game after Wembley '68.

MATCH FACTS

UNITED: VAN DER SAR, NEVILLE, FERDINAND, EVANS, EVRA, NANI, HARGREAVES (ANDERSON 62), FLETCHER, PARK (RONALDO 62), ROONEY, TÉVEZ (GIGGS 81)
BOOKED: TÉVEZ.
VILLARREAL: DIEGO LOPEZ, ANGEL, RODRIGUEZ, GODIN, CAPDEVILA, CANI (SANTI CAZORLA 46), EGUREN, EDMILSON, PIRES (IBAGAZA 67), FERNANDEZ, FRANCO (LLORENTE 77) [PELLEGRINI]
BOOKED: FRANCO, IBAGAZA, DIEGO LOPEZ.
ATT: 74,944 REF: WOLFGANG STARK (GERMANY) H-T: 0-0

OTHER SCORES

CELTIC 0 AALBORG 0,
CHELSEA 4 BORDEAUX 0, MARSEILLE 1 LIVERPOOL 2,
DYNAMO KIEV 1 ARSENAL 1

"Who creates more chances than us? Melchester Rovers?"

NEWS

GIANFRANCO ZOLA REPLACES Curbishley at West Ham. Interestingly he names Steve Clarke, widely regarded as a key player in Chelsea's recent successes, as his no. 2. Butch Wilkins replaces Clarke. Reported summer target David Silva says United would be the first club he'd sign for outside Spain. Which sounds good. But he'd rather go to Barcelona than anywhere else. Which doesn't. Coleen Rooney suffers an allergic reaction to eating lobster whilst filming her show *Coleen's Real Women*, causing filming to be delayed for 90 minutes. Order is only restored across the nation when an ITV source reveals: "Filming continued after the symptoms died down."

QUOTES OF THE WEEK

"I am physically fine, but mentally unhappy." – *You'd have to have a right hard-hearted bastard not to feel sorry for billionaire Thaksin Shinawatra, right?*

"It was a complete scandal, but we live in a crazy world. That sort of money is an insult to the intelligence and should be denounced.

It made me feel queasy. Around 20 per cent of Spanish people live on the breadline and they are talking about that." – *Spanish politician Miguel Angel Revilla lambasts Real for waving £80 million at Ronaldo.*

"Heads can be turned by the lure of money. I can understand that. I said that to Cristiano at the time of all the talk about Real Madrid. But we were in a strong position to dismiss Real Madrid because the boy has got four years left on his contract. And we are also in the right position at this club to ensure that Cristiano stays happy. He enjoys his football at United and hopefully he will win more things" – *Fergie puts up a sterling defence of Ronaldo.*

DIG OF THE WEEK

"It will be interesting to see what they have on the pitch on Sunday. Maybe they'll have a combine harvester waiting for us this time." – *Fergie can't resist taking a sly swipe as United head to Chelsea for the first time since Paddy Evra started rucking with the groundsmen.*

LEAST FLATTERING QUOTE OF THE WEEK

"I have to work out whether I go with Evans' ability or Wes' experience" - *Fergie wonders out loud what defence he should pick for Stamford Bridge.*

RETROSPECTIVE QUOTES OF THE WEEK

"I cannot ever imagine leaving Manchester. My relationship with the club is perfect. Patrice Evra is my closest friend but the feeling I get from all the players is something I've not experienced before. I want to get the contract sorted and play for United for the rest of my career." – *Tévez.*

"Alex is very good with me and I really feel he loves me as a person. He is always a gentleman in the changing room. He has a lot of money but is very modest. I like people like him." – *Tévez again.*

"Carlos is not joining Manchester City. All this talk linking him with them is a complete load of nonsense" – *Tévez's advisor Kia Joorabchian.*

MAKING HIM PAY

Guess what Ronnie's been up to again… (from the News of the Screws)

"SOCCER star Cristiano Ronaldo's secret lover is a £2,000-night-drug dealing hooker. The Manchester United ace has NO IDEA, but cheeky prostitute Fernanda BRAGS of her famous conquest to London punters. As she offered a cocaine-fuelled threesome

Fernando showed off intimate pictures of herself with winking winger Ronaldo and purred: "We're REALLY good friends."

"Ronaldo has secretly dated Brazilian beauty Fernanda for years. But he'll go nuts to discover he's been sharing her with a string of seedy vice punters paying £460 a time."

QUOTE OF THE WEEK

"Who creates more chances than us? Melchester Rovers? We do create more chances. But we will hit form and we will start scoring goals. Last season was similar until we got a scrappy 1-0 win against Sunderland and we were away. It will happen." – *Fergie's expecting title take-off.*

FAPL 21/09/2008

CHELSEA 1 UNITED 1
Park 18, Kalou 80

IT HAD BEEN another crap British summer. But there was one place in the country where the sun never stopped shining. And that, according to the papers, was out of Phil Scolari's backside. The London press pack just couldn't stop slobbering over the Brazilian, their view being that Chelsea had bagged themselves an extra special one, a serial winner who, unlike Mourinho, could also entertain. So when Deco & co. started the season by steamrollering Portsmouth, City and Bordeaux (giants of the game, all), the papers were more or less ready to hand them the league. And pass on the title of the new kings of total football while they were at it.

The outpouring of praise was all massively premature of course. By the time autumn passed into winter, the wins had started drying up, Chelsea's air of invincibility at home had been shattered, Deco had disappeared, Drogba was off on another sulk, Essien was crocked and Scolari, whose English could never quite shake off its pigeon feel, was looking more like the new Ranieri than the new Mourinho. There was even talk that Chelsea would have been better off with Avram Grant.

And looking back this match was the first real sign that the

Scolari Chelsea revolution was nothing but a false alarm...

United arrived with no form behind them, an unfit Ronaldo on the bench, an out-of-touch Rooney leading the line and no Vidic. They also brought with them the psychological baggage of knowing that a defeat would leave them nine points adrift. And they responded by playing Chelsea off the park, for the first half-hour at least. In fairness Chelsea owned the second half and deserved their point (though would they have got it if Kuszczak wasn't so retarded in coming off his line?) but the moral victory was United's. 35 days into the season, had the race for number eighteen begun in earnest at last?

HOW THE MATCH UNFOLDED

TEAM NEWS: United have gone for a solid look with three hard runners in midfield and Hargreaves re-enacting his Moscow duel against Ashley Cole. Is Fergie's conservatism sensible? Or an exercise in damage limitation against an in-form team that will be crying out (crying... tears...Terry... geddit?) for revenge for Moscow? As for Chelsea they're at full strength apart from Deco who injured himself in the warm-up. Ballack, who scored that contentious penalty winner in the same fixture last year, plays in his place.

CHANCE! MISS! (9): So much for the pre-match assumption that United are going to be cautious. They're swarming all over Chelsea at the moment but they're lucky to escape here, Evra's mistimed mid-air bicycle-kick allowing Joe Cole a clear run on goal. He really should have buried it but with only Van der Sar to beat he loses his nerve and slashes the ball wide.

GOAL! PARK (18): United get their reward with an excellently worked goal. Evra makes the first move, bursting down the left and playing a one-two with Rooney. Evra then plays the ball back to Berbatov – standing roughly where the lawnmower nonsense started last year – and when his low shot is parried loosely by Cech, Park snaffles the rebound. Has Cech been the same since he started wearing that skull cap?

VDS. OFF. (31): For a minute Van der Sar looks like he's going to re-enact his Anfield nightmare, as he charges out of his area haphazardly and then fumbles Cole's centre. But the reason for his shakiness soon becomes clear. He's injured. On comes Kuszczak who is apparently the worst dressed player in the United squad as well as being almost certainly the worst player as well (or is that harsh?).

LET. OFF. (45): Chelsea end the half with the territorial advantage but United are still looking a danger on the break and they should really have finished the game off here. Rooney robs Terry near halfway and plays in Berbatov who should have instantly sent Park, who was undertaking him at speed, clear on Cech. Instead the ball goes behind Park and the chance is gone.

BIG GUNS ON (46/54): It had to happen. Malouda's off, the villain of Moscow, Drogba, is on to test out Evans. He's shortly followed by Ronaldo who replaces Scholes. It looks like United are going to try and finish things off. But first they've got to get their foot on the ball. And that's proving much more difficult this time around.

COLE. MISS. (66): Fortunately when Chelsea do make a chance they're falling to the wrong people. First Cole wastes Ballack's defence-splitting chip by smashing his shot straight at Kuszczak...

WHAT. A. MISS. (73): ... and then Anelka, standing unmarked 5 yards out with Kuszczak stranded, somehow allows Joe Cole's low centre to slip between his legs.

GOAL. KALOU (79): But just when you think it's going to be one of those days – for both teams – United concede. It's a sloppy, unnecessary goal too. Mikel floats a free-kick into the area, Kuszczak timidly stays on his line rather than clearing out the danger and the unmarked Kalou flicks in his header from 5 yards.

SEVEN UP: 90+1: Kalou tackles Ronaldo late, Ronaldo complains, Ronaldo becomes the 7th United player booked. It's an old cliché I know, but there's hardly been a bad tackle. Anyone else think that Mike Riley is trying too hard to prove he's not a United fan?

EEK. OFF? (90+2): Rio clashes with Drogba on the edge of the box, Riley blows his whistle, Rio blows his top and then walks off the pitch. Has he just got his second yellow? Several players surround the ref, a growling Fergie stomps on the pitch... and then it becomes clear that Riley has actually blown for full-time. So it's a draw and a point each. Which could have been better. And could have been worse.

MOMENT OF THE MATCH

PARK'S GOAL - Classic Evra. Classic United.

RUNNER-UP

The 'Fergie and the balloon' youtube classic. Mickey Phelan grabs a stray balloon and bursts it, without warning, almost giving Fergie a heart attack. The look he gives after is a picture (note to sensitive lip readers, please don't watch).

VIEWS FROM THE PRESSBOX
(have they all been copying each other)

"This fixture is an exercise in time travel. We may only be in late September, but both teams displayed the desperate ambition of men playing as if the title hung in the balance with just a few seconds left of the last fixture. Judging by the unyielding determination, these sides may be locked together once again in May.

"If it puts a terrible strain on United and Chelsea their suffering will be a spectacle to engross the rest of us. Here, the Stamford Bridge side held on to an intangible honour of profound importance. The unbeaten record at home in the Premier League now stands at 85 fixtures." – *The Guardian.*

"On the surface, Manchester United got what they came for: an away point and the brakes applied to Chelsea's early-season momentum. Underneath, the draw was worth considerably more, for it sent out a message regarding the size of the fight required to wrest the Premier League trophy from Old Trafford.

"There were seven Manchester United players booked, which suggests foul play, but this was a scrap between championship contenders, nothing more. That one of the teams started the day in fourteenth place and ended it in fifteenth is irrelevant. At the end of the match there was little doubt that United's fight for a third successive title is only just beginning. They will claw their way to the summit, or near by, from here, make no mistake, and that was the true worth of yesterday's performance. It said that the best is to come; and, until then, prepare for combat." – *The Times.*

"It is too early in the season for this to be a seminal match, but for an hour yesterday it felt like it could be. Manchester United, showing the form they have been searching for during the campaign's opening weeks, appeared poised to inflict Chelsea's first home League defeat for four-and-a-half years. That would have been a resounding psychological blow worth even more than the three precious points at stake.

"Then Chelsea's resilience, which seems part of their DNA regardless of who is in the dugout, surfaced again. Trailing to Ji-Sung Park's 18th-minute goal, they had lacked the fluency previously displayed under Luiz Felipe Scolari. But the best teams graft when the craft is missing and Chelsea pushed the champions back by force of will." - *The Indie*

MATCH FACTS

CHELSEA: CECH, BOSINGWA, CARVALHO (ALEX 12), TERRY, ASHLEY COLE, MIKEL, JOE COLE, BALLACK (KALOU 74), LAMPARD, MALOUDA (DROGBA 46), ANELKA [SCOLARI]

BOOKED: MIKEL

UNITED: VAN DER SAR (KUSZCZAK 32), NEVILLE, FERDINAND, EVANS, EVRA, FLETCHER, HARGREAVES, SCHOLES (RONALDO 55), PARK (O'SHEA 75), BERBATOV, ROONEY

BOOKED: SCHOLES, FERDINAND, NEVILLE, BERBATOV, ROONEY, EVRA, RONALDO.

STAMFORD BRIDGE ATT: 41,760 REF: MIKE RILEY H-T: 1-0

OTHER SCORES

LIVERPOOL 0 STOKE 0; BOLTON 1 ARSENAL 3.

LEAGUE TABLES

1. ARSENAL 12 (5); 2. CHELSEA 11 (5); 3. LIVERPOOL 11 (5); 15. UNITED 5 (4)

"The start United have had was not because of my absence, because last season we also started badly and I was playing."

NEWS

ROONEY BREAKS DOWN after filling Coleen's car with the wrong kind of fuel, Anderson is cleared of any wrongdoing after a notorious drug dealer was arrested at his home in Brazil. And that, as far as United, er, news goes, is about it. Elsewhere, the Premier League's youngest ever referee Stuart Attwell makes a name for himself – for all the wrong reasons - by awarding Reading a goal at Watford even though the ball had actually gone out for a corner, the FA rules in favour of Sheffield United in their claim for compensation against West Ham over the Carlos Tévez affair and Arsene Wenger has one of those moments when you think he might not be such a bad bloke after all...

QUESTION TIME

"I don't know why these people are in there. It doesn't look like they are there to make any money. So if they are not there to make money out of it, then are they buying it out of love? Well, I am not sure these people are supporters of Manchester City from a young age. So then comes a further question: Why are they doing it? Why have they bought the club? I can't really find a rational answer. If it is just a toy for them then it is even more dangerous" - *Wenger withdraws the welcome mat for the Sheikhs.*

THIS CHARMING MAN
Scouse-baiting football365-style:

Jamie Carragher continues to endear himself to the nation and takes another step in dismissing the lazy stereotype of Scouse scallies being nasty little violent scroats. In the latest extract from his autobiography, as serialised in The Daily Mirror, *Jamie tells a charming tale about the company he keeps.*

'When my leg was broken in an horrific tackle by Lucas Neill in September 2003, my mates were ready to hunt him down if I gave the go-ahead. A few weeks later I received a phone call. "You won't believe this, Jay. We're in the Trafford Centre and Lucas Neill is walking straight towards us. What do you reckon?"

'Did I really want Neill to take a crack? "There's only one problem," added the voice. "Little Davey Thommo is with him."

'That was that. I could hardly let one of my best mates, David Thompson, now a Blackburn player, become a witness to an assault. Besides he'd have recognised the attackers. The impromptu mission was aborted and I sent a text to Thommo telling him Neill should give him a hug of thanks.

'As word got back to Blackburn about the near miss, or should that be hit, their coach Terry Darracott, a Scouser, appealed to one of my friends to call the boys off. I agreed.'

NOW WHAT COULD POSSIBLY GO WRONG THERE?
From the Daily Star:

'Booze addict Paul Gascoigne is on tour with hell-raising rockers Iron Maiden. The football idol has just spent two months in rehab. But he has hooked up with the heavy metal giants to 'clear his head' after his rekindled romance with ex-wife Sheryl hit the rocks'.

'COR BLIMEY' SHOCK OF THE WEEK

"The start United have had was not because of my absence, because last season we also started badly and I was playing." - *Ronaldo proves he can be modest.*

TENUOUS LINK OF THE WEEK

'She may look like an all-American girl, but Britney Spears' ancestral lineage has been traced back to Tottenham in north London - so there is every chance her family have Spurs in their blood' - *The Daily Mail. Oh dear.*

23/09/2008
CARLING CUP 3RD ROUND
UNITED 3 MIDDLESBROUGH 1
Ronaldo 25, Johnson 56, Giggs 79, Nani 90

ALF INGE HAALAND might disagree. So might anyone who was in the ground when the North Stand was a building site and a young Gary Neville finished on the wrong end of a mad lunge from 'mad' Marco Boogers. And Fred the Red won't need reminding of the time he was gang tackled by most of the 1994 title winning team. But for the life of me I can't remember a worse challenge at Old Trafford in the Ferguson era than this. Emanuel Pogatetz, a journeyman player who glories in the nickname 'Mad Dog', was once banned for 24 weeks by the Russian FA for a tackle which left an opponent with a double fracture. But if it was any worse than this cowardly, double-footed, over-the-top lunge on Rodrigo Possebon it must have been truly barbaric.

Fortunately there was a silver lining amidst the blood and fears. First, United made the most of the extra room created by Pogatetz's sending off to cruise to victory with a gift goal apiece from Nani and Giggs. More importantly, Possebon, who was stretched off the pitch with a deep gash on his shin, a suspected broken leg and almost certain knee ligament damage, was back in the team for the next round of Carling Cup matches. So instead of mourning the loss of a potentially excellent young talent, we could spend the rest of the week enjoying the news from the Withdene Stadium, where Brighton had just turned over City. It was a welcome reminder that however much oil money they have, they'll always be City...

MATCH ACTION

1-0 (25): It's easy to forget, given the deluge of goals which followed, that it took Ronaldo until the Wigan 4-0 on October 6 to get off the mark at Old Trafford last season. This year it takes him barely a half of football. Giggs swings in a corner from the right, Ronaldo outmuscles and outjumps two defenders and plants a low header into the net. He looks pretty happy with himself too, punching the air, crossing himself, pointing to the heaven, hugging Giggs respectfully and then, for a second, even hinting at a smile.

1-1 (56): Middlesbrough snatch an unexpected equaliser, Johnson latching onto Vidic's headed clearance and banging in a fierce volley that beats Amos via a crucial deflection off Brown. The goal revitalises Boro who had looked there for the taking for most of the first half. But their chances of forcing extra-time or worse fade dramatically once Pogatetz does this...

HORROR TACKLE! RED! (65): Imagine a road-test dummy being struck in both shins and sent cart-wheeling into the air by a speeding car. Well, that's basically what happened to Possebon as he went in for a 50-50 challenge with Pogatetz. The Austrian and sections of the Boro bench make themselves look stupid – and send Fergie into purple-nosed apoplexy - by arguing he'd touched a minute piece of the ball en route to touching a whole lot of Possebon. Needless to say his defence doesn't wash with the referee who waits for the medical team to arrive and then sends him off.

2-1 (79): Pogatetz's departure, and two embarrassing defensive gaffes, see United's superiority restored. Riggott is the guilty party first time round, making a complete hash of a routine long ball and presenting Giggs with a free run on goal. A cheeky chip does the rest...

3-1 (90): Wheater is the guilty man second time round, prodding Manucho's weak pass into the path of Nani who zig-zags round the keeper and rolls the ball into the empty net.

WHAT WAS GOOD?

THE KIDS – The last time we played Carling Cup football Fergie's latest batch of fledglings looked out of their depth against, er, Coventry. For Bardsley, Dong and Martin, among others, it would prove a terminal performance, at least as far as their United careers were concerned. This years newbies – Welbeck, Amos, Possebon and Rafael - looked a class apart, even if they were helped by the presence of so many big names in the team. Welbeck caused plenty of problems alongside Tévez up front while Possebon looked neat, cultured and intelligent next to Anderson and Giggs.

RONALDO – One start this season, one goal.

CITY – Since they won the League Cup in 1976 they've only made it past Christmas in the competition four times (the last time was in 1995 when they got whupped 4-0 at Palace). In the last 4 years they've been dumped out by Brighton, Doncaster and Chesterfield.

POSSEBON WASN'T AS BADLY INJURED AS FIRST FEARED – though it did take him a while to regain his form and composure afterwards.

WHAT WAS BAD?

POGATETZ – The type of no-mark thug you wish had been around in the old days when every team had someone who could have sorted him out.

THE FA – how many extra games did Possebon get for a thuggish act that could easily have ended a young man's career? None.

BORO – THE VERBALS

"For the kid to make his first-team debut and get an injury like that was pretty horrendous. For the ten minutes after, I think everyone was numb about it. It killed the momentum a bit, too.

"The thing about these challenges is it always seems to be a case of the opponent claiming his innocence. Pogatetz should have walked right off – that's what I couldn't understand – and one of their bench is out screaming... that there was nothing wrong with the boy." – *Fergie fumes about Pogagetz – and the Boro bench.*

VIEWS FROM THE PRESSBOX

"There was a point last night when this looked like the perfect evening for Manchester United: Cristiano Ronaldo had scored on his first start of the season and Sir Alex Ferguson's youngsters were demonstrating why they are so highly rated at Old Trafford. But then one of them, Rodrigo Possebon, went into a 50-50 challenge with Emanuel Pogatetz and everything after that suddenly felt inconsequential.

"To describe Pogatetz's challenge as reckless would be an understatement. The notoriously combative Austrian defender went over the top of the ball and followed through, at speed, with his studs raised.

"As he headed for the tunnel, still protesting his innocence, his

19-year-old opponent was lying on the floor with blood seeping from a suspected broken leg. It was a moment that made the rest of this tie feel almost irrelevant." – *The Guardian*

MATCH FACTS

UNITED: AMOS, RAFAEL DA SILVA, VIDIC, BROWN, O'SHEA, NANI, POSSEBON (GIBSON 72), ANDERSON, GIGGS (MANUCHO 84), WELBECK, RONALDO (TÉVEZ 61).

MIDDLESBROUGH: JONES, HOYTE, WHEATER, POGATETZ, TAYLOR, DOWNING, DIGARD (RIGGOTT 72), O'NEIL, SHAWKY (A. JOHNSON 46), ALIADIERE, ALVES (EMNES 85) [SOUTHGATE]

SENT OFF: POGATETZ (66)
BOOKED: A. JOHNSON.
CC3 ATT: 53,729 REF: A.MARRINER H-T: 1-0

"Life was only PlayStation, movies on TV and sex."

NEWS

UNITED GET QPR in the next round of the Carling Cup. Ronaldo gets the kiss and tell treatment. Again. And just when you think Newcastle can't make themselves look any more ridiculous, they appoint Joe Kinnear as their new interim manager. Yes, that's the same Joe Kinnear who's been out of the game since he left Nottingham Forest in 2004, has a long history of heart problems and who's most obvious motivational talent is to swear like Tim Howard on speed. I know I should be concentrating on United but the press conference outburst he gave in the first week of his Newcastle reign is too good to miss...

BEST START TO A PRESS CONFERENCE. EVER.

KINNEAR: Which one is Simon Bird?
BIRD [*Mirror hack*]: Me.
JK: You're a ★★★★.
BIRD: Thank you.

ASTERIX ATTACK

*The best of the rest of JFK's (Joe F****** Kinnear) rant :*

"I think I am bright. I have had a good football career. I have won f***ing European Cup medals. I have got international caps. I am no f***ing mug, you know what I mean."

"I'm no mug. I know I'm going to get crucified and everything else, but I'll take it on the chin. There's always someone who wants to stab you in the back but bollocks to that, I'll stand up for myself. I've only been here five minutes and I'm branded a cockney. How am I a cockney? I was born and reared in Ireland."

"It is none of your f****** business. What the f*** are you going to do? You ain't got the balls to be a f****** manager. F****** day off. Do I want your opinion. Do I have to listen to you?"

STAT OF THE WEEK

46 - the number of swear words Kinnear fired off during his press conference (just in case you're interested, it featured 36 F-words, 4 C-words and 6 B-words).

UNEXPECTED RUMOUR OF THE WEEK
From the Mail:

"Top referee Mark Clattenburg was suspended after allegations he had sent an email threatening the family of a business associate. Clattenburg, 33, was dramatically dropped from refereeing last month's Community Shield clash at Wembley just hours after the FA and the PGMOL, the referees' professional body, were alerted to the accusation. He has been suspended ever since." *Honestly I never thought he had it in him…*

QUOTES OF THE WEEK

'You are missing the bigger picture. Check you can use our companies (sic) money to fund your legal crusade against me. If not, taking me to court might cause your family some pain.' – *What Clattenburg, (who I always presumed would still be shacked up with his elderly mother) allegedly said in his email.*

"I pointed out to him how much better it would be to leave like Eric Cantona, with the fans loving and appreciating him." – *Fergie reveals the tactics he used to talk round Ronaldo.*

"Mike is a big mate and he is getting even bigger by the looks of him." – *Gary Megson on Mickey Phelan.*

"Jonny will be a future centre-half for Manchester United, there is no doubt about that." – *Fergie on Evans.*

SO HOW DID THAT GO THEN?

September 22: "We're ecstatic, we're on a high, we're buzzing and we are really looking forward to our next few games coming up with the form that we are in. At the moment we feel we are invincible, we are going from strength to strength and we are in great form" - *Stephen Ireland*

September 24: League One side Brighton beat City 5-3 on penalties.

UNDERSTATEMENT OF THE WEEK

"We have to point out – his calendar's a bit gay." – The Sun *on Ronaldo's new calendar (It couldn't have been much gayer if he'd grown a handlebar moustache and dressed up as a construction worker).*

SPURNED LOVER OF THE WEEK

"The city is a little bit sad and the nightclubs close early. Life was only PlayStation, movies on TV and sex." – *Ronaldo's off-on-off girlfriend Nereida Gallardo on life in Manchester. And the problem was?*

FAPL 27/09/2008

UNITED 2 BOLTON 0
Ronaldo 60(p), Rooney 77

OK, WE WERE lucky with the penalty. Really lucky. And Rob Styles probably deserves all the abuse he gets, if only for the smug officiousness he brings to every game he referees. But no one can tell me there would have been all this fuss if the incident had happened in a game between two mid-table no-marks. Or if the player who 'won' the penalty hadn't worn the name Ronaldo on his back. And there would have been virtual silence if United would have been on the receiving end, as there was when Styles denied us stonewall penalties against Blackburn, Newcastle and Fulham last season.

No, if the roles had been reversed, the papers would have focused not on the penalty injustice but on how bravely Bolton had defended and on how United shouldn't be blaming poor refereeing for their failure to make their quality count. So, sorry Gary Megson. I know you feel robbed. I know it was a bad one. But you're not the first manager to get a duff refereeing decision. And you won't be the last. And remember one more thing when you keep on muttering about 'cataclysmic cock-ups' and Robbie Styles playing for United. There were still 30 minutes left when the penalty was given. And Rooney, Scholes, Nani and Giggs still had their trackie tops on...

GOAL ACTION

1-0 (60): Ronaldo cuts in from the right and Jlloyd Samuel produces a textbook display of watching the ball rather than the stepovers before timing his slide to perfection. There's no dive from Ronaldo and no appeal but Styles somehow spots a foul and points to the spot. Ronaldo picks himself up and sends Jaaskelainen the wrong way.

2-0 (77): A couple of years back, Ronaldo and Rooney combined for a sensational goal against Bolton, relaying the ball the length of the field before Rooney applied the final touch with a delicate dink. This Ronaldo-Rooney collaboration wasn't quite as dramatic but it still earned high marks for artistic impression. Ronaldo draws two defenders to him before back-heeling the ball to Rooney. Rooney makes to shoot, drops his shoulder and then passes a beautiful curler into the far corner.

WHAT WAS GOOD?

FABRICE MUAMBA'S FIRST HALF MISS – It was hard enough for United to break Bolton down at 0-0. If Muamba hadn't sidefooted an open goal chance wide from almost inside the disabled stand just before the break, we might have needed more than Rob Styles.

FERGIE'S POST-MATCH MIND-F*** with Rob Styles (see the verbals)

ARSENAL 1 HULL 2! (And Arsenal were 1-0 up)

GARY NEVILLE - man of the match in many papers, looked like his old self for the first time since his injury (suffered against Bolton back in 2007).

WHAT WAS BAD?

FABRICE MUAMBA'S FIRST HALF MISS – Seriously, how can a professional footballer get is so wrong?

THE 'UNITED GET ALL THE DECISIONS' OUTRAGE THAT FOLLOWED STYLES'S PENALTY BOOB – Predictable, boring and untrue. Every objective observer knows we get plenty of stinkers too.

RONALDO CHEAT CLAIMS - Predictable, boring and untrue. How on earth can a player be expected to stay on his feet when he's slide-tackled from the side at pace?

BOLTON – THE VERBALS

"It wasn't a penalty, it wasn't even close. It was a nonsense decision and it changed the game. We had to open up and it gave a world-class team the space to have a go at us." – *You could understand what Megson was saying here...*

"A cataclysmic cock-up" – *And here...*

"He [Styles] blew the whistle and then didn't know what to do. It was a nonsense decision which changed the game." – *And here...*

'Respect for the ref'. There will be more respect if he [Styles] holds up his hands and says he's made a big mistake." – *And here...*

'I can't imagine there is any side in the world where you have to play against the likes of Berbatov, Ronaldo, Tévez and Rooney and yet it was 0-0. Unfortunately, you can add Rob Styles to those four." – *...But I'm not so sure about here. Is he saying that Bolton are the only side in the world who could have kept us to 0-0?*

'I was surprised. I haven't seen it again but it looked to me as if their player got his foot on the ball. None the less, Rob turned down four or five for us last year, so maybe we got payback today - but he still owes us four!" – *Fergie's in classic form, accepting that Styles did us a favour while also reminding him that he owes us some more. Like the way he calls him Rob too. When else would he call a referee by his first name?*

"Ronaldo was on the floor saying, 'I didn't want a penalty'. Darren Fletcher was going, 'It's not a penalty', Carlos Tévez was going 'It's not a penalty'. There were 20 players in and around the box and every one of them knew it wasn't a penalty. But the other guy was wearing black and, somehow, he thought it was." – *Bolton captain Kevin Nolan becomes the first Englishman to understand what Carlos Tévez is saying.*

VIEWS FROM THE PRESSBOX

"In the keen football mind of Sir Alex Ferguson, referees obviously find themselves embroiled in an ongoing score chart of debts owed and repaid. Yesterday, Rob Styles repaid a huge one to Manchester United with an outlandish penalty decision that put the defending champions on course for their first home league win of the season." – *The Observer*

"Despite Styles' aberration, United were full value for a victory that was assured when substitute Wayne Rooney responded to his manager's new squad rotation policy by stroking in a superb second goal, six minutes after coming on as a 71st minute replacement." – *The Observer again.*

"A good referee is usually one who goes unnoticed. In which case, it is easy to understand why so many football people are wondering how the Premier League can continue to tolerate Rob Styles. When a referee is attracting more publicity than Wayne Rooney, Dimitar Berbatov, Cristiano Ronaldo and everyone else, there is clearly something wrong."

"Styles's influence on this game was so outlandish it is almost impossible to take issue with the online petition, set up in 2002, that demands he is 'removed from the referee's list for the sake of football'. Styles is a familiar subject for students of refereeing demonology. Controversy sticks to him like ticks on the side of an old mountain goat." – *The Guardian isn't 'Rob's' biggest fan.*

"Rob Styles could not have a more appropriate first name, could he? He has been robbing teams for so long now it is wonder that, as of yesterday, there were only 141, 163 and 209 signatures respectively on the three known petitions demanding his removal from the referees' register." – *The Times goes to town on Styles too.*

MATCH FACTS
UNITED: VAN DER SAR, NEVILLE, FERDINAND, VIDIC, EVRA, RONALDO (NANI 80), FLETCHER, ANDERSON (SCHOLES 71), PARK, TÉVEZ (ROONEY 71), BERBATOV
GOALS: RONALDO 60 PEN, ROONEY 77.
BOLTON: JAASKELAINEN, STEINSSON, CAHILL, ANDREW O'BRIEN, SAMUEL, DAVIES, NOLAN, MCCANN, MUAMBA, GARDNER (SMOLAREK 73), ELMANDER (VAZ TE 66) [MEGSON]
BOOKED: ELMANDER, MCCANN, DAVIES.
ATT: 75,484 REF: R.STYLES H-T: 0-0

OTHER SCORES
ARSENAL 1 HULL 2, STOKE 0 CHELSEA 2, EVERTON 0 LIVERPOOL 2.

LEAGUE TABLE
1. CHELSEA 14 (6) 2. LIVERPOOL 14 (6) 3. ASTON VILLA 13 (6)...
11. UNITED 8 (5)... 17. BOLTON 4 (6)

*"I didn't punch him strong enough.
I should have punched him harder."*

NEWS

ONE-PACED BOLTON old boy Alan Thompson reveals he could have joined United in 1998 but opted to move to Villa instead. Which makes Darren Anderton's decision to turn us down in 1995 look like the height of reason. Rob Styles apologises to Bolton for the penalty that never was. Funnily enough I never heard him apologise to United for the 4 or 5 penalty gaffes that counted against us last season...

SO WHO ASKED YOU AGAIN?

El Tel – a man who's never been known to chase the moolah, remember – goes off on one about Berbatov in The Sun*:*

"Berbatov kept telling us he had a dream. Well good for you Dimi! You had a dream with a few extra noughts added to your bank balance. But don't you think Spurs had a dream too? Don't you think that when they bought you and helped you blossom into one of the best strikers in the world, you had a duty to reward them by helping them fulfil THEIR dream.

'You got your way but your poisonous presence at the start of this season - the pouting, the brooding and the reluctance to play - has cost the club that believed in you.' *Blah, blah, blah..*

QUOTES OF THE WEEK

"I went looking for him but he ran away pretty quick" - *Keano reveals how he dealt with a terrace dissenter last season.*

"You think about the game and, if you can watch it, you watch it again. But there were certainly enough ingredients in the game to make me physically sick again" - *Wenger struggles to digest Arsenal's amusing home defeat to Hull.*

YOUSE ARE ALL BLEEPING BLEEPS

"I gave you access in South Africa and I shouldn't have given you access. It won't happen again. From now on, no matter how many miles you travel to get an interview, you won't get one." – *Fergie imposes his 335th media ban, apparently after his summer comments about the age of Chelsea's team (he said he couldn't see the likes of Lampard and Ballack improving hugely at their age) were misrepresented.*

IT WOZ CHELSEA

"There is an exaggerated perception of how well Liverpool and Everton fans used to get on 20 years ago but, equally, I have noticed a much meaner atmosphere at more recent derbies. As someone who has been a Blue and a Red, I feel qualified to say where it all went wrong and I feel the responsibility lies mainly with the way Everton fans reacted to their barren spell" – *Jamie Carragher lives the cliché in his autobiography.*

MISJUDGED CHANT OF THE WEEK

"2-0 to the murderers." – *Liverpool fans try to go ironic at Goodison. Someone should tell them that irony doesn't work anywhere near as well if it's based in fact.*

QUOTE OF THE SEASON

"I didn't punch him strong enough. I should have punched him harder." – *Eric's big regret about the Matthew Simmons affair.*

CL GROUP E 30/09/2008

AALBORG 0 UNITED 3
Rooney 22, Berbatov 55, 79

YOU CAN ALWAYS tell when United are playing against true Euro no-marks. The match is hidden away on the sort of Freeview channel that normally survives on a diet of police chase shows, Heartbeat repeats and Arsenal games. And armchair Reds are subjected to 90 minutes of Jim Beglin, the Scouse 'legend' who's most famous for, er, breaking his leg. This game had Beglin and ITV4 written all over it from the moment the draw was made. And in truth it didn't deserve a better stage. Aalborg were willing enough, and they caused us a few problems early on, particularly when the prima donnas up front decided not to track back. But from the moment Rooney converted

Giggs's peach of a through-ball, it was so easy it was embarrassing. "Welcome to Hell", the flag draped behind one goal said. If this is hell, we'll all take a piece of that.

MATCH ACTION

1-0 (22): Giggsy's passing has always been imaginative. It's just that he used to see balls that were never on (for a great player he's spent far too much of his career passing the ball straight to an opponent). But in recent years he's added accuracy and subtlety to his passing and the throughball which sent Rooney haring away for the opening goal was a masterstroke. Rooney's first time finish is immaculate, a hard, low shot into the right hand corner.

2-0(55): The moment of the night. Berbatov, who'd missed a sitter in the first half, is gifted the ball by some atrocious Aalborg defending and fires a right-foot volley past Zaza for his first United goal. Most players in that position would have been flashing teeth all over the place. Berbatov walks off like he's just crashed and burned with the town minger at the school disco. He might not play like Cantona, but, boy, he's going to be every bit as watchable...

3-0(79): Berbatov's second goal was so coolly taken even he couldn't help offering a sheepish smile. Ronaldo destroys Aalborg on the right, Berbatov leans back, pulls back his right foot and lashes a volley into the net.

DOING THE DECENT THING (82): Aalborg's fans stop pretending and pull their 'welcome to Hell' banner down.

WHAT WAS GOOD?

RAFAEL – No idea if he can defend yet. But what a player he looks going forward. He was in the six-yard box waiting for a cross at one stage. Gary Nev didn't make it there for 3 years. And here's the really exciting bit. Experts in Brazil reckon Rafael's brother, Fabio, is even better.

GIGGSY – If he could have passed like this when he was 25 how good would he have been?

BERBATOV GETTING OFF THE MARK.

BERBATOV'S GOAL CELEBRATION. Fascinating...

THE BENFICA '68-STYLE BLUE AWAY KIT – the best yet?

WHAT WAS BAD?

MORE INJURIES – Rafael, Rooney and Scholes all picked up knocks, with Scholes's damaged knee ligaments set to keep him out for 10 weeks. Scholesy's injury means that Fletcher is the only fit recognised central midfielder on the books.

AALBORG – THE VERBALS

"If I am not happy here, I cannot be happy anywhere 'Hey, I am at Manchester United. I am the happiest guy. It is a wonderful thing'." – *If this is Berbatov being deliriously happy God knows what he's like when he's in a mood.*

"The boy has got something special" – *Fergie's as excited about Rafael as everyone else (Brown and Neville aside).*

"I was still angry and disappointed with myself over the first one I missed. I was embarrassed." – *Berba explains why he didn't celebrate his first United goal.*

"It's a goal like any other. It was a tap-in and that was it, 3-0." – *Dimitar Berbatov, the king of the understatement.*

VIEWS FROM THE BROADSHEETS

"United should have had six, maybe even more. Ronaldo, in particular, will wonder how his own performance did not include a goal. He and Nani shimmered with menace on the wings, Rooney was alert and impressive and Ryan Giggs, Scholes's replacement, delivered a masterclass in the centre of midfield." – *The Guardian is a bit too impressed by United. Let's not forget, Aalborg were pants.*

WORST HEADLINE OF THE DAY

'Aarghlborg' - *The Daily Mirror makes a play on United's injury crisis. Get it?*

MATCH FACTS

AaB: Zaza, Bogelund, Olfers, Beauchamp (Caca 38), Pedersen, Augustinussen, Risgaard, Curth, Johansson, Enevoldsen, Saganowski [Rioch]
Booked: Johansson, Zaza
United: Van der Sar, Rafael (Brown 66), Ferdinand, Vidic, Evra, Ronaldo, Scholes (Giggs 16), O'Shea, Nani, Berbatov, Rooney (Tévez 59)
Aalborg Stadion Att: 10,346 Ref: Olegario Benquerenca (Portugal) h-t: 1-0

OTHER SCORES

Villarreal 1 Celtic 0, CFR Cluj 0 Chelsea 0, Liverpool 3 PSV 0, Arsenal 4 Porto 0

"Sometimes you can't find love, sometimes you can, but it's still not right, you want more, you want to give, you want to receive."

NEWS

HARRY GREGG'S BRAVERY at Munich is marked with a Special Recognition award at the *Daily Mirror*'s Pride of Britain ceremony. Absurdly it's the first time his actions have ever been officially recognised. 18 year-old Bursaspor forward Sercan Yildirim – the leading scorer in the Turkish league so far - claims that United are after him. Fletcher, the surprise star of the season so far, signs a new 4-year contract while Scholesy extends his for another year. And as they prepare to square up for the first time as managers at Ewood Park Fergie publicly ends his feud with the Guv'nor...

MAKING UP

"I regret saying that [*that Ince was a big time Charlie*]. That was a mistake. We let a camera into our dressing room, which we had never done before, and it won't happen again." – *Fergie repents.*

"It wasn't a personality issue with Paul. With Paul you could not have a honeymoon all the time, because he was such a volatile character, but he never let us down." – *That's not what he said after the Nou Camp '94 and Wembley '95 mind...*

QUOTES OF THE WEEK

"In Fletcher's case, it was the relief of the season to get him on a new contract. There were a lot of clubs trying to buy him and he only had a year left on his contract. But Darren is a United player and in big games he is outstanding. He does a great job for us in big games." – *Fergie's delighted Darren Ferguson, I mean Fletcher, isn't going to jump ship.*

"[Finding the right club is] like a woman: sometimes you can't find love, sometimes you can, but it's still not right, you want more, you want to give, you want to receive." – *Who else could it be but Eric?*

"I'm not sure that I would like to be with a woman who is like some of the chairmen I met." – *Eric's spot on. I wouldn't fancy dating women who liked peering under toilet doors either.*

"Fear is a funny thing, isn't it? I think when you drive, you have a fear. In heavy traffic. When it's going quickly" – *Fergie has a zen moment.*

FOOTBALLER OF THE WEEK

"Athletic Bilbao's Joseba Etxeberria has signed a one-year contract extension with the club which will see him play the final season of his career for nothing. The former Spain international agreed the deal with his current contract due to expire at the end of this season." – *bbc.co.uk*

COMMENTARY OF THE WEEK

"Transylvania. Famous, of course, for Count Dracula which was created by Irishman Bram Stoker. Another famous export from these parts is The Cheeky Girls whose biggest hit was called 'touch my bum'. Hopefully the players won't be up to anything like that this evening." - *RTE's Stephen Alkin goes left-field with his preview of Chelsea's Champions League game in Cluj.*

FAPL 04/10/2008

BLACKBURN 0 UNITED 2
Brown 31, Rooney 64.

OK, I WOULDN'T have said this when he joined Liverpool. And when he was diving into the Kop in injury time in '99 I could have quite easily dived in after him... with a knife. But I like Paul Ince. No, 'like' isn't the right word. It's a stronger feeling than that. Why? Because he was part of the United team I'd been waiting for all my life, the first United team I saw that made life feel better (admittedly, winning the title helped in that too). And he wasn't just part of that team, he was the driving force, the explosive dynamo who finally allowed us to stop pining for Robbo at his peak... the arrogant, pacy, wrecking ball who took on Barcelona on his own in '94, who scored that overhead at QPR and who, for the short time they played together, outshone even Roy Keane (the re-written version of United history takes Keano's superiority for granted but if he was a better player than Ince, it wasn't by much).

So for me the decision was simple. Once Ince left his Scouse treachery behind him he wasn't Charlie or the Guv'nor. He was a United legend [flawed but a legend all the same]. That's why I was really pleased to hear Fergie publicly rebuild bridges with him before this game. And that's why I didn't join in with the 'Charlie, what's the score?' taunts that broke out as United cruised to their best victory at Ewood for years. Mind you if Ince follows a similar career path to the last Red to take the job here, there's every chance I'll be changing my mind...

THE MOMENTS THAT MATTERED

1-0 (31): We're used to seeing Blackburn keepers – actually, one keeper, Friedel – perform miracles against us at Ewood. So it made a change for us to get a helping hand this time. Jason Brown fails to collect a long cross under pressure from Vidic and Wes Brown's downward header does the rest. Ince argues long and hard that Vidic impeded Brown and in fairness it falls into the 'seen them given' category. But Brown is as guilty of bumping against Vidic as the other way round so he can't feel that let down.

2-0 (64): In fairness to the Blackburn Brown he was almost faultless from then on as United turned it on in the Ewood rain. But there was nothing he, nor any keeper, could have done to stop United's second. Berbatov, of all people, wins the ball back in the left-back position. 18 seconds, and 12 touches from Fletcher, Anderson, Giggs, Brown and Ronaldo later, Rooney is looping the ball into the net, 'Bobby Charlton against Benfica' style.

TÉVEZ (66): OK it didn't really matter, and it only lasted 11 minutes. But when Tévez came on, the Awesome Foursome of Berbatov, Tévez, Rooney and Ronaldo were on the pitch for the first time.

THE BEST OF THE GUV'NOR
– Top 10 Ince memories
1. Posing in a United shirt while still a West Ham player.
2. The bloodied 'Guinness' bandage look on England duty in Rome.
3. Playing Barcelona on his own at Old Trafford in '94.
4. The run and finish at Palace on the night we all but won the first Premier League.
5. Selflessly squaring the ball for McClair to score in the '94 Cup Final.

6. The equaliser and frenzied celebrations at the Upton Park return in '94.

7. That gay goal celebration with Giggs.

8. Licking his top lip before he speaks.

9. Threatening Fergie with a gun (jokingly).

10. Having his pants pulled down by Gazza on England duty.

EWOOD – THE VERBALS

"'If the referee can't see it then he shouldn't be a referee" - *Ince calls for the sacking of Steve Bennett after he failed to penalise Vidic's challenge on Jason Brown just prior to Wes's opener (Ronaldo for one wouldn't argue with that idea).*

"I didn't get a great view but the ball was in the air long enough, the goalkeeper had a chance to collect it." – *Fergie can't see what all the fuss is about.*

"I think the bigger teams do get the bigger decisions. I played for Man United so I know. I've had it happen to me. I'm not saying all officials should be banned [for a bad mistake], but players get banned for being sent off and things like that. Referees are on professional contracts as well, so why not?" – *Ince won't let it drop...*

"It's scary, isn't it? You can spend all week discussing tactics and personnel, and I probably thought about playing 20,000 different teams, but at the end of the day when a team is that good, sometimes you can't do anything about it. We tried hard and went in there with a lot of confidence, but when they play like that they're awesome." – *But finally acknowledges the real difference between the teams.*

VIEWS FROM THE PRESSBOX

"The good news for the other Barclays Premier League clubs is that Paul Scholes, Michael Carrick and Owen Hargreaves are injured and Cristiano Ronaldo has yet to find his best form. The bad news is that Wayne Rooney and Dimitar Berbatov are starting to hit the high notes, Darren Fletcher and Anderson are no mugs in central midfield, Ryan Giggs continues to defy the years, Rio Ferdinand appears to be impregnable at the back and Ronaldo will start destroying the opposition, as he did so often last season, soon." – *The Times says United are back.*

"Despite this glowing assessment, Ince reiterated his belief that the 1993-94 Double-winning United team he was a part of was Sir Alex Ferguson's finest since the Scot became manager almost 22 years ago. They certainly had strength and guts in himself, Roy Keane and Mark Hughes, deadly pace through Andrei Kanchelskis and Ryan Giggs and a little je ne sais quoi with Eric Cantona. But that team was a simpler beast than Ferguson's current crop, one designed for the straight lines of the Premier League rather than the sophistication of the Champions League. The 2008 model, by contrast, is as chic as a Parisian boutique." - *The Guardian wades into the never-ending 1994 v today debate. Was it Fergie's best XI? Well it was the only one never to lose...*

WHAT WAS GOOD?

THE PERFORMANCE – the best of the season so far (and the first time we've won both halves)

BEATING THE EWOOD JINX - Despite playing some good stuff here in recent years, this was only United's second win in the last 8 visits.

WHAT WAS BAD?

THE RAIN?

MATCH FACTS

BLACKBURN: BROWN, OOIJER, SAMBA, NELSEN, OLSSON, EMERTON, KERIMOGLU (ANDREWS 68), WARNOCK, PEDERSEN (TREACY 58), DERBYSHIRE, ROQUE SANTA CRUZ (ROBERTS 50) [INCE]
BOOKED: PEDERSEN, SAMBA.
UNITED: VAN DER SAR, BROWN, FERDINAND, VIDIC, EVRA (O'SHEA 71), RONALDO, FLETCHER, ANDERSON, GIGGS (TÉVEZ 66), BERBATOV, ROONEY (PARK 77).
BOOKED: FLETCHER.
EWOOD PARK ATT: 27,321. REF: STEVE BENNETT H-T: 1-0

OTHER SCORES

SUNDERLAND 1 ARSENAL 1; CITY 2, LIVERPOOL 3; CHELSEA 2 VILLA 0.

LEAGUE TABLE

1. CHELSEA 17 (7); 2. LIVERPOOL 17 (7); 3. HULL 14 (7); 8. UNITED 11 (6)

"Have you ever seen an eagle in Manchester?"

BOY WITH THE BLUES
Noel Gallagher, easily the best Gallagher after Frank, opens up about City:
ON CITY BEING RICHER THAN UNITED: "I'd rather be in debt and have their trophies, than our money and have nothing."
BEST/WORST MOMENT AS A CITY FAN? "When we beat United 5-1 and then they beat us 5-0. We'd always had that 5-1 over them. And on that night they beat us 5-0, I actually met the woman who would become my ex-wife. The dark wife."
ON CITY'S BADGE: "If you win the Champions League you get a star, or the World Cup or ten championships or something. We haven't won anything, but we put three stars on our badge. And an eagle. Have you ever seen an eagle in Manchester?"

REWRITING HISTORY, CHELSEA-STYLE
According to The Independent, *the final copies of Didier Drogba's autobiography show some subtle changes from the initial version...*

"I hope I am in my last year at Chelsea. I don't know what the future holds for me but I let it be known I wish to leave because I want to start again from scratch, try something new." – *What Drogba said before the censors got to work.*

"I hoped I am in my last year at Chelsea. I didn't know what the future held for me but I let it be known I wished to leave because I wanted to start again from scratch, try something new." – *What Drogba 'said' after the censors got to work.*

JOURNALIST OF THE WEEK
Nuts journalist Adam Ralph quizzing Denis Irwin...

Q: "Denis, do you remember where you were when United won the Treble in Barcelona in '99?"
A: "Oh yes, son. I was playing left back."

SHOCK OF THE WEEK
Joe Kinnear only let out one expletive during his weekly press conference

NON-FOOTBALL NEWS OF THE WEEK
As reported on bbc.co.uk:

An investigation from the London School of Hygiene and Tropical Medicine found that 36% of Scouse men and 31% of Scouse women walks around with bacteria from faeces on their hands. In Newcastle the figures were 30% for women and 53% for men (presumably the other 47% had already weed the faeces off).

DELUDED QUOTE OF THE WEEK

"The credit crunch is not having a negative bearing on United. We continue to benefit from the sell-out of Old Trafford." – *A spokesman for the Glazers, the same Glazers who've left United in more desperate need of cheap credit than just about any club in history.*

RUNNER-UP

"I know Ronaldo is fast - he scores goals, has a great technique, everything - but I am still a different player and in some ways I can be better than him." – *West Brom journeyman Roman Bednar makes himself sound silly.*

POT. KETTLE. RIO.

"Croatia were fined a few thousand quid. What good is that going to do? That is not going to stop people shouting racist or homophobic abuse." - *Ferdinand after FIFA hand Croatia – and their racist chants – a derisory fine, 2009*

"You're a faggot." - *Ferdinand after Chris Moyles asked him if he'd rather go out with Alan Smith or Scholesy, 2006*

GLASWEGIAN SMILES
From The Sun:

'Bigoted yobs who trashed the cars of Rangers ace Allan McGregor and his fiancée were branded "moronic idiots" by the star's pals last night - after they MISSPELLED their taunts.

'The vandals tried to scratch 'Holy Goalie', nickname of McGregor's Celtic rival Artur Boruc, into the bonnet of the keeper's Bentley - but ended up with "HOLLY GOALY".'

RUMOUR OF THE WEEK
Methinks someone might be getting paranoid… (from The Daily Mail).

'When you have a personal fortune of £11.7billion, you can perhaps be forgiven for feeling the need for protection. In Roman

Abramovich's case, the solution is to order an armour-plated mega-yacht with missile detection system to offer early warning of attack by pirates or terrorists. At 550ft long, the vessel, costing more than £200million, will be the largest private yacht ever constructed.

'The yacht will include radar equipment designed to warn the crew of incoming rockets, together with bullet-proof windows and armour plating on the bridge and around the 41-year-old Russian tycoon's cabin. There will be twin helicopter pads and anti-bugging equipment, while the crew of 70 will include former SAS and Special Boat Service personnel. If intruders make it on board the Eclipse, named because it is intended to overshadow all other private boats, Abramovich and his girlfriend Daria Zhukova, 26, could escape in a yellow submarine which can dive to 160ft'

FAPL 18/10/2008

UNITED 4 WEST BROM 0
Rooney 56, Ronaldo 69, Berbatov 71, Nani 90

It's FUNNY. Just a few short weeks ago Wayne Rooney was supposed to be treading water. He hadn't come on since he was a teenager, his head was all over the place, he didn't score enough goals, he smoked, he was fat and he was in danger of becoming the greatest lost talent since Gazza. Now, after scoring a few goals against the assorted might of Bolton, Blackburn, Belarus, Kazakhstan and West Brom, he was the real deal again, the great white hope of the English nation, the first £100 million man.

Of course neither cap fits Rooney's newly scalped head just yet. The stick he got at the start of the season was ridiculous, particularly considering he started the new season with a nasty virus – and United started it without a midfield. The superlatives currently being vomited from the pressbox were equally over the top. As Fergie pointed out, this isn't the best Rooney's ever played, it's just another example of what he can do. And that's why he's not a true great yet. Because unlike the likes of Ronaldo, Kaka and Messi, Rooney only gives flashing tastes of his true ability, going through purple patches that fade as unexpectedly as they start. When he turns it on every week for months on end, it'll be time to put him on a pedestal. Until then let's enjoy his good days while they last.*

*(*and we'll wait for as long as it takes. Remember, even Maradona wasn't recognised as a true great until Mexico '86 when he was 25. Rooney won't be that old for another 3 years.)*

GOAL ACTION (CONDENSED VERSION)

Fergie was mildly irritated when no one asked him a question about West Brom in his pre-game press conference. But the way the Baggies rolled over in the second half, after defending diligently for most of the first half, effectively made the journalists' point for them. After all, what's the point of building up the chances of a team that doesn't believe they have a chance themselves?

The game was effectively over the moment Berbatov set Rooney on his way to hit a rolling bomb past Carson just before the hour. 13 minutes later Fletcher moved the ball to Rooney, Rooney moved it to Ronaldo and a miserable looking Ronaldo moved it into the net. Two minutes on and Berbatov scored his first league goal, nonchalantly flicking in Nani's centre at the far post. And it was Nani who finished things off, adding the final touch to a length-of-the-pitch move featuring Giggs, Berbatov and Rooney.

THE BAGGIES – THE VERBALS

"The players have now got the legs to play 90 minutes and the rhythm and tempo as well. The speed of our game was terrific today. That was our best 90 minutes of the season. I reckon we are back on track and playing more like the real Manchester United." – *Fergie clearly wasn't concentrating in the first half (when we were no more than OK).*

"I don't think it is the best Wayne has played. I know there is this English thing about Wayne Rooney at the moment, to look upon him as the saviour of English football, but Wayne was part of a team today. As good as he was, there were others just as good." – *Fergie trys to dampen down the latest bout of Rooney euphoria...*

'Wayne tends to go in spurts and that's probably a sign of his immaturity. When he gets older, his goalscoring will spread out better - that's a natural thing that will happen. But, at the moment, when he is on one of these spurts, he is fantastic.' – *But can't help drool over him a little.*

"What a pro, what a player. You simply can't fault him." – *Jonathan Greening gets in on the drooling act, this time over Giggs*

MATCH REPORT OF THE WEEK

From the Birmingham Mail (who are clearly still stuck in the early '80s):

"LET'S face it, an Albion victory at Old Trafford is a bit like a couple from the West Midlands winning a speedboat on Bullseye but forgetting to claim the cash.

"Yes, there is an instant thrill of winning Bully's Star Prize and getting nothing for 'two in the red' or whatever it is.

"There may even be an overwhelming sense that better times are around the corner. Today a speedboat, tomorrow an ocean liner and then, eventually, the world.

"But then reality bites.

"Owning a speedboat is fairly futile in the West Midlands. There's very little open water for starters.

"And, to make matters worse, the electricity has been cut off – and all because you didn't win enough prize money during the game to keep the meter running.

"And this, in many ways, is a bit like Albion's playing field in the Premier League."

WHAT WAS GOOD?

GIGGS – looks born to play in the midfield maestro role

FLETCHER – what happened to that one-paced, one-dimensional, pasty-looking kid who used to make large swathes of Old Trafford groan?

WHAT WAS BAD?

THE NEW WAVE OF SURLY GOAL CELEBRATIONS. I don't want to come over all *Daily Mail* here but would it be asking too much to ask Ronaldo to show some pleasure when he scores for the biggest club in the world? See below. .

VIEWS FROM THE PRESSBOX

"The scoreline may have flattered United slightly, but Wayne Rooney's performance most certainly did not flatter to deceive. The England forward's remarkable renaissance continued as he took his scoring tally to eight goals in the past six games for club and country.

"Statistics, however, do not do justice to Rooney's current dominance of his profession and any opponent unfortunate enough to come across his path. Rooney started the eventual rout at Old

Trafford, but also had a perfectly valid first-half effort ruled out for a phantom push on Gianni Zuiverloon and assisted on goals for Cristiano Ronaldo and Nani, with strike partner Dimitar Berbatov scoring the other. Add his recent displays for England, and the fact that Rooney does not turn 23 until Friday, and the young Scouser may currently be the most irresistible force in European football."
- *The Observer on one of United's famous 'R's...*

"Too much can be read into a goal celebration, but compare Ronaldo's glower with Rooney's double knee-slide or the sunrise of a smile that crossed Berbatov's face after he had turned in Nani's cross to make it 3-0. Nani himself went in for a back-flip. Yet Ronaldo spent so long over the summer trying to get a move to Real Madrid there are times when he looks as if he is here against his will. And that alone will have taken the gloss off this victory for some of United's supporters." – *The Guardian on the other.*

MATCH FACTS

UNITED: VAN DER SAR, RAFAEL DA SILVA (NEVILLE 65), FERDINAND, VIDIC, EVRA (O'SHEA 36), RONALDO, FLETCHER, GIGGS, PARK (NANI 70), BERBATOV, ROONEY.

WEST BROM: CARSON, ZUIVERLOON, DONK, OLSSON, ROBINSON, MORRISON, KOREN (MOORE 72), BORJA VALERO, GREENING, BRUNT, BEDNAR (MILLER 53) [MOWBRAY]

BOOKED: ZUIVERLOON

ATT: 75,451 REF: MARK HALSEY H-T: 0-0

OTHER SCORES

ARSENAL 3 EVERTON 1, LIVERPOOL 3 WIGAN 2, BORO 0 CHELSEA 5.

LEAGUE TABLE

1. CHELSEA 20 (8) 2. LIVERPOOL 20 (8) 3. HULL 17 (8) 4. ARSENAL 16 (8) 5. UNITED 14 (7)... 10. WEST BROM 10 (8)

"I am not the Chelsea manager any more and I don't have to defend them any more, so I think it's correct if I say Drogba is a diver"

WHERE'S RIO?

THE SHORTLIST FOR the Ballon D'Or is announced, minus the name of Ferdinand, arguably Europe's finest defender.

GOALKEEPERS: BUFFON, CASILLAS, VAN DER SAR
DEFENDERS: PEPE, VIDIC, ZHIRKOV, RAMOS
MIDFIELDERS: BALLACK, FABREGAS, GERRARD, LAMPARD, SENNA, VAN DER VAART, XAVI
FORWARDS: ADEBAYOR, AGUERO, ARSHAVIN, BENZEMA, RONALDO, DROGBA, ETO'O, TORRES, IBRAHIMOVIC, KAKA, MESSI, RIBERY, ROONEY, TONI, VAN NISTELROOY, VILLA

COME AGAIN

"Joey's disciplinary record hasn't been too bad" - *Joey Barton's agent Willie McKay as the ex-lag prepares to make his return from his 6 game ban for assaulting Ousmane Dabo.*

QUOTES OF THE WEEK

"It's been a bit s★★t" - *£15 million flop David Bentley doesn't waste words as he sums up Tottenham's start to the season – the worst in their history.*

"They had Jan Venegoor of...whatever you call him" – *Fergie gets flummoxed by the longest name in football as he recalls Celtic's last trip to Old Trafford (a game where Jan Venegoor of whatever scored the first goal).*

"Cristiano will win both [World] player of the year awards, I am sure of it. If he doesn't, I want to sign the guy who does." – *Fergie doesn't think Pepe, Zhirkov & co. should get too excited by their nominations for the Ballon D'Or.*

"I am not the Chelsea manager any more and I don't have to defend them any more, so I think it's correct if I say Drogba is a diver" - *Jose Mourinho says nothing and everything.*

"He is a player we like and does seem to be very interesting." – *Fergie comments on the speculation linking United with a move for Brazilian wonderkid Douglas Costa. Though as they appear in Marca, he's probably never even heard of him.*

NEVER SURRENDER

"Manchester United have pace, power, height, ability and determination and I'm not sure our players have all five of those assets." – *Gordon Strachan's idea of a rabble-rousing speech before the Battle of Britain.*

"Yeah, we're trying to find Snow White to lead us out. If we can get hold of her, we might be all right."- *Strachan tries his usual sprinkling of witty fun as he contemplates playing without his injured target men, Georgios Samaras and Jan Venegoor of, oh, ask Fergie (he's suggesting that Celtic are dwarves – geddit?).*

"If we are playing one-for-one in the middle of the park then I'll beat him [Fergie]. I'm fitter than him, there's no doubt about it. He wasn't a good defender and I was quite a good attacker so it will be no problem. So if it was me and him playing tomorrow then I would be delighted. But unfortunately he has a lot of world class players behind him." – *I think they call it gallows humour.*

WISHFUL THINKING

"I have seen the match on video and I believe I should not have been sent off with three minutes to go. If I had punched him, I would have understood. Now I wish I had." – *Drogba bravely threatens Vidic from the safety of his autobiography. For the record I wish I'd punched Jason Harding when he broke my Grifter* in the park when I was 6 (I didn't because he was 11)*

QUOTE OF THE WEEK

"It's comical. It's just such a big surprise that Derby went down to 10 men and won a game" - *Paul Jewell on the FA's announcement that they will investigate the Rams' win over Norwich following match-fixing claims (actually Derby have been so bad under Jewell, the FA might have investigated them if they won the game with 11 men on the pitch).*

RANT OF THE WEEK

"Who is Souleymane Diawara? If he went to play in Saudi Arabia, people would ask 'what kind of ketchup is that?' Me, I'm known everywhere. I'm on Puma's A-list along with Samuel Eto'o. I was one of the best 100 players of the century" – *El Hadji Diouf is spitting mad after his compatriot, Souleymane Diawara, criticizes him for his performances for Senegal.*

P.C. PLAYER OF THE WEEK

"I wouldn't go for a walk on my own around White Hart Lane. A lot of dark-skinned people live there. So naturally the crime rate is higher than anywhere else. It's not nice to be a robbery victim. So I suggest that Roman doesn't walk but drives around that area" – *Former Spurs man Sergei Rebrov offers some friendly advice to new boy Roman Pavlyuchenko.*

*if I'm honest it was a Budgie (my parents could be right b**tards)

CL GROUP E 21/10/2008

UNITED 3 CELTIC 0
Berbatov 29, Berbatov 51, Rooney 77

WHAT CELTIC WERE crying out for before this game was the sort of up-and-at-them rabble-rousing from their manager that another famous ginger, Churchill, used to specialise in. Instead Gordon Strachan sent out a wave of weak one-liners and excuses - mostly based on the absence through injury of strikers Jan Vennegoor of Hesselink and Georgios Samaras (yes, that one) – and effectively arrived in Manchester waving a white flag. The result was as predictably one-sided a match as many punters had feared. Celtic couldn't even bring themselves to moan too hard that United's first two goals were offside because, as many of their players openly admitted afterwards (check out McGeady's quote below), anything less than a 3-0 scoreline wouldn't have even come close to reflecting the gulf that exists between the two teams.

GOAL ACTION

1-0 (29): United took a while to shift gears but they were right in Celtic's faces by the time Berbatov opened the scoring with his fourth goal in as many games. Nani whips in a corner from the left, O'Shea stabs the ball goalwards and, from six yards out, Berbatov beats Boruc with another lazy waft of his right foot. Replays showed that the Bulgarian was just offside when he scored, though the hacks who wrote that his sheepish goal celebration suggested he knew it missed the point. Berba would look sheepish if he'd just banged in an overhead kick from the corner flag.

2-0(51): United kill Celtic off, once again with the help of a linesman. Ronaldo slams a swerving free-kick straight at Boruc which the Pole can only push back out into the box and Berbatov, who was marginally offside when the set piece was taken, does the rest.

3-0(77): Moments after Berbatov's second it's United's turn to fall foul of a dodgy offside decision as Rooney is denied a good goal after Ronaldo tees him up to walk round Boruc. 20 minutes later he makes up for it, banging a low shot from inside the D that arrows through Loovens's legs and into the bottom left corner. It's Rooney's ninth goal in his last seven England and United games.

WHAT WAS GOOD?

THE TRAVELLING JOCKS BEHAVE THEMSELVES. Every Mancunian with a sense of smell breathes again (after Rangers were here the streets reeked of piss for days)

UNITED'S HOME RECORD IN THE EUROPEAN CUP SINCE 2006: P14 W13 D1 L0 F33 A7

WHAT WAS BAD?

CELTIC'S AWAY RECORD IN THE CHAMPIONS LEAGUE: P19 W0 D1 L18 F10 A40

QUOTE OF THE NIGHT (SHORT VERSION)

"The 3-0 result probably does reflect the game because they gave us a bit of a doing to be honest with you." – *Celtic's Aiden McGeady*

QUOTE OF THE NIGHT (LONG VERSION)

"We've played some terrific sides over the past few years, but that Manchester United side here tonight was the best we've faced. Wayne Rooney, for one, was unplayable — world class in fact — with ten other great players backing him up. Also, physically, we couldn't match them. We were blown away at set-pieces and just didn't have the balance to cope. As I say, we've played some terrific teams in this competition, but that's the best I've ever seen in my time at Celtic." – *Strachan slaps on the praise.*

CELTIC – MORE VERBALS

"My players cannot be faulted for guts or effort, and we didn't get some decisions, but I'm a football man and I know when we're well beaten." – *Many managers would have attempted to hide behind the two offside calls. Gary Megson would still have been moaning about them in 2015. So full marks to Strachan for refusing to follow suit.*

"This is the first time we have made a mistake in 52 international matches." - *Assistant referee Alex Verstraeten – one third of the team of officials responsible for getting three major offside decisions wrong - thinks we're stupid.*

"They were brilliant. They are probably the best side we've played against. They are the best side in Europe and it was a test for us and a great experience." - *Celtic's Stephen McManus on the class gap.*

"The gap was embarrassing. I was not expecting it to be quite so easy for United." – *Paul Ince in the TV studio.*

"It was a bad night for Celtic. I just felt we were always on the attack. The speed of our play was very good and we have to think a result in Glasgow will get us through." – *Fergie in the tunnel.*

HEADLINE OF THE DAY
From football365:

'See You Dimi' - *The Daily Mirror goes for a pun/lazy national stereotype combo for the Manchester United v Celtic game.*

WORST HEADLINE OF THE DAY

'Dimi Roo Well' - *The Sun. If you listen carefully, you can even hear Brucie groaning at that one.*

VIEWS FROM THE PRESSBOX

"Two goals from Dimitar Berbatov and a further strike from Wayne Rooney only indicates a little of the chasing of shadows that Celtic were subjected to over these 90 minutes. If it was understandable, given the differences in the two clubs' wealth, it was still a little ignominious for Celtic and Scottish football. The United fans taunted their visitors with chants of "Are you Rangers in disguise?", thus somehow managing to ridicule both halves of the Old Firm in the same moment." – *The Times.*

"It is a curious experience to be both outplayed and wronged. A wry Celtic supporter struck the correct balance in a well-constructed complaint. "They weren't the ones needing help from the officials," he said in mock indignation. The Dimitar Berbatov goals that put Manchester United 2-0 ahead had been taken from marginally

offside positions." – *The Guardian*

MATCH FACTS

UNITED: VAN DER SAR, NEVILLE (BROWN 59), EVANS, VIDIC, O'SHEA, RONALDO (PARK 82), FLETCHER,
ANDERSON, NANI, BERBATOV (TÉVEZ 60), ROONEY
CELTIC: BORUC, WILSON, LOOVENS, MCMANUS, NAYLOR, NAKAMURA (HARTLEY 61), SCOTT BROWN,
CALDWELL, ROBSON (MALONEY 61), MCGEADY, MCDONALD (SHERIDAN 77) [STRACHAN]
BOOKED: HARTLEY, LOOVENS
ATT: 74,655 REF: FRANK DE BLEECKERE (BELGIUM) H-T: 1-0

OTHER SCORES

VILLARREAL 6 AALBORG 3, CHELSEA 1 ROMA 0,
ATLETICO 1 LIVERPOOL 1, FENERBAHCE 2 ARSENAL 5

GROUP E LEAGUE TABLE

1. UNITED 7 (3) 2. VILLARREAL 7 (3) 3. CELTIC 1 (3) 4. AALBORG 1 (3)

"Whenever you leave Manchester United it is a step down but, if we have to look at it this way, Everton is a good step down."

NEWS

DAVID BECKHAM JOINS AC Milan on loan and becomes the first player to play for Madrid, United, Milan and, er, Preston. Are Milan trying to build the best seniors team ever? The FA decide not to take action against Drogba for his quotes about hitting Vidic in Moscow. Now I don't think he should have been punished (what he said was pretty tame) but can you imagine what would have happened if Keane had written something like that? Lubos Michel, the referee who sent off Drogba in Moscow, retires at 40 and Bruce Rioch is sacked as manager of Aalborg after last year's Danish champions slip to second bottom of the league.

IMMODESTY BLAZES

"If you assess what I did over the course of the season, I think I did more than everyone. What else should I have done to win the Ballon d'Or and the Fifa award?" – *Looking back, it would have been fun to see Ronaldo's face if he hadn't won the Ballon D'Or...*

PORK LIFE

"It is forgotten, not only for January but forever" - *Ramon Calderon 'brings an end' to the Ronaldo-Madrid saga.*

THE BARTON FILES

Say what you like about Barton, but he certainly makes for good copy:

"I've got sort of a quirky personality" - *Joey Barton. Well that's one way of saying it.*

"He's got a big heart and is a good character" – *Kinnear's messing with us right?*

"My reputation will always precede me until the day I die. For some people that probably can't come quickly enough" - *Whatever else he is, at least Joey Barton is not delusional.*

OPTIMIST OF THE WEEK

"Champions League football in three years? It's achievable" - *Mickey Walker, Doncaster Rovers Director of Football, inadvertently puts himself up as a candidate for a top job at City.*

QUOTES OF THE WEEK

"After Inter I will return to England" - *Jose Mourinho. Interesting...*

"Madrid is not doing anything to disturb a 'friend club' like Manchester. We are two very big clubs. We want to be good friends forever. We are in the same market. I have a lot of respect for Manchester. I have a good relationship with David Gill and I want it to be like that for a long time." – *Ramon Calderon, presumably the sort of bloke who'd sleep with your girlfriend and still want to be best mates.*

"I used to want to be like Rio Ferdinand, but he was too good." – *Stoke's former Red, Ryan Shawcross*

"For obvious reasons, Saturday is a big game for me. It is always nice for any player to score 100 goals and if I can do that back at Everton... it would be really pleasing. But it wouldn't really matter if it was my first or my 100th, it would still be really sweet." – *Rooney, fresh from his 99th career goal against Celtic, looks forward to Goodison on Saturday.*

BETTER THAN BRAZIL

Strachan's still raving about United. Pull yourself together man, we weren't that good…

"I was speaking to Gary Caldwell, Stephen McManus and Shunsuke Nakamura after the match. Gary and Stephen have played against France and Italy and Naka against Brazil. I asked them to tell me where United rank compared to the national teams and they told me United are better than any national side. A million miles better. They have it all. Did you see the size and strength of them? Did you see the workrate of Carlos Tévez when he came on? They can also all make that 10 or 15-yard pass. United destroy you if you give the ball away."

QUOTE OF THE WEEK

"Whenever you leave Manchester United it is a step down but, if we have to look at it this way, Everton is a good step down." – *Louis Saha, the man who could have been king.*

FAPL 25/10/2008

EVERTON 1 UNITED 1
Fletcher 22, Fellaini 63

As ROONEY HIMSELF said, this was going to be 'sweet'. He was going to celebrate his 100th career goal in front of the Gwladys Street and in the process give the Merseyside police a proper reason for starting these matches at noon (how come Everton games at Old Trafford don't have to kick off so early?). United meanwhile would ease to their seasonal win at Goodison and ramp up the pressure on table-topping Chelsea and Liverpool just before they went head to head at Stamford Bridge.

So much for the script... Rooney managed to wind up the Everton fans all right by kissing the United badge but that only served to convince Fergie to bring him off. As for United, they contrived to throw away their third winning position in their last four league aways. If anything, this was even more frustrating than the Anfield suicide and the missed opportunity at Chelsea. United were so superior to Everton in the first half it was embarrassing. But they didn't get the buffer of a second goal and that allowed Everton to scrap, foul and play their way back into the match after the break. And though an off-colour Ronaldo had two great chances to win it late on, Everton deserved their point. In fact, if it hadn't been for Vidic, who had to effectively man the defence on his own as Rio and Wes's heads went AWOL after half-time, they could easily have sneaked all three.

GOAL ACTION

1-0 (22): When United were good - as they were for virtually the entire first half - they were very, very good. And although Berbatov was excellent, there's no question who the best player on the pitch was. Giggs was sensational in central midfield and the goal he created was a mini-classic, Fletcher running on to his slide-rule pass, taking Lescott out of the game with his first touch and sliding the ball under Howard with his second. You could tell what a good goal it was - even Ronaldo smiled.

1-1 (63): And when United were bad – as they were for long stretches of the second half – they were... well, you know the rest. Ferdinand, who made more brain-dead mistakes in one afternoon than he has for two years, set the tone by missing a straightforward clearance and allowing Yakubu to run clear. United snuffed out that danger but then switched off at a throw-in, allowing Pip Neville to clip in a cross that the freakish Belgian, Fellaini, headed past Van der Sar.

FREAK SHOW

I don't want to go on about Fellaini. But he really is a strange looking boy. And that got me wondering about the oddest looking players to score against United. I'm guessing there are plenty of better candidates from the 70s but here's the top 6 I can remember:

BEARDSLEY (PREDICTABLE) – scored hat-trick at Anfield in 1990.

FOWLER – scored on Eric's return in 1995.

TÉVEZ – scored the winner for West Ham in 2007.

LE TISSIER – scored in the 6-3 at The Dell. Also practically ended Taibi's OT career with that pea-roller in 1999.

WANCHOPE – looked like bambi on ice before he waltzed through from halfway for Derby in 1997.

JANCKER (ok he didn't score but he hit the bar in the Nou Camp)

CROUCH – FA Cup winner at Anfield in 2006.

WHAT WAS GOOD?

THE FIRST HALF.

GIGGS, MIDFIELD MAESTRO (AGAIN).

BERBATOV (FIRST HALF).

WHAT WAS BAD?

THE SECOND HALF.

RIO'S RELAPSE.

RONALDO – he's either not fit, in pain, frustrated he's playing like a mere mortal or sulking he's not at Madrid. Either way he's acting like a p★★★k.

THE OTT TREATMENT Everton dished out to Berbatov and Ronaldo.

ALAN WILEY – for allowing Everton to get away with the rough stuff (see above), plus his crowd-pleasing decision to book Rooney for next-to-nothing.

MAKING SCOUSERS HAPPY... AGAIN.

VIEW FROM THE PRESSBOX

"A familiar sound bellowed down the players' tunnel at Goodison Park and, for the first time this season, it was not the jeering of disgruntled Evertonians. It was Sir Alex Ferguson employing a customary diversionary tactic from the self-indulgence that cost Manchester United more valuable ground in the defence of their title.

"Witnesses reported the United manager accusing the referee Alan Wiley after the final whistle of failing to protect his players, when the champions' run of six successive victories stalled against Everton's spirited second-half revival. Wiley would have been well within his rights to remind Ferguson that it is not the referee's job to immunise European champions from the complacency that produced their latest meagre return from Merseyside. Or the lack of discipline in Wayne Rooney. Or the embarrassing antics of Cristiano Ronaldo. Or the costly lapses in concentration from Rio Ferdinand." – *The man from the Guardian is wrong to ignore some of Everton's bullyboy tackling but there can be no arguments elsewhere...*

POT. KETTLE. LAWTON.

"Where does Sir Alex Ferguson begin to dissect this morning a performance that so reeked of self-satisfaction it made a mockery of the belief that his champions had found again their old hard edge?

He might, who knows, begin with his own decision to preserve the illusion that Cristiano Ronaldo can do any more for Manchester United than stew in his own self-regard.

"It may be true that the roots of United's slide from absolute control ran deeper and wider than Portuguese narcissism, but it was still impossible not to note the comparison with the Ronaldo of last season and the one who fretted and pouted his way through a match that came within a heartbeat of being surrendered.

"Last season Ronaldo was plainly on an extraordinary mission, and even if a lot of the motivation may, as it turned out, have been to do with his own standing in the world of football – one which he is currently announcing as unquestionably without a challenge – there could be no questioning its prime value to United's renaissance.

"On the evidence provided here, Ronaldo's mission appears to be complete, at least in his own mind and on this island. His body language would have looked disenchanted on the back of a lorry filled with disconsolately homesick fruit-pickers." – *The Independent's James Lawton has a nerve accusing anyone of being self-satisfied (has a writer ever spent so much time, and so many words, pleasuring himself?) but he's right about Ronaldo. We want to love him again, we want to forgive him, but when he pouts and preens like this, how can we?*

EVERTON – THE VERBALS

"Got carried away at times and that's why he was substituted." – *Mickey Phelan doesn't waste words explaining why Rooney was taken off*

MATCH FACTS

EVERTON: HOWARD, NEVILLE, YOBO, JAGIELKA, LESCOTT, ARTETA, FELLAINI, OSMAN, PIENAAR, SAHA (ANICHEBE 90), YAKUBU (VAUGHAN 88) [MOYES]
BOOKED: JAGIELKA, YOBO, FELLAINI
UNITED: VAN DER SAR, BROWN, FERDINAND, VIDIC, EVRA, RONALDO, FLETCHER (TÉVEZ 78), GIGGS, PARK (ANDERSON 67), BERBATOV, ROONEY (NANI 71)
BOOKED: VIDIC, ROONEY, BROWN
GOODISON PARK ATT: 36,069 REF: A. WILEY H-T: 1-0

OTHER SCORES

CHELSEA 0 LIVERPOOL 1, WEST HAM 0 ARSENAL 2, CITY 3 STOKE 0

LEAGUE TABLE

1. LIVERPOOL 23 (9) 2. CHELSEA 20 (9) 3. HULL 20 (9) 4. ARSENAL 19 (9).. 6. UNITED 15 (8)...14. EVERTON 9 (9)

"I am with Manchester United body and soul"

NEWS

RONALDO GETS WHAT he's always wanted. No, not his move to Real. But a nice shiny FifPro World Player of the Year award with his name on him. And to think, we would all have been so proud of him just a few months ago. Harry Redknapp trashes his reputation in Portsmouth for the second time by moving to Spurs in place of the newly sacked Juande Ramos. Amusingly the news breaks just hours before he is due in Portsmouth to receive the freedom of the city. United are linked with 19 year-old Vallodolid keeper Sergio Asenjo, CSKA Moscow right winger Milos Krasic and Bordeaux's former Milan playmaker Yoann Gourcuff while an interesting Mourinho rumour is splashed across the Sunday papers...

A SPECIAL KIND OF LOVE
From the News of the World (quoting a 'highly-placed Chelsea source'):

"Jose always made his love of United very clear, in fact he was obsessed with them and talked about being in charge of the biggest club in the world. He wanted to test himself in Italy when he left the Bridge, but it was obvious to most people he wanted to come back here with United to haunt us."

STAYING

"I'm a northern lad and I'd like to think I could stay here for the rest of my career. As for moving abroad can you ever see me playing for a foreign team?" − *The White Pele.*

STAYING?

"I am with Manchester United body and soul. Only God knows the future but I insist that I am a Manchester United player and now I think that next year I will continue here. I want to respect this club, my team-mates and the fans, and I prefer not to talk of other teams at this moment." − *The Orange Ronaldo.*

TEAM OF THE WEEK

FIFPRO WORLD XI: CASILLAS − RAMOS, TERRY, FERDINAND, PUYOL − GERRARD, XAVI − KAKA, RONALDO, MESSI − TORRES.

ASKING FOR IT
From The Guardian's Fiver:

"Harry Redknapp has had a huge impact on this city. I was thinking, what do I call him?" - *Portsmouth council leader Gerald Vernon-Jackson at that civic reception for last season's FA Cup winners this afternoon.*

"Judas!" - *a quick-witted heckler comes up with a suggestion.*

PUNDIT OF THE WEEK

"Harry Redknapp has showed dare and nerve in taking the Tottenham job. He was very happy at Portsmouth, working with good people, living close to the training ground and, let's get it right, doing an outstanding job." – *Who says Jamie Redknapp can't be impartial?*

ABOUT TURN OF THE WEEK

*Just last week Fergie told the press 'youse ***** will never get any f****** help out of me again'. And then he does an interview with GQ that contains enough nuggets for the press to bite on they wouldn't need to make any Ronaldo/Tévez mischief for, er, days:*

"Di Canio would have been capable of becoming a truly great player at Manchester United. We make heroes quickly here. Di Canio could have been in that category." – *Nugget number one. Interesting...*

"I think Sepp Blatter is in danger . . . or has reached a point now, where he is being mocked within the game." – *Fergie turns on the FIFA president, who angered just about everyone by agreeing with Ronaldo's summer bleating that his contractual situation with United was akin to being a slave.*

"Whether he's getting too old, I don't know. But things can happen to people in power. Look at some of the despots in Africa." - *Ooh this is good...*

"He has uttered so many ridiculous statements that he is in danger of seriously damaging his credibility. So when he came out with that stuff it created a furore and rightly so, the year after the commemoration of the 200th anniversary of the abolition of slavery." ... *real good.*

"No. Definitely not. Peter Kenyon? He wasn't a loss." – *Fergie almost brings up his breakfast when he's asked if Cuddly Pete's departure was a major blow.*

And now for the juiciest morsel of all, the idea that Real only snapped up Heinze to bring in Ronnie:

"When we sold Gabriel Heinze to Real Madrid in 2007, we

knew it [Madrid's campaign to pinch Ronaldo] was going to happen, because Ronaldo was very close to Heinze. I knew what they were doing. I don't believe they were interested in Heinze. The endgame was to get Ronaldo.

"What made it really obscene was that Madrid, as General Franco's club, had a history of being able to get whoever and whatever they wanted, before democracy came to Spain." – *First he compares Blatter to Mugabe & co. Then he labels Madrid a bunch of fascists. The man's a legend...*

QUOTES OF THE WEEK

"To be honest I don't even like going down to London. I am not comfortable there." – *Rooney rocks.*

"If I smile it is because I smile. If I don't, it's because I don't. People are always writing things about me. It is up to them; for me it is not a problem. I will just try to play well and do my best. I am just focused on playing good football." – *Ronaldo responds to the criticism (some harsh, most fair) that his surly body language and sulky pout has received this season.*

"This theory of Ferguson's - that I went to Real so the club could persuade Cristiano [to sign] the following summer - is a work of absolute science fiction." – *In fairness, Heinze's probably right. After all, the only reason he ended up at Madrid was that we were absolutely desperate not to sell him to Liverpool (though judging how slow he is these days that might not have been such a bad idea).*

RETROSPECTIVE QUOTE OF THE WEEK

"That was the result I wanted" – *Like most Reds, Fergie is delighted that Liverpool finally ended Chelsea's epic unbeaten home run. Now how could anyone possibly get upset by that? (see pxx if you haven't guessed already).*

SURPRISE STAT OF THE WEEK

Chelsea's 86 game unbeaten run in the league at Stamford Bridge deservedly earned them the plaudits. But here's the interesting bit. Since the run began back in February 2004, Chelsea have won 63 matches at home in the league. United have won 65...

FAPL 29/10/2008

UNITED 2 WEST HAM 0
Ronaldo 15, 30

FERGIE RECKONED HE'D pay 'double the money' to see Berbatov's bewitching touchline spin and pass for Ronaldo's second. Which was easy for him to say as, unlike the rest of us, he isn't already paying double the money he was just a few years back. Unfortunately the rest of the night rarely felt like money well spent. In fairness it wasn't United's fault. We were excellent for half an hour, when Nani, Berbatov and Ronaldo were at their hottest. But West Ham were such feeble opponents that we couldn't quite get up for it after half-time. So instead of watching United take chunks out of Chelsea's goal difference advantage, we had to settle for talking about Rooney's haircut - and pondering the question why it looks so strange under floodlights. I'm sure Jaap's baldie head didn't glow so much in the dark...

GOAL ACTION

1-0 (15): Nani's centre is too good for Neill. Ronaldo scores and then makes a big song and dance of celebrating in front of the hack pack (who'd been giving him grief all season for his default pouty body language). Judging from the match reports the next day most of them believe his celebration is genuine. A look at the replays – and Ronaldo's stern face – suggests he's winding them up.

2-0 (30): Can you remember when Redondo mesmerised Berg en route to setting up a tap-in for Raul when we lost 3-2 at home to Real in 2000? (if it helps, it was the night that Keano scored the crucial own goal opener). This was even better. At first it looked like Berbatov would do well to even keep Anderson's through-ball in play, eventually reaching it only a few inches away from the white-wash. It's what happened next that made Old Trafford go weak at the knees. With no room to play with, Berbatov spins, pirouettes and dances away from Collins and then coolly squares the ball for Ronaldo to bundle in. Brilliant.

WEST HAM – THE VERBALS

"I'm going to have to see it again to understand how he [Berbatov] did it. You'd pay double the money to watch that - fantastic imagination, control and balance." – *Fergie on that turn*

"The first half was magnificent and after that I was looking forward to more of the same. I was hoping they could add to their goals tally because that could be important at the end of the season. But they took their foot off the pedal and played at a couple of gears below what they are capable of. They ended up too lax for me." – *If Fergie had been a paying punter you get the feeling he'd have been on the M60 before the final whistle too.*

VIEWS FROM THE PRESSBOX

"The biggest compliment that can be paid to Berbatov is that, even in a stadium with the rich nostalgia and sepia-tinted memories of Old Trafford, it was difficult to remember a more sublime piece of penalty-area skill - even from Ronaldo. Sir Alex Ferguson used such adjectives as "stunning" and "magnificent" and nobody at Old Trafford will ever tire of seeing the television replays of how Berbatov deceived his marker, James Collins, to leave Ronaldo with an open goal". – *The Guardian on the moment of the night.*

"How would he celebrate? Old Trafford's amateur psychologists waited to analyse his body language and, after a dramatic pause of which Robert de Niro would have been proud, there was an explosion of unrestrained joy. Point made." – *The Guardian falls for the Ronaldo wind-up...*

"Cristiano Ronaldo picked up the FifPro World Footballer of the Year award before kick-off last night and proceeded to show West Ham United just why his fellow professionals voted him the best player on the planet. As gratefully received as his two goals were, it was the return of a smile to the Portugal forward's face that will have heartened Sir Alex Ferguson, the United manager, as much as it will have sent a shudder down the spines of opposition defenders.

"Ronaldo's sullen body language, coupled with a reluctance to celebrate previous goals scored this season, had hinted at a player struggling to accept that his immediate future lies with United after a much-publicised courtship with Real Madrid in the summer, but on this evidence, such troubles finally appear to have been put to bed." – *So does The Times .*

MATCH FACTS

United: Kuszczak, Rafael Da Silva (Neville 81), Ferdinand, Vidic, Evra, Ronaldo, Fletcher (Carrick 69), Anderson, Nani (Rooney 70), Tévez, Berbatov
Booked: Evra
West Ham: Green, Faubert, Collins, Upson, Ilunga, Behrami (Boa Morte 44), Bowyer (Sears 69), Mullins, Etherington (Collison 46), Di Michele, Bellamy [Zola]
Booked: Collison, Collins.
Att: 75,397 **Ref:** P.Walton **h-t:** 2-0

"Our season is not beyond my wildest dreams because they usually involve Elle Macpherson"

NEWS

Radcliffe Borough sign 25 year-old striker Luiz Henrique Pereira Da Silva, the older – and clearly less talented - brother of twins Fabio and Rafael. Rooney gets a police caution for spitting at a paparazzi photographer in London in the summer (no wonder he doesn't feel comfortable down there).

Mental Argentina name Maradona as their new coach. His first match in charge will be against Scotland – which should at least guarantee him a good reception. Russell Brand and Jonathon Ross finally knock the credit crisis off the front pages by making a rude phonecall to Andrew Sachs. Spain reacts with fury. No, not to the idea that Russell Brand shagged Manuel's granddaughter. But to Fergie's suggestion that, having been the plaything of General Franco, his dictatorial ways are now fused in Madrid's DNA. As if...

HATED IN MADRID. LOVED IN BARCELONA.

"Ferguson, what is he going to say? We went for everything in Europe and at that moment the Franco government ruled. And what were we meant to do? Throw the games away? We had to win." – *Real legend Alfredo Di Stefano disappears down a blind alley.*

"Ferguson Chochear" – *The headline in Marca, roughly translated as Ferguson has gone senile.*

"I'm not going to waste any time answering him, I admire his record, but he is getting old." – *Calderon aims the same barb.*

"Calderon has a few strange things to say every week. There is a lot of hot air comes out of that man. I am not getting involved but the nub of it is he is very disappointed he did not get Ronaldo. I am delighted to say he is still here and I will keep repeating that." – *Fergie wins the verbal battle hands down – and at the same time proves there's no shrewder mind game merchant in the game. Now he's spent so much time accusing Madrid of being the bad guys in the Ronaldo saga, it's easy to forget that Ronaldo was just as much to blame...*

HOW DID THAT GO AGAIN? PART I

OCTOBER 28: "They would do really well. I'm sure they would get a point" – *Cesc Fabregas considers how Arsenal Ladies team would get on against Tottenham's males.*

OCTOBER 29: *Spurs score two injury-time goals to get a point against Arsenal at the Emirates.*

QUOTES OF THE WEEK

"A part of the supporters show themselves to be more unhappy than others. But I hope to change their minds. When I put on the United shirt I give my maximum. Nobody can condemn me on this. I hope it will be similar to when I came back to England after the 2006 World Cup and I can win the fans back." – *A month ago Ronaldo was cocksure we'd fall madly in love with him just for pulling on the shirt. Now he just hopes he'll hear 'Viva Ronaldo' again.*

"Our season is not beyond my wildest dreams because they usually involve Elle Macpherson" – *Hull chairman Paul Duffen asks for trouble with Mrs Duffen on the eve of their first visit to United since 1987.*

"I'm very happy for him. It's going to be funny." - *Tévez on the Maradona bombshell.*

CONFUSED FOREIGNER OF THE WEEK
Blackburn new boy Carlos Villanueva:

"You don't get the time to blink here. As a striker I am constantly coming up against opposing defenders, and I have to laugh when I see my legs covered in cuts and bruises. The football is very physical, and I have to run a great deal. The fact that I don't speak English, and can't communicate with others, limits me in many ways. As a result I spend a lot of time watching TV in my apartment, eating nothing but frozen food. I have lunch at the club, but at night it's deep-frozen pasta for me, pure and simple."

"As most of my teammates live in Manchester, I decided to get a flat in the south of the city. Virtually none of them live in Blackburn. It was hard for me to get used to driving in England. The first week was like giving birth to a baby - I was not used to being in a car with the steering wheel on the right."

FAPL 01/11/2008

UNITED 4 HULL 3
Ronaldo 3, Cousin 23, Carrick 29, Ronaldo 44, Vidic 57, Mendy 69, Geovanni 82p

IT DIDN'T LAST of course. But for a couple of months in the autumn Hull were just about the best thing about the league. And this game, perhaps above any other, showed why. Most teams, even those packed with big-money international names, come to places like Old Trafford with a dreary, 'let's try and pinch something' attitude. Phil Brown – who'd just engineered a famous victory at Highbury and was about to blow a hole in Liverpool's title pretensions at Anfield – just seemed to tell his players to go out and have a go. The result was one of the most enjoyable – and perplexing – Saturdays of the season. After Ronaldo had put us 3-1 up before the break it looked like we were going to win by an absolute landslide. 40 minutes later we were looking down the barrel of an embarrassing draw. It was crazy, knockabout stuff (Fergie would have called it careless and unprofessional too). But for the first time at Old Trafford in what seemed like ages football felt how it should do… fun.

MATCH ACTION
(with so many to get through I'll keep it quick)

1-0 (3): I don't know if they meant it, but if they did this was one of the best one-twos ever. Ronaldo backflicks a long ball to Berbatov, he half-volleys it back to him and Ronaldo swivels and scores with a low left-footed scuffer.

1-1 (23): Cousin equalises with a glancing header from Andy Dawson's inswinging free-kick from the right

2-1 (29): But it's not long before United score again with a goal that travels the length of the pitch. Vidic punts a clearance out of the United area, Berbatov carries the ball another 25 yards and slips in the overlapping Carrick. His low left-footer goes in the exact same place that Ronaldo's did.

3-1 (44): Game over? Ronaldo scores the sort of goal that makes him unique, attacking Nani's corner at the far post and heading it in via Myhill's arms.

4-1 (57): Comedy Hull defending allows Vidic to volley in Nani's corner at the near post.

4-2 (69): But comedy United shooting and finishing allows Hull to creep back in the goal with a neat lob from Mendy.

4-3 (82): Ferdinand's shove on Mendy gives Hull a soft penalty. Former Blue Geovanni scores from the spot.

4-3 (90): Old Trafford descends into nervous silence, Rooney almost blows his newly bald top but Hull don't manage to create a proper chance. Thank god for that.

WHAT WAS GOOD?

BERBATOV'S FIRST TOUCH. A wonder of the modern world.

DESPITE HIS INJURY-DELAYED START TO THE SEASON Ronaldo already has more goals (7) than did at this time last year.

UNITED ARE ABOVE HULL for the first time all season

WHAT WAS BAD?

SEE FERGIE'S RANT BELOW

HULL – THE VERBALS

'We should have won by 10 goals, but ended up scrambling. They only had two chances in the match and scored three goals. We had 10 or 11 clear chances and frittered them away. We were almost left embarrassed.' – *Fergie doesn't know whether to praise his players or switch on the hairdryer.*

"As a footballer I was never really encouraged to play and that probably restricted my career," *said Brown, a former journeyman right-back.* "But I have belief in my players. I encourage them to pass the ball and I know we're capable of good football." - *Phil Brown, back in the days before he did a David O'Leary and turned weird.*

"Tactically United had problems with us when we switched from 4-3-3 to 4-4-2. When we went one on one on them, they didn't know what to do. We had them rocking." – *George Boateng, who's got a history of talking out of the back of his shorts, gets carried away.*

VIEWS FROM THE PRESSBOX

"It had to happen, and finally it did. Four days before Bonfire Night, helped by two more goals from Cristiano Ronaldo and in spite of a spirited second-half recovery by the visitors, Manchester United climbed above Hull in the Premier League table. They inflicted Hull's first away defeat too, without managing to make it sting. For some reason, 4–3 always sounds like a thriller, but this was never quite that. United should have been out of sight by the time the visitors made the last 10 minutes more interesting than they had a right to be. As at Everton last weekend, far too many clear opportunities were spurned and Hull were virtually invited back into the game." – *The Observer*

MATCH FACTS

UNITED: VAN DER SAR, NEVILLE, FERDINAND, VIDIC, EVRA, RONALDO, CARRICK (GIGGS 72), ANDERSON (O'SHEA 8), NANI (TÉVEZ 64), BERBATOV, ROONEY.
BOOKED: ROONEY, TÉVEZ.
HULL: MYHILL, MCSHANE, TURNER, ZAYATTE, DAWSON, MARNEY, HUGHES (MENDY 59), BOATENG (FOLAN 86), GEOVANNI, KING (HALMOSI 63), COUSIN [BROWN]
BOOKED: TURNER, MENDY.
ATT: 75,398 REF: MIKE DEAN H-T: 3-I

OTHER SCORES

STOKE 2 ARSENAL I, SPURS 2 LIVERPOOL I, CHELSEA 5 SUNDERLAND 0.

LEAGUE TABLE

I. CHELSEA 26 (II) 2. LIVERPOOL 26 (II) 3. UNITED 2I (I0)
4. ARSENAL 20 (II)... 6. HULL 20 (II)

"It was paradise watching George play football, just as it is with Ronaldo now."

WAG OF THE WEEK

'I DIE FOR FOOTBALLERS. When I want a player I simply become a goddess. I cover myself with vanilla and chocolate essence so they want to eat me whole. I dream that they scratch me all over. I am insatiable with men.' - *Tévez's alleged new bed buddy, Mariana Paesani, really should work on her quality control.*

STILL AT IT

"United are the best team in the world in terms of ability. Italy would have no chance against Man. United. France? No chance. Man United are far better. Roma lost 7-1 to them. It's unbelievable what they can do to other teams." – *Is Strachan making anyone else feel nauseous?*

STAT OF THE WEEK

3 – the number of goals Jamie Carragher has scored for Spurs (after his crucial goal in Liverpool's defeat at the weekend)
4- the number of goals he's scored for Liverpool in 540 appearances

HOW DID THAT GO AGAIN? PART 2

31 OCTOBER: "We will counter it by attacking the ball in the air and by not making too much of a fuss of it. They score one goal every one or two months and it is not like a penalty, it is a throw-in" - *Arsene Wenger dismisses the threat of Rory Delap,*
1 NOVEMBER: Rory Delap's long throw-ins set up both Stoke goals in their 2-1 win over Arsenal,

ULTIMATE PRAISE

Sir Bobby sides with Ronaldo over Best:

"George had the ability to turn people inside out, and beat anyone he liked. He was as good as anyone you will see. He used to embarrass players time and time again. It was paradise watching George play football, just as it is with Ronaldo now. The difference is that Ronaldo is stronger and faster."

FAT QUOTE OF THE WEEK

"If I could have looked after my weight the way Frank Lampard has, and eaten a few nibbles and nuts instead of a burger, I would have played for Real Madrid" – *Kiddo's favourite centre-forward, John Hartson.*

RUNNER-UP

"I couldn't have got any fatter, I was running out of clothes.

Everything on the table is nice but it makes you put on weight"
– *Ronaldo, the fat one.*

QUOTE OF THE WEEK

"He said: 'We went one v one on Saturday to see how good they
were.' We've just won the European bloody Cup. Can you believe
that one?" – *Fergie can't stop laughing about George Boateng's dribblings
after the Hull game.*

05/11/2008
CL GROUP E

CELTIC 1 UNITED 1
McDonald 13, Giggs 84

IT'S ONE OF the great mysteries of football. All pitches are roughly
the same size, only the Russians are allowed to play on anything
but grass, the goals are the same size, the rules don't change. So why
do even the best teams do so much better at home than away? Take
United. They have a squad packed with great players, they travel
in first-class comfort, they have the support of an army of trainers,
masseurs and chefs, they are used to playing in hostile atmospheres.
But even in the last year's title winning season we barely won half as
many games away (10) as we did at home (17). If last season's away
form had been maintained over 38 games we wouldn't be playing
our Euro games on ITV or Sky this year – we'd be stuck with City,
Villa and Colin Murray on Channel 5 on Thursday nights.

But if United tend to struggle to repeat their home form on
their travels, they've got nothing on Celtic. Celtic's away record in
the Champions League group stages is a shambolic one draw and 16
defeats. But their home record is amazing. Before this game they'd
only lost one out of 16 home games. They'd beaten Milan, Juventus,
Lyon, us and Porto. And they almost beat us again here, even though
we had an enormous 76% of possession, created a chance from just
about every set piece and spent the entire second half zig zagging the
ball round the pitch like Brazil 1970 on fast forward.

So how do they get away with it? Is it because the support of
60,000 screaming banshees lift them to levels they wouldn't normally
achieve without illegal supplements? Is it because Celtic fans don't

mind them playing 5-5-0 football at home (if United played Alamo stuff all the time, the Red Army would mutiny)? Is it because opponents have psychological problems playing at a stadium where the home team always seems to get a result? Or is it simply because they just keep on getting lucky?

It's probably a mix of all four. But after watching United boss Parkhead to a ridiculous degree – and each time waste golden opportunities with almost the last kick – for the second time in 3 years it's really tempting to plump for option D...

THE MOMENTS THAT MATTERED

0-1 (13): Celtic might have played ugly but their goal was anything but. A Celtic free-kick gets recycled to Scott McDonald on the left angle of the United box, he kills the ball with his first touch and lobs the ball exquisitely over Foster with his next. Maybe it wasn't quite as impressive as Nakamura's free-kick in 2006 but it was pretty close.

1-1 (84): United, by contrast, played the beautiful game all night but when the equaliser finally came it was a scruffy one. Boruc misjudges Ronaldo's wobbling 25 yarder, the ball drops invitingly in front of the onrushing Giggs and he bundles it in with his head. That's the 13th straight seasons that Giggsy's scored a goal in the Champions League. Incredible.

2-1 NO! (90+): In 2006 Saha missed a last-gasp penalty at Parkhead. This time it's Berbatov who wastes the chance to wreck Celtic's night, the Bulgarian hooking the ball wide from under Boruc's nose.

WHAT WAS GOOD?

THE PARKHEAD ATMOSPHERE. Say what you like about Glaswegians – and violent parade-wrecking drunks would be a decent start – but they certainly know how to make some noise. And this according to the locals might just have been their loudest night yet.

CELTIC'S BACKS-TO-THE-WALL DEFENDING. What happened to the cumbersome surrender monkeys from two weeks ago?

BEN FOSTER: finally got a chance to show what he can do in a big game

UNITED'S PASS AND MOVE EXHIBITION IN THE SECOND HALF

RONALDO'S BODY LANGUAGE. He was enjoying himself here, no doubt about it. I think we can put the 'his head's not here' debate to bed for a while now.

AALBORG'S 2-2 DRAW WITH VILLAREAL. Barring a four-goal Aalborg win at Old Trafford, it meant that United were through to the knockout stages. It also meant that United stayed top despite the dropped points here.

WHAT WAS BAD?

UNITED'S OVERELABORATION in the first half (OK, I'm being picky)

BEN FOSTER: didn't get a chance to show what he can do in a big game (apart from picking McDonald's perfect lob out of his net, I can't remember a United keeper having less to do)

PARKHEAD – THE VERBALS

"At least we made them work for it. I am happy that we are not boys, as some people have said. Whatever we are, we are men. You cannot play like that if you are not men because they are a million miles ahead of us technically. We should never be called boys, that's for sure, because boys do not fight like that." – *Strachan's proud.*

"You have to consider it a good result. If you're 1-0 down with only a few minutes to go you think you're not going to get anything out of the game. Credit to the players, our second half performance was very, very good." – *Fergie's satisfied.*

"Christ, I don't know where they pick them from nowadays." – *Fergie on the ref, the soon to be infamous Tommy Ovrebo (he was the referee Chelsea held responsible for losing their Champions League semi against Barcelona – he was also the man who gave Roma a joke penalty at Old Trafford in last year's competition).*

"We were having a bit of a laugh about it afterwards. I have never defended that much in my life before and maybe Manchester United will feel hard done by." - *Celtic defender Mark Wilson.*

VIEWS FROM THE PRESSBOX

"The English have an unpleasant habit of looking down their noses at Scottish football, the more so as the financial gulf between the two leagues widens. If Celtic's meek 3-0 defeat at Old Trafford last month represented a low point, this result, albeit achieved with an approach more associated with lower-division teams on FA Cup third-round day, will restore a little pride among Celtic's fans not only in Glasgow but also around the world." – *The Times.*

"Match statistics said that United had more than 73 per cent of the possession — almost unheard of at this level of football, particularly for an away team — and had struck 30 shots to Celtic's six. It felt even more one-sided than that at times, but, with Celtic defending heroically, Ferguson was gracious enough to say that Gordon Strachan's team deserved something, if only for their spirit and for the sublime skill that McDonald showed in putting them ahead, lobbing Ben Foster, who is regarded by many, not least Ferguson, as the next England goalkeeper." – *The Times again.*

WORST HEADLINE OF THE NIGHT

"Ry Fawkes" – *The Sun. The match was played on Bonfire night – geddit?*

MATCH FACTS

CELTIC: BORUC, HINKEL, CALDWELL, McMANUS, WILSON, HARTLEY, BROWN, ROBSON, MALONEY (O'DEA 75), McDONALD (HUTCHINSON 81), SHERIDAN (DONATI 63) [STRACHAN]

UNITED: FOSTER, RAFAEL DA SILVA (EVRA 66), FERDINAND, VIDIC, O'SHEA, RONALDO, FLETCHER, CARRICK, NANI (BERBATOV 46), TÉVEZ (ROONEY 71), GIGGS

BOOKED: NANI

PARKHEAD ATT: 58,903 **REF:** T.OVREBO (NOR) **H-T:** 0-1

OTHER SCORES

AALBORG 2 VILLAREAL 2, ROMA 3 CHELSEA 1,
LIVERPOOL 1 ATLETICO MADRID 1, ARSENAL 0 FENERBAHCE 0

GROUP E TABLE

1. UNITED 8 (4) 2. VILLARREAL 8 (4) 3. CELTIC 2 (4) 4. AALBORG 2 (4)

"What they saw tonight was an impersonator, a clown, a self-indulgent idiot really, doing crazy things."

NEWS

THE SUN RECKONS we'll swoop for £5m Leeds kid Fabian Delph in January. United move reserve games back to Altrincham from Northwich Vics after crowds drop below 400 and the floodlights pack up. Fergie snuggles up to Wenger again (what's the old fox up to?) by appealing for United fans to stop singing *that* song. Chelsea lay off 15 scouts as part of a series of cost-cutting measures. Is it the start of the end of the big spenders? Or are they just going to go back to their old tactics of signing everyone our scouts find?

INSENSITIVE JOURNO OF THE WEEK

From the Observer's Q & A session with Bobby Charlton

Q: Have you ever spent a night in hospital?
A: After the Munich air crash I was in hospital for a week.

FOAMING AT THE MOUTH PART I

Ronaldo gave perhaps his liveliest performance of the season at Parkhead. But that didn't stop Eamon Dunphy - a regular Ronaldo beater in the past - going off on one on RTE:

"Can you imagine Tiger Woods or any of the great sportsmen; Lewis Hamilton, Padraig Harrington, Ruby Walsh the jockey - going out in front of a paying audience and playing like that - while they are world player of the year? It's an absolute disgrace to the game.

"What they saw tonight was an impersonator, a clown, a self-indulgent idiot really, doing crazy things. He's a petulant brat Bill, poncing around all night....If you say that's showbiz, this is showbiz Bill (points at self). If you really want to make it showbiz, take your gear off.

"This is the World Footballer of the Year and his performance tonight in terms of his professionalism, his clowning around, was a disgrace to the game of football. I go back to Pele, Maradona, Best, Charlton, Giles, Law, Keane: would you see Keane do that tonight? No way baby! What they saw tonight was an impersonator, a clown, a self-indulgent idiot."

(And yes, apparently he did say 'No way baby'. For god's sake, get the man his pills...)

FOAMING AT THE MOUTH PART II

The Leeds Lucifer (Johnny Giles) joins in with the Ronaldo beating after hearing Sir Bobby's pre-match quote that he was better than Best:

"I always say that Bobby Charlton is the best player I played with and the best player I played against. I must say I'm disappointed by some of his comments about football today. I've never seen George Best do some of the things Ronaldo did tonight and in other matches. I've seen Georgie Best have poor games, but I've never seen him indulge himself in the way that Ronaldo does and I'm actually surprised at Bobby's comments."

QUOTES OF THE WEEK

"Everyone was trying to impress him. I hope he'll go back to Argentina and say he's seen a great player — Rio Ferdinand!" – *Rio goes ga-ga after Maradona nips into Carrington to see Tévez.*

"I am a bit surprised. But this is the FA. They were probably dying to send me a letter" - *Fergie reacts to his latest disrepute charge, for giving a mouthful to Mike Dean after the Hull game (he was upset about Hull's penalty).*

"Maybe I will get a chance to give my views to the FA. But the last time I was charged by the FA, they had a murder lawyer in against me, so it's going to be a hard case to win" – *Keano doesn't fancy his chances of beating his own FA rap (for having a pop at the referee during Sunderland's 5-0 hammering at Chelsea).*

FAPL 08/11/2008
ARSENAL 2 UNITED 1
Nasri 22 & 48, Rafael 90

IT'S ONE OF the unsolved mysteries of the last couple of years. Why don't Fergie and Wenger hate each other any more? Why, after years of exchanging insults and air handshakes are they now exchanging pleasantries and post-match embraces? Is it because Mourinho – the only manager to really break Wenger's cool façade - replaced Fergie as Wenger's number one enemy? Is it because they're both united in their antipathy towards Benitez? Is it because Arsenal just aren't the danger they once were? Is it because they looked in the mirror, saw the grey hair and glasses staring back at them, and finally thought all this aggro was ridiculous? Maybe, maybe. But perhaps the main reason for the entente cordiale is this… English football just isn't the game it was three or four years ago. In today's football, winning ugly is king. 4-4-2 has turned into 4-5-1 or even 5-5-0, the goals have dried up, so has the entertainment. In many cases the weaker teams don't even try and attack. And here we have the two grand old men of the game flicking two fingers at the managerial roundheads – the Megsons, Benitezes and the rest - and giving the watching billions a reminder of everything that's good about the beautiful game.

Of course the fact it was an absolute belter of a match didn't make this defeat any easier to take for us Reds. The points matter too much for that to be the case, particularly when it's November and you're already trailing Chelsea by 8 points. But Fergie was right when he said magnanimously: "Sometimes you just have to hold your hands up and say 'if you're going to get beaten, just make sure it's someone who's going to play football' and Arsenal played good football at times."

GOAL ACTION

0-1 (22): The first goal is always crucial in these sort of games. On this occasion it was even more important than usual. If United had scored first – and they really should have done when Rooney skied Ronaldo's cutback – then memories of Arsenal's recent surrenders against Spurs and Stoke would surely have strangled their play, while United would have jumped at the chance to take them apart on the break. As it was it was Arsenal who grabbed the psychological advantage with a marginally fluky goal, Nasri's casual volley flying in off Gary Neville.

0-2 (48): The half-time score really could have been anything as both teams indulged themselves in basketball football, surging from end to end to take potshots at goal. United certainly deserved to have at least one goal to their name at the break when Clichy handballed but Howard Webb chose, a la Wenger, not to see it. And that error took on an even greater significance when Arsenal scored a classy second right at the start of the second half, Nasri smashing the ball past Van der Sar after a 45 second spell of intricate passing.

1-2 (90): Even at 2-0 United weren't out of it. Ronaldo should have scored within a minute of Nasri's second, steering Park's centre wide from close range. Chances for Rooney, reverting to type by not scoring in five matches after his flurry of goals in October, came and went. It wasn't until Rafael connected with a beautiful left-footed volley that United finally scored but not even this Arsenal team – who had conceded 2 injury-time goals in the 4-4 with Spurs – could allow themselves to be struck by lightning twice. So for the third time in three Emirates visits United had played a full part in a sensational game. And for the third time it was Arsenal who were left celebrating at the end.

QUOTE OF THE DAY

"Today it was a game for people who love football." – *Wenger*

EMIRATES – THE VERBALS

"It was fantasy football, it was like playground stuff - you attack, we attack. I don't think you'll see a game as good as that anywhere else in the country." – *Unnervingly, Fergie raves about the quality too. Where's the moaning, the mind games, the excuses, the siege mentality..?*

"It's our second defeat of the season, but we have had a lot of tough away games. They say the league's not handicapped, well I'm not so sure about that. We're playing every game away from home after a European tie. It's not easy going up to Celtic Park and playing in that atmosphere and the intensity of that game, and having to come to Arsenal for a lunch time kick-off is difficult. But that wasn't a problem today because the players showed great energy and desire, everything that you expect of a Manchester United team. On another day we'd have won." – *Now that's more like it.*

'We'd got beat. And when you lose against Arsenal it does your head in. I was going back to meet my family in a hotel for my birthday. It was meant to be a really happy time. So I thought before I go back maybe I'll go and have a couple of drinks in a pub. So I told the driver to stop off at some London pub. And he was like, "No, I can't let you can't go in there." I had my Man United tracksuit on in a West Ham area. I said, "Nah, just drop me off, leave me. Stop the car." So he did, and I went in. And to be honest everyone was looking. I could see people going, "What's he doing in here?"

'I ended up having a couple of drinks, three packets of crisps and sat in the corner watching the football results coming in on the TV. Then I got up and went home. Players do do normal things. People think we don't, but we do.' – *Some people will never forgive him for the contract saga – and for being a Londoner – but can anyone still doubt Rio's commitment as a Red?*

WHAT WAS GOOD?

WE'VE GOT OUR THREE BIGGEST AWAY GAMES OUT OF THE WAY – and it's only just November

RAFAEL. Great potential. Great goal. .

THE EMIRATES SEATS – big and comfortable, the antithesis of Old Trafford's placcy knee-scrapers.

WHAT WAS BAD?

WE'VE ONLY GOT ONE POINT FROM OUR THREE BIGGEST AWAY GAMES - 3 less than last year.

ANDERSON'S GOAL DROUGHT – this was his 50th United game and he still hasn't scored (Rafael is a right-back with 5 starts to his name and he's already off the mark).

THE GENTS AT THE EMIRATES – an orderly single-file queue, no clouds of cigarette smoke, no pushing, people using the wash basins to wash their hands in? What the hell is going on?

WATCHING GARY NEVILLE FAIL TO LIVE WITH THE PACE. Is he still rusty after his long layoff? [hope so] Or have his legs gone? [hope not]

VIEWS FROM THE PRESSBOX

"Arsenal played angelic football and found some hope that they will receive their reward for it long before they get to heaven. Arsène Wenger's side must already feel soothed to be above Manchester United in the table, even if Sir Alex Ferguson's team has a game in hand. The greatest boon of all, however, came to onlookers across the world who were reminded that this sport, in its modern form, can cause excitement and awe in equal measure.

"Seldom has nostalgia for the football of bygone decades looked more deluded. Athleticism and technique were at the same uncanny pitch on Saturday. The energy served the game instead of undermining it. This spectacle was always likely to be too pure for the losers' taste, with Ferguson and his backroom staff rueful about the unchecked nature of the action. United did acquit themselves fairly well and could have shared the points, but Arsenal deserved to hog the glory." – *The Guardian*

"Wenger once referred to his philosophy as playing sans frein à main – without the handbrake – and it was the perfect description for a game such as this. When it comes to the propaganda battle, this kind of spectacle – arresting, compelling, magnificent stuff right up until the sixth and final minute of stoppage time – can help to restore faith in football played "the right way", but, as the dust settled, there were nagging feelings of doubt.

"This may, in terms of technique and flair, have been the finest exhibition of football in the Barclays Premier League this season, but can either of these teams hope to win the title playing this way? Or does the handbrake have to be applied once in a while, for safety's sake?" – *The Times*

MATCH FACTS

ARSENAL: ALMUNIA (FABIANSKI 78), SAGNA, GALLAS, SILVESTRE,

CLICHY, WALCOTT (SONG BILLONG 77), FABREGAS, DENILSON, NASRI, DIABY (TOURE 86), BENDTNER [WENGER]
BOOKED: GALLAS, SAGNA, CLICHY.
UNITED: VAN DER SAR, NEVILLE (RAFAEL DA SILVA 63), FERDINAND, VIDIC, EVRA, RONALDO, ANDERSON (GIGGS 72), CARRICK, PARK, ROONEY (TÉVEZ 77), BERBATOV.
BOOKED: EVRA, CARRICK.
THE EMIRATES ATT: 60,106 REFEREE: HOWARD WEBB H-T: 0-1

OTHER SCORES

LIVERPOOL 3 WBA 0; BLACKBURN 0 CHELSEA 2

LEAGUE TABLE

1. CHELSEA 29 (12); 2. LIVERPOOL 29 (12); 3. ARSENAL 23 (12); 4. UNITED 21 (11)

"They say the league's not handicapped but it is handicapped."

NEWS & GOSSIP

OWEN HARGREAVES IS ruled out for the season after United finally bow to the inevitable and send him off for a double knee operation in the States. It's a bad blow that, particularly remembering how useful his pace and versatility were in the run-in last season. United are linked with moves for Portsmouth's £12m-rated Diarra and Standard Liege's 19 year-old rated midfielder Axel Witsel. I still haven't figured out if that's a sex anagram or not. Thaksin Shinawatra has his UK visa revoked after he's sentenced to two years for corruption. Yes, that's the same Thaksin Shinawatra who had no problem passing the 'fit and proper person' test. And in another award-winning scoop *The Mirror* reveals that Anderson put a field mouse down the back of Gary Nev's shirt in training. He didn't like it.

RETRO REVELATION OF THE WEEK
From popbitch:

"Remember Dani Behr, the husky voiced vixen who used to share a toothbrush with Giggsy 300 years ago? Well, when she was dating Les Ferdinand, 'his favourite "thing" apparently was to ask her to dress up as Princess Diana'." Weird.

RANT OF THE WEEK

"I wouldn't trust them to walk my dog. There are ex-players and ex-referees being given air-time who I wouldn't listen to in a pub. OK, there will be one or two who've done something in the game whose opinion you would take on board, but I'm on about every Tom, Dick and Harry" – *Keano lashes out again, this time at TV pundits… and inadvertently goes on to confirm he'd be a great one:*

BISH: "Will Arsene Wenger be remembered in 100 years' time for what he has done for football? Bet your life he will. Will these people on the television be remembered for what they've achieved? None whatsoever."

BASH: "I was asked by ITV to do the Celtic-Man U game but never again unless I fall on hard times. I think I've done it once for Sky but I'd rather go to the dentist."

BANG: "You're sitting there with people like Richard Keys and they're trying to sell something that's not there. I tell people any time they watch a game to switch the commentators off, don't listen to experts, gather your own opinion."

NOT OK, COMPUTER

"They say the league's not handicapped but it is handicapped. Every game after a European tie is away from home. We've got the top 10 teams from last year's league all away from home in the first half of the season." - *Fergie rages at the fixture list. Though hopefully he won't mind so much when we play all the worst teams away in the title run-in.*

PREDICTABLE OUTBURST OF THE WEEK

"You'll be fined!" – *Chief funster Gary Neville's reaction to Anderson's mouse prank.*

CC4 11/11/2008

UNITED 1 QPR 0
Tévez 76(p)

WHY DID IT take us so long to put this one to bed? Why did QPR not at least give it a go? What did the 7,000 travelling fans think about their team playing 5-5-0? How can no-marks like QPR dictate to us what we have to pay for Carling Cup games? Who were more negative, QPR this week or Celtic last? Are Chelsea and Liverpool's Carling Cup exits good news or not? Did you ever think there'd be more Brazilian kids than local lads playing in the same United team? Why didn't Manucho and Welbeck get more of a chance? Is Rafael now the number one right back? How good must Fabio be if he really is better than his brother? Can we really win all four? Were there really 55,000 Reds in the ground? How good is an attendance over 62,000 for a full-price reserve team game? When was the last genuinely interesting Carling Cup game at Old Trafford? When was the last great Carling Cup memory*?

And now for the biggest question of all... why the hell didn't I opt out of the Carling Cup games when I had the chance?

GOAL!

1-0 (76): After knocking on the door all night, United finally make the breakthrough. Nani slips in Welbeck, he's taken out by Ramage and Tévez – using the same pacy, angled run-up he did in Moscow – side-foots the penalty firmly into the right corner.

QUOTE OF THE NIGHT

"It was not really Brazilian weather, but I think the performance was like Brazil" - *Rodrigo Possebon gets carried away with the 1-0 victory over QPR. Good to see him back in the team though.*

VIEWS FROM THE PRESSBOX

"On a night when most of Sir Alex Ferguson's A-list footballers were watching from the stands, Carlos Tévez could be forgiven if he had mixed feelings about turning out in the Carling Cup, against strange opposition, in a typically Mancunian downpour, but the Argentinian can at least reflect on a decisive contribution, with the goal that sent Manchester United into the quarter-finals.

"It came from the penalty spot, 14 minutes from the end of an otherwise soporific match in which Queens Park Rangers seemed so intent on keeping out their opponents they seemed to forget that opposition teams are allowed to attack United, too. It was a pity they were so defensive because, with a touch more imagination, they could have troubled this youthful, experimental side." – *The Guardian can't believe QPR's tactics either.*

★TOP 10 CARLING CUP MEMORIES AT OLD TRAFFORD (GOOD AND BAD)

1. Giggs rolling in from impossible angle against Sheffield Wednesday (semi-final '94)
2. Giggsy lob against Chelsea (2005)
3. Giggsy getting booed against Blackburn (2003)
4. Outclassing the Arsenal kids (2004)
5. Sparky's hat-trick against Southampton (1991)
6. Lee Sharpe settling the Boro semi in the rain (1992)
7. Pat McGibbon sent off in the 3-0 York disaster (1995)
8. The 0-0 against Southampton in Big Ron's last Old Trafford game (1986)
9. Pogatetz's assault on Possebon (2008)
10 Skiddy Giddy – John Gidman - scoring for Everton (1985) [and yes, I'm really scraping the barrel now]

MATCH FACTS
UNITED: KUSZCZAK, RAFAEL DA SILVA, NEVILLE (VIDIC 89), EVANS, O'SHEA, GIBSON, POSSEBON (WELBECK 72), ANDERSON, NANI, TÉVEZ, PARK

QPR: CERNY, RAMAGE, HALL, STEWART, CONNOLLY, BUZSAKY (AGYEMANG 33), ROWLANDS, MAHON, COOK (DI CARMINE 7, PAREJO (LEDESMA 46), BLACKSTOCK [AINSWORTH]

ATT: 62,539 REF: P.DOWD H-T: 0-0

"He likes his body to be smooth all over."

NEWS

TO BE HONEST, apart from more tiresome rumours about the futures of Tévez and Ronaldo, there isn't any. Believe it or not, these were the three biggest United stories of the week – and you thought the Anderson-Neville mouse 'scoop' from last week was a waste of space...

NOTHING STORY OF THE WEEK #1
From Now magazine:

"'Cristiano Ronaldo is so obsessed with looking good he removes all his body hair", claims his ex Nereida Gallardo.

"'He likes his body to be smooth all over and would even use a hair removal cream,' Nereida says.

"'He would also use tubs of moisturiser, coating every part of his body at least twice a day. His house is full of mirrors so he's always walking around glancing at himself.'

NONSENSE STORY OF THE WEEK #2
From the Sun:

FOREIGN birds are driving Cristiano Ronaldo wild again . . . after Manchester United's training ground was invaded by Canada geese.

The fowl keep dive-bombing Ronaldo and team-mates including Rio Ferdinand and Ryan Giggs as they practise.

Their antics have achieved something that no footballer would ever dare to try — interrupting one of Sir Alex Ferguson's training sessions.

A club insider revealed: "The geese have been returning for the past couple of years and can dive better than Cristiano!"

[Yes, I'm sure they did.]

NOTHING STORY OF THE CENTURY
From the Liverpool Daily Post:

AFTER more than a decade in football management, former Southport manager Peter Davenport recently added a new coaching qualification to his CV – as a coarse angling instructor.

WHERE ARE THEY NOW?

Peter Davenport is busy catching fish. But what happened to the rest of the team that lost Big Ron his job (losing 4-1 away at Southampton in the League Cup)?

CHRIS TURNER – midget keeper helped Wednesday beat us at Wembley in 1991. Is now a journeyman manager with stints at County, Wednesday, Hartlepool and Orient behind him.

MICKEY DUXBURY – will forever be fondly remembered for nobbling McMahon at Anfield. Now working at Bolton junior school.

ARTHUR ALBISTON – Was a junior coach at United and manager of Droylsden. Now a regular on MUTV.

KEVIN MORAN – pundit on Irish TV channel TV3.

PAUL McGRATH – the world's most famous domestos drinker – and the finest centre-half we ever gave away. Had a stamp issued in his honour in Ireland in 2002.

Graham Hogg – the first United player to score for both United and Barcelona? Played for West Brom, Portsmouth, Notts County, Brentford and Hearts where he had his nose broken by team-mate Craig Levein.

Remi Moses – First black player to score for United – against Boro in 81/2. Punched Olsen in training. Coached the Manchester Warriors U-20 inline skating side to win the GB Inline Hockey League.

Norman Whiteside – Peaked early, left early. Still a United legend.

Colin Gibson – Lingered on at United till 1990. Few noticed him leave. Now a football commentator on BBC Leicester.

Frank Stapleton – Rumours he smiled in late 2006 have never been proved. Is miserable on TV for a living.

Peter Davenport – loves fish.

Jesper Olsen – Now in Australia thankfully recovering from the brain haemorrhage he suffered in 2006. Still has a place in Danish lexicon – a rigtig Jesper Olsen (a real Jesper) – for his disastrous mistake against Spain in the 1986 World Cup.

MENTAL IMAGE OF THE WEEK

"Big Ron remains a good friend and being called racist was a terrible representation of the man. In my time at Coventry, he treated me with utmost respect. Big Ron doesn't mean any harm to anyone. Well, apart from one time, when he hit Steve Orgrizovic in the face with a fish during a club fishing trip" – *Former Coventry winger Peter Ndlovu on his old boss.*

15/10/2008

UNITED 5 STOKE 0
Ronaldo 3, Carrick 45, Berbatov 49, Welbeck 84, Ronaldo 89

Rory Delap and his bionic arm had made Stoke one of the surprise packages of the season so far. But the hacks and punters who noisily backed them to rough up United, as they had done Arsenal a couple of weeks before, were not so much barking up the wrong tree, as plain barking. Sure Delap can throw a hell of a ball but it's one thing taking a throw at the Britannia, where the ballboys are primed to fluff up the ball and you're allowed a 20 yard run-up, and quite another doing it at Old Trafford where you've got a couple of feet to play with and a slope to navigate. And yes, Arsenal had failed to cope with the aerial barrage but United's defence is made of far sterner stuff than theirs. But the biggest barrier to Stoke's chances was this. For Delap's missiles to have a decisive impact on the game, his team-mates would a] have to spend a decent amount of time inside the United half and b] have to stop United banging them in at the other end. And when Ronaldo destroyed Sorensen inside the opening three minutes you just knew that wasn't going to be the case...

GOAL ACTION

1-0 (3): Stoke fans – or at least those who'd avoided being kidnapped by the GMP (see page 106) – gave a decent account of themselves, noise-wise, but they should perhaps have thought twice before aiming so much stick in the direction of Ronaldo. So far this season he'd been OK but nothing particularly special, a slower, more agitated version of last year's model. The sound of Stoke fans, of all people, hurling abuse at him seemed to add a yard to his pace and, as Sorensen found out to his cost here, extra devilery to his free-kicks. The papers reckoned the Stoke keeper should have saved Ronaldo's first effort – his 100th goal for United – on the basis that it was aimed straight at him. Watching it speed and wobble through the air like a fighter plane in a gale, mind, you've got to say he made a smart choice getting out of the way.

2-0(45): In fairness to Stoke, they made a decent recovery from the shock of conceding so early and managed to frustrate United for most of the first half. The real killer was United's second goal, struck left-footed by Carrick from the edge of the box on the stroke of half-time.

3-0(49): After that it was all United. First the A-team turn it on, Tévez crossing, Berbatov volleying home...

4-0(84): Then it's the youth team's turn, Welbeck, the great Mancunian hope*, thumping in a stunning first ever United goal high into the net from 25 yards...

5-0(89): And fittingly it's Ronaldo who has the final word, taking advantage of a badly-positioned wall to drive home goal no. 101.

QUESTION OF THE DAY

How did Stoke's journeymen giants beat Villa and Arsenal at home and hold Liverpool 0-0 at Anfield? *(I'm guessing we'll find out the answer at the Britannia on Boxing Day)*

RUNNER-UP★

Why doesn't Manchester produce more great footballers? And is Scholesy the greatest ever Mancunian player (apart from Paul Lake of course)?

GETTING OFF THE MARK

Welbeck's goal was a beauty. But who's scored the best first United goal? Here are 5 suggestions:

NEIL WEBB – lovely curler in the 4-1 opening day thrashing of Arsenal in 1989.

MICHAEL KNIGHTON – nice juggling, beautifully executed half-volley, also against Arsenal in 1989.

RAFAEL – one touch to set himself up, one swing of his left boot to volley it into the net (at the Emirates a week ago).

TÉVEZ – near post diving header against Chelsea in September 2007.

NANI – 25 yard screamer (slightly deflected) against Spurs in August 2007.

QUOTE OF THE DAY

"It was lovely, especially coming from Manchester, especially in front of the Stretford End. I wouldn't say I've dreamt about it but I've thought about it every minute of my life." – *Danny Welbeck*

CENTURION CLUB

Ronaldo is the 20th player to score 100 United goals and he did it in the 12th quickest time (253 games). He's only the fifth member of the United centurion club not to have played all his football as an out-and-out striker (the others are Charlton, Best, Scholes and Giggs).

STOKE – THE VERBALS

'Fantastic. He's back, right on song. His speed has come back. He was taking his time, but every game he is getting better. That is nine for the season now. His acceleration is marvellous and he has scored his first goals from free-kicks this season. We have been waiting for that to happen. Today, we saw the real power of him.' – *Fergie's glad to see the real Ronaldo again.*

"I feel very proud. One hundred goals is a great achievement. I have 101 for this club now. This is my sixth season here so I think that is fantastic." – *Ronaldo on his ton (though he obviously didn't think it was that big a milestone in the summer)*

"What a goal. To come on and score a goal like that must be beyond his wildest dreams. I'm sure he'll build on that. He's got bags of ability and good temperament, so he suits playing for us. I'm not sure about the celebration, but he can work on that!" – *Carrick on Welbeck's dream start. He had a point about that celebration (a Henry-style 'look at me' type shrug) too.*

"He's no doubt a Manchester United player, but he's only young. He needs time, but he's got a lot of marvellous things about him. He's a local boy, which is nice too." – *Fergie's mad about the boy too.*

WORST HEADLINE OF THE DAY

"Fergie's boys are Berba toffs" *(from the News of the Screws). Why?*

VIEW FROM THE PRESSBOX

"So that's the secret of putting Stoke in their place. Score an early goal, force them to come out and play and pick them off. Stoke, who smothered Liverpool to a goalless draw at Anfield and outmuscled Arsenal at the Britannia Stadium, were ill equipped to engage United in conventional football. Their Brazil kit suggested a devilish sense of humour or desperate delusion." – *The Telegraph with the 'no shit Sherlock' spot of the day.*

MATCH FACTS

UNITED: VAN DER SAR, O'SHEA, VIDIC, EVANS, EVRA, RONALDO, CARRICK, FLETCHER (GIBSON 63), PARK (WELBECK 63), TÉVEZ (MANUCHO 74), BERBATOV
BOOKED: EVRA.
STOKE: SORENSEN, GRIFFIN (WILKINSON 79), ABDOULAYE FAYE, SHAWCROSS, HIGGINBOTHAM, OLOFINJANA (CRESSWELL 31), DIAO, AMDY FAYE, DELAP, FULLER (KITSON 68), SIDIBE [PULIS]
BOOKED: FULLER, DELAP.
ATT: 75,369 REF: PETER WALTON H-T: 2-0

OTHER SCORES

ARSENAL 0 VILLA 2, BOLTON 0 LIVERPOOL 2, WEST BROM 0 CHELSEA 3

LEAGUE TABLE

1. CHELSEA 32 (13) 2. LIVERPOOL 32 (13) 3. UNITED 24 (12)

4. Arsenal 23 (13)… 15. Stoke 14 (13)

"I am the first, second and third best player in the world."

NEWS

Fergie gets a two-game touchline ban and a £10,000 fine for piling into Mike Dean after the Hull match. Drogba gets a 3-match ban for lobbing a coin thrown by Burnley fans during the recent Carling Cup tie back into the Burnley end. Tévez agrees a permanent move to Real Madrid. *Marca* says it so it must be true. Berbatov considers retiring from international football after once again being lambasted by the Bulgarian press for not trying hard enough. His cause isn't helped by the fact he limped off half an hour into Bulgaria's most recent game – a disastrous 6-1 defeat by Serbia - having moved less than 2 kilometres (if an average person walked for 30 minutes they'd move 2 miles).

The gossip columns link us with new sponsors (Saudi Telecom), a new Scholes (the brilliant Xavi who's apparently in a contract dispute with Barcelona) and a new Solskjaer (Valarenga striker Moa Abdellaoue). The GMP is forced to apologise after holding 80 Stoke supporters in a pub in Irlam and preventing them from attending the United game (on the spurious basis that they posed a risk of alcohol-related disorder – doesn't everyone in a pub?). And nine months after his infamous sulk at Birmingham blew a hole in Arsenal's title charge, William Gallas goes weird again, attacking an unnamed Arsenal player for telling him to speak more quietly. Is there a stranger man playing football today?

SLEUTHING IT

So who was Gallas jabbing his finger at in the Arsenal dressing-room? Let's take a look at the evidence…

"The youngsters from the Euros seem cheeky, very sure of themselves." – *So he's a cocky youngster who played in Euro 2008. Walcott's out then. So the early favourite is Bendtner.*

"Faced with his contempt, I raised my voice. The young player said: 'Lower your voice, speak less loudly'. "I replied: 'How are you speaking to me?" – *Gallas, who's had the odd Taxi Driver haircut, comes over all Robert De Niro.*

"'Who do you think you are? You are only 20 years old. I am not your friend'. "He said: 'Me neither, I am not your friend'." – *Now things get interesting. This whippersnapper was at the Euros and he's only 20. It's not the pizza thrower then. He's 21.*

"I am trying to defend myself without giving names, otherwise I take all of the blame. It's very frustrating. I'm 31 and the player in question is six years younger than me" – *That's all very well Billy boy but you've given away too many clues already...*

So who is it? I'm not pretending to know for sure. But as Samir Nasri was the only Arsenal player aged 20 during Euro 2008...

WE BELIEVE YOU

So Gallas didn't do the best job of hiding who he was naming and shaming. Which will come as no surprise to anyone who's familiar with the Frenchman. As former French international Jerome Rothen reveals in his new book, 'You're Not Going To Believe Me', our Billy isn't exactly the sharpest tool in the box... I don't think William Gallas will mind me talking about how he used to be a no-hoper. At school he was a right wally - he would sit at the back of the class as far away from the blackboard as possible. One day the maths teacher gave us a test - she knew that William understood nothing about maths, so she allowed him to use the textbook. But even with the book under his nose he still only got four out of 20!"

AND HE HASN'T FINISHED THERE...

Rothen also goes on to say that Gallas, who was a fellow trainee at Caen, was nicknamed Pierre Richard – the French equivalent of Mr Bean.

AND FINALLY, THE BIGGEST BOMBSHELL OF ALL...

Rothen exposes Gallas as the lowest of the low, the dressing room thief – and a stupid one at that:

"One evening, Eric Sitruk burst into my room and shouted, 'Someone has stolen my bank card and taken out 1,500 francs (£150)'.

"Furious, he accused five of us. It made sense because we were all very close, we had the keys to each other's rooms and knew the codes to our bank cards so we could lend each other money. Next evening, Eric said he had gone to the bank and a surveillance camera had filmed the person using the card.

"He said, 'I know who is guilty'. It was a bluff. But an hour later, William knocked on his door and admitted his mistake.'

Sounds like a great guy (though there's plenty worse – see below)

LIKELY STORY OF THE WEEK

"Even if I wrote notes, I wrote good things. I praised [those] people" *- former Spurs defender Gica Popescu defends his role as an informer for Romania's secret police in the late 1980s.*

INTERNATIONAL REDS

Carrick produces his best international performance as an England side packed with reserves beats Germany 2-1 in Berlin. Park captains South Korea to first win against Saudi Arabia for 19 years in a World Cup qualifier. Berbatov limps off with a hamstring strain as Bulgaria get humiliated by Vidic's Serbia. Ronaldo and Nani also have a night to forget as Portugal get battered 6-2 by Anderson's Brazil. (I wonder if Queiroz is regretting leaving us yet). Evra's France draw 0-0 at home with Diego's Uruguary. Tévez plays the full game as Argentina's Maradona era gets off to a 1-0 start against Fletcherless Scotland. Gibson and O'Shea's Republic side (why doesn't anyone say Eire any more?) lose 3-2 at home to Poland. Evans' Northern Ireland go down 2-0 at home to Hungary.

WHINE OF THE WEEK

"He's a malicious guy and if I hadn't jumped out of the way he would have broken my leg. He just lost it because we snuffed him totally out of the game. He had the nerve to say he didn't touch me but that's only because I got out of his way"- *Brazilian 'tough guy' Tiago Silva cries about Ronaldo.*

MARADONA WINS AGAIN

"England won a World Cup with a goal that never crossed the line. It was plain to everyone who saw it that it never went in, so I don't think it's fair that everyone should judge me when stuff like that [his Hand of God goal] went on." – *Diego plays up to the Scottish audience.*

PUTDOWN OF THE WEEK

Before the Scotland-Argentina game, Terry Butcher – who's now in charge of putting out the cones for the Scottish team – made a minor fool of himself by announcing that he'd refuse to shake Maradona's hand (particularly if it was the one that scored back in '86). Diego's

putdown was perfect: "Who is Terry Butcher?"
(He was the big lanky Englishman you heard panting behind you, Diego)

ON THE BUSES

"He sat downstairs as if it was the most normal thing for a multi-millionaire footballer to do. Word quickly went round about who he was. Nobody quite believed it and some just stared open-mouthed." - *A disbelieving onlooker after Robinho and his girlfriend travel by bus to the Trafford Centre, presumably to gaze open-mouthed at the fountain.*

ME, MYSELF AND I

"I am the first, second and third best player in the world." – *Who else could it be but Ronaldo?*

FAPL 22/11/2008
ASTON VILLA 0 UNITED 0

WHAT A LETDOWN. The afternoon matches couldn't have gone much better if Fergie had bought the referees. Crap travellers Fulham drew at Anfield. Newcastle, who are crap in most places, drew at Stamford Bridge. And crap Arsenal got battered at City. Another win at our luckiest ground and we'd be right back in the title race, six points off the leaders with a game in hand and almost all our toughest away games out of the way.

Instead we got a first 0-0 draw in a year and a performance that didn't deserve any more. OK, there were excuses. The pointless friendly internationals had taken their toll. Berbatov was back in Manchester, his sore hamstring propped up on a pillow and a pile of half-written resignation letters to the Bulgarian FA scattered next to him. Ronaldo, Anderson and Nani had all been to Brazil in midweek – and given what they used to get up to in Poynton, that always looked like spelling trouble. Rooney didn't look fit and Tévez still looks like he desperately needs to know if he's staying or going. And it wasn't a terrible performance. Some of the possession play was brilliant in the first half. But the second half was a major disappointment. At the very least you expected Brad Friedel, the bane of so many trips to Ewood, to have to add to his collection of miracle saves. But apart from one, admittedly glorious, Rooney chance, he hardly had to get a frown on. So we ended up winning the game on points, but sharing the points that mattered. And that hasn't happened in these parts for donkey's years...

WHAT WAS GOOD?

WE DIDN'T LOSE. And we didn't finish the day even further off the lead.

THE ARSENAL CRISIS. Five defeats already – and their worst defence in a generation (good work agent Silvestre) - suggest they're already out of the running for the league.

WHAT WAS BAD?

THE SECOND HALF PERFORMANCE WAS POOR AGAIN. In our five big away games so far this season – at Liverpool, Arsenal, Everton, Chelsea and now Villa – we've won the first half twice, drawn it twice and lost it just once. Our record in the second half reads won 0 drawn 2 lost 3.

WE COLLECTED 10 POINTS FROM THOSE 5 AWAY GAMES LAST SEASON – we've only managed 3 points this time.

UNITED'S AWAY RECORD. We've only won 2 out of 7 aways. Chelsea have won seven out of seven.

VILLA'S SAFETY-FIRST TACTICS AT HOME. Does anyone still think Martin O'Neill is the right man for us?

VIEWS FROM THE PRESSBOX

"Come back Dimitar Berbatov, all is forgiven. Manchester United have created and missed so many chances in recent weeks that people have started to wonder whether the classy Bulgarian is a luxury they do not need, a bit like Rodney Marsh at City all those years ago.

"United's first goalless league game for a year gave the lie to that idea. In Berbatov's absence, they struggled to create any chances at all and, with Park Ji-Sung and Carlos Tévez failing to rise to the occasion, and Wayne Rooney and Cristiano Ronaldo below their best, Villa held the champions quite comfortably to move above Arsenal into fourth." – *The Observer*

"Manchester United have got into the habit of treating their lopsided Premier League programme as a penance. The idea seems to be to suffer now and enjoy radiant performances later. It could all work out but the champions should reflect on their sub-standard efforts in that arduous string of away games." – *The Guardian*

SWITCHED ON JOURNO OF THE DAY

"Villa Park is a pleasingly down-to-earth place. The club have a package that will let two adults and two children see Saturday's match with Fulham for £40. Deals of that sort for Premier League fixtures do not seem to crop up at Old Trafford, Stamford Bridge, Anfield or the Emirates." – *The man from the Guardian fails to twig that Villa have to offer deals like that... otherwise they wouldn't get most of their fickle fans into the ground.*

MATCH FACTS

ASTON VILLA: FRIEDEL, REO-COKER, DAVIES, LAURSEN, LUKE YOUNG, SIDWELL (CAREW 81), PETROV, BARRY, MILNER, AGBONLAHOR, ASHLEY YOUNG [O'NEILL]
BOOKED: DAVIES.
MAN UTD: VAN DER SAR, O'SHEA, FERDINAND, VIDIC, EVRA, RONALDO (ANDERSON 82), PARK, CARRICK, GIGGS, ROONEY, TÉVEZ (NANI 71).
VILLA PARK ATT: 42,585 REF: CHRIS FOY H-T: 0–0

OTHER RESULTS

CHELSEA 0 NEWCASTLE 0, LIVERPOOL 0 FULHAM 0, CITY 3 ARSENAL 0

LEAGUE TABLE

1. CHELSEA 33 (14) 2. LIVERPOOL 33 (14) 3. UNITED 25 (13) 4. ASTON VILLA 24 (14) 5. ARSENAL 23 (14)

"I was actually supposed to have dinner one night with Sinatra and we lost to Charlton, and I cancelled him at home."

NEWS

THE GOVERNMENT KNOCK a couple of percent off VAT on the basis that saving £2.50 on £100 will get us all out buying fridges, TVs and cars and instantly solve the economic crisis. I'm not sure about that but at least we get a few quid off the United ticket – and a few pence off the half-time pie and Double Decker (don't United realise most people stop eating them the same time as jam and Wotsit sandwiches?). Wenger strips Pierre Richard, I mean Mr Bean, I mean Billy Gallas of the Arsenal captaincy following his 'respect the elderly' rant. He gives the armband to Fabregas instead, a sure sign that Arsenal are worried he's going to do one. Valerenga reject United's offer to take the next Ole, striker Moa Abdellaoue, on trial. I'm not so sure about all these 'new Ole' stories anyway. It took Norway their entire history to produce one Ole Solskjaer. Why does everyone think they'll produce a second in little more than a decade? Someone, probably from Nike, reveals that Ronaldo turned down the chance to wear their new pink boots. A refreshing sign of good fashion sense? Or was he worried that the shocking pink would clash with his orange tan?

STORY OF THE WEEK

Fergie reveals he was so obsessed with turning United around in his early days at the club that he once bombed out on a night out with Frank Sinatra:

"Well, you can't beat Sinatra, can you? Ole' Blue Eyes. I was actually supposed to have dinner one night with him and we lost to Charlton [in April 1989], and I cancelled him at home. I wasn't in the mood to meet anybody that night, so it was back in the bus."

FRANK BOUGH?

"Tell me someone who likes getting abused? Will you please point them out to me?" – *Fergie defends Ronaldo after he reacted angrily to the Villa fans who taunted him as he limped off the field at the weekend.*

QUOTES OF THE WEEK

"My only plan at the moment is not to have a plan" - *Fergie on his future.*

"I love my pink boots. I've wanted to play in that colour since I was young. I think it's an outstanding colour and it looks amazing." – *Nike finally find someone willing to pull on their pink boots – Niklas Bendtner. To think that Brucie let him sniff around his daughter...*

"I've seen criticism of Ronaldo saying that he couldn't take it on Saturday but I wonder how many people would take it if they were walking down the street and so many people hit them over the head with a baton? He was tackled many times on Saturday, most of the time fairly, but a few occasions they weren't good and he didn't get the decisions he deserved. But that's the mantle you carry as a great player." – *More from Fergie's defence of Ronaldo.*

GUT-WRENCHING IMAGE OF THE WEEK

"Oh, I just sat in my hotel room watching porn" - *Robbie Savage is disturbingly honest as he describes how he spent his free time while on loan at Brighton.*

FOOTBALL RUMOUR OF THE WEEK
From The Guardian:

"Chief Inspector Parm Sandhu, the highest-ranking female Asian officer in the Metropolitan police, is being investigated after she was reportedly involved in a scuffle with another female spectator at a football match in Sevenoaks, Kent."

UNDERSTATEMENT OF THE WEEK

"Everyone makes mistakes" - *Al Ahli coach Mohammed Ahmed, sticks up for star striker Faisal Khalil after he was arrested on suspicion of casting "black magic" spells on other players in order to maintain his place in the United Arab Emirates national team.*

25/11/2008
CL GROUP E

VILLARREAL CF 0 UNITED 0

ON THE FACE of it, Villarreal should be the sort of team everyone has a soft spot for. They're a small club from a small town. They spent the first 75 years of their existence in a mix of regional leagues, only making the top league in 1998. They keep on upsetting the superpowers of Europe and Spain. And to cap it all they have a cool little nickname, the Yellow Submarines.

But then you get to see them first hand and the warm feelings quickly fade away. Like Wimbledon, Villarreal have come very far, very quickly. And just like Wimbledon, they've been in such a rush they seem to have forgotten to develop any class on the way. Sure, against lesser teams they might look the part. But four meetings with United have shown what they're really like. And that's a cross between Butch Wilkins, Robert Pires (how fitting is it that that diving cheat has finished up here?) and an old-school Argie hatchet man. Once again, Villarreal only passed forwards when they really needed to, they threw themselves to the floor at the slightest opportunity and aimed high whenever Ronaldo got on the ball.

Fortunately, this year's 0-0 double was nowhere near as costly as it was in 2005. In fact Villarreal's unwillingness to come out and play on their home turf – they didn't make a chance all night – played right into United's hands. A Villarreal win would have condemned us to second place and put us in line for a springtime date at a Nou Camp or San Siro. The draw means a win against Aalborg at Old Trafford will clinch top spot. And, if history is any guide, that means we'll spend the last week in February dodging the gendarmes in some provincial town in France...

THE MOMENTS THAT MATTERED (SORT OF)

41 – The first chance of the game and it's almost worth the wait. Rooney cushions Anderson's crossfield ball into the path of Ronaldo whose crashing drive is superbly tipped onto the bar by reputed United target Diego Lopez.

80 – The second, and final, chance of the game. Rooney bursts down the left, his deflected cross loops over Lopez and it needs Capdevila's contortionist act to keep it out of the net.

82 – Capdevila's next lunge, a knee-high assault on Ronaldo (whose joints were targeted all night), is nowhere near as admirable and Roberto Rossetti, the overly-pampered Italian ref, deals him a straight red.

WHAT WAS GOOD?

JONNY EVANS. Cool, composed and hardly gave United old boy Giuseppe Rossi a kick.

WE'RE THROUGH. And we only need to beat Aalborg to secure top spot in the group.

WHAT WAS BAD?

GIUSEPPE ROSSI – In fairness he wasn't terrible but he did nothing to justify all the pre-match talk that Fergie would sign him up instead of Tévez. He's slippy enough and his goal record is good but he's just too small, too one-footed and too easy to outmuscle to make the grade with us.

KUSZCZAK – The Pole in goal looked edgy all night even though he didn't have anything to do. Why is he getting valuable experience ahead of Foster?

THE TREATMENT DISHED OUT TO RONALDO. Does he really think life will be easier for him – and his ankles/shins/knees – if he gets out of England (see below*)?

AND WORST OF ALL... Villarreal saw the visit of the European champions to rip off the Red Army, charging £102.50 for the best seats in the away section and a ridiculous £50 for those with a restricted view.

VIEW FROM THE PRESSBOX*

"Whatever he might try to convince himself on those cold and muddy afternoons when he is subjected to rough-house treatment from hatchet men in the Barclays Premier League, it would be no different for Cristiano Ronaldo wherever he plied his beguiling trade. His is a talent that inspires resentment and attracts aggressive tackles wherever he goes and, if he thinks it would be any different if he were playing in Spain for his beloved Real Madrid, an arduous evening here at the Madrigal should tell him otherwise.

"Playing out a goalless draw for the fourth time in as many meetings in the Champions League, Manchester United and Villarreal secured their progression to the knockout stages, but for Ronaldo, in particular, this was far from the convivial occasion that conspiracy theorists in Glasgow might suspect. The United forward was subjected to some horrible challenges, with Joan Capdevila, the Spain full back, sent off for the worst of them with eight minutes remaining." – *The Times makes some good points.*

QUOTE OF THE NIGHT

"Four times we've played each other and there hasn't been a goal yet. Uefa will hope we don't meet in Rome." – *They're not the only ones Fergie...*

MATCH FACTS

VILLARREAL: DIEGO LOPEZ, JAVI VENTA, RODRIGUEZ, FUENTES, CAPDEVILA, SANTI CAZORLA, SENNA (BRUNO 46), EGUREN, PIRES (FERNANDEZ 65), ROSSI (FRANCO 78), IBAGAZA [PELLEGRINI]
SENT OFF: CAPDEVILA (82)
BOOKED: JAVI VENTA, EGUREN, FUENTES
UNITED: KUSZCZAK, O'SHEA, FERDINAND, EVANS, EVRA, RONALDO, FLETCHER (GIBSON 80), CARRICK (TÉVEZ 86), NANI (PARK 85), ANDERSON, ROONEY
BOOKED: EVRA, RONALDO

El Madrigal Att: 26,000 Ref: Roberto Rosetti (Italy) h-t: 0-0

OTHER SCORES

Aalborg 2 Celtic 1, Arsenal 1 Dynamo Kiev 0,
Liverpool 1 Marseille 0, Bordeaux 1 Chelsea 1

GROUP E TABLE

1. United 9 (5) 2. Villarreal 9 (5) 3. Aalborg 5 (5) 4. Celtic 2 (5)

*"If they were winning trophies, it would irritate me,
but while they are still lingering in mid-table,
I am not really too bothered about it."*

NEWS

Just a couple of days after Partizan Belgrade deny any contact with United, United announce they've been granted a work permit for £3 million left-winger Zoran Tosic. Details about the new boy are sketchy but we do know he's nicknamed Bambi, he's got a wand of a left foot, he's 21 and he grew up with a United flag on his bedroom wall. Oh and he's got less muscle than Paris Hilton.

United get dumped out of the FA Youth Cup by last year's finalists Chelsea, Danny Welbeck and 15 year-old Ravel Morrison scoring in a 3-2 defeat at Old Trafford. And the richest club in the world adds a 2-0 UEFA win in Schalke to their weekend hammering of Arsenal. As the giddyometer reaches danger levels, Stephen Ireland names the current City side as the best ever. Now I know there's not much competition but to claim you're the best when you're beneath Hull in the table takes some beating...

BULLSEYE

The Sun's Steve Howard hits the nail on the head after Ronaldo gets an old-school continental kicking in Villarreal...

'This Ronaldo-baiting is now absurd. The real animosity started when he winked after Wayne Rooney's red card against Portugal at Germany '06. Incredibly, that was deemed a greater event than Rooney kicking Ricardo Carvalho in the crotch.'

...Though his place on the moral high ground looks less secure if you recall which paper printed a Ronaldo dartboard and encouraged its readers to 'give

the sly senor one in the eye'. (Just in case William Gallas is reading this, it was The Sun).

FRAULEIN OF THE WEEK

"Would all Man U fans please stay in their seats after the final whistle." – *The PA girl at the Schalke-City game can't get her head around the idea there's another team in Manchester. Classic.*

A HARD KNOCK LIFE

"Money can be a burden. I could choose what I wanted and so I ended up indecisive... And we had a massive house that I couldn't control or clean, it took all day." – *Joe Cole's fiancée Carly Zucker gives an insight into the hardships of being filthy rich on I'm [sleeping with] A Celebrity, Get Me Out Of Here.*

BLEEDING HEART II

"You can say the last six months have been the worst of my career. It's been really tough for me." - *Poor Didier Drogba is feeling sorry for himself too. Though his depression didn't stop him – reportedly - from cuddling up with Inter officials on a late night dinner date.*

GLAD THAT'S CLEARED UP

"I do not sleep with him. Where he was last night? I don't know. I am not a policeman for my players" – *Phil Scolari declines to discuss Drogba's whereabouts after news of the Inter date.*

'MASSIVE' QUOTE OF THE WEEK

"Looking at our squad now, it's probably going to be the best City team to line up against Manchester United ever because we have so many big names. Every derby is massive. We look at Manchester United and what they've achieved and that's what we aspire to. That is our target." - *The massively deluded Stephen Ireland.*

SPOT THE DIFFERENCE

IPSWICH'S DAVID NORRIS is fined £5,000 by the FA for making a handcuff gesture in support of a friend – Plymouth keeper Luke McCormick – convicted of causing death by dangerous driving.
LIVERPOOL PLAYERS go unpunished for wearing t-shirts with the slogan 'Free Michael Now' in support of a fan – Michael Shields – convicted of attempted murder in Bulgaria.

Now I know that as a fan you'd appreciate your team giving

such support for a fellow fan. And there might be some truth in the public perception that Shields was stitched up. But how can the FA allow Liverpool players to make a public statement on something they don't have a clue about? Gerrard & co. weren't in Bulgaria when the incident happened. Honest witnesses or not, at least the people who gave evidence that Shields hit the victim with a seven-pound paving slab were.

QUOTE OF THE WEEK

"It will be nice to show them who are the kings of Manchester. It doesn't irritate us that City are getting all this publicity. If they were winning trophies, it would irritate me, but while they are still lingering in mid-table, I am not really too bothered about it." – *Excellent work from Rooney.*

RUNNER-UP

"It was uncharacteristic of Wayne. He apologised to me afterwards and said he didn't mean to do that. He said that he thought the defender was going to challenge him and was expecting the challenge. It was unfortunate really. I think he has been watching Robert Pires too much. At least he apologised to the Villarreal players. You would never see Pires do that" - *Fergie transforms a gentle jibe at Rooney's aberration in Spain (when he went down too easily a couple of times) into a dig at a favourite old target.*

FAPL 30/11/2008

CITY 0 UNITED 1
Rooney 42

THIS WAS CITY's chance to lay down a marker. To tell the whole world – and that immortal Schalke announcer – that there is more than one team in Manchester. To back up Stephen Ireland's hilarious claim that they are the best City team ever. To give an indication of the damage they're going to do once they've had a proper chance to spend their oil billions. And what did they do? They did what City really are the undisputed kings of, money or no money. They cocked up. Even when Ronaldo was sent off – ludicrously, again – United were in pipe and slippers mode. When it was 11 v 11 this was like a rerun of the last trip to Eastlands. Except this time United didn't just annihilate City with their football, they scored.

Oh, and one more thing. City fans. In February you accepted the nation's thanks and praise for respecting the minute's silence at the 50th anniversary game. Nine months later you're singing Munich songs. Take your tea towels off your heads and hang them... in shame.

THE MOMENTS THAT MATTERED

1-0 (42): Last year's Eastlands derby was effectively played in City's half. So was this one. Last year Geovanni scored. This year Rooney did. Park finds Carrick, Hart does well to save his low shot but he can only palm the ball out to Rooney who makes no mistake from a yard. That's 100 goals in his club career, 83 for United.

YELLOW (58): Shaun Wright-Phillips is getting a bit of treatment from United here – though the post-match talk that he was the target of systematic fouling was well wide of the mark – but this trip by Ronaldo was completely accidental. That doesn't stop Howard Webb reaching for his pocket...

YELLOW! RED! (67): ... all of which becomes far more significant when he sends Ronaldo off for deliberately handling Rooney's corner. The ABU camp defend Webb's decision. After all, the rule book says that deliberate handball is a yellow card offence. Two yellows make a red, right? Reds and neutrals aren't so sure. Ronaldo didn't try to score with his handball, he didn't seek an unfair advantage, in fact by batting down the ball with both hands he denied himself a decent goalscoring opportunity. Ronaldo himself claimed that he acted after hearing a whistle. And judging by his look of abject astonishment at the decision, he'd have to be a hell of an actor to be lying.

ESCAPE! (92): In theory Ronaldo's dismissal should have tipped the balance of the game from blue to red. In fact it merely allowed United to show their dominance in another way. Most teams would have tried to kill the game by sitting deep and when possible holding the ball in the corner. United merely showed that nine outfield players can keep the ball just as well as ten. City hardly saw the ball in the final 20 minutes and Van der Sar had nothing serious to worry about until this, deep into injury time. City get a corner, Hart joins everyone else in the box, the ball pinballs around, Dunne sends a toepoke goalwards. And Evra clears off the line.

ESCAPE! (93): As City switch off and Hart starts a 90m run back to his goal, United break, Giggs turns down the opportunity of a punt at open goal from long range (actually, you rarely see Giggsy kick the ball miles – maybe those hamstrings won't let him) and instead passes possession on to Rooney who immediately aims and fires. His 50 yard shot has power and accuracy but it doesn't quite have the height and Hart manages to get back in time to tip it behind. As he wheezes to his feet, Webb blows up. United's record at Eastlands now reads a symmetrical LWLWLW.

WHAT WAS GOOD?

ROONEY, THE CENTURION. It's no coincidence he wasn't in the team when City won their derby double last season.

UNITED'S FULL-BACKS. Evra did more attacking than Wright-Phillips, Rafael had Robinho in his pocket. Before the game he wasn't well known in Brazil. He is now.

CHELSEA & CITY LOSE, LIVERPOOL DRAW AND WE WIN. Oh and Leeds lose to Histon in the FA Cup.

AFTER 3½ MONTHS OF DECENT RESULTS but unmemorable games it finally feels like the season's started. Does it always take this long for the anti-climax to wear off after a European Cup-winning season?

WHAT WAS BAD?

CITY'S SUPPORT (see above).

HOWARD WEBB. Became the second referee of the season – after Mike Riley at Chelsea – to give United 6 yellow cards. And most of them were a joke. Rafael was booked for tossing the ball gently in the air after he was penalised for winning the ball, Evra was booked for, actually, no one's quite sure and Ronaldo was sent off for an accidental trip and an accidentally deliberate handball.

EASTLANDS – THE VERBALS

"He was protecting his face, he was shoved and he heard a whistle" – *Fergie tries to cover all the bases as he explains why Ronaldo handled.*

"It never entered my mind that the referee would show me a yellow card because for me I had not done anything wrong. To the contrary after Richards yelled I thought he was hurt and needed assistance. I heard the whistle, so I took the initiative and stopped the match. I understood the referee wanted to talk to me but maybe influenced by the fans, he put his hand in his pocket and sent me off." – *Ronaldo offers a more plausible explanation.*

"If he thought it was going to hit him in the face, why didn't he head it?" *It's weird, I never thought Hughesie would end up being so annoying. Mind you, I never thought he - or Schmeichel for that matter - would end up at City. Will it taint his United legacy?*

VIEWS FROM THE PRESSBOX

"Do not put money on United winning the Fair Play League but, equally, think twice before questioning whether they have the battling qualities to come from behind in this season's title race. They won the 150th Mancunian derby because they passed the ball better and had a centre-forward who decided he had waited long enough to score the 100th goal of his career. Wayne Rooney was the outstanding performer, although an honorary mention goes to Michael Carrick. Between them, they dictated the pattern of a game in which the margin of victory was flattering to Mark Hughes's team." – *The Guardian*

"It was with a dismissive, disdainful air that Sir Alex Ferguson, Wayne Rooney and others had shrugged off the idea of an uprising in the blue half of Manchester. To pour scorn on a highly mobilised underclass is to pour oil on the flames of revolution, but Manchester City are not yet in any kind of position to overthrow the establishment. Let them eat cake? Let them sign Kaká and see what difference that makes.

"For the aristocrats of Manchester United, this victory, restoring the natural sense of order in the city after two derby defeats last season, was more straightforward than the scoreline suggests. Not even a red card for Cristiano Ronaldo, for an inexplicable second bookable offence, could throw Ferguson's team off course after they took a deserved lead in the 42nd minute through Rooney's first goal in eight games." – *The Times*

"Cristiano Ronaldo may need to be convinced but, when the dust settles, Manchester United will cherish the day they reminded their nouveaux riches neighbours who should be known, in the words of the match-winner Wayne Rooney, as "the real kings of Manchester". Ronaldo's red card removed some of the gloss but, ultimately, that kind of thing is only a minor irritation when you have just beaten the club who have been shouting from the rooftops about changing the order of world football." – *The Guardian again.*

RIDICULOUS REDS

If I was Ronaldo I'd make damn sure I got sent off for a proper reason next time. All 4 of his red cards in English football so far have been harsh, at best:

VILLA (A) MAY 2004 – Ronaldo gets a soft booking for an alleged dive and then a second for kicking the ball away seconds after Rob Styles had blown his whistle. Fergie called the decision "Bizarre" before adding, "People are going to laugh at that when they see it on TV".

CITY (A) JANUARY 2006 – Ronaldo is taken out badly on the touchline, jumps to his feet and then jumps in one-footed in the vague direction of a City player. Steve Bennett sends him off, presumably for damaging the pitch.

PORTSMOUTH (A) AUGUST 2007 – Ronaldo nudges heads with Richard Hughes, he collapses pathetically and that man Bennett shows a red. In fairness to the poor man's Ed Harris this one falls into the 'some they give, some they don't' category.

MATCH FACTS

CITY: HART, RICHARDS (STURRIDGE 76), KOMPANY, DUNNE, GARRIDO, WRIGHT-PHILLIPS, IRELAND, HAMANN (ELANO 46), VASSELL (ZABALETA 46), ROBINHO, MWARUWARI [HUGHES]
BOOKED: IRELAND, VASSELL
UNITED: VAN DER SAR, RAFAEL DA SILVA, FERDINAND, VIDIC, EVRA, RONALDO, CARRICK, FLETCHER, PARK (O'SHEA 90), ROONEY, BERBATOV (GIGGS 83)
SENT OFF: RONALDO (68).
BOOKED: RAFAEL DA SILVA, FLETCHER, RONALDO, EVRA, CARRICK.
EASTLANDS ATT: 47,320 REF: HOWARD WEBB H-T: 1-0

OTHER SCORES

LIVERPOOL 0 WEST HAM 0; CHELSEA 1 ARSENAL 2

LEAGUE TABLE

1. CHELSEA 33 (15); 2. LIVERPOOL 33 (14); 3. UNITED 28 (14);
4. ARSENAL 26 (15)

"We are very proud. Manchester United have been waiting for this for 40 years."

AND THEN THERE WERE FOUR

RONALDO GETS WHAT he always wanted (part II). No, not legs that stay permanently hair-free. Or a girlfriend who doesn't kiss 'n' tell. Or that nice new gaff in Madrid. He gets the Ballon D'Or, the original and still the best of all the honours heading his way this year. After scoring 46 goals, shining in Moscow, reinventing the free-kick and getting a massive 77 out of the 96 first votes cast, you'd be hard pushed to argue that he didn't deserve it. But that didn't stop the usual suspects in the press pack having a damn good try...

Check out this twaddle from James Lawton, peering and sneering down from his desk at *The Independent*:

"Ronaldo is displaying the gravitas and self-awareness not of great men like Pele and Cruyff, who once beat England at Wembley while hardly crossing the half-way line, but a drastically under-trained pup."

"Right now football has a supreme and beautiful exponent★ -- and it is not the superstar who, whatever you think of the rights and wrongs of his eventual dismissal last Sunday (against City), behaved in a way that made a travesty of Ferguson's ultimate praise."

"After his brutal (come again?) tackle on Shaun Wright-Phillips, Ronaldo displayed contempt for referee Howard Webb that came out of the top drawer of petulance. He announced that, as far as he was concerned, he could make his own rules and give himself the benefit even of the most outrageous levels of doubt."

"His body language remains, mostly, sour. He has this season only just got round to celebrating any success achieved by his team-mates. He is happy to dish out punishment but writhes and moans when he is on the receiving end."

"In the wake of his magnificent goal - and penalty miss - in the Champions League final against Chelsea in Moscow last May, he put on a post-game performance of stunning surliness."

So there it is. Ronaldo is cocky, he's surly and he's got no gravitas or self-awareness. That might be true enough (and many Reds would argue that he's got far worse personality traits than that). But what's indisputable is that for two seasons he's treated us to the longest sustained spell of attacking and goal-scoring brilliance Old Trafford has possibly ever seen. And if that doesn't make him a worthy winner of the Ballon D'Or then god knows what will.

★ He's talking about Messi (yes the same Messi who was injured for large stretches of last season when his Barca side bombed)

WHERE'S RIO?
Here's the 2008 Top 10, plus some honourable mentions...

1. RONALDO (446 POINTS) 2. MESSI (281) 3. TORRES (179) 4. CASILLAS (133) 5. XAVI (97) 6. ARSHAVIN (64) 7. VILLA (55) 8. KAKA (31) 9. IBRAHIMOVIC (30) 10. GERRARD (28) 13. ROONEY (11) 21. VIDIC (3) 24. VAN DER SAR (2)

FROM STAN TO THE MAN
All the European Footballers of the Year from 1956 to today:

MATTHEWS – DI STEFANO – KOPA – DI STEFANO – SUAREZ – SIVORI – MASOPUST – YASHIN – LAW – EUSEBIO – CHARLTON – ALBERT – BEST – RIVERA – MULLER – CRUYFF – BECKENBAUER – CRUYFF – CRUYFF – BLOKHIN – BECKENBAUER – SIMONSEN – KEEGAN – KEEGAN – RUMMENIGGE – RUMMENIGGE – ROSSI – PLATINI – PLATINI – PLATINI – BELANOV – GULLIT – VAN BASTEN – VAN BASTEN – MATTHAUS – PAPIN – VAN BASTEN – BAGGIO – STOICHKOV – WEAH – SAMMER – RONALDO (THE TOOTHY ONE) – ZIDANE – RIVALDO – FIGO – OWEN (HOW?) – RONALDO (THE FAT ONE) – NEDVED – SHEVCHENKO – RONALDINHO – CANNAVARO – KAKA – RONALDO (THE ORANGE ONE)

BRIT AWARDS
The British-based players who've featured in the top 5 (Reds in bold if you haven't guessed):

1ST – MATTHEWS (56), LAW (64), CHARLTON (66), BEST (68), OWEN (2001), **RONALDO (2008)**

2ND – BILLY WRIGHT (57), CHARLTON (67), CHARLTON (68), BOBBY MOORE (70), KEEGAN (77), DALGLISH (83), LINEKER (86), BECKHAM (99), HENRY (2003), LAMPARD (2005), **RONALDO (2007)**

3RD – JOHNNY HAYNES (61), JIMMY GREAVES (63), JIMMY JOHNSTONE (67), BEST (71), CANTONA (93), SHEARER (96), GERRARD (2005), HENRY (2006), TORRES (2008)

4TH – EDWARDS (57), LAW (63), BOBBY MOORE (66), KEEGAN (76), STRACHAN (83), RUSH (84), GAZZA (90), OWEN (98), HENRY (2000), HENRY (2004), HENRY (2005), DROGBA (2007)

5TH – CHARLTON (65), BILLY BREMNER (73), SHILTON (89), SCHMEICHEL (92)

BALLON D'OR IN NUMBERS

0 – number of English-based foreign players to win the award before Ronaldo.

0 – number of winners from Liverpool when they were at their pomp (fair play to the panel for recognising that success isn't the same thing as style).

0 – number of times Roy Keane was voted in the top 10. Robbo never featured in the top 5 either but he did at least get 4 mentions in the top 10.

1 – number of goalkeepers who've won the award (Lev Yashin in 1963). Schmeichel's best was 5th in 1992, the year he won the Euros with Denmark.

2 – number of winners from English clubs apart from United – Matthews (Blackpool 1956) and Owen (Liverpool 2001).

3 – most wins by a single player – Van Basten, Cruyff and Platini all achieved the hat-trick.

3 – number of winners from Portugal – Eusebio (1965), Figo (2000) and Ronaldo.

3 – number of defenders who've won the award – Beckenbauer (1972 & 76), Sammer (1996) and Cannavaro (2006).

4 – number of winners from United – Law (1964), Charlton (1966), Best (1968), Ronaldo (2008)

4 – number of English winners - Matthews (56), Charlton (1966), Keegan (1978 & 79), Owen (2001)

7 – number of times Bobby Charlton was voted in the top 10. Only Beckenbauer (11), Cruyff (9), Gerd Muller and Platini (both 8) have featured more.

10 – number of medals (in other words, 1st, 2nd and 3rd place finishes) won by United. Only Barcelona (18), Madrid and Milan (17), Juve and Bayern Munich (16) and Inter (11) have won more.

17 – number of medals won by English players – only Germany (27) and France (19) have produced more medal winners.

23 – the number of medals won by players playing in the English league – Italy (48), Spain (36), Germany (25) are the 3 leagues to have provided more.

Stats from Rob Moore, Karel Stokkermans and RSSSF 1995/2008

SHOCK OF THE WEEK

United don't get Villa in the 3rd round of the Cup. We're off to Saint Mary's instead. Which means we'll have to sit through a load of 1976 reruns, and read all about the tragic life of Bobby Stokes (he later became an alcoholic and died of pneumonia in 1995), in the New Year. All the other former European Cup winners get an easy ride too, with Villa, Liverpool and Forest paired with Gillingham, Preston and City.

SPOT OF THE WEEK
From football365:

Undaunted by Blackburn's shoddy form, the pressure growing on his fledgling managerial career and the poor record of all Fergie's former charges against him, Paul Ince seems fairly bullish about his side's prospects at United tonight [in the Carling Cup].

He says in *The Times*: "We had a situation when I was at Macclesfield where we were bottom of the table and had to go to Walsall, who were top of the league. We beat them 1-0 and it lifted everybody and we went on a long unbeaten run and ended up staying up by the last game of the season. If we can go to Old Trafford and get something, it could just lift everybody and put us on a run."

Yes Paul. Playing Walsall is exactly like going to Old Trafford.

QUOTES OF THE WEEK

"It's one of the most beautiful days in my life. Thank you to my team-mates, who helped me to be the best. This morning, arriving at the training session, I will be the same lad." – *'Surly' Ronaldo after being named no.1.*

"We are very proud. Manchester United have been waiting for this for 40 years. His award is beyond all possible dispute … and his best years are all ahead of him." – *If only Fergie could guarantee they'd be spent with us…*

"ITV are f******* s***" – *Chant heard during ITV's coverage of Histon's Cup win against Leeds after fans grabbed a pitchside microphone. It's not a subtle barb, admittedly but you can't say they're too far off the mark. Sometimes they get so bad I even find myself missing Brian Moore.*

CC Q/F 03/12/2008

UNITED 5 BLACKBURN 3

Tévez 36, Nani 40, McCarthy 48, Tévez 51(p), Tévez 54, Derbyshire 84, McCarthy 90, Tévez 90 +

TAKE A LOOK at the score and this looks like a Roy of the Rovers style thriller. It wasn't. Another late bout of defensive carelessness apart, this was a walk in the park for United and a massively chastening experience for the Guv'nor on his managerial debut at Old Trafford. And the player most responsible for pushing Ince's head precariously close to the chopping block? Carlos Tévez. Like the other players signed in the summer of 2007 - Nani, Anderson and Hargreaves - Tévez had been struggling with second season syndrome for most of the autumn. But this – Tévez's first hat-trick for United and his first four-goal haul ever - was an eloquent reminder of his talent. Mind you, how he managed to keep that first goal god only knows...

MATCH ACTION

1-0 (36): In the old days the ball could go in off the referee's backside and still the centre-forward would be able to claim it. But then the Dubious Goals panel arrived to spoil their fun. But it appears they get time off in Carling Cup weeks. Which is good news for Tévez. He might have been near Giggs's free-kick to the far post, his presence might have been the reason Mokoena ended up putting the ball into the net, but he sure as hell didn't touch it.

2-0 (40): Nice. Nani plays a quick one-two with Tévez, bursts into the box and gets off a quick shot that Robinson can only help into the net. It's weird. United were pretty miserable for the first 35 minutes. But now they're two goals ahead.

2-1 (48): Where did that come from? Blackburn looked like dead men walking when they came out for the second half. But then Santa Cruz flicks on, McCarthy makes a mug of Neville and buries his shot inside the near post.

3-1 (51): Blackburn's travelling fans – all 800 of them – are only just back in their seats when the lumbering Ooijer takes out Tévez in the box. Tévez slides his spot-kick into the bottom right corner.

4-1 (54): Just 3 minutes later Tévez grabs his second, I mean his third. And it's no ordinary goal either. Anderson kicks things off, drilling the ball to Giggs, who immediately returns the favour. Anderson and Tévez then rip a hole in the Blackburn defence with a swift one-two before Anderson (who could do with a goal himself) draws Robinson out of goal and rolls the ball into the path of Tévez.

SUB (76): The funniest moment of the night. Fowler wobbles onto the pitch. How long has he been past it for now?

4-2 (84): Blackburn are getting embarrassed. But again lax defending allows them to get a goal out of nothing. Derbyshire gets behind Evra, sorts his feet out neatly and pokes the ball under the advancing Foster.

4-3 (90): Hold on a minute, what's going on here? In a repeat of the Hull finale, Blackburn get another sloppy goal. Neville and Foster misread the speed of Derbyshire's daisycutter centre from the left and McCarthy's toe does the rest.

5-3 (90): But just when the Blackburn fans start feeling guilty about giving Ince so much grief, Tévez finally kills the game off, waiting for Anderson's crossfield pass to sit up and then hammering it past Robinson on the volley.

WHAT WAS GOOD?

TÉVEZ – Started the season better than any other forward but has since struggled to cope with the Berbatov factor, scoring just a single league goal. Could this goal rush be the turning point of his season?

HEARING FOWLER GET BARRACKED BY BOTH SETS OF FANS.

THE OTHER RESULTS mean that Spurs are the only Premier League team left in the competition.

WHAT WAS BAD?

THE AWAY TURNOUT - QPR bring 7,000 fans the length of the country, Blackburn bring 800 fans the length of Gary Neville's drive. Can you believe these no-marks used to be our main challengers?

OLD BOYS – FIRST RETURNS
(all in the Premier League unless stated)
COPPELL – lost 1-0 in League Cup with Palace in 1985/86
ROBSON – lost 2-0 to 10-man United with Boro in 1995/96 (Keane got sent off)
HUGHES – drew 0-0 with Blackburn in 2004/5

Bruce – lost 2-0 with Birmingham in 2002/3
Keane – lost 1-0 with Sunderland in 2007/8
McClaren – won 1-0 with Boro in 2001/2
Strachan – lost 3-1 with Coventry in 1996/7

BLACKBURN – THE VERBALS

"Carlos was marvellous — his energy and commitment were brilliant. I don't think you could ask for a better performance than that." – *Fergie (who was probably already planning to leave him on the bench for the weekend) praises his 4-goal man.*

"You're not fit to wear the shirt" – *Blackburn fans to Fowler. Be fair lads, he's hardly fit to get off the sofa.*

"You don't know what you're doing" – *Blackburn fans to Ince when he brought on Fowler for Santa Cruz. You can see their point...*

VIEWS FROM THE PRESSBOX

"Strap a polygraph to Sir Alex Ferguson and he might just be forced to admit that he often finds the Carling Cup a hindrance in an already cluttered fixture list. At this stage of the competition, however, the good outweighs the bad and Manchester United will not overly mind the extra dates in their calendar when they reflect on the possibility of another Wembley final.

"There was certainly plenty for United supporters to relish last night as Carlos Tévez's hat-trick helped them into the semi-finals and Paul Ince became the target of sustained and voluble criticism from Blackburn's small band of fans. Ince may once have represented United with distinction but his popularity in these parts has rapidly diminished over the years and the Stretford End had little sympathy as the first tinny cries of "we want Incey out" emanated from the away end." – *The Guardian*

MATCH FACTS

United: Foster, Rafael Da Silva, Neville, Evans, O'Shea (Evra 66), Nani, Gibson, Possebon (Scholes 66), Anderson, Giggs (Manucho 71), Tévez.
Blackburn: Robinson, Olsson, Nelsen, Ooijer, Warnock, Treacy, Kerimoglu (Pedersen 70), Mokoena, Emerton (McCarthy 46), Derbyshire, Roque Santa Cruz (Fowler 76) [Ince]
Booked: Nelsen.
Att: 53,997. **Ref:** Alan Wiley h-t: 2-0

OTHER SCORES

CARLING CUP QUARTER-FINALS: WATFORD 1 SPURS 2

"Of all the things the FA have done to us down the years that is one of their biggest."

NEWS

UNITED GET DERBY in the semi-finals of the Carling Cup. Spurs get Burnley. No one gets excited. Keano walks out on Sunderland on the eve of his return to Old Trafford. Was he worried about taking a spanking? Is he cut out for management? Can he handle dealing with mere mortals? Has he blown his chance of taking over from Fergie? Will Triggs survive another bout of street pounding? United kid keeper Ron Robert Zieler joins Northampton. And 8 months after the farcical 'Battle of the Bridge' the FA finally gets round to shafting Pat Evra...

THE NEW OUTCASTS

United have been banging heads with the FA for as long as they've been banging balls into the net. When the FA wanted to turn footballers into slaves and ban the fledgling Players' Union it was Charlie Roberts and his merry band of rebels who stopped them. When the FA ordered clubs not to mix with Johnny Foreigner in the European Cup, it was Sir Matt and United who told them where to go. When the FA kangaroo court banned Ferdinand before he was convicted of his drugs charge, who was it that was hell-bent on leading the England team's first strike? That's right it was Comrade Neville, of United.

No other club has stood up to the FA like United. None has given them as much grief. And because of that no other club has copped so much grief going the other way. The history of United is littered with FA pettiness, overreaction, injustice and blatant bias. Think of the FA Cup winners from 1909 – turned into football outcasts for refusing to bail out on the Union. How about Enoch 'Knocker' West – banned from playing football until he was well past his 60s? Or big Frank Barson – the finest centre-half of the 1920s who couldn't get a game for England? The Lawman, Eric, Rio and Bestie all got special treatment from the FA. So did Rooney and Scholesy as recently as last year. Even Sir Bobby got turned over when he was ordered not to play in the European Cup semi in Milan in '58 – the same semi the Babes had sacrificed their lives to reach.

Fast forward 40 years and now it's Evra's turn to gag on justice, FA-style. Let's get reacquainted with the details. Fuming United players who've just lost a crucial late-season match courtesy of a dubious late penalty are warming down on the Stamford Bridge pitch. They're met by the biggest convoy of lawnmowers seen since, well, I just don't know. It's like Frogger out there. There is a coming together between players, groundsmen and self-important no-marks in luminous jackets. Verbal insults are exchanged and a couple of fists look to be swung. It's handbags really, the sort of non-event that happens in schoolyards every other day.

If it had been just any other club the FA would have barely raised an eyebrow. Except it wasn't, it was United. This was another chance to settle some old scores. So, after dragging their heels long enough for everyone's memories to go hazy, they call in the two main protagonists – Evra from United and groundsman Sam Bethell from Chelsea. One of them looks certain to be found guilty of kicking the whole thing off. Except here's the thing. Bethell can't be punished by the FA because Chelsea left the relevant clause out of his contract. So as he takes his seat next to Mo Watkins, Evra knows that his is the only head on the block. Laughable but true.

Then the hearing begins. Now none of us found out exactly what was said – not even when the FA took the unprecedented step of publishing their findings (without United's knowledge of course) just a few days later. But here's a good guess. Everything coming out of the red corner is ignored. Everything Chelsea staff say starts the panel nodding like the Churchill dog. Evra must know he's in trouble but at least he knows that his excellent disciplinary record – no red cards in almost 3 years in England – will save him from anything more than a fine and a heavy slap on the wrist. And then the panel announce their verdict. Bethell and his mower gang are cleared of any wrongdoing. United are effectively found guilty of provoking the incident themselves – as if a bundle with groundstaff is an integral part of their post-match routine. And Evra gets 4 games. He'd have got fewer if he'd slapped Drogba under the ref's nose and fired a snot torpedo – a la John Terry - into his hair as he walked off. It's ridiculous, a sham. But when the FA's involved, what else can you expect?

REACTION OF THE WEEK

"Of all the things the FA have done to us down the years that is one of their biggest. I could not believe it....

"You could never tell what these people (the FA) are doing. Even if I was sitting having breakfast with them, I would not know what they were thinking." - *Fergie's gobsmacked.*

DO THE MATHS

THROWING COIN INTO CROWD - Didier Drogba - 3 match ban
ALTERCATION WITH A GUY ON A LAWNMOWER - Evra - 4 match ban
FRACTURING A PLAYERS' SKULL AND CAUSING INTERNAL BLEEDING - Chris Morgan - 0 match ban*

RUMOUR OF THE WEEK

"Sir Alex Ferguson's disdain for the FA has been deepened yet further by learning that the man responsible for handing Patrice Evra a four-game ban recently is an Arsenal season-ticket holder'" - *The Daily Mail*

FORUM COMMENT OF THE WEEK
from Bunter [Red News]

"A guy smashes an opponent's skull, and the FA are powerless to take any further action, yet Evra gets four games for relatively nothing. Absolutely stinks, I can just see the self-effacing, sanctimonious, smug twats patting each other on the backs for sticking it to United yet again. If you want your Warholian 15 minutes of fame, what better vehicle than (picking on) United, FA *******."

QUOTES OF THE WEEK

"To serve a ban which is longer than one imposed for a career-threatening tackle or throwing an object into the crowd indicates that the disciplinary commission made a very poor decision." – *United fume about the Evra ban.*

"Patrice is a wonderful character and I believe him 100 per cent when he says he never hit the groundsman. He has our full support. We don't like the decision and we don't think it reflects other improper conduct charges. But we move on." – *So does David Gill.*

"I'm very angry because I didn't touch anybody, yet I have a four-game ban. But sometimes bad things happen in life - now I'm focusing on the Club World Cup because I want to be a world champion." – *Enjoy your Christmas off Paddy.*

'TRY SAYING IT TO HIS FACE' QUOTE OF THE WEEK
Self-important former journeyman Tony Cascarino gets involved in the Keane debate in the Times:

"He instigated the problems in Saipan in 2002 and he got away. He instigated the problems towards the end of his time at Manchester United by criticising the players in an interview on MUTV. He instigated the problems last Friday to do with his present team and the doubts around himself, and I think it was all [an attempt] to open the door to walk away. Maybe he doesn't want to face Fergie; maybe he doesn't like the fact that Fergie might stare him down and give him his comeuppance. This is the end for him. He'll not manage again. No one will give him the opportunity to manage a football club because they won't trust him. That's the bottom line"

UNLIKELY HEADLINE OF THE WEEK
From football365

'Saha Set For Quick Recovery' - *The Mirror. The world has gone mad.*

QUOTE OF THE WEEK

"Football is a better place when Roy is in it." – Brucie. Hear hear.
*Sheffield United centre-back Chris Morgan was only booked for an elbow on Barnsley's Ian Hume that left the striker in a high dependence unit. To the disbelief of many, the FA decided not to take any further action.

FAPL 06/12/2008
UNITED 1 SUNDERLAND 0
Vidic 90

IN SOME WAYS it seems harsh not to feel sorry for Sunderland for what United did to them here. After all, Keano walked out on them so close to the game that the *United Review* still had a 'Welcome back Roy' double-spread in the middle. They'd won only one of their last six league matches – a run that included a 4-1 thrashing by Bolton of all people the previous week. And former United men Ricky Sbragia and Dwight Yorke had only had one training session to sort them out. In the circumstances they deserved better than to go down to United's brutal injury-time goal, right? Actually, no, no way, not at all. It's one thing to turn up at Old Trafford, refuse to be cowered and put up a fight. It's quite another to stand in front of your goal like a red-and-white Maginot Line and show absolutely zero interest in crossing the halfway line, never mind scoring a goal. As Red Nev said afterwards, "I thought Sunderland's attitude to the game was appalling. It is difficult for teams to come to Old Trafford and you don't expect them to roll over. You do expect them to come out and play football and they got what they deserved." Nothing...

GOAL!

1-0 (90): Sunderland's lone striker Kenwyne Jones wins them their first corner – after 89 minutes. The need to commit no fewer than two players into United's half – one to take the kick, the other to try and keep it in the corner – blows apart Sbragia's 9-0-1 master-plan and finally gives us a gap to attack. Rafael squares the ball to Carrick, his 25 yard shot spins off Anton Ferdinand past a wrong-footed Fulop and rebounds off a post. Vidic, now playing as an extra centre-forward, slams the ball into the empty net and then windmills away in celebration. Sensibly his team-mates stay away from him. Just a glancing blow with those forearms would have finished them.

STATS OF THE DAY

28% – the amount of possession Sunderland enjoyed (pathetic).
22-0 – the score in shots on goal (United got the 22 if you weren't sure).

MATCH REPORT OF THE DAY
Excellent stuff from The Guardian:

"Everyone has a favourite Roy Keane story and they don't come much better than the time Phil Taylor came across him on a tour of Manchester United's training ground. This was 2003, the one year out of 11 when the PDC world championship trophy was not on Taylor's mantelpiece and he was introduced to the players as world darts champion. Keane was injured, in one of his coalmine-black moods, pounding away on an exercise bike. He lifted his eyes for only a second. "Ex-champion," he replied, then started pedalling again.

"That was the thing about Keane: he liked to say it how it was. Sometimes it endeared him to us; at other times you found yourself wincing. Mostly, Keane made sense in a sport where so many other managers tend to say nothing and see even less. He had no time for the cliche claptrap or PR gimmickry in which other football people indulge.

"So what would Keane, as a man whose managerial status now also includes the prefix "ex-", have made of a match in which his old side managed zero efforts at goal compared with 23 for the opposition? The answer will probably never be known as Keane embarks on one of his Trappist-like periods of silence, but it is fair to say he would not have fallen into the trap of thinking Sunderland played with distinction. Competitive courage, yes. But distinction? Not in a game in which, attacking-wise, they contributed absolutely nothing."

'MOUNTAIN MEET MOLEHILL' MOMENT OF THE DAY

Many of the papers, including the Sunday Times (below), get their knickers in a twist after Ronaldo effectively subbed himself in the second half:

"Ronaldo, who appeared one dropped lollipop away from a tantrum from the moment the game kicked off, took a blow to the ribs when attempting to convert a chance created by Dimitar Berbatov early in the second half. A quarter of an hour later, after much wincing and limping, Ronaldo just walked off the field. He was prompted by seeing Anderson getting stripped for action and the fourth official holding the substitutes board but replacing Ronaldo was not the switch United had in mind. A puzzled Anderson looked on and a flustered Mike Phelan made a hasty phone to Ferguson, in the stand because of a touchline ban, as Ronaldo walked straight off the field of play and down the tunnel with barely a look to his bench. While the re-calculating was being done, two minutes elapsed with United having 10 players on the field. Eventually Anderson came on for Ji-Sung Park and Ryan Giggs for Ferguson's departed No 7."

A more accurate – less sensationalist - write-up would have gone as followed. Ronaldo gets injured, does his best to play on, sees Anderson getting ready to come on, presumes he's coming on in his place (or decides to get off the pitch before United mistakenly leave him on), kicks the ball out and limps off. No drama. No problem. No story.

SUNDERLAND – THE VERBALS

"I think the pictures tell the story! My favourite goal is my one against Everton [another winner, in September 2007), but this one, scored with my left foot, is probably the most important. It's always nice to score." – *Veni, Vidi, Vidic, as the T-shirt says.*

'There was no need. He got a kick on the hip and it was important to get treatment straight away." - *Fergie instantly dispels the Ronaldo nonsense.*

USELESS TRIVIA OF THE DAY

Sunderland goalkeeper Martin Fulop's dad, Ferenc, played centre-forward for the Nazis in Escape to Victory.

MATCH FACTS

UNITED: VAN DER SAR, RAFAEL DA SILVA, FERDINAND, VIDIC, EVRA, PARK (TÉVEZ 57), FLETCHER (ANDERSON 68), CARRICK, RONALDO (GIGGS 68), BERBATOV, ROONEY
BOOKED: ROONEY.
SUNDERLAND: FULOP, CHIMBONDA, FERDINAND, COLLINS, BARDSLEY, YORKE (TAINIO 60), MALBRANQUE, WHITEHEAD (EDWARDS 76), REID, DIOUF, CISSE (JONES 69) [SBRAGIA]
ATT: 75,400 REF: MARK HALSEY H-T: 0-0

OTHER SCORES

ARSENAL 1 WIGAN 0, BLACKBURN 1 LIVERPOOL 3, BOLTON 0 CHELSEA 2

LEAGUE TABLE

1. LIVERPOOL 37 (16) 2. CHELSEA 36 (16) 3. UNITED 31 (15)
4. ARSENAL 29 (16)... 18. SUNDERLAND 15 (16)

"I think I have gone down in history. And I am only 23."

SAY WHAT?

BRILLIANTLY MISJUDGED STUFF from Rosenborg's Alejandro Lago who prepared for last week's UEFA Cup match with Valencia by calling the visitors 'little girls who can't take the cold', and describing his team's defence as a 'wall of real men facing Valencia's homosexuals'.

FINAL SCORE: 'Rosenborg 0 'Homosexuals' 4

WHILE WE'RE ON THE SUBJECT

Sheasy dismisses the gay rumours:

"The Man City fans think I'm gay. I've been gay for about five years according to them. I laugh every time we play City and they sing a certain song at me. I just brush it off – it doesn't annoy me"

"What can you do? What can the FA do – put a load of stewards in and throw loads of people out? It's ridiculous, but it's just a bit of banter really."

(INEVITABLE) CANINE RUMOUR OF THE WEEK

'One of the unsung casualties of Roy Keane's reign at Sunderland is the family golden labrador Triggs. He is understood to be tired out and unable to last the course of the frequent long walks on which his master likes to mull over his football life. However, Keane now has a German shepherd who is fit and available if selected to replace Triggs in the starting walkies line-up' - *Daily Mail*

NUMBERS OF THE WEEK

Get out your P60, read what you earned last night, pour yourself a drink, sit down. And cry. Here's how the Rooneys get by... (Figures come from a writ issued against the Rooneys by their agents, Proactive Sports Management)

3.55 – how many millions Wayne has banked already for his 5-book deal

18,933.97 – the bill for his stag week in Ibiza

41,667 – the amount Coleen gets paid a month by OK mag

90,000 – Wayne's basic weekly salary from United

118,689.57 – the cheque he gets from computer giants EA twice a year

283,334 – how much his missus got for her book deal

600,000 – the wedge Coke give the Rooneys every 4 years

760,000 – Wayne's image payment from United every 6 months (and his agent gets £152,000 of that)

1,000,000 – what Nike pay him every year to risk his metatarsals

QUOTE OF THE WEEK

"I think I have gone down in history. And I am only 23." – *Go on, guess who.*

10/12/2008
CL GROUP E

UNITED 2 AALBORG 2

Tévez 3, Jakobsen 32, Curth 45, Rooney 52

VILLARREAL'S DEFEAT AT Celtic made everything that happened here irrelevant. Which was just as well. Because this was worse than disappointing, as sloppy a display as United have produced in Europe for years. But if Reds went home unhappy after watching us almost get embarrassed by a team that had turned up at Old Trafford like open-mouthed tourists, spare a thought for Aalborg sporting director Lynge Jakobsen. Before the game he'd promised to fly home naked if his side managed to grab a draw. Now all he could do was sit back and hope that the air hostesses kept a steady hand whilst serving the coffee…

MOMENTS THAT MATTERED (NOT A LOT)

1-0 (3): Giggs to Rooney, Rooney to Giggs, Giggs to Tévez, Tévez to the goal. 'That's the Manchester United we all love,' says Dion Dublin on TV.

1-1 (32): Sloppy. Unmarked Michael Jakobsen flicks a right-wing free-kick from Anders Due past Kuszczak with the back of his head.

OUCH: Rooney, visibly irked by United's testimonial approach, gets in an awkward tangle with Kasper Risgard and, in his attempts to get away, lands both sets of studs on his chest. It looks bad but a second viewing shows that Rooney's feet had nowhere else to go.

1-2 (45): More disastrous marking as Jepp Curthy arrives late to head Due's deep cross from the left across and past Kuszczak.

2-2 (52): Rooney collects Anderson's beautifully weighted throughball and sends a crisp shot past Karim Zaza – great name – to salvage a point, and extend United's unbeaten Euro run to 19 games, equalling the Champions League record set by Ajax in 1996 and Bayern Munich in 2002.

QUOTE OF THE NIGHT

"I'll look forward to tea and biscuits with Ramón Calderón" – *Fergie on the prospect of playing Madrid in the next round.*

RUNNER-UP

"He has got some problems now. Maybe he can give some money to the team and we will let him keep his tie on.", Aalborg caretaker boss Allan Kuhn on the soon to be naked Lynge Jakobsen.

VIEW FROM THE PRESSBOX

"From the pre-match warm-up, which they spent gazing up at the vertiginous stands, to the flight home, on which one of the club's senior officials threatened to sit naked as a forfeit for their heroics, this was a night that the little-known footballers of Aalborg will never forget. They will take home a thousand memories of the evening on which they briefly led at Old Trafford and it is just a shame that for one of them, Kasper Risgard, the souvenirs came in the form of the stud marks left on his chest by Wayne Rooney." - *The Times*

MATCH FACTS

UNITED: KUSZCZAK, NEVILLE (RAFAEL DA SILVA 76), FERDINAND, EVANS, O'SHEA, NANI, GIBSON (PARK 46), ANDERSON, GIGGS (SCHOLES 46), ROONEY, TÉVEZ

AAB: ZAZA, BOGELUND, OLFERS, JAKOBSEN, PEDERSEN (SORENSEN 76), CURTH (CACA 74), ENEVOLDSEN, AUGUSTINUSSEN, RISGAARD, DUE (KRISTENSEN 65), SAGANOWSKI [KUHN]

BOOKED: CURTH.

ATT: 74,382 REF: LAURENT DUHAMEL (FRANCE) H-T: 1-2

OTHER SCORES

CELTIC 2 VILLARREAL 0, CHELSEA 2 CLUJ 1, PSV 1 LIVERPOOL 3, PORTO 2 ARSENAL 0

FINAL STANDINGS

GROUP A: 1. ROMA 12 2. CHELSEA 11 3. BORDEAUX 7 4. CLUJ 4

GROUP B: 1. PANATHINAIKOS 10 2. INTER 8 3. BREMEN 7 4. ANORTHOSIS 6

GROUP C: 1. BARCELONA 13 2. SPORTING LIBSON 12 3. SHAKHTAR 9 4. BASEL 1

GROUP D: 1. LIVERPOOL 14 2. ATLETICO 12 3. MARSEILLE 4 4. PSV 3

GROUP E: 1. UNITED 10 2. VILLARREAL 9 3. AALBORG 6 4. CELTIC 5

GROUP F: 1. BAYERN 14 2. LYON 11 3. FIORENTINA 6 4. STEAUA 1

GROUP G: 1. PORTO 12 2. ARSENAL 11 3. KIEV 8 4. FENERBAHCE 2

GROUP H: 1. JUVENTUS 12 2. REAL MADRID 12 3. ZENIT 5 4. BATE 3

"You know Hercules? He was hefty and
muscular but sometimes he fell."

NEWS

So that's another dream over. Adelaide United beat Waitekere United
FC in the World Club thingy which means United won't get the chance
to play the pride of New Zealand for another year at least. Van der
Sar extends his United contract until 2010. The OFT confirm they are
investigating MUST's complaint about the ACS (that'll be the automatic
cup rip off). And, ignoring the fact that he'd have needed to levitate
to avoid him, there's loads of nonsense in the papers about Rooney's
'stamp' on Aalborg's Risgard. Honestly, sometimes you'd think that the
press has nothing better to do than stir sh*t with United...

NO BALLS

Unlike Bernie Slaven (who promised to show his backside in a shop window
if Boro won at Old Trafford back in 1998), Lynge Jakobsen refuses to
follow through on his naked flight promise following Aalborg's draw at Old
Trafford:

"It was a joke," he insisted. "I am lucky that I have the body to
get away with it, and it probably wouldn't be that bad if I were to
show it off occasionally."

RANT OF THE WEEK

"I am not going to discuss Wayne Rooney. I think you press guys
have created most of it and you are not getting anything from this
club on Wayne Rooney. So that's it, finished" - *Fergie goes off on one*
after the press call for Rooney to be banned for treading on Risgard.

AND THERE'S MORE...

When someone dared to challenge him over Rooney, he ranted: "You play
your part - don't get lippy. You sit there playing the innocent party
but you know the part you play, you are never off that phone to
Uefa." *Brilliant.*

DIG OF THE WEEK
From The Guardian:

"'Are you a mastermind when it comes to all things LFC-related? Do you know your Alan A'Court from your Alun Evans, your Peter Thompson from your Phil Thompson and what links the tiny hillside village of Glenbuck with the greatest football club in the world?" – *Liverpool official website's advert for their online quiz. Recipients might need to know what on earth the greatest football club in the world has got to do with Liverpool.'*

FERGIE QUOTES OF THE WEEK

"His experience, temperament, professionalism and performance level have not changed one bit since he has been with us. Obviously, it will be his last year. He will be almost 40 then, which is a great credit to the lad." – *SAF on VDS.*

"Next season, in fairness to Ben [Foster] and Tom [Kuszczak], we've got to make it more competitive. It'll be who is the best man for the job next year." – *Sounds fair enough. But if the Pole in goal makes it at United I'll fly naked to Warsaw... strapped to the wing.*

QUOTE OF THE WEEK

"You know Hercules? He was hefty and muscular but sometimes he fell." - *Ronaldo's mouth is in fine form again as he explains why he's partial to a tumble.*

FAPL 12/12/2008

SPURS 0 UNITED 0

OK, IT WASN'T the worst result in the world. And once Chelsea had failed to win like everyone else, it actually looked pretty decent. Even so, this was still one of those games that takes the edge of your Saturday night takeaway and bugs you when you open the papers the next morning. United should be making fools out of messed-up clubs like Tottenham. Full stop. Ronaldo should be too good for journeyman midfielders/ makeshift full-backs like Zokora. Berbatov and Tévez should be too good for a defence held together by the likes of Dawson and big-boned midfielder Huddlestone. United should be able to ping the ball around the pitch. They should be able to force an error out of Gomes, the most disaster-prone keeper of the season so far. They should have a bit more about them. But once again this season they pushed on the gas and found there was nothing there. So instead of adding to the long list of classic White Hart Lane memories - Tévez twirling his shirt after last season's late equalizer, teenaged Giggs slaloming and scoring in '92, that nutty 5-3, William Prunier committing career hari kari - we got this. Ronaldo's goal from a corner disallowed for handball, Ronaldo flicking out at Dawson a la Becks in 98 and Gomes tipping Giggs's late free-kick over the bar. It wasn't a lot to keep us going during the Japan-enforced break to Stoke. But it would have to do.

WHAT WAS GOOD?

WE GOT AWAY WITH IT AGAIN.

WHAT WAS BAD?

IT FELT LIKE WE GOT AWAY WITH IT AGAIN.

BERBATOV'S WHITE HART LANE RETURN – It can't be easy to come back to your old club, particularly when you're as welcome as a fart in a spacesuit, but Berbatov (who was an increasingly peripheral figure as the autumn wore on) made it look more difficult than most. The OPTA stats man responsible for counting his touches would have had a ball...

AT THE MOMENT VIDIC LOOKS OUR MOST DANGEROUS FORWARD.

REDKNAPP AND SPURS – Just like Villa, they played one man up front and packed the midfield at home. That's OK for Bolton and the rest. But it's a bit sad coming from proper clubs like Villa and Spurs, right?.

SPURS – THE VERBAL

"We were nice on the ball, but there was not enough pressure." – *Van der Sar sums the game up in a sentence.*

VIEWS FROM THE PRESSBOX

"Sir Alex Ferguson doffed his ill-fitting woolly hat to the crowd near the end of this contest, his attempt to retrieve a bouncing ball on the touchline having prompted whoops of laughter from those behind the dug-out as the game drifted towards an unsatisfactory conclusion. The Manchester United manager's gruff persona mellowed as he played the clown with a smile. His only regret was that his team continue to veer from their own more customary script.

"United's dazzling array of attacking talent is spluttering at present. There have been only two goals in four league games since the destruction of Stoke City at Old Trafford. That is hardly catastrophic, but it is now proving costly with Saturday's blank at Tottenham Hotspur offering an anti-climactic note upon which to depart for the Fifa Club World Cup in Japan. The squad had 11 hours to stew over their inability to puncture Spurs on the flight to Japan yesterday." – *The Guardian picks up on United's impotence.*

"Some billed it as Dimitar Berbatov's return to White Hart Lane, but the Bulgarian was never more than a sideshow. He worked harder to engineer his transfer to Old Trafford than he ever did on the pitch towards the end of his spell as a Spurs player and the residual ill-feeling towards him was reflected not only in the home fans' ritual booing but also in the fact that he was the only United player who did not have a pen picture in the match programme." – *The Sunday Times.*

MATCH FACTS

TOTTENHAM: GOMES, CORLUKA, DAWSON, WOODGATE (HUDDLESTONE 10), ASSOU-EKOTTO, LENNON,
ZOKORA, JENAS (O'HARA 62), BENTLEY, MODRIC, PAVLYUCHENKO (BENT 54) [REDKNAPP]
BOOKED: HUDDLESTONE
UNITED: VAN DER SAR, RAFAEL DA SILVA, FERDINAND, VIDIC, O'SHEA, PARK, FLETCHER (SCHOLES 69),
CARRICK, RONALDO, BERBATOV, TÉVEZ (GIGGS 69)
BOOKED: RAFAEL
WHITE HART LANE ATT: 35,882 REF: M.DEAN H-T: 0-0

OTHER RESULTS

CHELSEA 1 WEST HAM 1, MIDDLESBROUGH 1 ARSENAL 1,
LIVERPOOL 2 HULL 2

LEAGUE TABLE

1. LIVERPOOL 38 (17) 2. CHELSEA 37 (17) 3. UNITED 32 (16)
4. ASTON VILLA 31 (17)…15. SPURS 19 (17)

*"The English live badly, eat badly
and their women do not wash their genitalia."*

NEWS

GAMBA OSAKA PIP Adelaide 1-0 in the Club World Cup finals to set up a semi clash with United. As expected, LDU Quito beat Mexican outfit Pachuca in the other semi. United continue to fume about Paddy E's suspension but decide not to appeal because a] there are no guarantees he won't get an even more outrageous ban if he does and b] even Sheasy can be trusted to do the business against Stoke, Boro, Southampton and Derby (the games Evra's missing). UEFA and the FA deal a blow to the media campaign to get more United stars banned by deciding not to act against either Rooney's 'stamp' against Aalborg or Ronaldo's air-kick at White Hart Lane. And just days after Calderon crosses his fingers and says he's no longer interested in Ronaldo, one of his cronies 'accidentally' reveals that we've agreed to flog him to Madrid in the summer. You knew right away that Fergie would just love that...

MARCA MYSTERY

"If you are asking me what we are going to do now then I would tell you that we have already signed the best player for the summer. The best of the best. It is Cristiano, there is no other. It is better that we do not say anything at the moment, though." - *Real Madrid director Pedro Trapote somehow allows the press to hear him say something it was better for him not to say. Now how on earth could that have happened Pete?*

PREDICTION OF THE WEEK

From Stan Collymore's column in The Daily Mirror *on Monday December 15:*

'Manchester United head to the FIFA Club World Cup to continue their quest for five trophies this term, but I fear they will be thwarted in Japan...they will be up against some very good opposition, like Al Ahly from Egypt.

'Their domestic game is very strong and I am going to stick my neck out and say the Egyptians will be crowned the best club side in the world.' *Yes, Stan, that's the same Al Ahly who had already been knocked out of the competition 4-2 by Pachuca last Saturday.*

NEWS PART II

A week after Keane quits Sunderland, Blackburn quit on Paul Ince. The decision means we're back to one black manager in the whole of the league – Keith Alexander at Ince's old club Macclesfield. Ridiculous eh?

Sir Bobby gets a lifetime achievement award – and one of the most moving standing ovations you'll ever see - at the BBC Sports Review of the Year. The rest of the show plots a predictable course with Fergie being pipped for the coach of the year award by the guy who coached the GB cycling team. In another sign that the world has gone mad, Chris Hoy gets the main award (I know he got 3 golds but cycling quickly in a circle is hardly the same as winning the Tour de France is it?).

SPOT THE DIFFERENCE

"You have to start somewhere. Who is to say what this tournament will look like in 40 years? Over time, I am sure it will be recognised as a competition of major significance." – *David Gill does his best to big up the Club World Cup...*

"It's one of those things. We managed to win the European Cup last year and sometimes afterwards you have to do things maybe you don't want to do" – *True to form, Scholesy can't be bothered.*

QUOTE OF THE WEEK

"If they want to go to England then in the end they're going to go, but they need to understand this: the English live badly, eat badly and their women do not wash their genitalia. To them, a bidet is a mystery" - *Napoli president Aurelio De Laurentiis warns his players of the perils of moving over here.*

18/12/2009
CLUB WORLD CUP SEMI-FINAL
GAMBA OSAKA 3 UNITED 5
Vidic 28, Ronaldo 45,Yamazaki 74, Rooney 75, Fletcher 78, Rooney 79,
Endo 85 p, Hashimoto 90

OK, SO THIS Club World Cup semi-final had all the tension and nerve-biting excitement of a game of knock-a-door run at an old people's home. But it did at least end up providing decent entertainment for the hordes of Ronaldo-worshipping locals in the stadium and the band of Reds who emptied their Christmas club accounts to join them. And for that our thanks must go to Gamba forward Masata Yamazaki. Before his neat goal with 16 minutes left, this game wasn't exactly stinking the place out but it was certainly leaving a bad smell. When the ball arrowed past Van der Sar, United snapped out of cruise control mode, Rooney got busy and both teams went goal crazy with United banging in three in no time and Gamba replying with two more consolations of their own. Like the Blackburn game the week before, the late goal rush didn't make this a classic, and you'd have to say some of the defending was bordering on the kamikaze, but after weeks of 1-0s and 0-0s back home, you'd have to be a right Hansen to start complaining...

GOAL ACTION

1-0 (28): Remember the old clichés about Asian teams being weak at set pieces? It looks like Gamba haven't. The first goal is a virtual gift, Vidic heading Giggs's inswinging corner almost unchallenged...

2-0 (45): And the second is almost as bad, Ronaldo heading in powerfully following a trademark run to the near post.

2-1 (74): Yamazaki's moment. United switch off down the left, the ball gets squared twice and Yamazaki steers the ball past Van der Sar's left hand.

3-1 (75): Rooney's moment (part I). Gamba's cente-backs allow themselves to be bamboozled by Fletcher's simple chip over the top and Rooney, who'd only been on long enough to see Gamba score, screws a left-footer past Fujigaya.

4-1 (78): Nani and Evra open up Gamba on the left and Fletcher, jogging into the box, easily heads in Evra's cross.

5-1 (79): Rooney's moment (part II). Nani bursts from deep and flicks the ball to Giggs, he adjusts his body position superbly to sidefoot Rooney clear and Wayne's toepoke does the rest. Brilliant stuff.

5-2 (85): Love this. United are 5-1 up in a game that doesn't really matter when the referee penalises Neville for a non-existent handball. Most players would smile and shrug it off. Red Nev goes mental. He's still chuntering and gesticulating at the ref when Endo slides the penalty low into the net.

5-3 (90): Hasimoto rounds off the goal frenzy, banging one in on the break.

WHAT WAS GOOD?

THE SIGHT OF RONALDO ENJOYING HIMSELF playing in front of a crowd that had come to cheer him, not jeer him.

THE SCORES BACK HOME.

WHAT WAS BAD?

NOTHING REALLY – though it's still weird to hear Japanese fans going crazy when Ronaldo attempts his 33rd pointless stepover. Shouldn't they be getting more football savvy by now?

VIEW FROM THE BROADSHEETS

"All continents are now equal in Fifa's re-structured Club World Cup but some remain more equal than others. Manchester United cruised into the competition's final against Gamba Osaka in Yokohama to set up the traditional Europe versus South America contest, against Liga de Quito of Ecuador. Fifa's vision of a truly global event will have to wait.

"United's victory had more of the air of lively and spirited testimonial than a do-or-die semi-final with six goals in the final 16 minutes producing the spectacle Fifa and a crowd of 67,618 craved. The spectators got the individual cameos they demanded too, with Nemanja Vidic and Cristiano Ronaldo heading United into a comfortable interval lead before Wayne Rooney emerged from the bench to score twice and collect the European champions' only booking of the game." – *The Independent*

MATCH FACTS

GAMBA OSAKA: FUJIGAYA, KAJI, NAKAZAWA, YAMAGUCHI, ENDO, MICHIHIRO YASUDA, MYOJIN, HASHIMOTO, BANDO (TERADA 85), LUCAS, YAMAZAKI.
BOOKED: YAMAGUCHI.
UNITED: VAN DER SAR, NEVILLE, FERDINAND, VIDIC (EVANS 69), EVRA, NANI, ANDERSON, SCHOLES (FLETCHER 67), RONALDO, GIGGS, TÉVEZ (ROONEY 73).
BOOKED: ROONEY.
YOKOHAMA STADIUM ATT: 67,618 REF: BENITO ARCHUNDIA TELLEZ (MEXICO). H-T: 2-0

OTHER SCORES (BACK HOME)

ARSENAL 1 LIVERPOOL 1, EVERTON 0 CHELSEA 0

LEAGUE TABLE

1. LIVERPOOL 39 (18) 2. CHELSEA 38 (18) 3. VILLA 34 (18)
4. UNITED 32 (16)

"No chance. I would not sell them a virus."

A SPECIAL ONE

Everyone was half expecting the Champions League draw to give Fergie another chance to endear himself to the Madridistas. Instead United are handed arguably the hardest tie of all in the shape of Jose Mourinho's Inter. Elsewhere, Liverpool get Madrid, Chelsea are paired with Juve and Arsenal meet United's bunnies, Roma. And Villarreal, bloody boring, spiteful, horrible Villarreal are rewarded for their negativity by getting what looks like a free pass into the quarters in the shape of Panathinaikos.

QUOTE OF THE WEEK/MONTH/YEAR

"No chance. I would not sell them a virus." – *The legendary Alexander Chapman Ferguson (when asked about the rumours United had agreed a deal to sell Ronaldo to Madrid).*

RUNNER-UP

"No. That's bollocks." - *Fergie shoots down a Japanese journalist who asks whether United will retire the shirt numbers of Gary Nev, Giggs and Scholes when they end their careers.*

NEVER SAY NEVER AGAIN

"It is sad that a professional with the career of Mr Ferguson can make declarations like these, in addition to some of the other unfortunate things in the last few months. Despite that, Real Madrid will never respond with a lack of respect to Manchester United, to any of their directors, nor of course to their fans, for whom everyone has the greatest of respect." – Ramon Calderon's riposte to Fergie's 'virus' jibe would seem a classy one if that last bit didn't smell so bad…

NEWS

Blackburn remind everyone how far they've fallen by naming Sam Allardyce as their new manager. In another sign that fronting up to Fergie is bad for your health, Benitez and Scolari both undergo operations for kidney stones in the same week. And the FA dump fuel on the flaming anger United feel over the Evra affair by slapping a transcript of the case on their website – without United's knowledge, of course - and accusing the United delegation, particularly Mickey Phelan, of presenting ropey evidence…

SHORTS SHRIFT

'In the first [Phelan] statement Mr Bethell and Mr Evra are already squared up close to each other, in the course of the second altercation, when the remark is made. But in the second statement the remark comes before Mr Evra has even started to run back for the second Bethell–Evra altercation." – The FA on the 'inconsistent' Mickey P.

HEADLINE OF THE WEEK

'Liverpool 1, Chelsea 3 - *Benitez bags one as Scolari nets three.'* – *Yes, The Sun really did splash a 'kidney stone' score all over their front page.*

AND IT GETS WORSE…

'You'll never pass a stone!" – *The Sun disgrace themselves on their website (It sort of sounds like You'll Never Walk Alone, geddit?)*

WORRYING STAT OF THE WEEK

P 12 W 6 D 5 L 1 F A (Mourinho's record against Fergie)

RUNNER-UP

P 5 W 0 D 1 L 4 F1 A 11 (United's record in the San Siro)

NON-UNITED QUOTE OF THE WEEK

"I must admit I have a dressing room curiosity over Beckham. I want to see if he is equipped as he is in the Armani underwear adverts" – *Milan striker Marco Borriello makes himself sound weird. But what would you do?*

RUNNER-UP

"I told the referee that I had another shirt on so he shouldn't book me for taking it off, but he told me that the yellow card was for taking my shorts off, which annoyed me" – *Roma striker Mirko Vucinic after scoring the winner against Cagliari.*

21/12/2009
CLUB WORLD CUP FINAL
UNITED 1 LIGA DE QUITO 0
Rooney 72

CHAMPIONS OF ENGLAND. Champions of Europe. And now Champions of the World. Say what you like about FIFA's new Club World Cup – and any competition that sets up a scuffle between the best team in Europe and the best team in South America sounds good to me – but that's certainly got a nice ring to it.

Oh, and one more thing. I know we should be above these sorts of things, I really do, but listen to this. Just a few hours before United were being crowned the best team in the world, Leeds were losing 3-1 at Milton Keynes Dons. Life is sweet my friend. Life is sweet...

RULING THE WORLD –
A MINUTE-BY-MINUTE GUIDE

So what do we know about Liga de Quito? Their full name is Ligo Deportiva Universitaria de Quito (LDU for short). They're from Ecuador's capital, Quito. They're the first ever Ecuadorian side to win the Copa Libertadores, having beaten Fluminese on penalties.

They beat Mexican side Pachuca in the semis of this tournament. And they like eating guinea pigs.

GROUCHY: Gamba Osaka hardly made a tackle in the semi. La Quito start off the final as if they mean to re-enact the Estudiantes wars from 1968. First, right-back Campos gets away with an ugly lunge from behind on Ronaldo. Then centre-forward Claudio Bieler gets booked for a wild shoulder-block, also on Ronaldo.

WHAT.A. MISS. 3: But just when you start thinking LDU aren't even interested in the ball they create, and waste, the chance of the match. Alkejandro Manso, the black-haired playmaker who's got something of a guinea pig look about him (which must be a worry for him back home in Quito) whips in a low in-swinging free-kick from the right. United don't react, the ball just evades one Quito leg and falls perfectly for Campos, on his own in the penalty area, who panics, gets his legs in a tangle and prods the ball limply wide.

8: Ronaldo goes on his first run and the Tokyo crowd swoons en masse.

9: United's first chance. Carrick picks out Rooney with an inch-perfect 40-yard pass, Wayne chests it down and smashes a volley that keeper Jose Cevallos beats away.

10: Ronaldo lines up a free-kick. It doesn't go anywhere in particular but the crowd still goes mental. They'd have cheered him farting tonight.

14: Carrick lets rip with another touchline pass, this time to Park who looks suspiciously like he's pushed on the edge of the Quito box. The ball falls to Rooney who smashes a low screamer that effectively hits Cevallos and goes behind for a corner. The keeper's a lucky boy there.

18: Another chance. Ronaldo picks up a mislaid cross on the left, shimmies back onto his right foot and curls in a centre that Tévez lunges and heads to Cevallos's left. It needs a great save to keep it out. You get the feeling Cevallos is going to have to perform miracles if Quito are going to get anywhere near a result tonight. Their defence is getting a pasting here...

21: And their main problem is they don't have a clue how to cope with the movement of United's forwards when the ball is played over the top. This time Anderson assumes the quarterback role, sending Rooney clear. The backspin on the ball helps Rooney get to the ball first but it also gives Cavellos time to rush out and get in his face. Rooney's attempted lob is a good one but it never looks like coming down in time and lands on the roof of the net.

21: The commentator on Channel 5 digs up a good story about Tévez who, apparently, was once sent off whilst playing for Boca Juniors for impersonating a bird. After scoring against Boca's fierce rivals, River Plate, Tévez tore round the pitch flapping his arms around like duck's wings (a reference to the nickname Boca fans have for their rivals). The referee judged his antics overly provocative and gave him the red.

22: The camera pans to Sir Bobby in the crowd. Stan Collymore, co-commentating on Channel 5, says something about him being a great ambassador for the game. I guess it takes one to know one.

23: Before the game the scarf-wearing Quito coach Edgardo Bauza promised that his players would produce 'the game of their lives'. They're not. They're hardly getting in United's half, the midfield and attack are non-existent, they haven't created a single chance from open play and the defence can't cope with simple long balls over the top. The possession stats say it all. Quito have had 32%, United 68%.

34: Shock news. United don't do anything really dangerous for ten minutes. But what a move this is. Rooney turns and pirouettes past three Quito players and prods the ball to Tévez. Tévez controls and flicks it back to Rooney who immediately sends Park clear on the right. It's crying out for a low drive across the goal. Instead Park blasts his shot right at the overworked Cevallos and he shovels it behind.

35: Campos, who's having a half to forget, kicks through the back of Park and gets the yellow card he should have got for piling into Ronaldo right at the start.

40-41: How is this one still 0-0? First Rooney slides through Tévez who stings the palms of Cevallos. Then Cevallos makes another smart save from Rooney's speculative drive. Then Tévez just fails to get a toe on Rafael's low centre.

42: Cevallos is booked for time-wasting over a goal-kick. There are 50 minutes left. If anything sums up La Quito's approach here, that is it.

44: In the build-up to the game Fergie told Park to sharpen up his goalscoring record. But he's not showing any signs of improvement here. Once again Quito can't defend a long Anderson ball from United's half, the ball sits up nicely for Park to lob Cevallos but he misjudges the speed of the ball, almost runs past it and lobs it tamely wide.

HALF-TIME: United have stuffed La Quito 0-0. Surely all they have to do is make sure they don't do anything silly and the goals will come...

ELBOW! RED! 48: What was I saying about not doing anything silly? Vidic slide tackles Bieler, the Argentina forward falls on top of him and Vidic brushes him off with his elbow and arm. As Bieler grasps his face and begins rolling in the direction of United's goal, the Uzbekistan referee arrives on the scene with his red card held aloft. It wasn't an elbow elbow – if that makes sense – but Vidic's elbow definitely did make contact with Bieler so there can be no real complaints.

49: Mind you, the behaviour of Bieler leaves a sour taste. Vidic is almost in the dressing-rooms now and Bieler, who will have suffered far worse facial injuries shaving, is still rolling around on the pitch.

49:20: He's still going...

49:35: The Argentine is finally back up on his feet (was he getting dizzy on the floor?). Hang you head man, hang your head...

50: The commentator – Dave Woods – scored big points for the duck wings story. But he loses them for missing out on a curious stat here. United have only won the European Cup 3 times. But they've had 4 players sent off in these inter-continental affairs – Nobby Stiles in Argentina, Bestie in Manchester, Becks in Brazil and now Vidic In Japan.

51: Vidic's red card necessitates a reshuffle and it's Tévez who once again gets the hook. As he's replaced by Evans he gives a 'why the f*** me?' gesture to the bench. But you can't argue with Fergie's logic here. United are going to keep themselves solid at the back and wait for Rooney and Ronaldo to do something special on their own up front.

55: Quito have the extra man now but they're still not showing any signs of committing any more men forward. And still United are creating chances. Rooney plays a short pass to Ronaldo on the edge of the area, he cuts inside and sends in a looping, deflected shot that gets Cevallas hopping across goal.

63: At last a shot in anger from Quito, the human guinea pig, Manso, forcing Van der Sar into a fingertip save from 25 yards.

66-70: As both sides adopt a pragmatic approach – United out of necessity, gutless Quito out of choice – the game deteriorates into a spate of yellows. Calle gets the first for kicking Ronaldo, Anderson gets one for throwing the ball away and Araujo for taking out

Ronaldo (again).

DANGER 71: Evra undercooks a simple ball back to Evans and gifts Quito their best counter-attacking opportunity of the night. Manso gallops forward with Bieler in a 2 v 2 but he delays and delays his pass and is eventually bundled out of it by a lung-bursting covering run and tackle from Anderson. It feels like a big moment at the time. It feels like an even bigger one as the Ronaldo-Rooney plan comes together just a minute later...

GOAL! ROONEY! 72: Carrick spears a low ball to Ronaldo on the edge of the Quito box, he sends a spinning flick to Rooney who immediately powers the ball across Cevallos and into the far corner. It's an excellent finish and all but guarantees Rooney the giant 'man of the match' key that Giggsy had to lug home in '99.

83: Gary Nev comes on for the injured Rafael and in the process becomes the only survivor from Tokyo '99 to make it onto the pitch. United won on that occasion, 1-0 against Scolari's Palmeiras. And unless Quito somehow find the attacking spark they've been missing all game, the same score's going to be enough here...

88: It never really looks on the cards. Manso forces a second good save from Van der Sar from long range but that's the nearest they come to forcing extra-time. Quito promised us the game of their lives. Instead they left us wondering how on earth they managed to book their ticket here (did they only win the Copa Libertadores because they play their home games at altitude?). As for United, and man of the tournament Rooney in particular, it was a case of a job professionally done. Now let's see what this win means in the league...

LA QUITO – LOS VERBALS

"We're the best team in the world. If we hadn't won, it would have been difficult going back home. We would probably have been on a downer and it would have had a knock-on effect. Now we can go back with lots of confidence. I just looked at my phone and I had a message saying 'congratulations – you're a world champion'. To score the winning goal is a great feeling." - *Wayne Rooney, champion of the world.*

"I said from the start that in 30 years I wanted people to look back and see our name on this trophy. I will not be around by then, but maybe I will look at it with pride tomorrow instead." – *Fergie, feeling his years.*

"They didn't really want to play. When they broke, only four players came out and even in the second half they did not leave their shell." – *Van der Sar has a pop at LDU's negative approach.*

"We have played against better South American teams. They had nobody even as good as Yasuhito Endo, the playmaker from Gamba Osaka." – *Fergie didn't rate them much either.*

VIEWS FROM THE PRESSBOX

"Easy like a Sunday morning, Manchester United were crowned champions of the world in Yokohama yesterday. Despite playing almost the entire second half with ten men after the dismissal of Nemanja Vidic, the central defender, United were never less than settled against Liga de Quito, the first Copa Libertadores champions from Ecuador, and won with a stunning finish from Wayne Rooney.

"This has been Rooney's tournament and that much was confirmed when he was given the Golden Ball award for best player, for which he was presented with a car, although not one he would be seen dead driving. Not that Rooney is in need of modern transportation anyway, his best work, as ever, being done on Shanks's pony and running more smoothly than any limousine. It was not just that he scored again, his third goal in the tournament despite featuring for only 108 minutes, or the sublime manner in which he did so. No, the most impressive element of Rooney's display was the work he put in to ensure that United went global with their domination of the sport in the year 2008." – *Times*

"Manchester United had to go to the other side of the world to become champions of it and, in truth, jet lag was almost a bigger obstacle to winning the Club World Cup than Ecuadorean opponents who left any ambition back in the Andes. Fittingly, United did it with a goal from Wayne Rooney that was out of this world.

"Even here in Japan, in the land that celebrates inscrutability, there was no mystery as to why United had their legions of supporters singing "ob-la-dee, ob-la-da, Man United, champions of Planet Earth" long into the night. United won because Rooney craved victory with a hunger that shamed the lacklustre standard-bearers from South America, whose craven tactics of kicking Cristiano Ronaldo, wasting time and playing for penalties was wonderfully, deservedly destroyed by United's No 10." – *Telegraph*

FLYING THE FLAG

United are the only British side to have been crowned World Champions:

1967 – **RACING CLUB (ARG)** BEAT CELTIC 0–1, 2–1, 2–1

1968 – **ESTUDIANTES (ARG)** BEAT UNITED 1–0, 1–1

1980 – **NACIONAL (URUGUAY)** BEAT FOREST 1–0

1981 – **FLAMENGO (BRAZIL)** BEAT LIVERPOOL 3–0

1982 – **PENAROL (URUGUAY)** BEAT VILLA 2–0

1984 – **INDEPENDIENTE (ARG)** BEAT LIVERPOOL 1–0

1999 – **UNITED** BEAT PALMEIRAS (BRAZIL) 1–0

2005 – **SAO PAULO (BRAZIL)** BEAT LIVERPOOL 1–0

2009 – **UNITED** BEAT LDU QUITO (ECUADOR) 1–0

MATCH FACTS

LIGA DE QUITO: CEVALLOS; CAMPOS, CALLE (AMBROSI 77), N ARAUJO, CALDERON; REASCO, W ARAUJO, URRUTIA, LUIS BOLANOS; BIELER, MANSO [BAUZA]

BOOKED: BIELER, CAMPOS, CALLE, W ARAUJO.

UNITED: VAN DER SAR; RAFAEL DA SILVA (NEVILLE 85), FERDINAND, VIDIC, EVRA; PARK, CARRICK, ANDERSON (FLETCHER 87), RONALDO; TÉVEZ (EVANS 51), ROONEY

BOOKED: ANDERSON.

OFF: VIDIC.

YOKOHAMA STADIUM ATT: 68,682 REF: R IRMATOV (UZBEKISTAN) H–T: 0–0

OTHER SCORES

EVERTON 0 CHELSEA 0; ARSENAL 1 LIVERPOOL 1.

LEAGUE TABLE

1. LIVERPOOL 39 (18); 2. CHELSEA 37 (17); 3. VILLA 34 (18); 4. UNITED 32 (16)

"I don't know if I am the best left-back in the world. Maybe the people saying it are blind."

NEWS

Despite all the grief he's been getting from the press back home, Berbatov is named Bulgarian Footballer of the Year for a record-equalling fifth time (Hristo Stoitchkov also won it 5 times). *The Mirror* reckons we're lining up a move for 17 year-old Nigerian-born

AC Milan youngster Wilfred Osuji Chinoye. Osaka finish third in the Club World Cup with a narrow victory over Mexican outfit Pachuca...

Vidic gets banned from the first leg of the Inter quarter-final following his red card in the Club World Final. It seems a ridiculous decision whichever way you look at it. If you get sent off for an elbow you should get more than a one game ban. If you get sent off in what was effectively an exhibition game you shouldn't be made to miss out on a huge European night. A massive fine – and a ban from the next FIFA club tournament – would surely have been a better idea...

And the FA apologise to United for not informing them that the transcript of the Evra hearing would be made public. Which makes you wonder whether there might be a silver lining to the whole messy affair. After all they're going to have to be ultra-careful to do the right thing by us from now on, right?

NON-UNITED QUOTES OF THE WEEK

"Two things really irritate the hell out of me. In terms of goal celebrations, it is someone taking their shirt off having scored a goal. And secondly if anyone scores and gives me another baby celebration, then I will go ballistic. I don't care whether they have had twins, quadruplets or 19 children at the one time." – *Martin O'Neill, grumpy old manager (he's got a point about the baby thing though).*

"I was ashamed to say that I live near Stratford-upon-Avon and I'd never been to a production. But I went to see the RSC's production of Hamlet the other day. It was fabulous" - *Coventry's Jay Tabb, the stereotype-buster of the week.*

"Some of our younger supporters have never seen us win the title and the last time we did it I was an Everton fan!" – *Jamie Carragher on Liverpool's 18½ years.*

"I don't think there will be many Leeds fans voting for me!" – *Darren Ferguson laughs off the speculation linking him to the Leeds manager's job.*

'MOWERGATE' – THE FALLOUT:

"The staff involved have exemplary careers as professionals at the top of the game and Michael in particular has been associated with the Club for most of the last 20 years and in that time he has consistently demonstrated himself to be a man of the highest integrity." – *United steam about the FA's jibes about the reliability of Phelan & the other United witnesses at Evra's hearing.*

"Banning the groundsman for four matches was not going to have such an impact, was it?" – *Are you reading the same thing into FA Chairman Lord Triesman's words that I am?*

"I would like to thank the FA for my little holiday, it means I can spend more time with my family over Christmas. I have thought about the ban every day." – *Paddy Evra, the modern-day Denis Law (according to legend, he always made sure he was suspended for Christmas).*

BOOK OF THE WEEK

It's coming up to Christmas, the time of year when people eat, drink, get merry and buy bland football biographies. But Italian bad boy Antonio Cassano's book, 'Dico Tutto' (I'll Tell Everything), promises to be a much livelier read. In it he...

• Slags off Fabio Capello, his coach at Roma and Madrid, calling him "a worthless man, you're more fake than Monopoly money".

• Reveals that he's slept with between 600 and 700 women, with around 20 from 'the showbusiness world'.

• And fondly recalls his time at Madrid, particularly the arrangement he had with a waiter at the hotel he stayed in: "I made friends with one of the waiters. His job was to bring me 3 or 4 cornetti (an Italian pastry) after I had sex. He would bring the cornetti to the stairs, I would bring the girl and we would make a trade: he took the girl, I stuffed myself with cornetti. Sex plus food, the perfect night."

QUOTE OF THE WEEK

"I don't know if I am the best left-back in the world. Maybe the people saying it are blind." – *If Evra's not the best left-back in the world – and I haven't seen better – he's certainly the most quotable.*

FAPL 26/12/2008

STOKE 0 UNITED 1
Tévez 83

UNITED'S SEASON WAS always going to stand and fall by how well they dealt with the paraphernalia that came with winning the European

Cup. How they coped with the pressure of always playing catch up in the league as well as the demands of the extra three games. And, just as importantly, how they responded to the shock of playing in Tokyo one minute and Stoke the next.

In that respect this was one of the most important phases of football of the season. 70 minutes into United's first visit to the Britannia Stadium we were struggling. The effervescence that had carried us through with 10 men against LDU Quito was gone. We were huffing and puffing on a pitch that looked like it needed a good mow. Stoke really were proving as tough to play against (and watch) as everyone had warned. Riccardo Fuller and Danny Pugh – of all people – were looking a danger. Berbatov and Tévez weren't.

Then came two big moments that changed the game. Actually make that three. First, young full-back Andy Wilkinson loses his cool in the midst of a running feud with a tetchy Ronaldo (who was guilty of another of those annoying retaliatory taps that are creeping into his game) and piles into him from behind earning a brain-dead red card. Then a cracking tactical change sees Giggs moving to left-back in place of O'Shea to take advantage of the gaping hole that Wilkinson had left on Stoke's right. And finally, on 83, comes the moment of the match. Neville plays the ball into Berbatov, he digs out a volley across goal and Tévez hooks in from point-blank range. Fergie later said he was just about to give Tévez the hook and bring on Welbeck. A flawed piece of thinking if you ask me. Say what you like about Tévez's goal threat this season. And it should have been a lot better, particularly in the league. But as he showed last year against Lyon, Blackburn and Spurs, give him a chance in the last few minutes and he'll come up with the goods.

QUOTE OF THE DAY

"They're all huge players – I don't think there's anybody in the Stoke side who's shorter than 6ft. They were continually playing the ball forward, which was a bit of a throwback to some of the teams we used to play, like Crystal Palace and Wimbledon. But Manchester United are a tough team to play against, both in attack and defence, and we don't shirk anything." – *Gary Neville, a proud captain.*

VIEWS FROM THE PRESSBOX

"It was not the stuff of world champions, nor a result that would resonate in Tokyo, Quito or even in Bulawayo, but it was enough.

Sir Alex Ferguson has long argued that whether Manchester United are able to retain their Premier League title or not would be decided by the team's reaction when returning from the Club World Cup and this was the kind of result he had in mind. On paper, overcoming a Stoke City side that played the final 21 minutes with 10 men is not a big victory but in a month when points have been spilling from the big four it was gratefully received." - *The Guardian on the result of the month*

PUB TRIVIA QUESTION OF THE WEEK*

This was United's first visit to the Britannia Stadium. What are the previous 5 grounds we've visited (on official business) for the first time?

MATCH FACTS

STOKE: SORENSEN, WILKINSON, ABDOULAYE FAYE, SHAWCROSS, HIGGINBOTHAM, DELAP (DAVIES 74), WHELAN, AMDY FAYE (OLOFINJANA 89), PUGH, CRESSWELL (PERICARD 90), FULLER [PULLIS]
SENT OFF: WILKINSON (72)
BOOKED: CRESSWELL, WILKINSON, FULLER, WHELAN
UNITED: VAN DER SAR, NEVILLE, EVANS, VIDIC, O'SHEA (BERBATOV 64), RONALDO, SCHOLES (CARRICK 90), FLETCHER, GIGGS, ROONEY, TÉVEZ.
BOOKED: EVANS, NEVILLE
BRITANNIA STADIUM ATT: 27,500 REF: CHRIS FOY H-T: 0-0

OTHER SCORES

CHELSEA 2 WBA 0; LIVERPOOL 3 BOLTON 0; ASTON VILLA 2 ARSENAL 2

LEAGUE TABLE

1. LIVERPOOL 42 (19); 2. CHELSEA 41 (19); 3. UNITED 35 (17);

* *Yokahama Stadium, Aalborg Stadion, Luzhniki Stadium, Wembley, Stadio Olimpico*

'There's never been a better time to visit Southport!'

NEWS

As YOU'D EXPECT at Christmas, news slows to a dribble. United kid Craig Cathcart extends his loan spell at Plymouth to the end of the season. Ex-Red coach Ricky Sbragia is named as Sunderland boss.

The new range of Quality Street causes a commotion – and tests the teeth of every unsuspecting gran - in front rooms the length and breadth of the land (where've all these bloody toffees come from?). Oh and Gerrard maintains a Scouse Christmas tradition, started by Joey Barton last year, by getting himself arrested for assault. Now I don't care what happened that night at the Lounge Inn in Southport. I'm not fussed if Gerrard was doing some weird Chuck Norris shit on the poor DJ* or was sat on the loo all the time he was being beaten up (for the record Gerrard was later found innocent). The really important news here is what kicked it all off. So was the DJ hitting on someone's girlfriend? Did he take exception to Mark Lawrenson – another regular at the bar – pinching his bum? No, the trouble apparently started when he refused to agree to Gerrard's request for him to play a track from his favourite album? And which album's that? Phil Collins... Hits. Crikey, there can't have been a nightclub fight over a request like that since 1986.

* a United fan no less

FAMOUS LAST WORDS

"I think we've got to enjoy it. We will play our best football if we are relaxed and composed. I think it's important for us to remain humble, keep our feet on the ground and keep working hard." – *Steve Gerrard speaking after Liverpool won at Newcastle... and before he headed out for a night out with the boys.*

THE PLACE TO BE
Sharp work from football365:

According to the town's official website, 'There's never been a better time to visit Southport!' *Judging by the size of the press pack outside Southport's police station last night, they're not wrong.*

Meanwhile, the Lounge Inn's official site assures would-be customers that, 'You are guaranteed a warm welcome with personal and attentive service. Our late night bar allows you to enjoy the evening that little bit longer!' *Quite.*

COME AND GET ME

"I would like to play in the Premier League and, above all, at Manchester United. I like Manchester United, the way they play and they have great players. Before I wanted to play in Spain, but this has now changed." – *The supposedly sh*t-hot Udinese forward Alexis Sanchez*

QUOTE OF THE WEEK
By Rafael:

"Ronaldo is a sensational person. Very humble and he jokes with us all the time and is nothing like his public superstar image." – *There's a lot said and written about Ronaldo by people who've never met him and never will. And at times it's easy to fall for the public perception of the man (especially when he tries to leave your club). But it's worth remembering that those who know and play with him, from Fergie down, seem to think he's a pretty decent guy.*

FAPL 29/12/2008
UNITED 1 MIDDLESBROUGH 0
Berbatov 69

THIS WAS THE sort of night they talk about in clichés when championships are won and lost. It was cold, so cold you had to ram nuclear hot chips and gravy down your throat to survive the walk back to the car. We were playing Middlesbrough, serial irritants who've scored more Premier League goals at Old Trafford than any team apart from Chelsea. We'd fallen into a rut of creating few chances and converting even fewer. We'd been denied the most blatant penalty (Pogatetz's headlock on Ronaldo) since Denis Irwin was catapulted into a triple pike at Wembley in '94. And we were looking like copying Liverpool and dropping two vital points against a side we should be battering out of sight. But then came the moment we'd been waiting for since those shots of him sneaking into Old Trafford were splashed all over Sky Sports News back in August. I'm talking about a really important goal from Dimitar Berbatov. Previously his goals had amounted to a collection of disdainful flicks against a bunch of no marks. None of them had even tempted him into anything more than an embarrassed shrug. This one was different. It wasn't particularly difficult, not for a man with his poetic technique. But you could tell from the pumped-up celebration how much it mattered to him – and how big a goal it was in the context of United's season. If Carrick hadn't made it to the by-line, if Wheater hadn't sliced his attempted clearance, if Berbatov hadn't timed his mid-air prod just right, United would have finished an unforgettable year on a depressing low. Instead we finished it with another win – the 38th in 59 games – and a real feeling that 2009 was going to be a bad year to be a Scouser… yet again.

WHAT WAS GOOD?

BERBATOV COMES TO THE PARTY.

WHAT WAS BAD?

UNITED'S FINISHING (AGAIN) – 25 chances, 1 goal.

'MAD DOG' POGATETZ – You'd have thought he'd behave himself after his horrific assault on Possebon. He didn't, first all by choking Ronaldo in the area (ridiculously, Martin Atkinson didn't give United the penalty), then getting involved in a rutting match as the two walked off and finally throwing himself to the ground in an attempt to get Ronaldo booked (again Atkinson missed it).

RONALDO'S FORM - I blame the new lime green boots.

BORO – THE VERBALS

"He's a marvellous player and he took his goal very well. We missed a lot of chances, though, and that is a big concern. Credit to Middlesbrough, the way they played belies their league position and we had to turn to our most experienced players in the second half. We're in a good position at the turn of the year and our two remaining games in hand are both at home. I don't think Liverpool are a bigger threat than Chelsea, I think they are both the same, but it's how we do our own job that will decide the title." – *You get the feeling Fergie's going to enjoy his birthday.*

VIEWS FROM THE PRESSBOX

"He is the type of player who would rather miss the bus than be seen breaking into a sprint, but, as a sense of urgency grew around Old Trafford last night, it was the languid figure of Dimitar Berbatov who ensured that Manchester United did not fall further behind schedule in their hunt for a third successive Premier League title…

"Berbatov is not every United supporter's cup of tea and even Sir Alex Ferguson, his greatest advocate, must be frustrated by him at times, but, whatever he may lack in terms of dynamism or industry, there is no more composed finisher in the Old Trafford dressing-room. In many ways he is the antithesis to Carlos Tévez, who has returned to Argentina to address what Ferguson called a "family issue", but, in a season when errant finishing has posed the greatest threat to United's ambitions, it is little wonder that the United manager has usually found himself turning to Berbatov rather than Tévez." – *The Times*

"Manchester United may not be in the same free-flowing form as Liverpool at the moment but they can still dig out victories when they need to. This was a far from comfortable win for the side who started the evening 10 points behind the leaders and for an hour there was a doubt whether they would be able to take maximum points from the first of their games in hand. Yet at a point in the evening when Steven Gerrard might have felt like smiling for the first time in 24 hours the hitherto ineffective Dimitar Berbatov struck from close range and normal service was resumed. The debate over whether the £31.5m United paid Tottenham for the Bulgarian was money well spent has not yet been resolved but the home side created 25 chances and someone had to stick one away." – *The Guardian*

MATCH FACTS

UNITED: VAN DER SAR, RAFAEL DA SILVA (NEVILLE 62), VIDIC, EVANS, O'SHEA, PARK, FLETCHER (SCHOLES 62), CARRICK, RONALDO (GIGGS 84), ROONEY, BERBATOV.
BOOKED: PARK, SCHOLES.
MIDDLESBROUGH: TURNBULL, BATES, RIGGOTT, WHEATER, POGATETZ, ALIADIERE (EMNES 76), O'NEIL, ARCA, DOWNING, SANLI, ALVES [SOUTHGATE]
ATT: 75,294 REF: MARTIN ATKINSON H-T: 0-0

OTHER SCORES

ARSENAL 1 PORTSMOUTH 0; NEWCASTLE 1 LIVERPOOL 5; FULHAM 2 CHELSEA 2

LEAGUE TABLE

1. LIVERPOOL 45 (20); 2. CHELSEA 42 (20); 3. UNITED 38 (18)

THE 2008/9 SEASON: THE HALF-TIME REPORT

TOP 10 WINNERS

UNITED – World champions, in the semis of the Carling Cup and still well in contention for the league despite only playing well in a handful of games. Have also equalled the record unbeaten run in the history of the Champions League. And the amazing thing is it doesn't feel like the season's really started yet.

Liverpool – Benefitted from United's fixture burden, Chelsea's home jitters and the Arsenal crisis to lead the table. They shouldn't be genuine contenders – they drop too many points against ordinary teams at Anfield for that – but somehow they are.

Vidic – The man's a colossus. And he's taken over the mantle as our best defender. The only United star of last season to do better than this time around.

Fletcher – Bigger, stronger, faster, better, making dangerous runs into the box, scoring goals, captain of his country and the recipient of a bumper new deal at United... let's make this clear, he's 'The Scottish Player' no more.

Rafael – The breakthrough act of the season by far.

Park – Seemingly now United's no.1 winger after Ronaldo. Not sure how a player who can't stay on his feet or score gets in the United side. But you've got to love his effort.

Fergie – Great to see him back leading from the front, picking fights with everyone who gets in his way. His war of words with Calderon is a classic.

City – Were heading nowhere – or worse - under Shinawatra. Now they've got Robinho and more money than they can spend (literally, as it soon turned out).

Aston Villa – Given themselves their best ever chance to grab a Champions League spot.

Cassano – see his book revelations earlier.

Capello – Hated after England drew with the Czech Republic in August. Feted after they hammered Croatia in Croatia. It just shows what a balls-up McClaren made of it all.

TOP 10 LOSERS

City – All that money and they can't buy a win in the Cup. Embarrassed by Brighton in the Carling Cup in September. And 2009 starts with them being humbled 3-0 at home by Forest in the FA Cup.

United fans – We're watching winning football. But where's the style?

Maurice Watkins – Would you trust this man to defend you in court? Ferdinand and Eric got far longer bans than was expected. And now Evra is doing time for a crime he says he didn't commit.

Tévez – Love his personality, love his attitude. But he's never worth £35 million so why did we agree to that? Hardly played, hardly scored.

Ronaldo – Used to be hated by everyone outside Old Trafford and worshipped by everyone inside. Now many Reds are indifferent. And many others are actively hostile. Plus he doesn't look quite the same player after his operation. Yet.

Fergie's old boys as managers - Brucie's doing well at Wigan but Ince is gone, Keano's gone and Hughesie's under big pressure to get City's season back on track.

Scolari – Subject of a mass love-in in the summer and autumn. Now looks like he's losing his grip.

Deco – see Scolari.

Mike Ashley – Managed to make Freddie Shepherd look respectable.

North London – Arsenal aren't in crisis yet. But they could be heading that way. And Spurs are constantly in crisis. So far this season they've shot themselves in the foot over Berbatov, lost a pile of games, sacked Ramos and resorted to Redknapp. Portsmouth fans won't be the only ones celebrating if they go down.

The Portuguezers – Nani and Anderson (I know he's Brazilian but I like the word). Both bogged down by second season syndrome (especially Nani who's been pants).

Tony Adams – Talks slowly to show how intelligent (?) he is. Gets the Portsmouth job as soon as the money dries out. It'll drive him to drink.

Spurs £50 million old boys – Robbie Keane's been a major flop at Anfield. Berbatov's shown signs of his undoubted brilliance but also signs that his lacksadaisical ways might not fit in at OT.

(Full marks for anyone who spotted it was 11 winners and 15 losers, I got on a roll)

04/01/2008
FA CUP 3RD ROUND
SOUTHAMPTON 0 UNITED 3
Welbeck 20, Nani 48 pen, Gibson 81

SOUTHAMPTON HAVE HATCHED some barm-pot plans in recent years. The move away from the Dell was a belter. It crippled their finances and lost them the crucial advantage that playing in a shoebox gave them. Hiring England's rugby manager [Clive Woodward] as director of football was another. So was bringing in the manager of their most hated rivals [Harry Redknapp]. He took them down. This year's plan was to save money by cramming the team with kids. It wasn't such a bad idea in theory. But then you get to see the kids in the flesh and you just know they were just asking for trouble*. It's not as if Southampton were terrible. They were just, well, non-existent. Even when it was 11 against 11 this game had all the tension of a kickaround in the back garden. When beanpole centre-forward Matt Paterson was sent off for going over the top on Vidic it was almost cruel to watch, like football's version of child molesting. If United had really wanted to they could have scored a hatful, perhaps even pushing Anderlecht out of the record books. But as Fergie said, there was no need to humiliate them, so we settled for three.

GOAL ACTION

1-0 (20): Southampton keeper Kelvin Davis – the only Saints player you'd have the slightest chance of recognising in the street – does well to push O'Shea's close-range prod against the bar but can do nothing to stop Welbeck nodding in the rebound.

RED (36): 19 year-old forward Matt Paterson had already left his foot in on Evans. Now he lunges in studs-up on Vidic. There's no questioning the youngster's bravery, there's no questioning the resulting red card (no matter what potty Saints manager Jan Poortvliet ranted afterwards – see below).

2-0 (48): In fairness the ranting Dutchman had a better case here, a much better case. Nani curls in a free-kick, the ball deflects off David

McGoldrick in the Southampton wall and Mike Riley mistakenly rules he's used his hands (in fairness to Riley, the Saints midfielder had jumped with his arms raised and it took a good look at the replay to see that the ball hadn't actually hit them). Nani makes the penalty look easy.

3-0 (81): Rooney cuts the ball back, Gibson coolly finishes.

RANT OF THE DAY

The post-match dribblings of potty Poortvliet:

"Arsene Wenger says the 50-50 decisions always go with United — and I agree with him. The referee is always a help for the top teams. Too many decisions went against us, you need neutral people."

"I can't see any justification for the red card." – *Apart from the fact it was high, dangerous and a textbook dismissal...*

"He [Riley] is in favour of the top teams. He's a help for the top teams."

"Alex Ferguson got out of his seat once in the first half and, from that point on, every decision went their way. No one knows my players so they get no protection from referees especially when they are playing against big stars."

"I was disappointed during the game by the decisions and I still am after watching the replays on television. With the red card the boy made a tackle on the ball with one foot — not two as I was told. I know the boy well and it was a normal tackle." - *One foot or two it was still high, dangerous and a textbook dismissal...*

"It wasn't a red card, then the first goal was offside and it was never a penalty for the second goal, either." – *First goal offside? Huh?*

"Normally I never have a reaction to the referee but believe me this year they are not in favour of my team. It is part of the game to make mistakes but in a big game like this for us it had something to do with my boys being unknown. You need the decisions to be the same for both sides and that's what I missed today." – *How hard would it have been just to acknowledge that your boys were beaten by the far better team?*

VIEW FROM THE PRESSBOX

"In the upstairs-downstairs world of modern football, the FA Cup third round provides a welcome opportunity for the hoi polloi to rise up and remind the aristocracy of their presence. Not here. At the first hint of anyone climbing out of the serving hatch, Manchester United slammed the door shut.

"Any glimmer of an insurrection was brusquely ended in particular by Dimitar Berbatov, a magnificent centre forward who embodied the gulf between the champions of the world and the fallen Saints. At £30 million, Berbatov is valued even higher than Southampton's substantial debts." – *The Telegraph*

MATCH FACTS

SOUTHAMPTON: DAVIS, JAMES, PERRY, LANCASHIRE, SKACEL, SMITH (HOLMES 69), MCGOLDRICK, GILLETT (SCHNEIDERLIN 56), SURMAN, GOBERN (MCLAGGON 56), PATERSON [POORTVLIET]
SENT OFF: PATERSON (37)
BOOKED: SKACEL, JAMES.
UNITED: VAN DER SAR, NEVILLE, EVANS, VIDIC, O'SHEA, NANI, ANDERSON, CARRICK (GIBSON 56), GIGGS (POSSEBON 56), WELBECK (ROONEY 63), BERBATOV.
BOOKED: EVANS, O'SHEA.
ST MARYS ATT: 31,901 REF: MIKE RILEY (YORKSHIRE). H-T: 1-0

OTHER SCORES

FA CUP 3RD ROUND: RICHEST CLUB IN THE WORLD 0 NOTTINGHAM FOREST 3

★The kids plan didn't work. At the end of the season Southampton were relegated into the 3rd tier of English football for the first time in 50 years. Poortvielt wasn't around to see it. He was put out of his misery just 19 days after United's visit.

"I wish to become a world-class footballer wearing the United shirt."

"THEY COME FROM SERBIA..."

SAY WHAT YOU like about the Glazers – and most of it won't be good. But you can't deny that United's moves in the transfer market are now so much smoother and effective than they were in the plc days. So while the papers talk up rival interest from Madrid, United fly Serbian kids Zoran Tosic and Adem Ljajic over to Manchester and get them signed up. Tosic, the latest new Ryan Giggs, joins straightaway while Ljajic, dubbed the new Kaka, will arrive next January. Total cost? Unknown. But they reckon there won't be much change from £15 million.

SWEET DREAMS

"It all happened so fast. I am only 17 and have a lot of football dreams, but one has already come true – and that's to play for a club the calibre of Manchester United." – *The new Kaka.*

"I dreamed of playing for a club like Manchester United. Now the dream has come true and I'm very happy for it. I wish to become a world-class footballer wearing the United shirt and not miss my chance to be remembered for my contribution to the biggest football family" – *The new Giggs.*

OTHER NEWS

The media get strangely overexcited by the news that Nigel Clough is the new manager of United's cup semi opponents Derby. I know his dad was a legend but all Clough junior's done is tread water with Burton Albion for a decade. United kid midfielder Sam Hewson joins Hereford on loan. United are linked with 19 year-old Grenoble playmaker Sofiane Feghouli. And all the speculation about his future finally gets to Tévez when Fergie is quoted – falsely as it turns out – as saying that the Tévez camp is asking for too much cash, a whopping £125,000 a week. Ranting on the Radio Del Plata radio station Tévez denies that he's ever been offered a new deal, reiterates his love for us fans and the Argentina chants, queries why United have been dragging their feet and says he'll be speaking to any club who can offer him the full-time deal he's after. Well, I guess it had to happen some time…

RANT OF THE WEEK

"I haven't asked for what Ronaldo gets or what Rooney gets. I have never discussed this ever with either the manager, Alex Ferguson, or anyone on the United board. I have never said anything about what I should be paid because we have never had any talks. The club has always said they would offer me a deal but they haven't. How can I reject an offer I've never had? It's being suggested I'm creating a bad atmosphere but it's just not true." – *Carlitos spits his dummy out of his pants. In fairness, you could see why he did it. He's thrown his heart and soul into the club, he played a huge part in us regaining the European Cup and he's been rewarded with a year in limbo – at the same time as United have splashed the money they could have spent on him on Berbatov. But – and apologies for repeating myself - the cold hard fact remains that not even his biggest fan thinks he's worth £35 million.*

KLUTZ OF THE WEEK

From the Guardian:

"We were told thieves had taken a number of things, the most important one being the chequebook. Given what soccer stars earn, that was obviously a matter of great concern. Then we got a call back saying nothing was missing after all" - *A spokesman for Northumbria police reveals that Newcastle striker Shola Ameobi's hadn't been ransacked by burglars as was first feared... it was just very untidy.*

RETROSPECTIVE QUOTE OF THE WEEK

"There's no doubt that in the second half of the season they [Liverpool] will get nervous. With the experience we've got at our club, having won a couple of titles in the past couple of years especially, it helps you." – *Fergie tries some minor mind games. But not even he could have forecast the scale of reaction they'd provoke...*

"The players love me. They don't come in and say 'I love you' but I feel my relationship with my players. Your wife does not come in every day and say 'I love you, I love you' but you know she does. I know my players love me, because we've had situations where it is possible to know this" – *Under-pressure Phil Scolari.*

07/01/2009
CARLING CUP SEMI-FINAL (1ST LEG)
DERBY 1 UNITED 0
Commons 30

I KNOW UNITED were desperate to find a way to shift tickets for the semi-final second leg. I had no idea they were this desperate. Everyone expected a strong United team – Welbeck was the only kid on show, while both Ronaldo and Rooney were on long before the end – to cruise through against Derby's championship strugglers and make the second leg at Old Trafford the most pointless game of this, or any other season. Instead they were lucky not to lose by 2, 3 or 4. Oh well, at least the men in suits ended the night happy...

THE MOMENTS THAT MATTERED

0-1 (30): United were appalling all game, with many of the senior players playing like they thought the Fizzy Lager Cup was beneath them. But make no mistake about it, Derby were good and in diminutive winger Kris Commons they had the best player on the pitch by a distance. His winning goal was worthy of winning a much more prestigious affair than this, the Scottish international wandering into a massive gap in midfield and almost taking the leather of the ball with his left foot from 25 yards.

MISS! (80): Is this the moment Derby threw away their Wembley chance? Kuszczak parries Commons's shot into the path of Rob Hulse. It looks easier to score than miss but that's exactly what he does. And United, despite losing the game, remain odds-on favourites to get the job done at home.

PRIDE PARK – THE VERBALS

"The one positive is that we lost only 1–0. It's actually a fantastic result for us because we could have lost by four goals. I think we're lucky it's only 1-0. You need a bit of luck in the cup and we've had a bit of luck tonight. We just didn't play well at all." – *Who'd have thought Fergie would end the night saying that?*

"We didn't have a great game, we can be better in many positions. I give Derby credit. They played exactly the way they said they would in the press - they didn't lie! It was a hard game for us and I think Derby are going to play the same way and fight for every ball at Old Trafford." – *Captain for the night, Vidic.*

VIEWS FROM THE PRESSBOX

'For the English, European and world champions to manage only two shots on target against the team that was relegated from the Premier League last season with a record low points total was certainly bizarre. Ferguson was visibly aggrieved, pointedly complaining that his senior players had let down the younger ones, and saying the only consolation was that the damage was limited to Kris Commons's goal on the half-hour.' – *The Guardian*

'This was a joyous night for Derby, who have had precious little to shout about in the past 18 months, and with their new manager looking on from the directors' box, their only slight regret was that their place in the final was not already secured. Even after Ferguson sent on Cristiano Ronaldo and Wayne Rooney in the second half last night, Derby had enough chances to settle the issue, with Rob Hulse squandering the easiest of them from six yards with ten minutes remaining.' – *The Times*

JOURNO OF THE DAY

From football365: We're not sure what Kevin Garside of The Daily Telegraph *has been smoking, but we'd like a toke please. From his piece on Cristiano Ronaldo today:*

'At Pride Park on Wednesday night football rebooted through romance. We looked on via misty eyes as one of the great narratives of the English game turned a page. We mused about old Big 'ead looking down as Nigel Clough assumed the family mantle at Derby County.

'Victory against Manchester United was pre-ordained, delivered by a goal mistakenly awarded to Kris Commons. It was in fact the spirit of John Robertson concealed in the No 7 shirt that cut in from the right to set the net ablaze. 'Well done, young man,' echoed around the ground.' *Come again?*

HEADLINE OF THE DAY

'United Undone By The Nous Of Commons' - *The Metro. That's not bad at all.*

WORST HEADLINE OF THE DAY

'Cloughie Son 1, Ferguson 0' - *The Daily Mirror. Oh dear. Clough, who had only just arrived from Burton Albion, wasn't even acting manager that night. It was the head of Derby's academy, David Lowe.*

MATCH FACTS

DERBY: CARROLL, CONNOLLY, TODD (SAVAGE 87), NYATANGA, CAMARA, STERJOVSKI (TEALE 58), GREEN, ADDISON, COMMONS, HULSE, DAVIES (BARAZITE 81) [LOWE]
BOOKED: TEALE, CONNOLLY.
MAN UTD: KUSZCZAK, RAFAEL DA SILVA, VIDIC, EVANS, O'SHEA, ANDERSON (CARRICK 74), SCHOLES (RONALDO 63), GIBSON, NANI, TÉVEZ, WELBECK (ROONEY 63)
BOOKED: RAFAEL DA SILVA
PRIDE PARK ATT: 30,194 REF: PHIL DOWD HALF-TIME: 0-1

"I am not playing mind games, just facts."

NEWS

A STRANGE WEEK for Ronaldo. First he becomes the first English-based player to be named FIFA's World Player of the Year. Then he makes a right mess of his Ferrari in a tunnel near Manchester airport. Cue a crop of bad jokes comparing his car with this season's free-kicks (they both hit the wall). While City make bids for every famous name – from Kaka to Pele - with a pulse, United go leftfield by snapping up 20 year-old Belgian defender Ritchie de Laet on loan from Stoke. As his only appearances in English football came during a loan spell at Wrexham there's understandably no rush for 'Laet 44' shirts at the megastore. Mind you, Ben Foster's career took the same detour and it didn't do him any harm. And Fergie's gentle prods and moans about United's fixture schedule and Liverpool's ability to stand the title pace finally prove too much for Rafa Benitez. His tirade isn't in the Keegan class. But it doesn't half run it close…

RAFA'S RANT: THE FICTION FACTS

Here are best bits from Benitez's infamous press conference, where he read from a specially prepared 'Fergie dossier':

"I was surprised by what has been said, but maybe they (United) are nervous because we are at the top of the table. But I want to talk about facts. I want to be clear, I do not want to play mind games too early, although they seem to want to start.

'Allo 'allo, that sounds like fighting talk…

"But I have seen some facts. On November 1, they played Hull and Mr Ferguson had a two-match touchline ban and a £10,000 fine after confronting Mike Dean, the referee, for improper conduct.

Yes, so.

"We started the Respect campaign, and that was when (Javier) Mascherano was sent off (last season) at Old Trafford.

The same Mascherano who abused the ref constantly just days after Ashley Cole's infamous show of dissent against Mike Riley, right?

"The referee (Steve Bennett) was the referee when they played against Wigan - he could not see the handball against Wigan by Rio Ferdinand, he did not give a penalty. They won the game and they won the title in this game.

Hold on I thought we were talking about respect here. Steve Bennett favours us does he? Have you ever seen him referee Ronaldo?

"I think it will be the same referee who will be in charge of their game in hand this season (against Wigan).

You can't deny he's done his research here. What's the point though?

"During the Respect campaign – and this is a fact – Mr Ferguson was charged by the FA for improper conduct after comments made about Martin Atkinson and Keith Hackett. He was not punished. He is the only manager in the league that cannot be punished for these things.

Hmmm. Redknapp, Keane and Kinnear have all recently got off scot free after slagging off refs while Fergie copped a two game ban and a £10,000 fine for abusing Mike Dean. So Fergie has actually been punished more severely than everyone else.

"Then he was talking about the fixtures. Two years ago we were playing a lot of early kick-offs away on Saturdays when United were playing on Sundays. And we didn't say anything.

Yes, you did. You bleated like crazy, whining, in September '07, "We will be talking to the Premier League about this because it is not fair."

"Now he is complaining about everything, that everybody is against United. But the second half of the season will see them playing at home against all the teams at the top of the table, it is a fantastic advantage.

Not necessarily old boy. It's just as big a disadvantage to have all your hardest away games up first, especially if, like United, you're always playing catch up.

"But at Christmas, United played on the 29th and the rest of the teams played on the 28th. We were away against Newcastle two days after playing Bolton. They were playing about 40 hours later, they were not complaining then.

We had just flown in from Japan. And our opponents, Boro, had also had the benefit of an extra day's rest (and if we're being pedantic about the facts it was actually 31 hours).

"And about his behaviour with referees. The Southampton manager he knows how Mr Ferguson works and how he works, he was very clear. I am not playing mind games, just facts.

He's siding with Jan Poortvliet now. That bloke was one rant away from being sectioned.

"If he wants to talk about fixtures, and have a level playing field as you say in England. There are two options if we don't want more problems with fixtures.

"One is the same as in Spain, the draw for the first part of the league is known, everyone knows which weekend. In the second half everyone plays the opposite, so you all know.

Sure, but does that stop United playing all the big teams at home in the second half of the season?

"Sky and Setanta have the right to choose their games and it will be the same for everyone. So Mr Ferguson will not be complaining about fixtures and a campaign against United.

Yeah, but don't the TV companies want to show United more than anyone else?

"Or there is another option. That Mr Ferguson organises the fixtures in his office and sends it to us and everyone will know and cannot complain. That is simple.

Are you sure no one will complain? Oh I see, you're being funny...

"We know what happens every time we go to Old Trafford and the United staff. They are always going man to man with the referees, especially at half-time when they walk close to the referees and they are talking and talking.

Only at Old Trafford? Really?

"All managers need to know is that only Mr Ferguson can talk about the fixtures, can talk about referees and nothing happens. We need to know that I am taking about facts, not my impression. There are things that everyone can see every single week. Are they under pressure? Maybe they were not thinking that we would be at the top of the table in January. But we are at the top of the table and they are nervous.

"I am not telling the authorities what to do. But I have been here for five years and know how things are going on. I will be watching United's game with Chelsea. The result does not matter to us, if we win at Stoke that result does not matter.

And that would be a bigger 'if' than you originally thought...

"I was surprised United wanted to start the mind games too early, maybe it is because we are top of the table. But I only wanted to explain our position. It is a massive difference to play early on a Saturday, say, after a European match in midweek. But they will play the second half of the season with home matches against the other top teams, and that is a massive advantage to them."

Swings and roundabouts man, swings and roundabouts...

"They cannot complain about the fixtures after they were playing on December 29 while the rest played on the 28th.

Boro didn't.

"I have decided that I had a lot of information and I have been watching every single week what has been going on. Then they started talking about us, but every single week we know they will be talking. But we want to stay at the top and maybe they will talk about us right to the end.

"To hear someone talking when he has problems with referees every single week, and now complaining about the fixtures and complaining about everything, I think that is not fair. You can see every single week how they put (referees) under pressure, we know this. We have seen it before. We have seen players sent off at Old Trafford and we do not see our opponents sent off.

Hmmm again. Number of opposition players sent off at Old Trafford this season: 0. Number of opposition players sent off at Anfield: 5 (including Vidic of, er, United).

*FACT OF THE WEEK

0-0 – the score between Liverpool and Stoke the following day. *Still think the rant was a good idea Rafa?*

QUOTE OF THE WEEK

What Rafa said at the end of his rant, which lasted just under five minutes and more than 1,000 words:

"I would rather not talk too much about this, though, when we have an important game ahead." *Pinocchio may have left Anfield. But his spirit still lives on.*

FAPL 11/01/2009

UNITED 3 CHELSEA 0

Vidic 45, Rooney 62, Berbatov 85

*"Viva John Terry. Viva John Terry. Could have won the Cup
but he f***ed it up. Viva John Terry"*

SEVEN MONTHS ON from Moscow, Reds finally get the chance to salute the man who did more than anything else to ensure we brought the European Cup home. And boy did we love every single Terry-taunting minute of it...

TERRY-TAUNTING – A MINUTE-BY-MINUTE GUIDE

TEAM NEWS: Ooh that's a curveball from Fergie. Carrick is on the bench and Giggsy is playing in centre midfield alongside Fletcher. Will he be able to cope with the physical strength of Mikel, Lampard and Ballack? Elsewhere the teams line up as expected. Evra is back from his lawnmower ban, Evans replaces the injured Ferdinand, and Tévez, fresh from his unscheduled appearance on Radio Del Plata, is on the bench. So is another Moscow penalty hero – Nicolas Anelka.

0.16: If you're a cricket fan, you'll remember the first ball Steve Harmison sent down in the last Ashes series in Australia which almost took the fourth slip's face off. It set the tone for the whole series, a series which ended with England being mercilessly thumped. Was this the footballing version? As Viva John Terry echoes around Old Trafford, Chelsea kick off, immediately play the ball back to Carvalho who plays a couple of one-twos with Terry and Ballack before Ballack rolls the ball back to Cech who immediately slices it out of play. "I think that's an awful start. I hate to see it in teams when you get the kick-off and you end up on your own goalline," rants Andy Gray to Mart'n, who responds by muttering something about the weather being mild (in fairness Tyler's not as young (63) as he used to be – in fact he's only a couple of months younger than Motty and he's been past it for years).

7: That's better. Mart'n unveils the stat that Chelsea didn't lose an away league game in 2008, and are now unbeaten in their last 20 aways overall. He then points out that United have history when it comes to ending long records from London teams – cutting off Arsenal's unbeaten run at 49 games in 2004 and Chelsea's at 40 games in 2005. By the way did you know that Motty was born in Salford? Me neither.

10: Old Trafford's rocking, erupting into deafening cheers whenever Terry gets on the ball and equally loud boos whenever a Chelsea player doesn't pass the ball back to him.

11: Now OT echoes to the Russian version of Que Sera Sera...in Moscow we made it three. Imagine how different the atmosphere here would have been had Terry not slipped. Feel free to shudder at the thought. It's like that Bayern guy who miskicked the ball to Giggsy in '99 when the score was still 1-0. He can't have slept since.

15: Chelsea fans respond by chanting 'You should have died in the tunnel' at Ronaldo. Charming folk. Hope you enjoyed your night in those Moscow airports you slinked back to early on 22 May.

22: There's been plenty of midfield sparring but not much penalty box action so far. Hold on though...

PENALTY! NO! 22: Chelsea get lucky – very lucky - as Ashley Cole jumps up to block Ronaldo's centre and knocks it to safety with his left arm. The linesman – who's set for an interesting afternoon – gives the handball but conveniently decides it all happened a fraction outside the area. Replays show that Cole was actually on the line when he blocked the ball, which means Ronaldo should now be lining up his penalty kick. Instead Giggs curls in a free-kick that Cech punches clear comfortably.

PENALTY! NO! 27: At least you could understand why the linesman didn't give the last penalty. After all it was an extremely close call he got wrong. But even Rafa Benitez would have been hard pushed to turn down this one. Bosingwa gets himself a yellow for a lunge on Rooney out left, Giggs swings in the centre and Carvalho first wraps his arms around Ronaldo and then trips him up. So what does Howard Webb do? He awards Chelsea a free-kick and then, when Ronaldo and Carvalho square up, he books them both. Top work from Webb. Or 'top, top work' as Jamie Redknapp would say.

28: *Viva John Terry, Viva John Terry. Could have won the Cup but he f***ed it up, Viva John Terry.* Something tells me it'll take us a long time to get bored of this one.

CHANCE! BERBATOV! (30): So far the game's been open enough... until the ball gets near either area, when it tightens up dramatically. Finally United find a way of piercing the Chelsea defence. Van der Sar punts a ball onto Evra's chest, he bursts from halfway, Rooney flicks his pass to Berbatov who dumps his man on his backside with a lovely dummy but then scuffs his left-foot shot into the ground and into Cech's chest.

32: Vidic breathes on Ballack in the United box, Ballack collapses and is lucky not to be booked. For me, he's been one of the biggest disappointments in the history of the Premier League. He came as a shoe-in for the world's best XI. And he's done next to nothing apart from niggle, nark, collapse and get in referee's faces. I wonder how much he regrets not coming to us when he had the chance.

CHANCE! PARK! (42): The move of the match so far. High-speed interplay between Giggs, Berbatov, Park and Ronaldo sends Park in on Cech on the left side of the box. Terry spreads himself superbly to block Park's low left-footed shot.

PENALTY! NO! 44: This is getting ridiculous now. Mikel gifts Park possession on the left side of box, he tees up Ronaldo who miskicks the ball against Rooney's back. The ball ricochets back to Fletcher whose first time half-volley is blocked by Terry's spread-eagled starfish impression. United players go mad, Red Nev even arriving in the area to have a go at Webb. Webb just makes a shushing motion with his finger and awards a corner. And that's where things get really interesting....

GOAL! NO! 45: Hands up who's ever seen anything like this. Giggs saunters over to take the kick, then seems to take leave of his senses by dribbling the ball towards the penalty area and chipping in a centre that Ronaldo, on one of his trademark bursts into the box, heads past Cech. Non-plussed Chelsea players appeal, the linesman flags and Webb orders the corner to be retaken. Surely the right decision? Not once you've seen the replay. While most fans were still debating Terry's starfish – stop sniggering at the back – Rooney had placed the ball in the corner box, rolled it a couple of feet with his studs and made himself scarce. Which meant that when Giggs reached the ball, it was already in play. The goal should have stood. Take into account the three penalties we had turned down and we should be 4 up. Someone phone the injustice police, we're being robbed here. Actually wait a minute...

GOAL! VIDIC! 46: Unbelievable. One minute United are denied a blatant penalty. The next they're denied a perfectly good goal. And finally they score a goal that not even Webb & co can rule out. Giggs swings in the retaken corner, Berbatov gets a nice flick-on at the near post and Vidic heads the ball down and into the net via Cech's desperate goal-line lunge. "That one's going to count," Mart'n shouts before adding "First blood is red blood for Manchester United". Which sounds a good line... until you think it through and realise it doesn't make sense. By the way you'll never guess who should have been marking Vidic★....

★(clue – he's not scared of crying in public)

HALF-TIME: As the teams walk off the Sky cameras focus on the match officials. And guess what. Rafa's right. They are being man-marked by people from United. Oh hang on, they're security guards in United anoraks. That's not what's got the old boy in such a tizz is it?

Even Richard Keys, who's made a career out of saying absolutely nothing controversial, can't resist a dig at Benitez saying, "There is some man marking but no sign of anyone from Manchester United as the three officials come off. Fact." Which must have gone down like a sh★t sandwich amongst the Sky studio panel which, strangely for a United-Chelsea game, consists of Jamie Carragher, Gary McAllister and Jamie Redknapp – three Liverpool men, one of whom used to play for Leeds. I'm surprised they didn't go the whole hog and squeeze in Tommy Smith, Alf Inge Haaland and half of Bolton.

In fairness the Liverpool camp don't show any anti-United bias, all of them agreeing that Ronaldo's goal should have stood, though it was hard to tell exactly what Carragher was saying amid the phlegm, particularly when he was discussing Chelsea's man-markkkkkkkkkkkkkkking.

45: Scolari responds to United's goal – and Chelsea's chanceless first half – by replacing Deco with Anelka which means that all three players who missed penalties in the Luzhniki – Ronaldo, Terry and Anelka – are now on the pitch. Curiously Giggs is the only United player in action today who scored in the shootout.

47: According to Sky pitchside man Jeff Shreeves, the linesman flagged for the Ronaldo goal because Rooney hadn't told him he was taking the corner. But do you have to get permission to take a corner quickly? I always thought it was only direct free-kicks round the box.

47: As a boyhood United fan growing up in Barking, Terry must have dreamt of playing at Old Trafford and hearing the fans cheer his every move. But not like this. A shanked clearance from the sobbing hardman brings the second biggest cheer of the afternoon so far.

47: *Viva John Terry, Viva John Terry. Could have won the Cup but he f***ed it up, Viva John Terry.* It's still going.

49: Ashley Cole hits a hopeful long-ranger straight at Van der Sar. It was never going in. I only mention it because it's the first time the United keeper has been forced into any kind of action.

55: After all his brave words in his autobiography, its noticeable how much time Drogba has spent in the vicinity of Evans rather than Vidic. Finally the pair engage, Drogba laying off the ball under pressure from Vidic and then thumping his shot so wide it threatens the pressbox. He must have wished he'd hit that one harder/straighter. As the ball gets fished out of A stand, the camera pans to the Chelsea bench where Scolari looks like he's passing another kidney stone and Ray Wilkins, his glasses perched onto the end of his nose, looks like an elderly uncle in a Dickens drama. Well he does from the neck up. I'm not sure anyone from the 1800s ever sported a blue anorak.

57: Sky show a replay of the short corner incident. As Giggs and Rooney rush to remonstrate with the linesman you can hear Giggsy scream 'he took it, he took it'. Fortunately you can't hear what Rooney says. It might have made JFK blush.

59: As Ronaldo is bundled over by the one-paced Mikel (was he really billed as the new Gerrard?), the camera pans to Tévez who's getting a great reception whilst warming up. I must admit I'm a Tévez fan myself. Even so it's amazing how popular he is when in many ways he's no more than an exotic Alan Smith. Tévez responds by clapping the crowd and slapping the United badge on his trackie top. Which all but ended his chances of getting a runout today. Especially when this happens...

EVRA! ROONEY! GOAL! 62: So far the second half had played out just like the start of the first with all the best play squeezed into the middle third. But then United strike with a basic but beautiful goal. Ronaldo showboats the ball out to the overlapping Evra who whips in a cross first time. Berbatov gets the faintest touch on the ball, Terry seems to duck out of the way and Rooney takes advantage of the dozing Cole to sidefoot the ball in emphatically. "What a ball in," Andy raves. "What an absolute dream of a ball in."

63: "Are you watching Merseyside?" Old Trafford enquires. We know at least three Merseysiders are – up in their suits in the studio box. (What do you call a Scouser in a suit? A pundit). They must be choking on their complimentary refreshments watching this.

65: Rooney's goal comes at a price as Evra turned his ankle in the process of delivering that dream ball. As he hobbles off and Sheasy comes on, Sky shows a super slow-mo picture of Van der Sar celebrating. With his head titled back and thick hair flapping behind him he looks like a short-sighted lion.

73: Joe Cole cuts in from the right and scuffs his low shot straight into Drogba. Amazingly that'll count as one of Chelsea's best three efforts today. Actually it might be the second best. All I can remember is Cole's no-hoper drive at Van der Sar, an eyes-closed mishit from Lampard early on, Ballack's dive and Drogba's wild slice.

74: Viva John Terry picks up again. It's got to be the best bootleg version of Viva Ronaldo yet though Viva da Silva wasn't bad either.

75: United are having so much time on the ball in midfield it's ridiculous. Fergie was right with what he said in the summer. Ageing Chelsea really can't improve. And some of them are slowing down in front of our eyes here.

75: Need a reminder of the Viva da Silva lyrics? It goes "Running down the pitch, don't know which is which, Viva Da Silva". Then there's the *other* Viva Ronaldo bootleg: "Helps out in the Caff, Has seen Blanche in the bath, Viva Ken Barlow. Keeps shopping bags for litter, Enjoys half a bitter, Viva Ken Barlow." Nice.

STANDING OVATION 79: Carrick comes on for Giggs who's been sensational today, first standing up to Chelsea when they packed the midfield in the first half and then hogging the ball, shrugging off challenges and bursting through gaps as Chelsea thinned their ranks in the second half. As I said, Ballack's been a massive disappointment in England. But I've never seen him get as bad a chasing as this.

80: Terry miscontrols, much to the delight of the crowd, and then finally snaps, piling into Park and getting a yellow. Frustratingly, if Webb hadn't blown straight away, Rooney would have been through one-on-one against the last defender, Carvalho.

PENALTY! NO! HOW MANY TIMES? 81: Once again Ashley Cole gets away with a handball, throwing his arms in the air to block Ronaldo's free-kick. It might not be intentional but your hands shouldn't be there. It should be a penalty.

82: Mourinho is spotted in the crowd. I wonder what he thinks watching 'his' Chelsea play like this (9 of the 11 starters were

Mourinho players). Does he take pleasure from the struggles of the club who made the – let's face it - quite ludicrous decision to sack him? Or does he sit there grimacing like a top architect who's just watched his finest building get pebble-dashed?

GOAL! RONALDO! NO! (82): The amazing thing about this game is that United are sat here with a hugely comfortable lead. And they've had four penalties, one perfectly good Ronaldo goal and now another one ruled out. Rooney flicks the ball round the corner to Berbatov, he slips Ronaldo in behind Belletti and, while the linesman is still raising his flag, the Portugeezer beats Cech. Replays showed that Ronaldo was level.

83: Chelsea aren't just non-existent in midfield and attack. They're really falling apart at the back now. Ashley Cole plays Carvalho into trouble with a terrible ball across his area, Carvalho's control lets him down and Ronaldo blasts the loose ball just wide from 25 yards.

FOUL! FREE-KICK! GOAL! (85): And finally United break through again. Belletti fails with his first kick at Ronaldo but nails him with his second, earning himself Chelsea's fifth yellow card in the process. Ronaldo smashes in a low free-kick from the left, Berbatov darts to the near post and sidefoots a la Rooney past the unprotected Cech.

90: Berbatov wastes a 3 v 2 opportunity, sliding the ball to Carvalho instead of Ronaldo or Rooney but it doesn't matter. Scolari's first visit to Old Trafford ends with a flattering 3-0 defeat. And judging from what he had to say afterwards he already knew there wouldn't be a second...

CHELSKI – THE VERBALS

"If I lose my job, I will have another job. Maybe tomorrow, maybe after one year or two. I've worked for 25 years...I like Chelsea. I like Cobham, where I live, like the school my son is at, I like my job here and the people. It's not problem for me. I like every day in London. But if I go back to Brazil, I will like Brazil the same. When I was in Kuwait, I loved Kuwait. I had three fantastic years in Saudi Arabia. I love life and I work hard every day. If I lose or do not lose my job, I will be the same. I am the same" – *Big Phil could walk on water in the summer. Now he sounds like he's treading on thin ice.*

"I didn't see Chelsea. I saw people from Chelsea before the match, at half-time and after the match. But I didn't see Chelsea on the pitch. I only saw Manchester United" - *Mourinho damning verdict on his old side.*

"Ballack couldn't live with Giggs." – *Fergie on the man of the match...*

... *And on the goal that should have been but never was:* 'Celtic used it [the corner kick routine] in a European quarter-final in the year that they won it. Bobby Lennox and Jimmy Johnstone did it and I always hoped that I would be able to do it and pull it off at some stage of my career. I tried it when I was manager at Aberdeen but we never managed to score from it. And then we scored from it against Chelsea at last and it got chalked off!'

VIEWS FROM THE PRESSBOX

"Sir Alex Ferguson was red-faced with rage earlier this season when relatively innocuous remarks by him were, he says, misinterpreted as a snide suggestion that Chelsea's squad was too old to win the title this season The irony is that today Chelsea did play like a team that is past it.

"Finesse was not present for much of this afternoon and in its absence the fastest, most lively team triumphed. It is not an age thing – 35-year-old Ryan Giggs was as energetic and alert as anyone – it's a question of mentality and in that regard Chelsea looked jaded and stale. Michael Ballack and Deco were as lethargic as they have been for most of the season, and Joe Cole was doddery. This season they have revelled on the road by absorbing blunt pressure and springing sharply forward, but United's speed and dynamism – and certainly not their passing, which was often as erratic as Chelsea's – meant the visitors could not rely on that approach." – *The Guardian*

"This was a soul-destroying, possibly season-destroying afternoon for the Blues." – *The Telegraph*

"The stats made grim reading for Scolari, and not just the five cautions that will trigger a £25,000 fine at a time when the club are straining to cut costs. Shots on-target figures were 11-1 in the champions' favour, and there was a brief debate afterwards over actually what Chelsea's effort had been. Another fact deserved recording: this was surely the first time a Liverpool manager had done United's team-talk. Rafa Benitez's speech criticising Sir Alex Ferguson looks even less smart in the wake of Liverpool's drab display at Stoke City and then this comprehensive victory for a fired-up United." – *The Telegraph again. They're right about the team-talk too. Fergie must have been rubbing his hands when he heard what Benitez had to say.*

"'Whoever negotiated Ballack's £121,000-a-week contract

deserves businessman of the year; again, the German failed to impose talent seen so often with his country,' reflected Ferguson. Michael Essien cannot return soon enough.

"Chelsea are in a bad place right now, with only three wins in their past 11 games in all competitions, but their frailties were exposed quite brutally by a team who warmed to the idea of humiliating Scolari's players as the game wore on. As Chelsea heads began to drop – and, strangely, this seemed to include John Terry, mocked by the home supporters throughout, as well as the more usual suspects, such as Didier Drogba – United twisted the knife. By the time that Howard Webb, the referee, blew the final whistle, some Chelsea players looked relieved that United had stopped at three goals." – *The Times.*

STRAINED ALLUSION OF THE WEEK

"And Ryan Giggs? Unbelievable. Man of the match from central midfield. The only Premier League player mentioned in "The Simpsons", Giggs seems to have been around since Wallis Simpson but he effortlessly defied Old Father Time as well as Michael Ballack, Frank Lampard and John Obi Mikel. Giggs, 35 going on 25, kept nicking the ball, kept weaving through the midfield." – *The Telegraph's on fire this week (thiugh not sure about the Simpsons/Wallis Simpson link).*

MATCH FACTS

UNITED: VAN DER SAR, NEVILLE, VIDIC, EVANS, EVRA (O'SHEA 66), RONALDO, FLETCHER, GIGGS (CARRICK 79), PARK, BERBATOV, ROONEY
BOOKED: RONALDO, ROONEY, PARK.
CHELSEA: CECH, BOSINGWA (BELLETTI 64), CARVALHO, TERRY, ASHLEY COLE, MIKEL, JOE COLE (DI SANTO 85), LAMPARD, BALLACK, DECO (ANELKA 46), DROGBA [SCOLARI]
BOOKED: LAMPARD, BOSINGWA, CARVALHO, TERRY, BELLETTI.
ATT: 75,455 REF: HOWARD WEBB H-T: 1-0

OTHER SCORES

STOKE 0 LIVERPOOL 0; ARSENAL 1 BOLTON 0.

LEAGUE TABLE

1. LIVERPOOL 46 (21); 2. CHELSEA 42 (20); 3. UNITED 41 (19)

"He is obviously disturbed about something. When he reflects on it he must realise what a ridiculous thing he is saying"

NEWS

IN ANY OTHER week the papers would have been busy dissecting the beating we handed out to Chelsea. They might even have gone to town on the news coming out of Spain that Ronaldo had registered CR9 as a trademark. Or the surprise role Diego Maradona played in the Chelsea win. But forget the gossip about Ronaldo & co, we've got ranting Rafa to enjoy. Like everyone else, the press had a field day. They laughed, they giggled, they wondered what possessed him. And then, just when it seemed the story had been milked to death, he went and did it all again...

RAFA'S RANT II

Magnificent stuff as Rafa rants, raves, rambles and all but accuses United of being football's answer to SPECTRE, with David Gill of all people cast as Blofeld (minus the white cat). Enjoy:

"They [Fergie/United/Donald Pleasance] were saying we are a threat. Now they know we are, they are playing mind games. But I don't think it's a mind game when you have control over everything; it's a mind game when you have the same level as the other people, then you can show you are cleverer than the others.

"But when you have control of everything and your chief executive is powerful in the FA and things like this, then that is not mind games. Is there a conflict of interest with David Gill at the FA? That is another fact. It is a fact that one person has a lot of power and control, and is on a lot of committees in the FA. To me that is very strange."

OK, let's step in here. Most Reds thought it was strange when Arsenal had a man – David Dein – on the FA board, and the FA had a Liverpool fan – Brian Barwick – as chief executive. But a] there's nothing new or suspicious about these sort of arrangements and b] if Gill has that much of an influence with the FA why did Paddy Evra spend Christmas on his holidays?

"Maybe in 20 years nobody has said these things. Maybe a lot of people are thinking the same but they didn't want to say it. I don't regret saying it and I don't think it had any effect on the players. I've known him for five years now and people say that he was playing mind games but it's too early.

So you'd be fine with mind games later in the season, right?

"To talk too much about Liverpool isn't fair so he has to think about his own team, the problems they have and all the things they've been doing for the last 15 or 20 years, maybe they will think the same as me.

Getting a bit lost here. Why is it unfair to talk about Liverpool again? Does this bit make any sense?

"He started talking when we won at Chelsea and we'd done a favour to United because we are not contenders so maybe he's a little bit scared. I have a lot of respect for him because I think he's a great manager but he was talking too much about Liverpool so he has to stop.

Is this really what started this – Fergie saying he wanted Liverpool to beat Chelsea back in October? At the time Chelsea had been United's main contenders for years and felt they couldn't lose at home. Who else was he going to support?

"He started talking a long time ago. It won't have the same effect on me because if he talks too much and too quickly then I won't understand so I will be happy."

Ooh, saucer of milk for Mr B…

"Would I meet Mr Ferguson face to face? I don't have any problem. I have a lot of respect for him as a good manager. If he wants to talk about the weather we can talk about the weather."

Fergie hurriedly fills up his diary.

"I don't need to put pressure on Manchester United. They are under pressure, they know they are, because when you talk too much about another team that means you are under pressure. I need to change my mobile phone because it is blocked with messages.

… from people sniggering?

"Are they from managers? I can't talk to you about what they have said to me.

We'll give you an idea below.

"It was the right moment for me to say these things about Mr Ferguson. Mr Ferguson was talking too much about Liverpool and for too long a time so I think it was the right moment to say, 'enough is enough'".

Right moment? You were top of the league and under no pressure. Now people will be using 'Rafa's rant' as a stick to beat you with every time you have a bad result.

QUESTION OF THE WEEK
So who were these managers filling up Benitez's mobile?

STEVE BRUCE? "It is fantastic radio and television. I found it humorous like everyone else. There is always a little bit of banter going about and the mind games have started. How do you take him (Fergie) on? You don't. I think that is the motto." *Nah*

ARSENE WENGER? "It came as a complete surprise, because he is usually a quiet man and I would not like to comment further on that. I do not know what it was really about." *Nah*

JOSE MOURINHO? "I played at Old Trafford many times, including a few wins, and never saw anything strange [in terms of the referees being hounded by United staff]. It is only normal that a referee will feel under pressure in an atmosphere like that with 80,000 people." *Nah*

JAN POORTVLIET? *Maybe...*

P*SSTAKE OF THE WEEK
Nice work from The Telegraph the morning after the Chelsea game:

"So, Rafa, let's review the last few days shall we? Dealing, as you prefer to do, in facts (Bung unfolds A4 sheet of paper and clears throat....)

RAFA: 'United put pressure on referees at Old Trafford and all the decisions go their way.'

FACT: United have perfectly good goal disallowed when assistant referee chooses to make up rule about need to inform him about corner kick plans. (Supplementary question to that linesman - what the hell do you think Rooney would be doing over there if he WASN'T taking the corner? Blowing his nose on the flag?)

RAFA: 'United are nervous.'

FACT: United produce most emphatic display of the season in their biggest game of the season. United are now 8/11 to win the title, the shortest they have been all season.

RAFA: 'Attacking Mr Ferguson will not affect my team or put more pressure on my players.'

FACT: Liverpool fail to beat Stoke, the first time they have not won away against so-called inferior (non Big Four) opposition since November 1.

RAFA: 'We know what kind of player Robbie Keane is. He needs people around him to pass the ball well. I believe he will be OK'

FACT: Keane, who at £20.3 million cost more than Stoke's entire first team, was left on the bench despite the 0-0 scoreline as Benitez chose to make only two substitutions."

THE CIGAR OF GOD

The Sun reveals how United's efforts to beat Chelsea got help from an unexpected source:

'Chelsea's preparations for their match against Manchester United were disrupted in the early hours of Sunday morning by a fire alarm reportedly started by Argentina legend Diego Maradona's cigar. Luiz Felipe Scolari's side had to evacuate the Radisson Edwardian Hotel in Manchester after alarms sounded at seven o'clock, and players were spotted standing outside in freezing conditions, some wearing just towels and bathrobes.

"'It looks as though it was set off by Diego and his entourage smoking cigars on the 14th floor," a fireman told us.'"

QUOTE OF THE WEEK

"There was a lot of venom in what he [Benitez] has said. I don't understand where it has come from. He is obviously disturbed about something. When he reflects on it he must realise what a ridiculous thing he is saying" - *Fergie resists the urge to crack up laughing as he responds to Rafa's rants.*

RUNNER-UP

"I dedicate the victory over Chelsea to the English FA. I'm doing so because I am still unable to stomach having been given a four-match suspension by them. My break? I had a nice time with my family and a nice holiday." – *Welcome back Paddy E.*

FAPL 14/01/2009

UNITED 1 WIGAN 0

Rooney 1

UNITED-WIGAN FIXTURES are normally something to look forward to, mainly because the Pie Eaters let us score so many goals. This was different. Wigan were unrecognisable from the surrender monkeys Paul Jewell used to send out at Old Trafford. United were unrecognisable from the team that had just swarmed all over Chelsea. And the atmosphere inside Old Trafford was unrecognisable from the Terry-baiting bear-pit from the weekend. Just about the only really recognisable part of the night was the result, with United doing just enough to make it 12 points out of 12 since returning from Japan – and beat Wigan for the eighth time in a row.

GOAL!

1-0 (1): Overall the night was a real slog as Carrick and Scholes struggled to cope with the hounding of Cattermole and Palacios, and O'Shea got a roasting off the lightning quick Valencia. But the opening minute couldn't have gone any better. Berbatov curls a lovely ball to Ronaldo with the outside of his right foot, Ronaldo fizzes a low centre across the six-yard box and Rooney cannot miss.

WHAT WAS GOOD?

UNITED WERE 8 POINTS BEHIND LIVERPOOL - when they travelled to Tokyo 4 weeks ago. Now they'll go top if they beat Bolton at the weekend.

VIDIC. WHAT. A. DEFENDER.
WIGAN – their best performance at Old Trafford by a mile.
ANTONIO VALENCIA - We didn't know it at the time but the chasing he gave O'Shea here virtually sealed a summer move to United. Funnily enough, Ronaldo's transfer was also pushed through after he'd given O'Shea a seeing to (shouldn't prospective wingers have to pass a stricter test than that?).

WHAT WAS BAD?

ROONEY - pulled a hamstring just minutes after scoring and won't be back until February.

VIEWS FROM THE PRESSBOX

"Everyone has a take on what Rafael Benítez said about Sir Alex Ferguson and last night we had the Stretford End's opinion on the matter: "Rafa's cracking up," they sang gleefully. Not true, of course, but Manchester United's supporters could afford to gloat on a night when the only downside for the champions was the sight of Wayne Rooney going off with a hamstring injury that will keep him out for at least three weeks." – *The Guardian*

"Sir Alex Ferguson and his Manchester United side are cheerfully showing the pretenders to their crown just why they have already won ten Premier League titles and are likely to collect an eleventh come May. They are not yet playing with the swagger of champions, but the way United have risen up the Barclays Premier League in the past few weeks should fill their rivals with foreboding. United were eight points behind Liverpool when they travelled to Tokyo for the Club World Cup four weeks ago, yet they can overtake their North West rivals at the top if they beat Bolton Wanderers on Saturday.

"Little wonder that as Rafael Benítez and Luiz Felipe Scolari are laid low by kidney stones and Chelsea's great expectations respectively, Ferguson seems to be getting younger every day. This was a far from vintage United performance, but nevertheless, the sort of result on which championships are built." – *The Times*

"Tévez's commitment is appreciated by an Old Trafford crowd who again gave him a rapturous reception, but more influential figures at the club harbour doubts as to whether his honest endeavour adds up to much. The Argentina striker buzzed around as usual without offering much in the way of an end-product, other than to miss a great opportunity to double United's lead in the 25th minute when he was one-on-one with Chris Kirkland." – *The Times steps into the great Tévez debate. If he wasn't such an enthusiastic trier would he be anywhere near Old Trafford?*

WHAT'S THE LINK?

Aldershot, ASK Vorwaets, Barnet, Boavista, Brondby, Chester, Colchester, Crewe, Bordeaux, Debreceni, Dinamo Bucharest, Feyenoord, Gamba Osaka, Rangers, Halifax, Hartlepool, Hereford, Higher Walton, HJK Helsinki, Honved, Kettering, Kosice, Liga de Quito, Olympiakos, Oswaldtwistle Rovers, Palmeiras, Pecsi Munkas, Peterborough, Rochdale, Shamrock Rovers, South Melbourne, Southport Central, Spartak Varna, Staple Hill, Sturm Graz, Tranmere, Waterford, West Manchester, Weymouth Town, Workington, Wrexham, Yeovil, Wigan★

POINTLESS TRIVIA OF THE NIGHT

Did you know that Wigan, frustrated by their failure to be allowed into the English league, applied to join the Scottish second division in 1972?

MATCH FACTS

UNITED: VAN DER SAR, RAFAEL DA SILVA, VIDIC, EVANS, O'SHEA, RONALDO, SCHOLES (FLETCHER 85), CARRICK, NANI (ANDERSON 59), BERBATOV, ROONEY (TÉVEZ 8)
WIGAN: KIRKLAND, MELCHIOT, SCHARNER, BRAMBLE, FIGUEROA, VALENCIA, CATTERMOLE (KAPO 88), PALACIOS, TAYLOR (DE RIDDER 81), ZAKI (CAMARA 75), HESKEY [BRUCIE]
BOOKED: BRAMBLE, SCHARNER, ZAKI
ATT: 73,917 REF: STEVE BENNETT H-T: 1-0

United have beaten all these teams every time they have played them (out of those teams, Wigan are the ones we've beaten the most)

"Medals are more important to a player than money, without doubt."

NEWS

RAMON CALDERON RESIGNS as Real Madrid president amid allegations that his team manipulated the presidential elections. Who'd have thought it? United look set to swoop for another young Serbian, 16 year-old midfielder Filip Djuricic. Unused forward Manucho and kid midfielder Tom Cleverley are sent out on loan – to Hull and Leicester respectively. The Norwegians ask Ole if he fancies being the assistant to welly-wearing national coach Egil Olsen. Inter and Chelsea are the latest to be drawn into the 'oh my god will they never stop going on about this?' soap opera surrounding Carlos Tévez. The FA announce they'll take no action against the Chelsea fans who sang 'you should have died in the tunnel' to Ronaldo. Gary Neville becomes the last of the famous 'Class of 92' to become a dad – all the rest have had at least two kids. Reports suggest United are going to beat Liverpool to the signature of Fluminese centre-back Anderson. Milan confirm their heads have been turned by City's massive - and this time that's no joke - £107 million bid for Kaka. And, as every man and his dog has his say on the Kaka deal, Alan Shearer comes up with the funniest line of the year...

QUOTE OF THE WEEK/MONTH/YEAR/DECADE

"Medals are more important to a player than money, without doubt."

AHAHAHAHAHAHA. Stop it Alan, please, stop it.

PULLITZER PRIZE WINNING STORY OF THE WEEK
The Sun reveals that Rooney wants Mini-Me star Verne Troyer to win Celebrity Big Brother:

'An insider said: "Wayne loves Verne and has told the lads he will vote to keep him in the house if he has to. He cracks up at the photos of Verne at the training ground."'

RUNNER-UP
The Daily Mail breaks the news that Ronaldo looked annoyed when he got a parking ticket in Alderley Edge:

"The glum-faced footballer looked down in the dumps after finding the unpleasant surprise stuck to his windscreen."

QUOTES OF THE WEEK

"He is a proven goalscorer at certain levels," *says Phil Brown after snapping up Manucho. Proven at certain levels? Aren't we all?*

"The implications would be disturbance on the market, an inflationary trend in a deflationary world." – *Say what you like about Arsene Wenger – well, apart from that thing (it might get you arrested). But no other manager would answer a question about the Kaka fee like this.*

"I think it's absolutely brilliant for football - It's what sets our league apart from any other league in the world. You don't see Spanish La Liga managers doing things like that. It's fantastic viewing from the outside and it's going to be a fantastic end to the season I'm sure." – *Pip Neville's loving the Fergie-Rafa dust-up.*

DEAR DELUDED
David Gill responds to Benitez's sniping about his role with the FA:

"Benitez should understand how football structures work. I'm not the only person on the FA board representing the Premier League; we're elected every year by the Premier League clubs to represent them. He missed the boat completely."

BOLTON 0 UNITED 1
Berbatov 90+

BACK IN OCTOBER Bolton tried to lure fans into their game with Blackburn by offering them a free pre-match beer and cheap pies and £1.75 pints. It was a decent idea. But you'd need more than beer goggles to convince people to watch what counts for football at the Reebok these days, particularly when the big boys are in town. Gary Megson would argue that a team like Bolton can't be expected to come out and play against a side as strong as United. But is that really true? Can't professional footballers at least get stuck into us and give it a go, like Derby did? Anyway, everyone who despises the anti-football teams in the league will be pleased that Megson's zero-attacking philosophy didn't pay off. They might even take a perverse pleasure from the manner in which United won it. Bolton were just a couple of minutes away from the 0-0 they wanted when a defensive mix-up allowed Tévez to wriggle through on the right and stand up a cross that Berbatov headed unerringly past Jaaskelainen. Apparently the look on the face of Phil Thompson, commenting on Soccer Saturday, was absolutely priceless...

WHAT WAS GOOD?

TOP OF THE LEAGUE FOR THE FIRST TIME ALL SEASON. And we've got all our toughest away games out of the way.

WHAT WAS BAD?

BOLTON'S NO-MARK FANS - singing Munich songs on the same day that Ian Greaves, a Busby Babe and a great Bolton manager who died a few weeks ago, was remembered.

VIEWS FROM THE PRESSBOX

"He moves quietly through most matches, a drifter more than a hustler. The opponent who swaps shirts with him might not even have to wash the garment when he gets home. Like his approach to everything else he does on the pitch, Dimitar Berbatov measures each drop of perspiration before spending it. And of all the players in the game, he is the one you must judge by quality, not quantity.

"Yesterday's contribution was classical Berbatov. He had spent most of the game on the edge of the action but there were enough good touches and perceptive passes to remind us of his worth. And there were enough raised eyebrows and hand signals of irritation to remind his colleagues that he expected more of them. He is more general than foot soldier, and just as the game seemed certain to end scoreless, he turned up in the right place to deliver the 90th-minute winner." – *The Times*

"The last time we saw Sir Alex Ferguson dancing like this it was amid claps of thunder on a Sunday afternoon in Wigan after an elegant swish of Ryan Giggs's left boot had brought confirmation of a 10th Premier League title last May. You know the routine by now. A hop, a step, an uncoordinated little jump and clap of the hands, and suddenly the oldest manager in the business has gone all Gene Kelly on us.

"It needs something special to see this side of Ferguson, and it was not just the quality of Dimitar Berbatov's winning goal that made this feel like such a powerful moment, but the sense of timing, and what it said about the character of the reigning champions. It told us that this is a team that can hold its nerve when the pressure is rising dangerously close to intolerable. But then, we probably should have known that anyway. There are not many moments in football more dramatic than the last-minute winning goal and who could possibly dispute that United grip us in this way more than any other team on the planet?" – *The Guardian*

REEBOK – THE VERBALS

"Being top is not decisive at this stage but it is always nice because it is the best place to be." – *Fergie.*

"I was ready to take Carlos off and then he makes a goal. Danny Welbeck is a big lad and I just felt he might get us a goal from a cross. I am always prepared to gamble." – *At Stoke Fergie said he was planning to give Tévez the hook before he came up with the winner. And he was planning to do the same here. Seems like a flawed plan to me. As I said before, no other forward at the club has his Solskjaer-style knack of changing games at the death.*

"I was looking at the clock towards the end of the match and there was about a minute and 10 seconds left. But at this club you never think you're out of the match. You always know you'll get another chance. That's been the motto down the years: we'll always get a chance." – *Gary Nev.*

MATCH FACTS

BOLTON: JAASKELAINEN, STEINSSON, CAHILL, ANDREW O'BRIEN, SAMUEL, DAVIES, BASHAM, MUAMBA, GARDNER (PUYGRENIER 83), TAYLOR, MAKUKULA (OBADEYI 64) [MEGSON]
BOOKED: MAKUKULA
UNITED: VAN DER SAR, NEVILLE, VIDIC, EVANS, O'SHEA, FLETCHER (GIGGS 69), CARRICK, ANDERSON (SCHOLES 69), RONALDO, TÉVEZ, BERBATOV
BOOKED: O'SHEA.
ATT: 26,021 REEBOK STADIUM REF: ANDRE MARRINER (ENGLAND) H-T: 0-0

OTHER RESULTS

CHELSEA 2 STOKE 1, LIVERPOOL 1 EVERTON 1

LEAGUE TABLE

1. UNITED 47 (21); 2. LIVERPOOL 47 (22); 3. CHELSEA 45 (22)

"In my personal opinion, they bottled it,"

NEWS

WIGAN SPEEDSTER ANTONIO Valencia is heavily linked with a move to United. Under-pressure Benitez goes into hospital for another operation on his kidney stones. It's starting to sound like Sharpie's meningitis that. Fergie reveals how to tell the difference between the Da Silva boys. Fabio is married (at 18) and wears a ring. And to the relief of everyone who's ever admired him as a footballer and a man, Kaka does the honourable thing. And tells City he still belongs to Silvio (for now)...

THE NEW KENYON

It was always going to be interesting how City coped with their surprise status as the richest club in the world. Would they keep it cool and act with humility or career around Europe with their heads figuratively stuck out of the top of a limo like the nouveaux riche chavs they are? Garry Cook's high-pitched reaction, as he returned from Milan like Neville Chamberlain without his letter, might give you a clue:

"We had entered into a confidentiality agreement weeks ago but, in my personal opinion, they [Milan] bottled it." *Priceless.*

WORST HEADLINES OF THE WEEK

'Pawn Kaka' - *The Daily Mirror. What the hell does that mean?*
'Stabbed In The Kaka' - *The Sun. And that's just rubbish.*

QUOTE OF THE WEEK

"I haven't been a Manchester City player not even for one minute."
– Kaka.

RUNNER-UP

"We know that Arsene Wenger likes the look of Arshavin. But I like the look of Angelina Jolie and it doesn't always mean you get what you want" - *Dennis Lachter, agent of Arsenal target Andrei Arshavin.*

CARLING CUP SEMI-FINAL (2ND LEG) 20/01/2009

UNITED 4 DERBY 2

(United win 4-3 on aggregate)
Nani 16, O'Shea 22, Tévez 34, Barnes 80 (p) Ronaldo 89 pen, Barnes 90

IT'S WEIRD. Premier League teams can't buy a goal against us. Yet Derby can. Unfortunately for them they only started scoring, like Blackburn did in the last round, when the game was as good as over. Nani's screamer took us level, O'Shea's gift-wrapped side-foot put us ahead and Tévez's thumping header all but booked us a place at Wembley. Derby did well to stop the bleeding in the second half but the biggest talking point wasn't the late brace from Giles Barnes but Fergie's decision to bring on, and risk, Ronaldo (in the hope that a cheap goal here would get him scoring again). How different it could all have been though if Derby had got the goals they'd deserved a fortnight before...

MATCH ACTION

1-0 (16): When you see Nani do something like this it seems ridiculous he's only scored one league goal this season, and that was against West Brom. The wet-look winger runs onto the ball just inside the Derby half, drops a shoulder and thumps a 25 yarder into the top-right corner. Roy Carroll gets a decent glove on it so Derby fans might think he should have saved it. Reds who watched his regular Leighton impressions for 4 years are just impressed he got as near as he did.

2-0 (22): Welbeck's prod unlocks the worst offside trap of the season and O'Shea, who should have been yards offside, digs the ball out of his feet and passes the ball into the corner.

3-0 (34): All over. Rafael swings over from the right and Tévez's forehead does the rest.

3-1 (80): Or is it? Evans trips Green near the by-line, Barnes buries his penalty high into the top left corner.

4-1 (89): Carroll takes out Tévez and Ronaldo converts.

4-2 (90): Barnes curls in a tasty free-kick from 25 yards but there's no time for Derby to get the goal they need to force extra-time (what score would it have ended if they had?). United are back at Wembley for the Carling Cup final for 15 long years. Let's hope it goes better this time...

QUOTE OF THE NIGHT

'You're starting to score again, son. That's really good of you.'" – *Fergie to Ronaldo, who'd only scored once in his previous 13 games.*

DERBY – THE VERBALS...

"They will be playing in the final. I think that the important thing is to find out their temperament, and they've all proved that again. I think Wembley is a special place, our record in going to finals at Wembley is terrific. Just being there is always a great occasion, but you always want to win them because that's the only way you can enjoy it." – *Fergie vows to keep the kids in against Tottenham*

"I'm buzzing. I can't wait to go to Wembley." – *The mini-Carrick, Darron Gibson.*

"Fourteen wins out of 15 semi-finals is a great record. The club has done well in semi-finals down the years, and it is good to reach another final." – *Fergie.*

"The first goal knocked the stuffing out of us; 30 yards in the top corner ... you can't do much about those. Defending the second and third goals was disappointing. But it was a vast improvement on Saturday - even the first half. It would be very easy to give up the ghost, 3-0 down at Old Trafford, and we could have been on the end of five or six. I asked them to defend a bit better and have a go and I thought we did that." – *Nigel Clough*

VIEWS FROM THE BROADSHEETS

"There could be no better illustration of Manchester United's strength in depth than the sight of what was essentially a reserve team reaching the Carling Cup final, but the concern for Sir Alex Ferguson last night, as his dressing-room began to resemble a casualty ward, was that his vast squad will be tested to the limit if they are to continue their quest for success on all fronts over the coming weeks." – The Times on the bittersweet news that United's march to Wembley came at the cost of serious-looking injuries to Anderson, Rafael and Evans.

"Good news for Manchester United sometimes arrives before the last minute. Three first-half goals took the drama out of this contest, leaving Nigel Clough looking for his first win since stepping into the Derby dugout and the home side looking forward to a third Carling Cup final in eight years, while Dimitar Berbatov was among those enjoying a night off." – *The Guardian*

MATCH FACTS

UNITED: FOSTER, RAFAEL DA SILVA (FLETCHER 42), NEVILLE (CHESTER 67), EVANS, O'SHEA, NANI, GIBSON, ANDERSON, GIGGS (RONALDO 58), WELBECK, TÉVEZ
BOOKED: RAFAEL DA SILVA, FLETCHER
DERBY: CARROLL, CONNOLLY, ALBRECHTSEN, TODD (BARAZITE 62), STEWART, TEALE, ADDISON, GREEN, DAVIES (SAVAGE 46), COMMONS (BARNES 68), HULSE [CLOUGH]
BOOKED: ADDISON, GREEN, CARROLL
ATT: 73,374 REF: MIKE DEAN H-T: 3-0

> *"I still support United and always will.
> I will die with them in my heart."*

NEWS

UNITED ARE LINKED with 16 year-old Sochaux starlet Yven Moyo.

Harry Redknapp causes a fuss by threatening to pick a 'mish-mash' team for the weekend cup game at Old Trafford in order to save his best players for next week's game at Stoke. That's right, Stoke. Portsmouth magistrates ban four Spurs fans from attending football matches for three years after they plead guilty to shouting indecent chants at Sol Campbell. No arguments there but it's still weird to think that Big Brother isn't just watching you these days, he's lip-reading. With the Fed holding a gun to their heads, AIG wisely announce they won't be renewing their United deal when it runs out in 2010. Villa – and Martin O'Neill – blow their credibility by signing Emile Heskey. And City make up for the pain of losing out on Kaka by signing Craig Bellamy from West Ham and Nigel de Jong from Hamburg for a staggering £31 million. The £17 million fee for De Jong makes him the most expensive player ever to leave a Bundesliga club.

HAHAHAHAHAHAHA

"If we don't get Kaka it is not the end of the world. We got Craig Bellamy" - *Garry Cook.*

HAHAHAHAHAHA

Priceless stuff from Peter Kenyon:

"We're delighted not to be the richest any more and other clubs may spend more without having as much success on the pitch. This would dispel the idea that we have just bought our titles."

And why would the fact that Chelsea are now the third richest club in the land – behind City and QPR (and just how mad does that sound?) – dispel the idea that they bought their titles when they were still the richest club by far?

HAHAHAHAHA

"The perception that we are out there throwing money around is simply not true" – *Sure as night follows day, amusement follows when Garry Cook opens his mouth. Where do City find them?*

HAHAHAHA

"Robinho obviously lost his head when looking at all those figures and let money dictate. It was not a footballing choice. And now, at City, he has lost the happiness that football gave him. And, just as sad, is that he has lost the 'fantasy' in his football. He totally messed up. No one can choose to leave Real Madrid in order to go to a club like Manchester City! A top player aged only 24 can never leave Real Madrid like he did and for those reasons." – *Madrid technical director Arrigo Sacchi takes no prisoners.*

NOT BACKING DOWN

"I think what I said will help us for the rest of the season for different reasons. One is that it will take some of the pressure off the players. And I was really pleased to see the TV cameras following Mr Ferguson and the referees at Old Trafford last week! But the players are not distracted. They have been training really well." – *Benitez still reckons he was right to rant even though Liverpool have just dropped four crucial points against Stoke and Everton.*

EX-REFEREE OF THE WEEK

"I think the last CD I bought was Motörhead. Because my best friend is the drummer of this band" - *Former ref Anders Frisk wasn't all about the peroxide hair then.*

KEEPING IT REAL I

'Manchester City's prowess in the transfer market has taken another embarrassing knock after it emerged they could have signed Nigel de Jong for just £2.3 million at the end of the season. De Jong completed his move from Hamburg to Eastlands for £19m, signing a four-year deal' - *The Daily Telegraph. So much for the 'realistic market values' Hughesie was talking about at the start of the transfer window...*

KEEPING IT REAL II

July 10, 2007: West Ham pay £7.5million for Craig Bellamy.
January 19, 2009: After 24 appearances and seven goals in 18 months, Manchester City pay £14million for Craig Bellamy.

THE MAGIC OF THE CUP
football365 plays spot the difference:

"When I see it devalued like a couple of years ago when teams suddenly didn't want to get involved, like Manchester United did, it's very disappointing. As far as I'm concerned I've always had a go at the FA Cup wherever I have been. I've never been at a club where we weren't interested in winning the FA Cup. We start the season in two cup competitions where we have a chance of winning - the FA Cup and the Carling Cup - and we go for it. We're not going to win the Premier League at Portsmouth, so we need to have a go at the cup competitions" - *Harry Redknapp, April 13 2008.*

"The games against United really is so secondary to me now. If Alex is listening, I'm really going to send a real mish-mash team up there. I hope it doesn't upset the supporters, but we played extra-time [at Burnley] and we're out on our feet a little bit. The lads who didn't play will play at Old Trafford; I'm going to rest the key players who played against Burnley because I can't afford to lose any more to injuries. We're in a relegation battle and need to get a team together to play against Stoke on Tuesday." - *Harry Redknapp, January 21 2009.*

WELL-TIMED DIG OF THE WEEK
By Henry Winter in the Telegraph:

MEMO TO COOK 1: by suggesting to Kaka's representatives that City can make the former World Player of the Year an even better-known 'brand' around the globe ignores the reality that the Brazilian is already bigger in Latin America and the Far East than City themselves.

QUOTE OF THE WEEK

"I still support United and always will. I will die with them in my heart." – *Eric. Still the King.*

24/01/2009
FA CUP 4TH ROUND

UNITED 2 SPURS 1
Pavlyuchenko 5, Scholes 35, Berbatov 36

HOW MANY TIMES have you done it? Gone away on holiday and, while everyone else does their best to switch off and forget what's happening back home, you spend your whole time trying to find a way of watching United. For this game I spent the evening dragging a group of knackered skiers round the one-bar towns in the Dolomites, in north-east Italy. It was a tough task, particularly as Juventus were playing Fiorentina at the same time, but the locals couldn't resist our smattering of pigeon-Italian for ever and eventually the tactic of repeating 'Manchester televisione' over and over again paid off. Unfortunately by the time it did, half-time had long gone and this cup tie had a suspiciously polite feel about it. But this was what everyone – well, Teddy Sheringham on TV and my dad on the phone - reckoned happened first. Redknapp didn't send out the reserves he'd promised, Spurs surprised everyone (including themselves?) by taking the lead, Scholes burst their bubble with the equaliser, Carrick and Berbatov immediately concocted a brilliant second and then Spurs started thinking about their relegation clash with Stoke on Wednesday. Were they playing to lose respectably? Maybe. But let's face it, they weren't the first team to do that at Old Trafford this season. And they wouldn't be the last.

GOAL ACTION

0-1 (5): Almost a year to the day after Spurs took the lead at Old Trafford in the fourth round of the Cup they do it again. It's a decent goal too - from Spurs's point of view at least. Huddlestone dinks a cross over from the left, United defenders switch off and Pavlyuchenko glances a header into the bottom right corner with Foster rooted to his line.

1-1 (35): United respond by throwing everything they have at the Spurs goal, while Spurs respond by throwing everything they have in the way. Berbatov drills a shot narrowly wide, Tévez almost breaks the bar from 25 yards, the excellent Welbeck comes close to doing a Ricky Villa not once but twice and Alnwick saves brilliantly from Tévez and Ronaldo. Finally they break through with a goal nowhere near as impressive as the attempts that preceded it. A corner from the right is rolled to Scholes on the edge of the box and his low shot deflects past the unsighted Alnwick.

2-1 (36): But if the equaliser was, as Scholesy admitted, 'a lucky goal', the winner was a peach. Carrick picks out Berbatov's run through the inside-right channel with the first-touch pass of the season, Berbatov plucks the ball from the air and then thumps it across Alnwick from the edge of the area.

AL MURRAY MOMENT OF THE NIGHT

You know the pint of Guinness they have on the corner of pub TVs to show that the landlord's paid his bills and not wired up a link bounced from Namibia? Guess what they have on the TV in Italy? A cocktail glass. Unbelievable…

TOTTENHAM – THE VERBALS

"That's the nature of life now. It's a social disease, I think. We must be the only club left to actually welcome back our former players." – *Fergie after Berbatov gets booed by the travelling Spurs fans (at least it's better than him being booed by Reds).*

"How could you watch the game and say that? It's not easy coming here at the best of times. We've had loads of injuries and we lost the game because we had a bad two minutes in the first half. I don't think our keeper had a shot to save in the second half. I'm really disappointed to hear people like Teddy saying that. It is difficult to put them under pressure because you need the ball to do that. If we opened ourselves up, that's when we would get smashed up." – *Harry Redknapp adapts his default defensive position after Teddy Sheringham suggested that Spurs didn't seem to be trying.*

QUESTION OF THE DAY

Did Spurs try? Redknapp was offended by the suggestion. But he did leave himself wide open to the accusations of not trying with his pre-match whining about Spurs's workload and his threat to send out his weakest possible team.

VIEWS FROM THE PRESSBOX
The papers on the question of the day...

"The next time these clubs meet will be in the Carling Cup final and it would be nice to believe that Tottenham Hotspur will not hoist football's equivalent of the white flag as they did here. It was not the tamest surrender at Old Trafford this season but there are different ways of going out of the FA Cup and Tottenham's method was to put on their jacket and politely show themselves to the door." – *The Guardian reckons they're guilty...*

"Controversy may be following Redknapp around at the moment, yet this was a half-decent Cup tie in the end, or to be exact half a decent Cup tie. The first half was almost vintage Cup fare, even if the second half did look suspiciously like two teams keen to avoid a replay. After all the scare stories about two reserve teams contesting this tie, both managers named perfectly respectable line-ups, give or take Jermain Defoe on the bench for Spurs and a debut for Fabio da Silva in a United side much stronger than the one that started in the Carling Cup in midweek. If Sir Alex Ferguson and Redknapp had kept quiet about their strained resources, no one would have noticed much difference on the night, though then we would have missed the former Portsmouth manager's hilarious U-turn after pledging to field his weakest possible team." – *The Observer leans the same way.*

"It was unsatisfactory at all levels and to the irritation of their manager, Harry Redknapp, the television pundits had no intention of sugar-coating it with the usual banalities, with Teddy Sheringham questioning whether the eight-time winners had been "happy to go out" and Andy Townsend recommending that Tom Huddlestone stopped "mooching about" and watched a tape of the indefatigable Carlos Tévez to learn a thing or two. "Absolute rubbish," responded Redknapp, citing the fact that his young goalkeeper, Ben Alnwick, was largely untroubled in the second half. 'People are just jumping on the bandwagon.'

"The truth was somewhere in between. Yet the best defence lawyer in the land would struggle to find a hole in the case that says Redknapp spent so long talking about the tie being secondary to tomorrow's league relegation battle against Stoke City that, once Roman Pavlyuchenko had headed them into the lead, his players seemed to forget that a) the FA Cup is important to Tottenham and b) Manchester United's team-sheet was not as intimidating as usual." – *The Guardian won't let this one go.*

MATCH FACTS

United: Foster, O'Shea, Neville, Vidic, Fabio Da Silva (Eckersley 53), Welbeck (Fletcher 86), Carrick, Scholes, Ronaldo (Tosic 72), Berbatov, Tévez.
Booked: Vidic, Tévez.
Tottenham: Alnwick, Gunter, Corluka, Dawson, Assou-Ekotto, Bentley (Defoe 72), Huddlestone, Zokora, Bale (Taarabt 67), Modric (Giovani 46), Pavlyuchenko [Redknapp]
Att: 75,014 **Ref:** Peter Walton **h-t:** 2-1

"I thought he spoke German because his accent is different."

NEWS

Unbelievable. United get drawn against Derby – again – or Nottingham Forest in the 5th round of the Cup. Hoffenheim's

Nigerian striker Chinedu Ogbuke is linked with a move to Old Trafford. No me neither. Spurs let themselves down – again – by re-signing Pascal Chimbonda from Sunderland, the same Pascal Chimbonda who skulked out of the club a year ago saying, "It's all about the money ". But they straightaway make up for it by re-signing Robbie Keane for between £5m and £8m less than Liverpool paid for him in the summer. What is going on in Benitez's mind?

BEAN SPILLER OF THE WEEK

"Dino had arranged that people should turn on the stadium lights for us and he finally fulfilled his dream of having sex in the middle of a football pitch. It was very naughty" – *Model Nives Celzijus embarrasses her boyfriend, Croatian international Dino Drpic, on a Serbian chat show. And Becks thought he had it bad when Posh told Parky about his Goldenballs…*

HE'LL FIT RIGHT IN

"I have never been outside the top six in my whole career and I want that to carry on." – *Craig Bellamy signs for City and immediately tries to rewrite history. For the record Craig you started your career in the Nationwide with Norwich, got relegated with Coventry in 2001 and finished last season at 10th-placed West Ham.*

FRIGHTENING PROSPECT OF THE WEEK
From the People:

The boob-flashing cousin of WAYNE ROONEY and her cross-dressing brother have signed up for a reality show.

And the move has left the millionaire Manchester United ace and missus COLEEN fearing likely embarrassment.

They already shun blonde glamour model NATALIE ROONEY, 18, and her 23-year-old bruv STEPHEN for their outrageous antics. Now they fear At Home With The Rooneys, which the outcast cousins are about to start filming for Living TV, could cause more upset.

Coleen is especially worried as Stephen bases his drag act on her.

COUSIN OF THE WEEK

"I was absolutely s***faced. I wasn't wearing a bra - just a bit of t*t tape - so they came out pretty easily. Friends thought it fun but I've not heard from Wayne or Coleen since." – *Natalie Rooney reminisces* *about Wayne's 21st birthday bash in 2006.*

WHAT'S HE UP TO?
Carragher cosies up to United:

"I was an Evertonian as a kid, but I've never hated Man United. I've always had respect for them,"

"They're a proper club, like us, and they should have respect for us as well.

"Man United aren't blasé or big-headed. I think Chelsea are, or have been in the past, a little bit.

"At Man United, there isn't a player who you think: 'God, I f******* hate him.' They're all good lads, aren't they? Hopefully we come across like that. We're clubs from working-class areas."
Hmmmm...

QUOTE OF THE WEEK

"I thought he spoke German because his accent is different." – *Vidic on his first meeting with Rooney*

RUNNER-UP

"I'm as baffled as you are" - *Robbie Keane, who could be the first player ever to be relegated and win a league medal in the same season, on Liverpool's decision to sell him back to Spurs.*

FAPL 27/01/2009

WEST BROM 0 UNITED 5
Berbatov 22, Tévez 44, Vidic 60, Ronaldo 65, 73

OK, YOU'RE A football fan. And if you've read this far I'm guessing you've either got way too much time on your hands or you're a Red. So if I asked you to name the rival teams that you'd rather see wiped off the face of the earth, it goes without saying that Liverpool, City and Leeds would jostle for a place right at the top of the list. But what about the rest? Arsenal and Chelsea have to be in the shake-up, though it's amazing how much of the Arsenal antipathy has faded since they've stopped winning anything. Spurs deserve a mention for their hypocritical whining over Berbatov and also for giving a job to Harry Redknapp. So do Real Madrid for their poisonous political machinations and Ramon Calderon. Everton should be in there but no one quite cares enough about them – and anyway, on the basis that your enemy's enemy is your friend they haven't got a chance. Milton Keynes Dons aren't on United's radar but it remains one of the great scandals that they were allowed to emerge from another club's carcass in the way that they did. Roma deserve a nomination because of what their fans want to do to your backsides. Actually, it's probably best to include West Ham and Chelsea (again) for the same reason. Villa deserve a mention because they're world leaders in fickle fans. Newcastle because they're so deluded. Rangers cost us a victory parade. Coventry look like City, except worse. Villarreal play anti-football. Bolton and Blackburn – in fact anyone from an old mill town who get their kicks mimicking airplanes – just aren't worth bothering with.

So are West Brom. I know that. But there's just something about them that gnaws at my tits. Is it because of Adrian Chiles, or Lee Hughes? Is it because they turned on Robbo despite him being the only manager ever to keep them in the Premier League? Is it because Jonathan Greening is the only United player I've ever taken an instant dislike to? I really don't know. What I do know is it was an absolute pleasure to see United turn them over like this...

MATCH ACTION

1-0 (22): The red card Rob Styles thrust in the face of West Brom left-back Paul Robinson just before halftime gave the locals an excuse to cling to as they dragged their knuckles home. But the truth is that United's free-flowing football did far more damage to their victory chances than the sending off. Even so, they may have struggled to add as many goals to Berbatov's opener if the numbers had stayed even. If ever a goal was made in the image of its scorer it was this one. Berbatov and Carrick make a defence-piercing one-two look ludicrously easy, Berbatov ambles into the area and fires a low shot through Carson's legs.

RED! (40): Here's the sending off. Robinson piles into a slide tackle that rattles Park's ribcage. Mowbray calls it an honest collision, pointing out that his man didn't jump in or show his studs. Fergie calls it reckless and careless. Both have a point. As for Rob Styles, he might not have been right to send Robinson off, but he wasn't wrong either.

2-0 (44): A goal down, a man down... the last thing West Brom needed was for their keeper to drop them even further in it before they can get back into the dressing room for a breather. But that's exactly what the ludicrously overrated Scott Carson does next, dropping Giggs's corner at the feet of Tévez. He can't miss. He doesn't.

3-0 (60): Another Giggs corner from the right, another goal. This time Vidic bulldozes his way to the near post and butts the ball into the roof of the net.

4-0 (65): The goal of the night. Tévez plays in Giggs down the inside left channel, he instantly squares the ball for Ronaldo to score in the league for the first time since November 15. You can tell it means a lot to him – he celebrates with a grin rather than his normal 'front cover of Attitude' style posturing.

5-0 (73): You wait 2 months for one Ronaldo goal and then... Berbatov unpicks West Brom's disintegrating offside trap with a deft flick, Ronaldo runs left to right to meet the ball and then dispatches it through Carson's legs.

NEW BOY (77): Tosic comes on for his league debut. He's small.

WHAT WAS GOOD?

THE BIGGEST AWAY WIN SINCE THE FOREST 8-1... Ronaldo scoring again... Van der Sar breaking Chelsea's top flight record of 1,025 minutes without conceding... United 3 points clear at the top with a game in hand... and a brand new chant to taunt Scousers with (see below). Tell me something that isn't good.

CHANT OF THE NIGHT

"TOP OF THE LEAGUE, AND THAT'S A FACT"

THE HAWTHORNS – THE VERBALS

"We have shown a ruthlessness that has maybe not been there this season. We hoped it was going to come and we expected it because of the standard of forwards we have, but tonight was the first indication it was there." – *Fergie on the goals.*

"Van der Sar, who has achieved everything in the game, was as delighted afterwards as when he saved that penalty kick [from Nicolas Anelka] in Moscow. That tells you about his desire. He still has that ambitious streak and wants to win." - *Fergie on the record.*

VIEWS FROM THE PRESSBOX

"If United are in the grip of an injury crisis, heaven help the rest. Ryan Giggs was magnificent in central midfield, the defence was strengthened by Rio Ferdinand and the champions were utterly irresistible in front of goal, scoring through Dimitar Berbatov, Carlos Tévez, Nemanja Vidic and Cristiano Ronaldo twice. If Ronaldo is in the grip of a confidence crisis, heaven help the opposition when he really regains belief.

"Rafa Benitez's strange outburst against Ferguson looks more ill-judged with every passing game. "Top of the League – and that's a fact," chanted the huge congregation of United supporters, mocking Benitez's obsession with 'facts'. What is an undeniable fact is that Berbatov has brought United a new dimension, a composed presence in front of goal, a striker as adept at creating as finishing." - *The Telegraph*

"'Top of the league — and that's a fact.' The message from Manchester United's fans was aimed directly at Rafael Benítez and it is doubtful whether the Liverpool manager will find any consolation or humour from the retort from the West Bromwich Albion supporters, which was that he was right to question Sir Alex Ferguson's influence over referees.

"It was nonsense, of course. United went three points clear of Liverpool at the top of the Premier League — in the process breaking Chelsea's top-flight record of 1,025 minutes without conceding a goal — because, ultimately, they played superbly. Admittedly their task was facilitated by Rob Styles's decision to send off Paul Robinson, the West Bromwich captain, five minutes before half-time, but that was neither the outrage portrayed by the locals nor a notable turning point. United's free-flowing football did far more damage to their team's survival hopes than Styles, the supposed villain of the piece." – *The Times*

MATCH FACTS

West Brom: Carson, Hoefkens, Pele, Donk, Robinson, Zuiverloon (Morrison 64), Borja Valero, Koren, Brunt, Simpson (Bednar 64), Fortune (Cech 46) [Mowbray]
Sent Off: Robinson (40).
Booked: Koren, Bednar, Carson, Donk, Morrison
United: Van der Sar, Neville (Eckersley 71), Ferdinand (Brown 70), Vidic, O'Shea, Park, Carrick, Giggs, Ronaldo, Berbatov

(Tosic 77), Tévez.
Booked: Park, Carrick.
The Hawthorns Att: 26,105 Ref: Rob Styles h-t: 2-0

"Why was it crazy? Because it was crazy."

NEWS

Nothing much to declare, not from United's end anyway. UEFA announce that Wembley will host the European Cup Final in 2011. Charles N'Zogbia goes on strike at Newcastle after falling out with Kinnear over, er, I'll tell you in a second. Robinho is questioned over an alleged rape at a Leeds nightclub. The charges are later dropped. Is it another example of a famous footballer being stung? The ever-charming El Hadji Diouf seals his departure from Sunderland by threatening to stab Anton Ferdinand over dinner. Sam Allardyce, patron saint of all football outcasts, wastes no time picking him up. And after Wigan become the seventh side in ten league games to draw against Liverpool comes another Neon-lit sign that Rafa might be cracking up...

C.R.A.Z.Y.

"Why was it crazy? Because it was crazy. In the last three games there has been something in common that I don't like. I know what it is, but I can't say anything." – *We know that something got Benitez's goat at the JJB, we just don't know what. Or do we?*

After much investigation, the chaps at football365 find the 'crazy' common denominator between those three Liverpool games:

"The Spanish guy in the anorak at the side of the pitch making some frankly mental decisions."

NEEDLESS WONDER OF THE WEEK

"I don't like it, I think it's pathetic and you have to wonder about the intelligence of these people". – *Gary Megson fumes about the grief he's getting from his own fans at Bolton.*

NOT THAT TIGHT THOUGH

"There are five or even six teams who could still win the title. Do not rule out Aston Villa and even Everton. It is much tighter than people think." – *Arsene Wenger with the baffling claim of the week.*

CLOWN OF THE WEEK
It had to happen…

'A bungling Manchester City fan had "Kaka" tattooed on his chest – then the star shunned his beloved club. Christopher Atkinson, 25, was so confident the Blues would land the AC Milan ace in a record £100million deal last month that he secured his signature permanently. But he was forced into a cover-up when the Brazilian decided to stay in Italy.

Christopher, of Altrincham, Cheshire, hoped his secret was safe – but his mates found out. He said: "They haven't stopped taking the Mick. Kaka's one of my favourite players. I got carried away by the emotion of him coming here…It's taken a few weeks to see the funny side. At least I have a permanent reminder of how close City came to signing him. I won't get rid of it. I'll just hang back a bit next time, hopefully for someone like Lionel Messi from Barcelona" – *The Sun.*

ROW OF THE WEEK
It's CNZ V JFK:

"Insomnia…N'Zogbia…Charlie" - *Joe Kinnear gets things rolling by forgetting what his man's called…*

"It is clear what he meant. It is hard not to react when your boss calls you mad" - *Franck Peslerbe, N'Zogbia's agent doesn't know what insomnia means.*

"This is at best disrespectful and at worst deeply offensive, especially as insomnia is as difficult to pronounce as N'Zogbia. It's not good when people who should cannot remember your name. Ask Graham Taylor how he feels when he gets called Gordon Taylor. We are our name" – *Is PFA chairman Gordon Taylor taking the mickey?*

"Charles is a mixed-up kid. He needs to grow up. And his agent is full of s★★t" - *Joe Kinnear bids Insomnia (who was apparently always telling his Newcastle team-mates he was off to United or Arsenal) farewell as he sells him to Wigan.*

ASKING FOR TROUBLE QUOTE OF THE WEEK

"We are not even thinking of the word 'relegation' and it won't happen" – *What on earth was Newcastle's Steven Taylor thinking?*

UNDERSTATEMENT OF THE WEEK

"He used to come to my house to eat, drink, everything. I used to go to his house to play pool. Me and Anton never had problems. It's just when I'm mad I had a problem with him" – *The ever charming El Hadji Diouf gives his side of the story following his bust-up with Ferdinand jnr.*

FAPL 31/01/2009

UNITED 1 EVERTON 0
Ronaldo 44(p)

OK, IT'S CONFESSION time. I was there at Highbury in November when Samir Nasri lashed in Arsenal's winning goal. In fact I was sat right behind the goal – an exiled Red in the plush seats in the Arsenal end – as Van der Sar effectively waved the ball past him for the second time that day. And I can remember seriously considering whether he had it in him any more. Whether at the age of 39 he had the reflexes you need to make the really big saves, the saves that Schmeichel, even Barthez in his first couple of years, could be relied upon to make. And I've got to tell you, having just witnessed his record-breaking clean sheet victory against dour, dependable Everton, I feel a right tool for ever thinking it. Say what you like about the opposition United have faced recently (although it's not been as weak as the press box snipers like to make out). Say what you like about the strength of the defence in front of him. But you've got to be an unbelievably good keeper not to concede a goal in the Premier League for 1,122 minutes. And that's what Van der Sar has been and still is. He's not a showy keeper, he's not an egotistical match winner but he's technically excellent, he's got this incredibly cool aura about him and he might be the best footballing keeper there's ever been. Whisper it quietly but we could have as tough a job replacing Van der Sar as Schmeichel in '99*...

*(*though hopefully Foster won't turn out to be such a nob as that Australian fool)*

THE MOMENTS THAT MATTERED

TOSS-UP (0) – The captains meet for the toss. Which would have been wholly insignificant if they hadn't grown up sharing a bunk bed in Bury.

1-0 (44) – United played some really good stuff here so it was credit to Everton, coming off the back of a couple of useful draws at Anfield, that we needed a penalty to beat them. The outstanding Carrick powers into the box, Arteta clips his ankles and Ronaldo, who also scored a penalty winner the last time Everton were here, first stutters and then scores.

BEATING DEATH (72) – Van der Sar's clean sheet run reaches the 1,103 minutes mark, in the process beating the English league record previously held by Reading keeper Steve Death. By the end of the game the tally had moved to 1,122 minutes, just 74 minutes short of the British league record set by Rangers' Chris Woods.

WHAT WAS GOOD?

LOTS OF THINGS. But the performance of Carrick really stood out. It remains one of the mysteries of modern United why Carrick is so underappreciated. He's not going to go about geeing people up like Ince or Keane, he's not going to beat players with mazy runs like Giggs, he doesn't creep into the box to score like Scholes and he isn't going to make gays and girls go all giddy with his looks like Becks but his vision, his passing, his ability to keep the ball and nick it off the opposition mark him out as a player of genuine United class. And if you don't agree, listen to Robbo who was raving about him after the match: "It's his understanding of where to be on the pitch that has impressed me more than anything else. He knows the areas to be in, regardless of where the ball is, which is a priceless asset."

EVERTON. Overachieving under Moyes yet again. One to bear in mind when Fergie calls it a day?

WHAT WAS BAD?

WE'VE FORGOTTEN HOW TO KILL TEAMS OFF. This was the seventh 1-0 win in the last 10 league games, and two of the others finished 0-0. "When you have teams by the throat you have to kill them off," Ferguson moaned. "We had them by the throat several times and didn't do that. We never put it to bed."

QUOTE OF THE DAY

"Looking at them [United] close up made me drool – it was difficult to keep thinking up ways to stop them." – *David Moyes.*

RUNNER-UP

"You are trying to find ways of stopping them and attacking them ourselves but you look at it and at times I was saying it's nearly impossible. I was looking and saying 'well, it's very difficult, you've just got to hang in there sometimes.' Your goalkeeper makes a couple of saves, you hang in there and that's what we did. I think when you get on a run like they are part of them will be thinking 'we're not going to give this up'. There's a real determination not to give it up and I think you can see that in their faces. They're all capable of doing so much. The way they have got here just shows there is so much strength in depth." – *More praise from Moyes.*

LINE OF THE DAY

"A great stadium echoes to the expression of many things on the final whistle; triumph, relief, panic and even boredom. The sound of Old Trafford when Mark Halsey blew for full time was one of inevitability." – *The Guardian*

VIEWS FROM THE PRESSBOX

"If any team are to hinder Manchester United's increasingly convincing pursuit of a third successive Premier League title, they must first score a goal against them. It is proving a formidable task. Last night United and Edwin van der Sar set a new record for English football by passing Reading's previous best of 18 hours and 24 minutes without conceding a goal. More importantly in the bigger scheme of things, they held out for the remaining 18 minutes of the game, to record a 10th successive home victory and move five points clear at the top of the table." – *The Independent*

"The British record of 1,196 minutes without conceding, set by Everton's goalkeeping coach Chris Woods when at Rangers, is next in line while the world record for a single season, the 1,275 goalless minutes kept by Atlético Madrid's Abel Resino in 1990 91 is also vulnerable. Curiously, for all Resino's heroics, Atlético did not win La Liga that season, having to contend with the extraordinary Barcelona team created by Johan Cruyff. There is nothing nearly so formidable blocking Manchester United's path." – *The Guardian.*

"Liverpool and Chelsea can do their worst at Anfield today knowing that they may be playing for second place. Their best hope is that a log-jam of fixtures holds United up, but they could just as easily face the same problem themselves. What Sir Alex Ferguson's team have already done is overcome the disruption of the World Club Championship in Japan and now, a crop of injuries." – *The Indie again.*

"Unusually for a man whose mantra is that Easter is the critical time of any football season, Sir Alex Ferguson had identified the period between Manchester United's return from the Club World Cup and the resumption of the Champions League as the decisive phase of the domestic campaign. Between the end of December and mid-February, the Manchester United manager reasoned his players would be slightly disoriented after their return from Japan and weighed down by injuries. Their response has been seven straight victories with a collective scoreline of 13–0." – *The Guardian again.*

MATCH FACTS

UNITED: VAN DER SAR, NEVILLE (BROWN 56), FERDINAND, VIDIC, O'SHEA, RONALDO, CARRICK, FLETCHER (GIGGS 75), PARK, BERBATOV, TÉVEZ

EVERTON: HOWARD, HIBBERT, JAGIELKA, LESCOTT, BAINES, OSMAN, ARTETA, NEVILLE, PIENAAR, FELLAINI (ANICHEBE 68), CAHILL [MOYES]

ATT: 75,399 REF: MARK HALSEY H-T: 1-0

OTHER SCORES

LIVERPOOL 2 CHELSEA 0; ARSENAL 0 WEST HAM 0

LEAGUE TABLE

1. UNITED 53 (23); 2. LIVERPOOL 51 (24); 3. CHELSEA 48 (24)

"When you're in the tunnel and you hear on the speakers 'Please welcome the champions of England, the champions of Europe and the champions of the world' you just believe you are going to crush anybody that is in your way."

NEWS

As IF ITV's football coverage hasn't got a bad enough name already (I know plenty of Reds who are still fuming that they cut away from the Nou Camp in '99 when David May was still hanging off Lennart Johansson's shoulders), they score a massive own goal during the Merseyside FA Cup derby, bleeping out Everton's winner in favour of an unscheduled ad break. How much would you have paid to see Phil Thompson's face when the pictures returned to show Goodison going mental? The FA surprise no one and amaze everyone at the same time by deciding not to take action against Jose Bosingwa after his leg karate chop on Benayoun at the weekend. Fergie and Vidic are named Manager of the Month and Player of the Month for January (amazingly it's the only time a United player wins the award all season). And Derby beat Forest in their replay to set up the third in a trilogy of cup games this season. No sheep's heads were harmed this time★.

NON-FOOTBALL RUMOUR OF THE WEEK

At least ITV aren't the only TV company sitting on the naughty step.
From the Guardian:

'Since Janet Jackson's bejewelled right nipple popped out during the half-time show at the 2004 Super Bowl, the term "wardrobe malfunction" has become part of the rich history of American football's showpiece event.

'Yesterday, as this year's clash between the Pittsburgh Steelers and the Arizona Cardinals neared a thrilling climax, TV viewers in Tuscon, Arizona, witnessed an intimate exposure of a completely different order.

'Shortly after 7.30pm, with less than three minutes to play in a tightly fought final, the Cardinals had taken the lead with a crucial touchdown. Fans watching in Arizona would have been forgiven for scenting a victory for their team against the odds. Then the pictures from Tampa disappeared.

'Instead, viewers in the Tuscon area were astonished to see a woman unzipping a man's trousers to reveal "full male nudity" followed by what was described as "a graphic act" between the couple.' *For the record, ITV viewers got to see an ad for Tic Tacs.*

SPOT OF THE WEEK
From football365:

Top work from ITV, who published an apology from executive chairman Michael Grade on their website this morning for their 'coverage' of the Merseyside derby last night.

Eyes right to a banner ad plugging the ITV online media player, which brags: 'Amazing telly you can't miss'.

NEWS II

It's that time of the year we all look forward to. The time that Chelsea release their latest set of disastrous financial figures and Peter Kenyon has to stand there and pretend they're pleased with them (funnily enough it's not quite as amusing when David Gill does it). This year they try to brush over their £65.7m losses by making a song and dance about the news that Abramovich has agreed to convert around half the debt owed to him by the club into shares. Which would make more sense to me... if he didn't own all the shares in the club already.

HOW'S THAT GOING THEN?
More good stuff from football365:

DECEMBER 2, 2008 - Peter Kenyon announces: "The long-term plan here was always that we needed to be profitable, non-loss-making and self-funding...In terms of breaking even, I think it will be 2010-11 but, this year, we're very clear about achieving no-funding targets from the owner. It's a process we believe can be achieved by the end of this season."

FEBRUARY 13, 2009 - Chelsea release their annual accounts which show a loss of £65.7million.

INTERESTING
From the Press Association's story on Chelsea's losses:

'Chelsea chief executive Peter Kenyon has warned that any signings in the summer will have to be financed by selling players after the club announced losses of £65m.' *And how much money are they going to get for all those old players?*

QUOTES OF THE WEEK PART I

"After my comments about Mr Ferguson, we still knew we had to win at Stoke. Those words didn't change anything on the pitch. The same applies to other games this month that have followed some controversy." – *Benitez is still in denial.*

"Everything I do, I want it to be perfect." – *We sort of gathered that Dimi.*

"Half the people might like me, the other half might not, but throughout my life I've had high expectations for myself so I just try to make the non-believers into believers." – *Should Berbatov be trying harder?*

"In England I like the passion, the quality of the grass, the quality of the referees, the TV transmissions, the sincerity of the football and Wayne Rooney." – *Perhaps Michel Platini isn't such a bad sort after all.*

TRANSFER WINDOW ROUND-UP

Arsenal just manage to bundle Andrei Arshavin through the transfer window before it closes. At £10m – about half of what Zenit St Petersburg were asking Spurs for in the summer - it seems like a decent piece of business (if Arsenal needed another tricksy attacking type that is). Elsewhere Chelsea get Quaresma on loan from Milan and Everton bag Jo from City, the Brazilian completing the trip from record signing to loan signing in just 7 months. Overall, though, the January transfer window of 2009 was a story of two clubs – Spurs who panicked and bought back all their old players. And City who bought anyone they could.

THE TRANSFER WINDOW TOP 10

1. Nigel de Jong (City, £16m)
2. Jermain Defoe (Spurs, £15.75m)
3. Robbie Keane (Spurs, £15m)
4. Wilson Palacios (Spurs, £14m)
5. Craig Bellamy (City, £14m)
6. Wayne Bridge (City, £12m)
7. Andrei Arshavin (Arsenal, £10m)
8. Adem Ljajic (United, £9.5m*)
9. Shay Given (City, £8m)
10. Jimmy Bullard (Hull, £5m)
*massive add-ons included

QUOTES OF THE WEEK PART II

"What are you lot going to do now? All those Liverpool fans, especially in the local press. The way you build that side up. I bet you're all stunned tonight. We completely controlled the game" – *David Moyes laps up the derby win.*

"Liverpool are out of the FA Cup. And apologies if you missed seeing that decisive goal live..." - *Steve Rider does his best after the ITV Tic Tac scandal.*

"Liverpool winning didn't bother me. I would have preferred a draw. But the one thing I didn't want was a Chelsea win, because they are a bigger threat. Chelsea are a better all-round side than Liverpool. I honestly don't think Liverpool are a threat in the title race" - *Paddy Crerand does a Fergie. Rafa will be pleased.*

"Andy, you are wrong - why did you sell yourself to an English club? Now you will bring good feelings to England. England brings our country only harm. They have incited revolutionary feelings all over the world. Our thieves run there and our fugitive oligarchs who took Russia's money hide themselves there" – *You get the feeling Vladimir Zhirinovsky, leader of the Liberal Democratic Party of Russia, isn't best pleased that Arshavin's joined Arsenal.*

QUOTE OF THE WEEK

"When you're in the tunnel and you hear on the speakers 'Please welcome the champions of England, the champions of Europe and the champions of the world' you just believe you are going to crush anybody that is in your way [and land on Alan Keegan right?]. I get goosebumps every time I walk out at Old Trafford." – *DB9*

RUNNER-UP

"I saw the game between Stoke City and Manchester City [which Stoke won 1-0]. I noticed that millions have been invested by certain people there very badly. I saw that they can do absolutely nothing, even though they were very expensive" - *Bayern Munich general manager Uli Hoeness*
Before the first game, at Pride Park, sheep heads were thrown at two pubs in Derby. Apparently – and I'm not making this up – the Derbyshire police said they were investigating whether the incidents were connected to Derby's nickname, The Rams. I wonder...

FAPL 08/02/2009

WEST HAM 0 UNITED 1
Giggs 62

Do you remember Reading away last year? It was the day that Fergie did an up-yours sign at Stevie Coppell's assistant Wally Downes and then used one of his 'It's running down my leg'* excuses to get himself out of a scrape. It was the day that Ronaldo and Rooney ran the length of the pitch on their own to score the points-clinching second. It was also one of the last times I can remember a lesser team having a proper go at us. That game was played on 19 January 2008, 39 league games ago. Depressing isn't it?

In fairness, West Ham weren't as soullessly negative as most teams have been against us recently. They did try to play some football. They even got into our penalty area every now and then. And I might have imagined it, but I'm pretty sure they were caught offside once or twice. But they did play one upfront. They did overstock midfield with willing runners. They didn't really come close to a goal. And they got what they deserved – a decent write-up in the papers the next day but no points.

As for United, another weekend brought another big stat and another spot of bad news for a forgotten 70s keeper. Last week's clean sheet against Everton removed Reading's Steve Death from the record books. This week's notch on Van der Sar's goalpost wiped out Aberdeen's Billy Clark. And if that wasn't exciting enough for the statistically sensitive, Giggsy joined in the fun with a flashback to the days when his blood-twisting runs from the left were the most exhilarating in the English game (in the process scoring in the league for a staggering 19th season in a row). I've said it before and I make no apologies for saying again. We'll only appreciate just how bloody good he's been when he's gone. Even so, does anyone else think it looks like an accident when he scores with his right foot?

GOAL!

1-0 (62): After West Ham make an unnecessary drama of clearing a United corner, Scholes drills a crossfield pass to the feet of Giggs on the left. He cuts inside a sliding challenge from Cole, gives the same medicine to Parker and then curls a low right-footer through a penalty box crowd and past Green's left hand. Vintage stuff.

USELESS TRIVIA OF THE DAY

Did you know that Edwin Van der Sar is called Ice Rabbit back in Holland?

WEST HAM – THE VERBALS

"It's hard work from everybody. I had to make a couple of saves today but the defenders are incredible, how they defend, how they clear the balls... it's a team effort because everybody tracks back. It's a fantastic record and I'm very happy about it. But what really means a lot at the moment is the win. It was so important, especially after seeing Liverpool win yesterday" – *The Ice Rabbit on another record-breaking afternoon.*

"I'm just glad to have scored the winning goal. I get a right-footer and a header every season so hopefully there's a header still to come!" – *Giggsy leaves us scratching our heads trying to remember the other 18 right-footed goals he reckons he's scored (see 'the Wrong 'uns' below).*

"Ryan truly is a credit to the game. If anyone wants an example of how to dedicate themselves to football, you could have no greater example." – *Fergie on the legend that's Giggs.*

VIEWS FROM THE PRESSBOX

"This was just another ordinary afternoon in the extraordinary life of Giggs, an occasion that will barely merit a footnote when the time comes to reflect on the career of the most decorated player in English football history. But, at the venerable age of 35, in the autumn of his football life, his every contribution is to be savoured. The second-half goal that sent United back to the top of the Barclays Premier League was merely a minor classic — a couple of delightful body swerves and a right-foot shot that deceived Robert Green — but, in the wider context, coming on his 786th appearance for the club as he approaches the 18th anniversary of his first-team debut, it seemed to carry an additional symbolism." – *The Times*

"The United method nowadays is to exhaust teams and then defeat them. There is such confidence in the passing that the oppositions' lungs burn as they chase after the ball that is often withheld from them. The gung-ho United of old were more likely to trade blows, but the adjustment in philosophy has made the side more effective in the Champions League as well as the domestic scene. Sometimes, as was the case here, their display appeals more to coaches than spectators. Domination was carefully established, but United were not particularly incisive." - *The Guardian makes an interesting point. Two things have changed at Old Trafford this season. First, we don't know what our best team is (it's been a squad effort rather than a team one). And second, we've not been going for the throat from the first whistle, instead preferring to strangle our victims slowly.*

LABOURED ANALOGY OF THE WEEK

It is 1,212 minutes since Van der Sar picked the ball out of the net and he rarely looked like being beaten here, particularly with Carlton Cole failing to turn some enterprising approach work into a threatening finish. The more venerable observers among the Upton Park crowd might recall that 1212 was Scotland Yard's old telephone number, and it felt like a different era when Nasri scored way back when." – *The Telegraph's lovably posh Henry Winter.*

THE WRONG 'UNS

Giggsy's 5 most memorable moments with his right foot:
1. **COVENTRY AWAY 1997** – a floppy-haired Giggs smashes in a sensational right-footer into the top corner from the edge of the box
2. **ARSENAL 2003** – that miss
3. **JUVENTUS 2003** – Giggs's greatest Euro goal, a stunning dribble from halfway and a cool, slotted finish with his right foot
4. **UPTON PARK 2009** – see above
5. **NOU CAMP 1999** – Giggsy's best ever miskick sets up Sheringham for the crucial equaliser

MATCH FACTS

WEST HAM: GREEN, NEILL, COLLINS, UPSON, ILUNGA, BEHRAMI (TRISTAN 87), PARKER, NOBLE (NSEREKO 77), COLLISON, COLE, DI MICHELE [ZOLA]
BOOKED: NEILL
UNITED: VAN DER SAR, RAFAEL DA SILVA, FERDINAND, VIDIC, O'SHEA, RONALDO, SCHOLES, CARRICK, GIGGS, TÉVEZ (PARK 87), BERBATOV.
BOOKED: VIDIC.
UPTON PARK ATT: 34,958 REF: PHIL DOWD H-T: 0-0

OTHER SCORES

CHELSEA 0 HULL 0; PORTSMOUTH 2 LIVERPOOL 3; SPURS 0 ARSENAL 0

LEAGUE TABLE

1. UNITED 56 (24); 2. LIVERPOOL 54 (25); 3. VILLA 51 (25);
4. CHELSEA 49 (25)

In 1999 Fergie was cleared of illegally driving on the hard shoulder of the motorway because he said he was desperate for the toilet.

"If I get the job will I be getting me own tracksuit, all the gear with all me name on it and that?"

NEWS

GARY LINEKER REVEALS that he spoke to United in 1989 after leaving Barcelona but never really fancied us. Is that part of the reason why Fergie can't stand him? Anyway, it's his loss. He never got to play with Ralph Milne. United add the two Roman kids, Petrucci and Macheda, to the Champions League squad list. Steve Bennett – United's favourite referee according to Benitez's facts list – gets stung by the *News of the World* undercover hit squad. News emerges that Ronaldo is dating a girl – 18 year-old Olivia Saunders – who isn't on the game. Wow...

And it's a bad week for three struggling Premier League managers. Joe F***ing Kinnear has to have a triple f***ing heart bypass operation. I don't want to seem unkind but why didn't someone stop a man with his medical record – and ample frame - getting involved with a nuthouse like Newcastle? Tony Adams will talk into his chest for Portsmouth no more as he's replaced by Paul Hart after just 107 days. And Big Phil Scolari, the darling of the press as recently as November, becomes the fourth manager in five years to be dumped by Chelsea. Russia manager Guus Hiddink replaces him on a caretaker basis until the end of the season.

RIGHT BEHIND YOU (HOLDING THE KNIFE... AGAIN)

"It can't be a coincidence that the two most successful teams in England have some continuity in their staff. You don't want to sack a manager every year. First and foremost, you want some continuity"
- *Peter Kenyon, December 3.*

"We're here with a guy who we've brought in with great respect.

He's done a tremendous job and we shouldn't be questioning his role" - *Peter Kenyon December 4.*

"It's not working" — *What Peter Kenyon reportedly told Scolari when he asked him to do one, February 9.*

NO CHANCE

"There's no chance of him going to Chelsea as he very much likes what he is doing now" - *Guus Hiddink's agent, February 9.*

LOSING FRIENDS

"The manager has been a great signing for the club, he has been different class. He is a great man as well and gets on well with everyone away from the training pitch. He is like one of our friends, but on the training pitch he has the complete respect of the whole squad" - *John Terry, December 22.*

"Scolari had my support. Two or three other players will say exactly the same thing, I'm sure" — *John Terry, February 10.*

"He has proved he is a great coach but most recently there has been a lack of success at Chelsea. When that happens the blame comes down on to the weakest link in the chain: the manager" — *Michael Ballack sure isn't one of them.*

OPTIMIST OF THE WEEK

"I was devastated. But I'll never forget when Sir Alex let me leave United he said that he feared one day I would come back to haunt him. I'd love to think this is going to be that day. To beat them in the FA Cup would be very, very special." — *Former Fledgling Robbie Savage.*

RUNNER-UP

"Nothing's changed. The owner wants me to do the job and the chairman wants me to do the job. The players want me to do the job and the majority of the fans do." - *Tony Adams, two days before he was sacked.*

WIND-UP OF THE WEEK

For four painful minutes Dublin radio station FM 104 manages to convince Peter Kenyon they are Steve Staunton applying for the Chelsea job. Cuddly Pete only catches on when 'Staunton' asks: "Will I be getting my own tracksuit with my name on it?"

RUMOUR OF THE WEEK
From The Express

"Rafa Benitez has to win the Premier League title to save his job after co-owner George Gillett criticised the Liverpool manager.

"Gillett let it be known on a rare visit to Merseyside last weekend that he blamed Benitez for Liverpool's indifferent form. He told Anfield insiders during his flying visit that he had been dismayed at Benitez's recent attack on Sir Alex Ferguson – insisting that it had destabilised the club and given Manchester United greater incentive to retain their title. Gillett, who refuses to bow to Benitez's demands for complete control over transfer policy before agreeing to a new four-year contract, also believes that the Liverpool boss likes to be constantly linked with other big jobs."

LETDOWN OF THE WEEK

The *News of the World* get all steamed up and pleased with themselves for getting a tipsy Steve Bennett to slur insider secrets (described as an 'astonishing betrayal' by the paper) at a refereeing convention.

SO WHAT DID HE ACTUALLY TELL THEM?

He revealed that: "A top international Premier League star asked to be booked so he could get suspended and go on holiday with his family. ANOTHER tried the same trick because he wanted time off over Christmas. And a THIRD wangled a booking so he would miss a match at a far-flung ground where he didn't fancy playing." *Oh.*

THE REAL STORY
The Screws miss the real scandal, tucked away in the final paragraph:

"Just metres away [from where Bennett stood], colleagues Howard Webb and Mike Dean were singing Liverpool anthem 'You'll Never Walk Alone'. *What the *@*@!*

QUOTES OF THE WEEK

"If I get the job will I be getting me own tracksuit, all the gear with all me name on it and that?" – *'Steve Staunton' plays hardball in his contract negotiations with Peter Kenyon.*

"It is a sign of the times. There is absolutely no patience in the world now" – *Fergie, who's outlasted no fewer than 13 Chelsea managers*, tuts about Scolari.*

'A few weeks ago, we were in first position, then a certain individual from the club attacked another individual from another club, and, since then, we have lost form and slid down the league.' – *What George Gillett reportedly said to fans' action group,* Spirit of Shankly. *Who could he be talking about?*

"As a fan, they [the players] f*****g rip you off. You don't know half the things that go on . . . if they knew that, you'd be absolutely gutted, trust me." – *What Bennett slurred to the* News of the World.

★PUB QUIZ QUESTION OF THE WEEK

How many of the 13 Chelsea managers Fergie's outlasted can you name? (I reckon 7 are easy then things get hard)

MAKING AN IMPRESSION
(Andrei Arshavin style)

"As far as London's citizens are concerned, I didn't like them at all. They are very dirty, scruffy. London is a dirty city. The women don't care about themselves and what they look like. They are very scruffy." – *Arshavin's radio presenter partner Julia wastes no time making friends on Arshavin's website.*

"Sometimes I find it hard to hide my dislike of certain people. It may be bad but that's just me" – *Arshavin gets in on the act.*

"He trained with us for the first time last Tuesday and I was really surprised: he is really small" - *Gael Clichy – no giant himself - sizes up his new team-mate.*

★ *Hollins, Campbell, Porterfield, Webb, Hoddle, Gullit, Vialli, Rix, Ranieri, Mourinho, Grant, Scolari, Wilkins*

15/02/2009
FA CUP 5TH ROUND

DERBY 1 UNITED 4
Nani 29, Gibson 44, Ronaldo 48, Addison 56, Welbeck 81

THE MEDIA DID their best to build up this game, they made Nigel Clough out to be the reincarnation of his old man (rather than the league novice he really is), they even tried to make a story about the pantomime villain that is Robbie Savage. But the reality is that these underdogs had already had their day – back in the Carling Cup semi in January. This time United got their heads right straight from the start, stopped Derby's better players – particularly first leg hero Kris Commons – getting on the ball and effectively scored at will. Nani started things off with a flashing 20 yarder, Gibson volleyed in the second after Ronaldo's free-kick spiralled off the wall and Ronaldo headed in the third. Addison's header was a decent reward for Derby's willingness to keep going but there was no chance of a comeback, a point Welbeck underlined with a lovely first-time curler from just inside the box. The goal was just like Henry. The celebration – a 'what do you expect?' expression and a nonchalant shrug – was like Henry too. Cockiness and class, and that's from an 18 year-old kid. And they wonder why Fergie doesn't want to call it a day yet...

QUOTE OF THE DAY

"They [United] could pretty much score at will." – *Nigel Clough*

VIEWS FROM THE PRESSBOX

"Such is the speed and breathtaking movement of Manchester United that the Red Devils almost resemble the Red Arrows. Nani, Cristiano Ronaldo and Ryan Giggs all flew around Pride Park on Sunday afternoon, leaving Derby County choking on their vapour trails. Giggs, all touch and vision, was again magnificent. Nani and Ronaldo, such elusive scarlet pimpernels, both scored while United's phenomenal strength in depth was confirmed in well-taken goals by Darron Gibson and Danny Welbeck. Amid all this shimmering beauty lurked a real ruthlessness. United fans are loving it. They had clearly been busy with the sewing machines, creating banners to go with their chants. All Singers and songs, United's following filled the South Stand with messages, saluting everyone from Carlos Tévez to Nemanja Vidic." – *The Telegraph goes OTT...*

"It was an epic, lyrical performance, full of everything that is good about Ferguson's team and a reminder that "genius" is not too strong a word to describe Ryan Giggs's gifts. Giggs is 34 now, reaching the stage of his career when insecurity can appear on the horizon, but his left foot has gone beyond the stage of being described as "educated". A master's degree is surely called for, given the finesse of his touches. Gibson is not so refined but an honorary mention should also go to the Republic of Ireland international, while Darren Fletcher, Nani, Park Ji-sung and the rest of the supporting cast ensured this was a chastening experience for their opponents." – *The Guardian follows suit.*

MATCH FACTS

DERBY: BYWATER, CONNOLLY, ADDISON, ALBRECHTSEN, STEWART, BARAZITE (STERJOVSKI 63), GREEN, SAVAGE (PEARSON 82), TEALE, COMMONS, HULSE (PORTER 68) [CLOUGH]
BOOKED: CONNOLLY
UNITED: FOSTER, RAFAEL DA SILVA, FERDINAND, EVANS, EVRA (O'SHEA 55), PARK (WELBECK 55), FLETCHER, GIBSON, NANI, GIGGS, RONALDO (POSSEBON 72)
PRIDE PARK ATT: 32,103 **REF:** ALAN WILEY H–T: 2–0

OTHER SCORES

FA CUP: EVERTON 3 VILLA 1, WATFORD 1 CHELSEA 3.

"It has always been my greatest dream to have sex on the roof of Real's Santiago Bernabeu stadium"

NEWS

UNITED ARE DRAWN away at either Swansea or Fulham in the quarter-finals of the Cup (I won't keep you in suspense, we end up playing Fulham). 15 year-old United 'wonder-kid' John Cofie chooses to play for England rather than Ghana or Germany. And Danny Welbeck gets his first England under-21 call-up.

WAGS OF THE WEEK

"I do not like England. People are too reserved and it's dull. I do not like English cuisine. Finding the right food may turn into a problem." – *Arshavin's partner Julia really isn't pleased he's here.*

"It has always been my greatest dream to have sex on the roof of Real's Santiago Bernabeu stadium in my favourite city, Madrid" – *No it's not Ronaldo. It's Nives Celcius, the stadium sex lover, who's got some interesting plans should her boyfriend, Dino Drpic, make it as far as Madrid.*

"It was a good opportunity but I didn't accept because I do not want to spoil the good contact that I have with Deco at the moment" – *Deco's estranged wife Jaciara Dias explains why she turned down a six-figure offer to strip for Playboy.*

'FACT' OF THE WEEK

Benitez uses an old tactic to explain why Liverpool have won only one of the 14 main domestic trophies open to them since he arrived in 2004:

"I have enough data to bore you with it. But if you look at United, it wasn't just spending £32m on Dimitar Berbatov - they can spend whatever it takes for what they need every year. Last year it was £17m on Owen Hargreaves, £18m on Nani and £20m on Anderson. Seven years ago they paid £30m for Rio Ferdinand. In my five years, I've paid less in transfer fees than I've received, even though I spent £40m on Fernando Torres and Robbie Keane. It's as simple as that."

Unfortunately, as the chaps at football365 pointed out, maths doesn't seem to be Rafa's strong point:

"According to the excellent and thorough TransferLeague.co.uk, since Benitez took charge of Liverpool in 2004, he has spent an impressive £215,490,000 on players, receiving £98,030,000. Our rudimentary maths tells us that amounts to a net spend of the not inconsiderable sum of £117,460,000.

"If one is to be fair - and we are nothing if not fair - one should knock off the £14million paid for Djibril Cisse in 2004, as that was Gerard Houllier's deal, but even then Rafa's net spend tots up to £103,460,000.

"By way of comparison, those big money bullies Chelsea have a net spend of £131,150,000 in that time, while Manchester United - the trampling behemoths cited by Rafa - have splashed £93,300,000."

RUNNER-UP

"Since I arrived we have won four titles, played in seven finals and reached a Champions League semi-final. We are where we should be. The problem is the anxiety and the desire to win everything and that is not easy." – *It looks like Benitez is doing the old Houillier trick of counting the Community Shield. Or was it the Youth Cup? .*

QUOTES OF THE WEEK

"It's impossible to prepare for playing against them. We watched them for six consecutive games and they played six completely different teams with different ways of playing. You can watch them in 60 consecutive ways but then they'll just change who plays where" – *Cloughie jnr. on the problems of managing a team against United*

"Everyone has done so well that I'm beginning to dread picking the team. I feel guilty when I am forced to leave someone out" – *Fergie on the problems of managing United.*

"I had death threats. No one would sit here and say that was enjoyable. When I received them, I wasn't too sure with some of them. A couple were written in crayon" – *Birmingham's Martin Taylor reveals the abuse he received (from primary school kids?) following his leg-break challenge on Eduardo last February.*

FAPL 18/02/2009

UNITED 3 FULHAM 0
Scholes 12, Berbatov 30, Rooney 63

I'VE GOT ANOTHER confession to make, a dirty secret I've kept hidden away for as long as I can remember. Something that might make you want to track me down and boil my pets. And here it is... I don't mind Alan Green. Oh god, it's worse than that. Sometimes I'm actually pleased he's commentating on a game I'm listening to. I know he's an over-opinionated Scouse-loving t★★★. I know he's the only commentator out there – actually he could be the only person out there – who looks like a cross between a mad monk and a coconut (though that doesn't stop him criticising what players look like★). And I know he's got a terrible habit of moaning his way through bad games, completely forgetting that he's getting paid for the privilege of watching the biggest games – while the rest of us are paying through the nose.

But you've got to hand it to him. When it comes to painting a picture of the game, there's no one to touch him. When it comes to calling a game he puts most of the so-called experts – think no-marks like Bright, Beglin and Claridge – in the shade. And when it comes to getting himself off the fence and saying something sensible or controversial or both – the stuff that could provoke anything from a debate to a riot – he's different class. Tonight he managed the impossible. He managed to get a rise out of Fulham and their fans, a group I always figured would be amongst the most placid in the game. In fact he annoyed them so much that Fulham's communications officer ordered Roy Hodgson not to talk to the BBC after the game.

So what did Green do that got them so wound up? Did he make jokes about Jimmy Hill's famous features and Hugh Grant's film career, or say that Harrods sells overpriced crap? No... Apparently he peppered his commentary on FiveLive with barbs about Fulham's lack of fight and ambition and suggested that they shouldn't have bothered turning up. That's right, that's the same Fulham side who turned up at Old Trafford for the 4th year in a row, crapped themselves and walked off pleased it was only three.

It wasn't exactly holocaust denying was it...?

* *Stones and glasshouses Al, stones and glasshouses...*

GOAL ACTION

1-0 (12): Mark Schwarzer has given United fans plenty of fond memories over the years, none better than the butter-fingered howler that gifted Beckham his late, late winner against Boro back in 2000 (for those who don't remember it, it was the same day that Jaap's head veins nearly popped and Keano nearly ripped Andy D'Urso's arms off). This was another one to add to the collection, the Australian allowing Scholes's fine volley from a corner routine (a rerun of his effort against Spurs in the Cup) to squirm under him and over the line. Surprisingly, it was Scholesy's first league goal for 18 months, since the 1-1 draw at Portsmouth way back in August 2007.

2-0 (30): Schwarzer wasn't quite as culpable for United's second but he didn't half make himself look silly, first charging out of goal to intercept Scholes's deft flick, then getting beaten to the ball by the lunging O'Shea and finally scrambling across goal like a drunk alligator in a vain attempt to stop Berbatov tapping the ball into the empty net...

3-0 (63): And he was completely in the clear for United's third, Rooney turning Park's cross-cum-shot into the net at the far post.

WHAT WAS GOOD?

ROONEY'S BACK - Van der Sar jumps to sixth in the all-time list of clean sheets in league football with a 14th straight shut-out and Scholes rolls back the years in midfield, thumping in a volley that most mortals would never have attempted, running the legs off the Fulham midfield with his rat-a-tat-tat one-twos and vaporising their defence with 50 yard missiles on to the toes of Ronaldo. Like I say elsewhere, he might not be the man for the truly big games any more but what a player to call on for nights like this…

FULHAM – THE VERBALS

"I think they have played into our hands and that the title race now is going to be between ourselves and Liverpool. I was shocked that Chelsea should part so soon with a manager of such great experience and proven success as Phil Scolari." – *Fergie rules out Chelsea after their knee-jerk decision to dump Scolari.*

"Some of his [Scholesy's] switches of play were absolutely magnificent. He and Ryan [Giggs] remain great examples to young players in how they live their lives and we are proud to have them here. It was a fabulous hit." – *Fergie raves about his old guns.*

'We always co-operate with the media and never complain about fair criticism. But Alan Green's comments about Fulham appalled some of our fans, who made their views known on the message boards or contacted me during the game. I also listened to some of his commentary myself and remarks like 'Fulham should not have bothered to turn up' were insulting. In those circumstances, I didn't feel it appropriate for Five Live to speak to our manager.' *Fulham's head of communications, Sarah Brooks.*

VIEWS FROM THE PRESSBOX

"There is a fundamental difference of opinion inside Old Trafford. Sir Alex Ferguson chose Fulham's visit last night to declare the Premier League title race officially a two-horse contest. His Manchester United players, however, suggest there may be even fewer runners in the final straight. The reigning champions cashed in their game in hand for a five-point lead over Liverpool at the summit with a simplicity and authority that illustrated how slim the margin of error has become for Rafael Benítez's team. There was an exhibition feel to this defeat of Roy Hodgson's meagre travellers as Wayne Rooney scored within two minutes of his return from injury and the only concern for United lay in enhancing Edwin van der Sar's clean-sheet record. Untouchable, Arsène Wenger said of United this week, although title challenges should be more fraught than this." – *The Guardian reckons it's as good as ours.*

LINE OF THE DAY

"We showed up, rolled over, and went home." *The Fulham fans on the Craven Cottage Newsround website don't seem to have too big of an axe to grind with Alan Green.*

REVIEW OF THE DAY

Also from the Craven Cottage website...

"One of those games that is best forgotten about as quickly as possible – there is no point in worrying about a defeat like this. Manchester United exist on such a different level that a 3-0 victory against the tenth best team in the country is utterly routine and unexciting – the players barely celebrating their goals, the atmosphere amongst 70,000 spectators muted (at best), and the ground half empty with five minutes remaining. We never looked like upsetting the apple cart – perhaps lacking the necessary 'fight' and belief or perhaps simply hypnotised, and left hopeless, by our opponents' sublime play."

STATS OF THE DAY

VAN DER SAR has now gone 1,302 minutes without conceding in the league.

FULHAM STRIKER BOBBY ZAMORA hasn't scored in the league in 1,702 minutes.

MATCH FACTS

UNITED: VAN DER SAR, O'SHEA (EVANS 62), FERDINAND, VIDIC, EVRA, RONALDO, CARRICK (GIBSON 69), SCHOLES, PARK, BERBATOV (ROONEY 61), TÉVEZ
BOOKED: PARK.
FULHAM: SCHWARZER, PANTSIL (DACOURT 67), HANGELAND, HUGHES, KALLIO, BAIRD, GERA (BROWN 86), MURPHY (MILSOM 80), DAVIES, DEMPSEY, ZAMORA.
BOOKED: PANTSIL.
ATT: 75,437 REF: ANDRE MARRINER (W MIDLANDS) H-T: 2-0

LEAGUE TABLE

1. UNITED 59 (25) 2. LIVERPOOL 54 (25) 3. VILLA 51 (25)
4. CHELSEA 49 (25)...10. FULHAM 30 (24)

"My hero was Andy Ritchie, always has been and always will be."

NEWS

GARY NEVILLE GETS another year's contract. Fergie calls him amazing. But is it going too far to ask if he really deserved one – as a player at least? And does he really need the 'G' on his shirt any more? Ronaldo gets a £20,000 bill from Manchester Airport for crashing into the bridge. It sounds a bit steep... until you remember his day's wages will just about cover it. The FA announces that Mark Clattenburg, who's been suspended since the summer for allegedly sending those naughty emails, will be back refereeing (badly) shortly. I wonder if players will think twice about giving him stick now. Vidic is linked, not for the first or last time, with a move to Milan. And in news that must have sent Benitez's blood pressure rocketing, Arsenal fan Ian Watmore replaces Liverpool fan Brian Barwick as the FA's chief executive. To make Benitez's day even brighter, it turns out Watmore has got a son in the United academy.

STAT OF THE WEEK

United have not lost a league game in which Paul Scholes has scored since 2001. (And we've never lost a game in which Gary Neville's scored)

RUMOUR OF THE WEEK
From the Sun:

"ALEX FERGUSON dumped teen ace Danny Welbeck into the reserves for being too cocky. The Manchester United boss was incensed by the striker's Eric Cantona-style goal celebration in Sunday's FA Cup win over Derby.

"A United source revealed: "Alex was very angry about the way Welbeck celebrated his goal at Derby. He felt there was a touch of arrogance about it. Danny is just a kid and Alex does not like the thought of him getting too big for his boots.""

ABSOLUTE NONSENSE
Fergie wastes no time stamping all over the Welbeck rumour:

"One newspaper said Danny was disciplined for his goal

celebration at Derby. That's absolute nonsense. Danny needed football. He came on against Derby and now he's got a full game against Wigan's Reserves, where he scored two goals. He'll be available for the Carling Cup final."

UNNECESSARY WARNING OF THE WEEK

"Don't even think about Manchester United and Stoke in the same breath" - *Tony Pulis on Sky Sports News. Que?*

CONTRIVED INTRO OF THE WEEK
'Wordy' Henry Winter in The Daily Telegraph:
'Someone needs to tell Paul Scholes, Michael Carrick and Dimitar Berbatov that Old Trafford is a no-smoking stadium because they had the cigars out here on Wednesday night.'

QUOTES OF THE WEEK

"I don't think there is anybody else in the world like Paul Scholes." – *Dimitar Berbatov worships Scholesy.*

"My hero was Andy Ritchie, always has been and always will be." – *Scholesy worships Andy Ritchie.*

"I used to love Giggsy so much - and still do. I could say he's my idol." – *And Danny Welbeck worships Giggs.*

"Defeat at Manchester United was embarrassing — not just for me but for all of us. I can barely remember when we lost a game like that. " – *Six weeks on, Drogba's still struggling come to terms with Chelsea's thrashing.*

"He (Thaksin Shinawatra) had his problems back in Thailand. He just said after sacking me, 'Sven I love you'. And I actually still believe it was from the heart" - *Sven Goran Eriksson on his unlikeliest love affair since Ulrika.*

FAPL 21/02/2009

UNITED 2 BLACKBURN 1
Rooney 23, Santa Cruz 32, Ronaldo 60

IT TOOK VAN der Sar the best part of four months to make history. It took Tommy Kuszczak 32 minutes against Blackburn to cock everything up for him. But once the game was over, and the points were in the bag, it was clear it was no bad thing that the epic clean sheet run was finally over. It wasn't just that it was getting boring to read about the record. There was much more to it than that. Even Rio admitted the record was affecting how we were playing, leaving us in the mindset of conceding fewer goals than our opponents rather than scoring more. It just wasn't like United. Let's get back to piling everything into attack and not worrying about the odd slip at the back.

Mind you, most of us would have settled for another 1-0 for much of this game. United were brilliant early on. We were 1-0 up courtesy of Nani and Rooney, we had 81% of possession (the ball boys had most of the other 19%) and we had Blackburn just where we wanted them. By the throat. But then a comedy of errors combined to transform the afternoon. Nani fannied away possession in midfield, Scholesy acted as his accomplice and as the ball was slid into the area Kuszczak had a Leighton moment, getting his angles all wrong and taking out Ferdinand instead of Santa Cruz who easily scored.

Then something interesting happened – something that showed how important it was that United's clean sheet marathon didn't end in a bigger game, against a better team (Inter next Tuesday for example). United got a bad case of the jitters and Blackburn woke up and smelled blood. They could have scored when Nelson hit the post. They should have scored again when Pederson was taken down by Rafael in the area – though Pederson didn't help his cause by collapsing at the merest hint of a touch. But a mixture of good goalkeeping, bad refereeing and good luck allowed us to clear our heads. And that gave Ronaldo the platform to remind us of his supreme ability from free-kicks. So far this season most of his free-kicks had crashed against the wall (leading to a drearily predictable fit of posturing and dry-eyed blubbering as the referee refused a retake). While those that had gone in had come against small fry like Stoke or at times when they didn't really matter. This one was different. It mattered. It was also incredibly difficult. As Ronaldo did his trick with the valve and stepped backwards, it seemed almost ridiculous he was going to shoot rather than cross. But as soon as the ball exploded off his foot you just knew that Paul Robinson was a beaten keeper. And for a minute it felt that the Madrid nonsense had never happened. For the first time all season Viva Ronaldo was back in fashion again…

MATCH ACTION

1-0 (23): That was no exaggeration earlier about United enjoying 81% of possession in the first half-hour or so. But we only had this one goal to show for our complete mastery. Nani curls in a peach of a low centre into the no-man's land separating Robinson and his centre-backs, the lunging Nelson does well to get some sort of touch on the ball but he can only make it sit up for Rooney who can't miss.

1-1 (32): Nani and Scholes combine to allow Ooijer to seize possession and drive into United territory before sliding in Santa Cruz. Ferdinand seems to have the threat under control until the Pole in goal emerges from stage left, wipes out his captain and leaves Santa Cruz with an open goal gift. After 1333 minutes of Premier League action United are finally made to take a kick-off in the middle of a game.

2-1! NO! (45): There was plenty of Benitez-style griping after the game following the Pederson penalty incident and also Howard Webb's refusal to caution Ronaldo - who would later be booked for diving - for flicking out at David Dunn. One fact the conspiracy theorists conveniently overlooked was that United were victims of arguably the worst decision of all on the brink of half-time when Evans's thumping header from Nani's corner was ruled out for a phantom push.

2-1 (60): Evra's taken out on the left side of the Blackburn box. You know the rest…

PEN! NO!: Pederson gets in front of Rafael who puts his arms on the Norwegian. Pederson goes down expecting a penalty. Somehow he doesn't get one. Cue another bout of media hand-wringing about teams being robbed at OT. Yawn.

WHAT WAS GOOD?

THE FIRST 30 MINUTES AND THAT GOAL. The best of the season so far?

WHAT WAS BAD?

KUSZCZAK – Hasn't got a cat in hell's chance of making it big at United has he? And, as he showed here, his key weakness is his inability to pick the right time to leave his line. When there's a cross that's practically begging for him to come and claim (as was the case for Kalou's crucial equalizer at Stamford Bridge in September) Kuszczak looks like his boots are nailed to the whitewash. When forwards are running towards him he tears out of goal like a deranged mongrel. Santa Cruz might have scored his goal if he had stayed put. Kuszczak's rush of blood made it a certainty.

HOWARD WEBB – Another bad afternoon for England's 'premier' referee, who should have allowed Evans's goal, given Pederson his penalty and sent Rafael off. How long before the authorities twig that his physique and shaven skull make him seem a far better referee than he actually is?

RONALDO'S HABIT OF FLICKING OUT AT OPPONENTS. He'd already done it to Celtic's Scott Brown, Stoke nobody Andy Wilkinson and Michael Dawson of Spurs. Here he added David Dunn to the list. Now only a card-carrying member of the ABU Brigade would argue that any of the incidents were worthy of a red card on their own but the more he does it, the harder it gets to defend him...

UNITED'S DEFENSIVE NIGHTMARE (PART 17). Arguably the most impressive part of United's clean sheet marathon was that it was achieved in a season when United have been consistently short of bodies at the back. Only Vidic has managed to avoid the injury jinx which claimed two more names in this game – Rafael, who fractured his ankle, and Evans, who damaged his hamstring.

VIEWS FROM THE PRESSBOX

"When a thin, almost gawky George Best first began to reveal his genius, a journalist, noting the time of one of his goals, was told he should remember the date. When, at just after 6pm on 21 February 2009, Roque Santa Cruz became the first man since Samir Nasri three-and-a-half months before to score against Manchester United in the league the time of the goal seemed irrelevant.

"That it was not decisive was due to the intervention of a man with whom comparisons with Best do not seem ridiculous. On the hour mark, when Blackburn appeared almost in control and Sam Allardyce had just seen Ryan Nelsen drive a shot against the foot of the post, Manchester United won a free-kick by the left-hand edge of the box around 12 yards out.

"The angle was acute, the three-man wall seemed more than sufficient. Cristiano Ronaldo had perhaps one spot to aim at – the top right-hand corner of Paul Robinson's net and found it with staggering precision. He may not be the player he was last season

– and it would be impossible even for Sir Alex Ferguson to imagine he might scale those heights. And he might be bound for Madrid, but it is moments like these that make him precious." – *The Guardian on the genius of Ronaldo.*

"Ferguson has rarely strayed from his seat in the stands in recent months, such has been the ease with which United have brushed aside the opposition. It said everything about the threat Blackburn posed that the United manager was glued to the touchline in the second half, barking orders at Ferdinand for not communicating with Rafael, before throwing on Vidic in the hope of shoring up his defence after Evans limped out." – *The Times gives an idea of how nervy this one was.*

BLACKBURN – THE VERBALS

"We're having a nightmare with defenders this season – Gary, Wes, John O'Shea missed the game and now Evans with his ankle. Hopefully we can patch up for Tuesday because it does leave us very, very short. I just hope we can get two centre-backs out there. At this moment in time, it's very doubtful." – *Fergie frets about the Inter game. Richard Eckersley v Adriano anyone?*

MATCH FACTS

UNITED: KUSZCZAK, RAFAEL DA SILVA, FERDINAND, EVANS (VIDIC 64), EVRA, RONALDO, CARRICK, SCHOLES (GIGGS 82), NANI (TÉVEZ 64), ROONEY, BERBATOV
BOOKED: RONALDO, BERBATOV.
BLACKBURN: ROBINSON, OOIJER, NELSEN, GIVET, WARNOCK, GRELLA (MCCARTHY 79), DIOUF (TREACY 83), ANDREWS, DUNN (KERIMOGLU 73), PEDERSEN, ROQUE SANTA CRUZ [ALLARDYCE]
ATT: 75,000 REF: HOWARD WEBB H-T: 1-1

OTHER SCORES

ARSENAL 0 SUNDERLAND 0, VILLA 0 CHELSEA 1, LIVERPOOL 1 CITY 1

LEAGUE TABLE

1. UNITED 62 (26) 2. LIVERPOOL 55 (26) 3. CHELSEA 52 (26) 4. VILLA 51 (26)… 18. BLACKBURN 23 (25)

*"Another year wasted, another title campaign in ruins…
and that's a fact."*

NEWS

FOR THEIR LATEST publicity stunt Paddy Power pay out on United winning an unprecedented domestic treble. We haven't even got our hands on a single trophy yet. That's right Rafa, the Community Shield still doesn't count. Ole turns down the Norwegian coach's job. Darren Fletcher's fiancee and mother-in-law are victims of a nasty armed robbery at home in Bowdon. Jose Mourinho lies back and licks himself as the pre-Inter talk focuses on his record against Fergie – just one defeat in 12 games. And United's defensive crisis – Rafael joining Brown, Vidic, Neville and possibly Evans on the sidelines – leaves Reds in the strange position of praying that John O'Shea is fit to play in central defence in the San Siro. Here's hoping that Ibrahimovic really is as overrated as he looks against everyone else…

THE END OF FOOTBALL
Middlesbrough send a letter to their fans complaining – of all things - about them making too much noise:

'I am receiving more and more complaints from our own fans also seated in the area about both the persistent standing and the constant banging and noise coming from the back of this stand. Please stop, make as much noise as you like when we score, but this constant noise is driving some fans mad.' *By the way, I thought it was only us Reds who were guilty of persistent standing at the Riverside. Or was that just a thin excuse for Boro to give us less tickets for the one game they reckon they can actually sell out?*

'DIDN'T THINK THAT ONE THROUGH' COMMENT OF THE WEEK
From football365:

"You need to be trustworthy" - *Tahli Grobbelaar, daughter of Bruce, lists one of the qualities required by to be a football agent in BBC's 'Superagents'.*

SHOVE IT UP YOUR BOLLOCKS

Keano's rent-a-rants are normally entertaining. But I'm worried. This latest outburst – his first since leaving Sunderland – just makes him sound bitter...

"The day I walked into Sunderland, putting a smile on the faces of well-paid players was the last thing anybody wanted me to do. Players had been taking the piss out of the club for years. If they wanted them smiling all the time they should have employed Roy Chubby Brown.

"He [former Sunderland defender Clive Clarke] went on loan to Coventry, and on a night we got beaten in the cup to Luton the staff came in and said 'Clive Clarke has had a heart attack at Leicester'. I said, 'Is he okay? I'm shocked they found one, you could never tell by the way he plays'. But Clive Clarke goes and does a piece in some newspaper telling the world that I have lost the dressing-room. He wasn't there! How does he know? Clown!"

"Alex Ferguson. My old manager comes out and says, 'You never know what he is going to do next'. What did he think I was going to do? Go backpacking around Mexico? I've got five kids! Football is in my blood! I'd just had enough at Sunderland. Things had changed. End of bloody story." *Any need?*

CANCEL EVERYTHING

Big news, MUTV are launching a new programme (I like Paddy's quote though):

"SIR Alex Ferguson and his Man United stars are appearing in a COOKERY show — called Red Devils Kitchen. French defender Patrice Evra, 27, was first to woo judges, with a lobster ravioli last night on United's TV channel MUTV. He said: "I made it with all my heart." Also taking part are Bryan Robson and Denis Irwin." – from *The Sun*.

QUOTE OF THE WEEK

"I can't wait. I wore the red shirt for many years and now I play for Milan. How could I support anyone else?" – *Becks, slowly returning to his rightful position as a Red legend, looks forward to being an away fan in the San Siro.*

DEBATE OF THE WEEK

This week United announce they are going to ban autograph hunters at Carrington on the basis that they 'have had too many opportunists selling on signed merchandise'.

You can see their point. It's got to be irritating to see the same chancers popping up with stuff for you to sign every week. But what's better? Getting the better of a few scallies seeking to make a few quid? Or giving the next generation of Reds the chance to meet their heroes? I know which option I'd go for.

INTRO OF THE WEEK
Henry Winter, on form again in The Telegraph, *reporting on Liverpool's home draw with City at the weekend:* "Another year wasted, another title campaign in ruins… and that's a fact."

24/02/2009
CL LAST 16 (1ST LEG)

INTER 0 UNITED 0

ATTACK IS THE best form of defence, or so the old cliché goes. But, as Inter found out to their cost here, keeping the ball to yourself comes a close second. Before the game there was plenty of talk of what Ibrahimovic and Adriano would do to a United defence featuring Berbatov, George Schwitzer and Mickey Phelan (or whoever else Fergie – in classic smokescreen mode – had hinted would play). 90 minutes later it still wasn't clear. Neither of Inter's big-name forwards played up to their reputations, admittedly, but so tight was United's grip on the midfield that they never really had a chance. Giggs was excellent, so was Fletcher while Carrick - the English Pirlo - was simply princely. In fact just about everyone turned it on as United fashioned their finest ever performance at the San Siro (actually our only performance there - let's face it, we've basically stunk the place out every other time we've been here). The one downside was that we didn't force the result the passing, the interplay and the cascade of first-half chances deserved. And that spelt trouble, for two reasons. First, 0-0 is a dangerous score to bring back to Old Trafford, as Trezeguet's thunderbolt and Keano's own goal showed in previous Euro campaigns. Oh and then there was the Mourinho factor. He dashed off before the end here, ducking into the bowels of the San Siro even before he and Fergie could hug, but he'll be back in the limelight in Manchester alright. And planning another charge towards the East Stand...

MOMENTS THAT MATTERED
(the condensed version)

What. The. Heck. Fergie names his team and while Evans and O'Shea are in (great news), there's no room for Rooney (weird news). Fergie tells ITV that he's chosen Berbatov because he's better at defending set-pieces. Can you imagine Barcelona benching Messi because he can't mark giant centre-halves? Of course not. Anyway the absence of Rooney doesn't really matter as United fly out of the traps. Ronaldo sets the tone, slamming a free-kick straight down relieved keeper Cesar's throat and then thumping a header into his guts. Giggs makes and squanders the night's best chance, taking Vivas back to school with a neat turn but then getting caught between shooting and squaring and allowing Cesar to smother. Ronaldo's back in the spotlight, slamming a violent wobbler of a free-kick against the outside of the post and then heading wide with Cesar a spectator. Half-time arrives. How is it 0-0? Inter finally make a chance but Adriano scuffs his shot hideously from 8 yards. Ronaldo's burst and an absolute slut of a cross (it was begging for it) somehow evades Park, Berbatov and Giggs. Giggs, all feints and dropped shoulders, cuts in from the right but his shot is blocked by Cordoba's superbly-timed sprawl. Rooney comes on for Park and immediately makes an impression. He's booked. Ronaldo is taken down by Cordoba. He's booked. Ronaldo's free-kick thunders over the wall but straight at the impressive Cesar, who looks amazed that the ball's in his hands. And that's it. United fail to score for the 5th time in 6 visits to the San Siro. Inter get lucky. Roll on OT.

VIEWS FROM THE PRESSBOX (THE ENGLISH SIDE)

"So nearly 11 Special Ones. So nearly Manchester United's night. With the near faultless Michael Carrick leading the way, the European champions gave Jose Mourinho's disappointing Inter a masterclass in the art of possession, particularly in the first half. United left the San Siro goalless only because of Inter's superb goalkeeper, Julio Cesar.

"Carrick and company arrived back home in the small hours with plenty to declare. They could declare that, on this evidence, Premier League sides are more watchable than Serie A. They could declare that Inter's much-vaunted striker, Zlatan Ibrahimovic, still has to justify his rave local reviews. They could also declare a real pride in this mature display, in the way Carrick, Ryan Giggs and Darren Fletcher worked triangles around black-and-blue shirts. Mourinho's men chased shadows in red." – *The Telegraph*

"As this magnificent theatre was enshrouded with mist at the final whistle last night, José Mourinho performed a vanishing act, disappearing down the tunnel and leaving Sir Alex Ferguson looking mildly flummoxed. It was just about the only surprise that Inter Milan produced on an evening when they were outplayed on their own pitch, but no doubt it was a calculated act designed to leave the Manchester United manager with something to think about before the second leg at Old Trafford in a fortnight." – *The Times*

"In the end, they passed their test with distinction. Sir Alex Ferguson could have been forgiven if he had had misgivings about the fitness of Jonny Evans and John O'Shea, but the players of Internazionale were simply not good enough and not quick enough with their passing or their movement to take advantage.

"That was the lesson of the evening: that this Inter side, when you take away all the posturing of Jose Mourinho, are not actually that impressive. A better side would surely have done more to single out Evans on a night when the young centre-half had to play the biggest match of his life with a badly swollen ankle. Or they would have cottoned on much earlier to the fact that O'Shea, also playing after a late fitness test, might be vulnerable if Zlatan Ibrahimovic went directly against him.

"What could not have been expected was that United, facing such esteemed opponents and with Nemanja Vidic, Gary Neville and Wes Brown all unavailable, would look as comfortable as at any stage of that recent record-breaking run when they managed to go 1,334 minutes without conceding a league goal." – *The Guardian*

VIEWS FROM THE PRESSBOX (THE ITALIAN SIDE)

"This was an intense match, full of danger and suffering for Inter, who were kept on the ropes by a stronger and more dangerous squad. Ronaldo was a constant threat. His speed was hard to match and when Davide Santon succeeded, the fans cheered as if their team had scored." - *Gazzetta dello Sport*

"Ferguson yet again failed to beat Mourinho – this was their 13th meeting, with a single win for the Scottish maestro – but that was the only consolation for Inter from an evening when everything seemed negative ... there was overwhelming evidence of the technical and tactical superiority of the European champions ... the first half was terrible ... the only downside for United was their failure to score ... Inter returned to their changing room stunned by this display of great football ... Manchester gave the impression of being superior to Inter in every area." - *La Repubblica*

TOP MARKS

Interesting stuff from the Corriere dello Sport in their United ratings section:

FERGUSON: 7.5 – Another type of football compared to Mourinho's. Manchester keep the ball on the ground with quick passes and control possession. They play a genuine, beautiful and complete game. And if it's true that they attack more at Old Trafford.......

RONALDO: 7 – Where does Cristiano pop up from? From the wing? Maybe. Down the middle? Possibly. But sure enough he pops up all of a sudden, like a whirlwind creating no end of danger for Inter's defence. He started the game like the world player of the year should – stamping his class on the match. There was just one problem he faced: Julio Cesar. He tried beating him in all manner of ways: headers, free kicks, shots all to no avail.

EVRA: 7 – His linking with Park on the left was superb attacking and defending relentlessly creating problems for Zanetti.

PARK: 7 – Played out wide on the left causing problems for Inter throughout the game playing wide and deep, a striker that can defend. An all action player who never stops running.

FLETCHER: 7 – Manchester's playmaker together with Carrick. Closes down, covers and sets up play with skill and an excellent positional sense.

CARRICK: 7 – Fletcher's twin brother. They have built up an excellent understanding and gave a faultless display keeping the ball on the ground.

EVANS: 6.5 – Ferguson thinks very highly of this player and was a surprise selection. In the end he wasn't seriously tested by Ibrahimovic and Adriano and had a quiet night next to Ferdinand.

O'SHEA: 6.5 – Safe, careful and precise. Never caught out of position.

FERDINAND: 6.5 – The physical battle with Ibrahimovic and Adriano was rough but fair and he did well in front of the England manager.

GIGGS: 6.5 – Playing behind Berbatov the team missed his crosses from the left. Despite the passing of the years, his talent remains intact. Allowed Cordoba to recover when he had a great chance to score.

Berbatov: 6 – Given the nod over Rooney and Tévez as the lone striker but didn't leave his mark on the game.

MOURINHO – THE VERBALS

"The team that plays at home in the second leg is always happy to do so but in my opinion it is now 50-50 for both teams, United played with great intensity and great speed but they did not score. " – *Shock news… Jose's confident*

"My dugout is a special dugout because we have a door which gives me the chance to leave it directly. Yesterday I left a £300 bottle of wine in the hotel with a note saying we would meet each other after the game at Old Trafford. I am always close to him and we are always friends and I will be there for him after the second game." – *Mourinho plays down the lack of a handshake with Fergie. (PS: I love the fact the Special One has a special dug-out)*

"It seems to me that Ibra had a good match. Manchester aren't Bologna," *Mourinho tries his best to defend the performance of the man he claimed was better than Ronaldo (he's just not).*

SAN ZERO

United's record at the San Siro now stands at played 6, won 0, drawn 2 and lost 4, goals for 1, goals against 11.

Out of interest, here's our record away to Europe's other elite teams (surprisingly, before 1999 we hadn't won at any of them)…

Real Madrid P 4 W 0 D 2 L 2 F 5 A 9
Juventus P 6 W 2 D 0 L 4 F 7 A 9
Barcelona P 4 W 0 D 2 L 2 F 3 A 9
Bayern Munich P 3 W 0 D 2 L 1 F 4 A 5

MATCH FACTS

Inter Milan: Julio Cesar, Maicon, Rivas (Cordoba 46), Chivu, Santon, Zanetti, Cambiasso, Muntari (Cruz 76), Stankovic, Ibrahimovic, Adriano (Balotelli 77) [Mourinho]
Booked: Toldo, Chivu, Maicon, Cordoba
United: Van der Sar, O'Shea, Ferdinand, Evans, Evra, Fletcher, Carrick, Giggs, Park (Rooney 83), Berbatov, Ronaldo
Booked: Fletcher, Rooney
San Siro Att: 84,000 **Ref:** Luis Medina Cantalejo (Sp) **h-t:** 0-0

OTHER SCORES

Lyon 1 Barcelona 1, Arsenal 1 Roma 0, R Madrid 0 Liverpool 1, Chelsea 1 Juventus 0

*"They have an intensity to their game we don't have.
They are sprinters"*

NEWS

It's FAIR TO say it's not been the best of seasons for Wesley B. First he gets blamed for the Liverpool defeat, then Rafael arrives to take his place, then his old injury curse strikes again and this week he's banned from driving for shooting a red light. Three United supporters need hospital treatment for minor-ish injuries after being attacked by a group of Inter fans after the San Siro draw. The incident barely gets a mention in the press. Imagine what would have happened if three Italians had had their noses broken on Chester Road. Rick Parry, Liverpool's chief executive and piggy-in-the-middle in the feud between the club's owners Gillett and Hicks, finally walks away.

LIVING IN THE EIGHTIES

Corriere dello Sport explains why United fans often get a rough ride on the road. It seems that the continentals still presume we're going to kick off:

"Despite the presence of large numbers of English fans in the city centre (four thousand tickets were sent to Manchester with at least another two thousand coming from other sources) there were no violent incidents."

RIGHT HAND MEET LEFT

"Look at what's happened under Rick [Parry]. It has been a disaster... We have fallen so far behind the other leading clubs...You have to be able to work with the manager and Rick has proved he can't do that" - *Liverpool co-owner Tom Hicks, April 17 2008.*

"I would like to thank Rick for his significant service to the Club and the assistance he has given us since we joined Liverpool. He has been integral to the club's success over the past decade and leaves with our best wishes for the future" - *Liverpool co-owner George Gillett, February 27 2009*

SHHHHH
Nice Arsenal dig from football365:

Cricket is an altogether more genteel sport than the rough and tumble of football, and Test Match Special commentator Jonathan Agnew is more genteel than most, if his comments towards the end of the first day of the Test last night were anything to go by:

"With all this football chanting it sounds like the Emirates Stadium in London!"

Cripes Aggers - you really never have been to a football game, have you? *(In truth, apart from Chelsea the Old Trafford atmosphere has been nothing to write about this year)*

EMAIL EXCHANGE OF THE WEEK
Another quality spot from football365: The follow appeared on the 'Reader's Letters' section of the ever-entertaining Jeff Winter's website earlier this month. Enjoy:

'From: David Harris, 8th February 2009

You're a C★★t!

Jeff's reply:

"Thanks for your comments, much appreciated. Perhaps you should have added "rich successful c★★t who has actually made something of his life".

By the way who the f★★k are you? "

Best wishes

Jeff

David Harris responds:

"Thank you for your reply. It is amazing that you find time to reply, being such a busy and in demand man.

"Unfortunately, it appears that some 'joker' has used my email address to write a hurtful and entirely unwarranted comment to yourself. For that I can only apologise.

"I have long been a fan of you as a referee and in general as a human being. I often enjoy nothing more than turning on Sky Sports News to watch you give your highly valued and respected views on the major incidents that have occurred during the Premiership weekend.

"I now find myself watching for referees' mistakes and thinking to myself 'Would Jeff Winter have made that decision? I don't think so' or 'What would Jeff Winter do here?'.

"And I also never hold the fact you are a Middlesbrough fan

against you. In fact, it is an endearing feature that such a man supports such a lowly club.

"I would quite like to find out who has been using my email address to do such a thing. But rest assured, that comment was sincerely not my view in any way, shape, or form and I would like to extend my sincerest apologies to you. I have long admired the 'refereeing legend and top media personality Jeff Winter' and the 'prolific writer and radio broadcaster'. Best Regards"

RUMOUR OF THE WEEK
Has Rafa cracked up for the last time? From The Times:

'Some bookmakers announced yesterday that they had suspended betting on Benitez's alleged "imminent" departure, with a spokesman for William Hill claiming that they would be "very surprised" is he was still the manager by midnight on Sunday."

QUOTE OF THE WEEK

"They have an intensity to their game we don't have. They are sprinters" – *Jose Mourinho, United fan.*

01/03/2009
CARLING CUP FINAL

UNITED 0 SPURS 0
(United win 4-1 on pens)
Pens: Giggs, O'Hara [missed], Tévez, Corluka, Ronaldo, Bentley [missed], Anderson

IT's A STRANGE thing about United. On most pitches we're the most exhilarating sight British football has to offer. But time and time again Wembley's pitch takes the pace and pizzazz out of our game and makes us look ordinary like everyone else. It's hard to remember a great Wembley performance under any of the five managers who've taken us there – Sir Alex, Big Ron, Dour Dave, the Doc or Sir Matt. Sure, we banged in four goals against Blackpool, Benfica, Brighton, Chelsea and Newcastle*. But for every Brighton there's a Sheffield Wednesday ('91), for every Newcastle '96 there's a Newcastle '99 and for every Chelsea there's a Chelsea '06. So would our latest trip to the world's most overpriced stadium kick-start a new era of entertaining football? Not a chance. Frankly it was one of the most tedious games Tottenham and United - both entertainers by tradition - have ever laid on.

But sod it. We'd won the cup. And that – remarkably – meant we only needed to win three more games in the FA Cup to complete the set...

HOW THE CUP WAS WON
- A MOMENT BY MOMENT GUIDE
(don't worry, it won't take long)

PREAMBLE: Fergie picks a fairly strong team with a pair of kids, Welbeck and Gibson, mixed in with Ferdinand, Scholes, Evra, Ronaldo and Tévez. Woodgate, who scored the winner against Chelsea in last season's final, fails a late fitness test on his Achilles, otherwise Spurs are at full strength. Weirdly – considering both team's reputation as Cup Kings – this is the first time United and Spurs have ever met at Wembley.

POST! (13): What. A. Shot. Gibson shaves the outside of the right post from 30 yards with Gomes nowhere.

OOH (24): Ferdinand almost scores the best goal by a United defender at Wembley ever, knocking a loose ball up on his thigh and then sending in a dipping 35 yard volley that beats Gomes but just beats the bar. Actually can you remember the last time a United defender scored any goal at Wembley?

OH DEAR (50): Spurs, and the jet-heeled Lennon in particular, are having a decent pop at us here, but they just don't look like they believe they can score. This free-kick from Pavlyuchenko won't help them out with that. Remember Brian McClair's last-minute penalty miss at Arsenal in the Cup in 1988, the one that threatened birds, planes and satellite stations? This was worse.

OOH, LUCKY BOY (64): O'Shea, who's already been booked, clumsily clatters into Modric from behind. If it hadn't been at Wembley, if he hadn't had a yellow card already, he'd have been booked for that.

PENALTY! NO! (67): But if that was a controversial moment, it had nothing on this. Ronaldo cuts inside the penalty area, King stands on his toe and Ronaldo goes over. It's a clear penalty. But Chris Foy books him for diving. Aye yay yay.

SAVE! (71): Great stuff from Foster, beating out Lennon's far-post rasper.

POST! AGAIN! (90+3): It's certainly not Ronaldo's day. He does Assou-Ekotto on the inside and smashes a left-footer against the near post with Gomes beaten. If Nani had taken a touch he'd have found the net from the rebound. Instead he goes for a first-timer, is surprised by the pace on the ball, and finds the side netting.

FULL TIME: UNITED 0-0 TOTTENHAM

ZZZZZ (94): Extra-time has only just beguin. But you just know this one's going to penalties. Spurs are knackered and have stopped attacking but they've just got enough strength left in them to stop United doing anything with all their possession. At least the lack of action gives me time to get back to you about that United defender goalscorer question. It was Ronnie Johnsen against Chelsea in the 1997 Charity Shield.

FINAL WHISTLE: UNITED 0-0 TOTTENHAM

Just to think in the old days they'd have dragged both sets of fans back to watch a rerun of this. Who says penalties are a bad thing? Here we go.

1-0 – YES! Giggsy in off the right post.

1-0 – YES! O'Hara tries to repeat Giggs's effort but Foster stretches out his left hand to beat it down. Great save.

2-0 – YES! Tévez scores with his favourite penalty, low to the keeper's left.

2-1 – Corluka chips it down the middle as Foster dives to his right.

3-1 – YES! Ronaldo makes up for Moscow, sending Gomes to his left and the ball to his right.

3-1 – YES! Almost over. Bentley drags his penalty wide.

4-1 – WINNERS! Anderson strikes his penalty low to his right and becomes the first player to score a winning goal for United who's never scored for United (if that makes sense). But it's Foster who's the real hero here, a great save from Lennon in normal time followed by a great save from O'Hara in the penalty shootout.

VIEW FROM THE PRESSBOX

Even the pressboys couldn't seem to gee themselves up for this one. This was about as exciting as the Monday's papers got:

"No prizes for guessing which brand of lager was waiting for Manchester United's victorious players as, their shirts drenched in cheap champagne, they returned to their dressing-room with the Carling Cup yesterday. No prizes, either, for guessing that they passed up the sponsors' kind offer or indeed that their winners' medals barely merited a second glance as thoughts drifted to the far bigger prizes that lie ahead.

"Nobody at Old Trafford seems sure if United are on course for a quadruple, a quintuple or a sextuple — depending on whether the Community Shield and the Club World Cup, already under lock and key, are regarded as trophies or mere baubles — but what is certain is that Sir Alex Ferguson's players have the winning habit, lusting after silver so desperately their victory seemed inevitable as, after 120 minutes of deadlock against a spirited Tottenham Hotspur, they prepared to settle the dispute on a penalty shoot-out." − *The Times*

CARLING CUP WINNERS – THE VERBALS

"The future is his. The present belongs to Van der Sar. Given that experience in a final, that strengthens his belief. I think he'll be England's goalkeeper for the next number of years" − *Fergie on his match-winner, Foster.*

"Just before the shoot-out I was looking at an iPod and on it were Tottenham's penalties, including one from O'Hara. They just told me to stand up, be strong and it will probably go that way. It is a new innovation." − *Foster reveals his secret weapon, an Ipod prepared by goalie coach Eric Steele showing where the Spurs players like to stick their penalties.*

"It would be great to think we could do it, but my experience says we could go to Fulham and a deflected shot off someone's backside and we're out of the FA Cup." − *Fergie on the chances of us winning the quadruple/quintuple/sextuple.*

MATCH FACTS

UNITED: FOSTER, O'SHEA (VIDIC 76), EVANS, FERDINAND, EVRA, RONALDO, SCHOLES, GIBSON (GIGGS 91), NANI, TÉVEZ, WELBECK (ANDERSON 56)
BOOKED: O'SHEA, RONALDO, SCHOLES
TOTTENHAM: GOMES, CORLUKA, DAWSON, KING, ASSOU-EKOTTO, LENNON (BENTLEY 102), JENAS (BALE 98), ZOKORA, MODRIC, BENT, PAVLYUCHENKO (O'HARA 65) [REDKNAPP]
WEMBLEY ATT: 88,217 REF: CHRIS FOY H-T: 0-0

OTHER SCORES

ARSENAL 0 FULHAM 0; MIDDLESBROUGH 2 LIVERPOOL 0;
CHELSEA 2 WIGAN 1

In 1948, 1968, 1983, 1994 and 1996

"I remember when they cuffed us 5-0.
They are still selling the video."

NEWS & GOSSIP

VIDIC IS STILL going to Milan apparently. Still can't see it. And Frank Ribery's coming to United. Can't see that either. Remember how easy Bayern were to deal with over Hargreaves? Wes and Rio are both going to use owls to deliver the rings at their weddings. Why? The FA confirm that Ben Foster won't face disciplinary action for using his iPod at the weekend (as if anyone thought he should). Though if it had been Paddy Evra checking out how Spurs players took their pens he'd already be on a one-way ticket to the colonies...

STRAW CLUTCHER OF THE WEEK

ARSENE WENGER: 'United Don't Dominate Games Like My Arsenal"
NEXT WEEK: "And Walcott looks better than Rooney in Red"

TECHNOPHILE OF THE DAY
From football365:

Said Ben Foster after a video on an iPod helped him work out where the Spurs players would put their penalties:

"It had actual video on it and showed where players put things. Eric brought it when he came to the club. I have never seen anything like it...The iPod is Eric's innovation. It's an amazing tool, you can brush up straight away."

PREDICTABLE HEADLINES OF THE WEEK
(from the Carling Cup win)

'**THE KING AND I-POD**' - *The Sun.* 2/10
'**HAND OF POD**' - *The Daily Star and The Times.* 3/10
'**THE I-POD HERO**' - *The Daily Mail.* 1/10
'**POD OF GOLD**' - *The Daily Express.* 0/10

OUCH BITCH

"If Berbatov returned it would be taken quite differently. I heard tales that he was an arrogant snob who after a training session would just throw his dirty boots to the man who takes care of our footwear saying: 'Clean them for me!' No one likes such people" - *Roman Pavlyuchenko isn't the biggest fan of his predecessor.*

'WHAT'S THE WORLD COMING TO' STORY OF THE WEEK
From the Daily Telegraph:

'The Football Association has been urged to introduce a "mercy rule" in youth soccer that would result in games being stopped if a team opens up a nine-goal lead. Supporters of the proposal claim it would prevent young players being humiliated and becoming disillusioned with the "beautiful game"...

'Ron Westerman, chairman of the league, in which more than 6,000 children play, said: 'We'd not be taking away victory or defeat, merely lessening its severity. Scorelines of 25-0 don't do anyone any favours, especially at age eight to ten. We've asked the FA to consider bringing this in nationwide, but at the moment it's just one of many things up for consultation." *Groan. Next they'll be changing it so the fat and four-eyed kits get picked first.*

THEY NEED US SO BAD
Jack Warner, FIFA vice-president and bosom buddy of Roy Keane, on the strength of England's bid for the 2018 World Cup:

"England has the ability and means to surpass other countries in the bidding. Only one country has Manchester United, David Beckham and Richard Scudamore."

QUOTES OF THE WEEK

"You have to ask yourself, is Robbie Keane the most complete footballer in the Premier League?" – *John Motson confuses the word footballer with the phrase 'biggest waste of money'.*

"It's just a media thing. It would be great to think we could do it, but my experience says we could go to Fulham next weekend, there will be a deflected shot off someone's backside and we're out of the FA Cup" – *Fergie plays down talk of the quintuple.*

"It's a fine line. I have watched Man United get an opening here and there and they are a great side. But I don't feel they dominate the games like we do" – *Everyone thinks they've got a better team at home, Arsene*

"The future is his. The present belongs to Edwin Van der Sar, that is obvious, but that performance can only strengthen my opinion of Ben's ability and his own self-confidence." – *Fergie on his I-pod keeper. Here's hoping he can stay fit.*

"Foster didn't have an iPod for David Bentley's penalty because he hadn't taken one before. He didn't have an iPod for (Vedran) Corluka's penalty because he had never seen him take one. We make big stories out of these things. We knew where they were going to put their penalties but saving them is a different thing. Ryan Giggs hits one off the post so how are you going to save that? They had better penalty takers than we did, but we get carried away with these stories. If I'd had Defoe, Keane and Pavlyuchenko I would have been confident." – *Harry Redknapp gets his pants in a twist over nothing (is he getting defensive because he knew that Gomes should have been given the same tool?)*

DIG OF THE WEEK

"I remember when they cuffed us 5-0. They are still selling the video." – *Fergie looks forward to the latest win, I mean, game at St James's Park.*

FAPL 04/03/2009

NEWCASTLE 1 UNITED 2
Lovenkrands 9, Rooney 20, Berbatov 56

NEWCASTLE HAVE BEEN doing their best to take City's crown as the undisputed kings of the cock-up pretty much every year since they got rid of Bobby Robson. This year they've finally gone and done it. From appointing Wise and undermining Keegan to giving Joey Barton yet another chance and bringing in a hospital case in the making as manager, Newcastle's season has been a lesson in doing everything wrong. On the pitch it's been no better with a run of one win in 12 matches before this game leaving them deep in the brown stuff (I don't mean beer). So it's strange that United have found the Geordies tougher opponents this season than they have for years. Last year we banged in 11 against them, this year we managed a scruffy 1-1 home draw on the opening day and now this, an equally unconvincing 2-1 win at St James's. Not that anyone was too fussed that United's football on a greasy pitch and freezing night was more White Lightning than champagne. Our eleventh straight league win meant we were now seven points clear. One more win in our next league game at home to Liverpool and we'd have the league sewn up by mid-March. Well, it seemed like a decent theory at the time...

MATCH ACTION

0-1 (9): You sort of knew it was going to happen... Either Van der Sar would allow his record run to be ended by a goal-of-the-season thunderbolt. Or he'd drop an almighty bollock. He took the bollock option, spilling Gutierrez's run-of-the-mill daisycutter and allowing former Rangers winger Lovenkrands to knock in his first Newcastle goal.

1-1 (20): For the first time in weeks United looked frail but Newcastle, for all their energy, could only contain United's class for 10 minutes before Rooney did what he does best – break Newcastle hearts. O'Shea works a slick one-two with Park, he squares the ball to Rooney and he spins and shoots left-footed into the top left corner. It's Rooney's ninth goal in eleven games against the team who had the nerve to try and sign him in 2004.

RED? NO. HUH? (45): United were marginally the better team for the rest of half and should have stolen a half-time lead when Vidic put a free header wide from Carrick's corner. At the very least they should have gone in a man up after Steven Taylor made out like Joey Barton at a Christmas do, first kicking Ronaldo, then throwing an arm at his neck and finally taking out Carrick. Bizarrely his three yellow card offences only result in one yellow card from Steve Bennett.

2-1 (56): Now here's a 'what if' moment for you. If Bennett had done the right thing and reduced Newcastle to 10 men United would have probably gone on to win the game. But if Taylor hadn't been on the pitch they wouldn't have scored their winning goal, not like this anway. Rooney's Hollywood ball from right to left should have been easy meat for the Newcastle right-back but instead of taking the safe option and heading clear he chests the ball back to his keeper. Park is quick to take advantage, winning his race with Harper before setting up Berbatov for a sidefoot into the empty net.

WINNERS

DANNY VERLINDEN – Van der Sar's blooper (which ended his impregnable streak in the league at 1,311 minutes) means that his 1,390 unbeaten minutes with Bruges in 1990 is still the record for Europe's top-flight domestic leagues.

LOSERS

NEWCASTLE – Just one point above the relegation zone having played a game more than their rivals. And, amazingly, heading for the Championship.

CHILDISH EXCHANGE OF THE DAY
(As overheard between Ronaldo and Taylor as they made their way down the tunnel at half-time, shortly after Taylor had lost his head)
    Ronaldo: "You're a rubbish footballer."
    Taylor: "At least I'm not ugly."
    Ronaldo: "But you're a rubbish footballer."
    Taylor: "I know, but you're still ugly."
    Sheer poetry...

ST JAMES'S – THE VERBALS

"He is a different type of player to what we had last season. He has a patience and composure in the last third of the field that is helping us. That is quite a number of winning goals for us now. Eric Cantona used to score important goals as well and if he keeps on scoring important goals then it is an emphatic result for us." - *Fergie can't resist the Berbatov-Cantona comparisons...*

"We do seem to have the momentum, just as we did in 1999. The most pleasing thing is that changing the team is not affecting us now. I've said before this is our best squad and I still believe that." – *... and pops in a 1999 one while he's at it.*

"Edwin says himself he made a mess of it, and they had a couple of near things after that. It was going to happen some time, and it is out of the road now." – *... before generously letting Van der Sar off the hook for his first mistake in six months.*

VIEWS FROM THE PRESSBOX

"It was not to be the night that prised open the contest for the title, but at least there was a tremor of uncertainty. Manchester United conceded a goal and, what is more, fell behind in the process. While a recovery to re-establish their seven-point lead was then completed, this was not the normal show of mastery." – *The Guardian*.

"It is one thing to rock Manchester United back on their heels, one thing to achieve the rare distinction of scoring against Edwin van der Sar, but it is another thing entirely to contemplate stopping them at present. Few teams will cause them more problems than they encountered in the first half at St James' Park last night, but by the end of a bitterly cold evening, normal service had been resumed, leaving one United to continue their quest for success on all fronts and the other to face up to an increasingly fraught battle against relegation." – *The Times*.

WORLD BEATERS

Van der Sar is stranded in 5th place in the list of keepers who've gone the longest time without conceding a goal

1,816 - Mazaropi (Vasco da Gama, Brazil) -- 5/77-9/78
1,442 - Thabet El-Batal (National SC Cairo, Egypt) -- 4/75-12/76
1,390 - Dany Verlinden (Club Brugge KV, Belgium) -- 3/90-9/90
1,352 - José María Buljubasich (CD Universidad Catolica Santiago, Argentina) 6/05-10/05
1,311 - Edwin Van der Sar (Manchester United, England) 11/08-02/09 (32 minutes by Kuszczak)
1,325 - Thabet El-Batal (National, Egypt) 3/78-2/79
1,288 - Essam El-Hadari (National, Egypt) 2/06-8/06
1,275 - Abel Resino (Atlético Madrid, Spain) 11/90-3/91
1,266 - Gaëtan Huard (Bordeaux, France) 12/92-4/93
1,242 - Zetti (Palmeiras, Brazil) 4/87-5/87
(stats from iffhs)

MATCH FACTS

NEWCASTLE: HARPER, STEVEN TAYLOR, COLOCCINI, BASSONG, JOSE ENRIQUE, LOVENKRANDS, RYAN TAYLOR (CARROLL 77), GEREMI, GUTIERREZ, MARTINS, SMITH (LUALUA 82) [HOUGHTON]
BOOKED: STEVEN TAYLOR, GUTIERREZ
UNITED: VAN DER SAR, O'SHEA, FERDINAND, VIDIC, EVRA, RONALDO, FLETCHER, CARRICK, PARK, BERBATOV (GIGGS 90), ROONEY.
BOOKED: VIDIC, FERDINAND.
ST JAMES'S PARK ATT: 51,636 REF: STEVE BENNETT H-T: 1-1

OTHER SCORES

PORTSMOUTH 0 CHELSEA 1; LIVERPOOL 2 SUNDERLAND 0; WBA 1 ARSENAL 3

LEAGUE TABLE

1. UNITED 65 (27) 2. CHELSEA 58 (28) 3. LIVERPOOL 58 (28) 4. VILLA 52 (28)... 16. NEWCASTLE 28 (28)

"I am playing the penalty shoot-out of my managerial career. I know that."

NEWS

UNITED RAID FEEDER club Royal Antwerp for 15 year-old forward Charni Ekangamene. It's the first time we've used our arrangement with Antwerp to buy a player rather than send our kids to gain experience and learn how to attack referees. Argentine side Banfield claim we're interested in their 23 year-old midfielder Nicolas Bertolo. Fergie comes out in support of Sepp Blatter's plans to introduce a '6 plus 5' rule, restricting the number of foreigners each club can play to five. It sounds like a decent idea – as long as the Welsh, Scottish and Irish aren't counted as foreigners this time. 15 months into his United career, Manucho scores his first goal in English football – for Hull at Fulham. Ashley Cole gets himself in trouble, first, with his missus (for chatting up a blonde in a nightclub) and then with the police (for getting abusive to the paparazzo who snapped them while they were chatting). Perhaps the most charming aspect of the whole affair was that while Cashley was getting himself banged up, the nation's new favourite Cheryl was hauling what remains of her backside up Kilimanjaro for charity.

NOSE-STRETCHING CLAIM OF THE WEEK
From The Sun:

"A source close to the 28-year-old England left back [Cole] insisted he and the beauty had been engaged in "an intellectual conversation".

FACT OF THE WEEK

'It is a curious fact that, since he joined Chelsea in August 2006, Ashley Cole has proffered more official public apologies than he has scored goals for the club that made him the best-paid left-back in the world' - *The Independent.*

SPECIAL TIMES

`He can be outrageous and he can be entertaining and funny and he's got a lot of great media tactics. But he knows it's his black and blues against the reds and there's nothing you can do once they cross the line. I'll rely on what I've got on the pitch.' — *You get the feeling Fergie's enjoying pitting himself against Mourinho again.*

"The great thing about Jose is he can laugh at himself and is able to separate what happens on the pitch and off it. He might lose a game but you can still have a conversation with him about anything and everything after it. It is important for managers to be able to communicate with each other and forget the game no matter what the result." — *A dig at Benitez perhaps?*

HIM MATURE

From football365: From Steven Taylor's profile on the Newcastle Official Website:

'Steven, a dominating and mature centre-half...'

Hmmm. And this the chap who apparently stopped just short of saying 'I know you are, you said you are, but what am I?' to Cristiano Ronaldo.

QUOTE OF THE WEEK

"I fear the idea of retiring. I have been on the train for so long that when I get off I fear my system will collapse. I am playing the penalty shoot-out of my managerial career. I know that." — *Fergie's on fire this week.*

RUNNER-UP

"At the end of January, something interesting happened with Van der Sar. When he beat the unbeaten record for a goalkeeper, he absolutely wanted to get the match ball. And he was so excited that in the dressing room he went and kissed each of his team-mates. At 38, achieving that still meant a lot to him. This made me proud. It means that maybe I have brought something to my players. I am like the keeper of the temple. For 23 years, it has been my motto to never let the perfectionism go." — *Fergie again.*

07/03/2009
FA CUP QUARTER-FINAL

FULHAM 0 UNITED 4

Tévez 20, 35, Rooney 50, Park 81

"THIS UNITED SIDE is as good as any team I've seen. Our pitch is very difficult yet the quality of their technique was fantastic, their movement is very good and when they get into the lead, you know how difficult it will be to get back into it. They know how to defend those leads, how to pressurise and soak up pressure. And when there is space in the counter-attack they know how to use it and they did that against us." – *Roy Hodgson*

Managers often use this tactic when their team gets a hammering. They ladle praise on the other side in the hope that they'll escape a good shoeing from the press. Gordon Strachan was guilty of it big time when Celtic bottled it completely at Old Trafford earlier this season, making out that United were the best side that had ever drawn breath. But I'm not so sure if Roy Hodgson wasn't just telling the truth here. Once they'd seen off Fulham's strong start, United really were exceptional, as good as anything that Craven Cottage has ever seen for sure. Perhaps as good as anything the FA Cup has ever seen. Which makes it even more frustrating that all their good work counted for absolutely zero, nada, nothing by the time the semi came around.

MATCH ACTION

1-0 (20): No one gave them much credit afterwards but Fulham were decent early on, troubling United with the pace of Johnson and the brawn of Zamora. But the whole match got dumped on its head when United broke through. Carrick swings in a corner from the right, Rooney flicks a looping header towards the back post. Konchesky doesn't react and Tévez squeezes his header through the crowd.

2-0 (35): The miss of the match from Rooney (who managed to guide Park's cross against the far post from under Schwarzer's nostrils) is soon followed by the goal of the month. Tévez collects Fletcher's pass virtually on halfway, charges 30 yards, cuts inside – dumping Dickson Etuhu on his backside in the process – and spears a screamer past Schwarzer.

3-0(50): United had no choice but to buy another striker in the summer after Saha limped off to Everton. And if you want to keep winning the big prizes you just don't turn down the chance to add a talent like Berbatov to your squad. But when Tévez and Rooney play like they did here you wonder whether Fergie would have been better off replacing Saha with another squad player rather than a definite starter. This time it's Rooney's turn to find the net, beating Schwarzer with a beautifully weighted low curler from the edge of the box.

4-0(81): 3-0 was the cue for Fergie to send on the kids and protect the stars for the return game against Inter. But that doesn't signal the end of the scoring as Park pins his ears back, squares up his marker and sends a virtual replica of Rooney's effort into the far corner.

ODDS OF THE DAY

The bookies make United 6-1 for a record-breaking quintuple. Generous eh?

LINE OF THE DAY

From The Times:

"The home fans, once the game was out of reach, gawped at them [United] in a mix of incredulity and reluctant awe."

VIEWS FROM THE PRESSBOX

"'Are you watching Merseyside?' enquired the cocksure collective from Manchester, from the banks of the Thames. To be honest, every time Manchester United appear on the television, anyone of a Liverpool persuasion would be advised to look away. This team is not for turning. This squad is not for weakening. United may not get the luck in every competition this season, but they have just about everything else going for them. They cruised into the FA Cup semi-finals in immaculate fashion and looked so full of smart running and sweet passing that they could have managed another 90 minutes at full pelt straight after this one. No sweat.". – *The Observer*

"The strength of Manchester United's current squad may be unprecedented in the English game; the quest United are on certainly is. Winning a quintet of major trophies remains possible

— and indeed became just that little bit more likely — after Fulham were pillaged in their own stadium, where they had lost only twice all season." – *The Sunday Times*

"Mourinho's levels of self-confidence are ludicrous, but if he were to knock United out of the Champions League while they are in such breathtaking form, we would have to take his claims seriously. It would have been impossible, anyway, for United to have adopted a presumptuous stance in front of their 5,000 expectant and raucous supporters. The home fans, once the game was out of reach, gawped at them in a mix of incredulity and reluctant awe." – *The Times doesn't fancy Inter's chances at Old Trafford on Wednesday*

FULHAM – THE VERBALS

"Tévez was a jack-in-the-box all day. He used so much great energy, on the ball and with his movement. His second goal was fantastic. My biggest concern is picking the right team and I'm leaving out great players all the time and that is not easy for me. I hope by the end of the year we all recognise that everyone has made a great contribution." – *Fergie on his biggest selection problem.*

"We feel we can win all five. We know how easy it is to make mistakes and go out of competitions, like we did in the FA Cup against Portsmouth [last season]. This time, we won't make those mistakes again. We have a stronger squad and we are more concentrated. Winning like that [at Fulham] and playing like that was the perfect way into the Inter game. Now, we are even more confident." – *Parky's getting cocky.*

MATCH FACTS

FULHAM: SCHWARZER, PANTSIL, HANGELAND, HUGHES, KONCHESKY, DAVIES, ETUHU, MURPHY (DACOURT 57), DEMPSEY, ZAMORA (GERA 67), JOHNSON (KAMARA 60) [HODGSON]
BOOKED: PANTSIL, DACOURT.
UNITED: VAN DER SAR, O'SHEA (ECKERSLEY 52), FERDINAND (EVANS 46), VIDIC, EVRA, FLETCHER, CARRICK, ANDERSON, PARK, ROONEY (WELBECK 64), TÉVEZ.
CRAVEN COTTAGE ATT: 24,662 REF: MIKE DEAN H-T: 2–0

OTHER SCORES

FA CUP Q-F: ARSENAL 3 BURNLEY 0, EVERTON 2 BORO 1, COVENTRY 0 CHELSEA 2

"If you want me to rule out ever being Manchester United manager I can't. Special clubs need special managers so in theory it could work"

NEWS

UNITED ARE DRAWN to play Everton in one of the Wembley FA Cup semis, Chelsea get either Arsenal or Hull (so, Arsenal). So which teams get the 4pm Sunday kick-off? The London-based sides? Or the ones whose fans will be lucky to make it home for midnight IF the game is settled in normal time? It was never in doubt. It's us and Everton. Thanks for that. Beckham is set to stay at Milan in a 'timeshare' arrangement which will see him fanny around in the States between July and October and then return to Milan for the rest of next season. Apparently he was so desperate for the deal to go through that he agreed to pay most of the Milan's loan fee himself. United are linked with 'rising star' Takayuki Morimoto from Catania, yet another Brazilian wonderkid, Walter, and toilet seat thief Glen Johnson. Haven't the papers heard of Rafael? And United fans are left in the slightly unnerving position of enjoying a Liverpool victory as the Scousers follow up their 1-0 stroll in the Bernabeu by thumping Raul, Heinze & co. 5-0 at Anfield. What exactly does Ronaldo see in them again?

HOW DID THAT GO THEN?

"We will win 3-0 in the Bernabeu which will be a great party. Then we will win 2-1 in Liverpool." - *Real Madrid President Vicente Boluda, February 23.*

THE EGO HAS LANDED

A Mourinho treble:

"If you want me to rule out ever being Manchester United manager I can't. Special clubs need special managers so in theory it could work."

"Old Trafford now looks like home because for four years I came here a lot of times, semi-finals, Carling Cup, FA Cup semis. It became part of my life. I even know the grass-man★. He asked me to train on one side because that side has no sun. I know the man, he's a nice guy, so okay I do it."

"Yes, Manchester United are the best team in England but you have to ask how good has the Premier League been since I left? Manchester United have won it with ease since I have gone because no manager has put a team together that can rival them. But my teams always rival Manchester United and Sir Alex knows that."

PUB QUESTION OF THE WEEK*

Mourinho knows the Old Trafford grass-man. Do you? (Clue: it's not Keith Kent) How about the kitman, fitness coach, physio, groundsman and doctor? Answers at the bottom of the page.

PUTDOWN OF THE WEEK

"As far as I know, he is discussing something which he has a chance of winning, but which I have already won five times" - *Paolo Maldini puts Jose in his place.*

ALAN GREEN: DEFINITELY NOT A LIVERPOOL FAN
Top stuff from football365: Tuesday night's commentary on BBC Radio 5 Live from the, as ever, impartial Alan Green when Liverpool were awarded the most dubious of penalties...

Alan Green: "Stone-wall penalty."

Mark Lawrenson: "That's a very harsh penalty. Actually, it's the wrong decision. The ball clearly hits Heinze on the shoulder."

AG: "Who cares?!"

ML: "Well everyone should, it's a bad, bad decision and we don't want to see them. Especially in games like these."

AG: "Well, of course not, but from a Liverpool point of view it doesn't matter."

ML: "Not for me, it's a poor decision and it could easily go against you."

AG: "Still it's a great chance for Liverpool to put the tie to bed now."

Unfortunately, radio does not record whether Green then stood up, raised his scarf in the air and started mouthing the words to 'You'll Never Walk Alone'.

'GLASS HALF FULL' MOMENT OF THE WEEK
Another classic from football365:

Said Oldham chief executive Alan Hardy about said skirmish: 'Lee Hughes fights with Oldham manager John Sheridan at Belle

Vue dogs'. "The CCTV does show one or two confrontations, but apart from these incidents it was a very successful night."

Which, we think you'll agree, is a little like Fred Goodwin saying, "The books do show one or two problems, but apart from losing that £24.1billion, it was a very successful year for RBS."

QUOTES OF THE WEEK

"He was smug towards us" - *Coventry boss Chris Coleman finds a new complaint to be levelled against Steve Bennett after Chelsea beat them in the Cup.*

"At his age? He would probably collapse. It would be nice to see but I don't think our manager goes in for that type of thing. He will probably stand up, have a little clap and be pleased we have gone through." – *Scholesy on the chances of Fergie reenacting Mourinho's touchline sprint in 2004.*

"We are used to Jose, I'm not a little lad from the Govan alleys who finds himself on Fifth Avenue in New York. I'm not shocked by anything any more. Mourinho has a magnetic power over the media, everyone wants him because he goes from the amusing to the spirited to the offensive. He's a great media tactician." – *It takes one to know one Fergie.*

*Albert Morgan, Tony Strudwick, Rob Swire, Tony Sinclair, Steve Mc-Nally.

11/03/2009
CL LAST 16 (2ND LEG)

UNITED 2 INTER 0

(United win 2-0 on aggregate)
Vidic 4, Ronaldo 49

FOR 11 LONG weeks, ever since the draw for this match had been made, the painful memories had played over and over. The inept Russian linesman... Phil Neville's gormless push... Tim Howard's career-defining flap... and the swarthy Armani-clad coach giving it the big one in front of the Scoreboard End. Could the Special One do as much damage to us this time around? Would Inter be able to live with United's midfield this time? Would Ibrahimovic – the world's best player according to his manager - finally live up to the hype? Would United's clean sheet spree come to an end at the worst possible time? Would we regret not taking our chances in Milan? Would Ronaldo finally score in this season's Champions League?

Fortunately, the answers were no, sort of, not really, no and yes. United were sloppy, Inter and Ibrahimovic were OK but a pair of headers at the start of each half proved plenty. So there was no dancing down the touchline from Mourinho at the end of the night, just a fairly comfortable United stroll into the next round. But if we'd thought we'd banished the ghosts of Porto 2004 there was still some work to be done yet...

THE MOMENTS THAT MATTERED

1-0 (4): Inter had performed a minor miracle in stopping United converting their superiority into goals at the San Siro. But all their good work – and luck - was wasted within the opening four minutes at Old Trafford. The goal was almost ridiculously easy, the sort you're just not supposed to score against an Italian team – or a Mourinho one. Giggs floats a corner to the back post, Vieira – who, happy to say, played like a drain – spins around for no reason and the Red he was supposed to be marking, Vidic, can't miss.

2-0 (49): Sometimes early goals lift United and demoralise the opposition. On this occasion it had the opposite effect. United become more and more sloppy in possession and Inter, with their extra man in midfield, slowly ease their way back into the match. Ibrahimovic hits the bar with a free header he should have buried and then misses the target – admittedly from a tight angle – when diving winger Balotelli sends him clear. And within 4 minutes of the restart Ronaldo – a genuine candidate for the accolade of the world's finest – underlines just how important both misses were. Giggs starts things off, waltzing his way across the box before running out of room and passing the baton to Rooney. He shapes to go past Maicon but instead stands up a lovely ball that Ronaldo, making a Robsonesque surge into the six-yard box, heads powerfully past Cesar.

WHAT WAS GOOD?

MOURINHO'S ENTRANCE: The Special One probably isn't destined to be a United manager – he's too cautious and calculated for that. But if his teams replicated his own swagger and attitude he'd be a legend here. His entrance was pure theatre. Whereas most managers – especially former Chelsea managers – would have waited for the teams to come out before making their way to the dugout, Mourinho couldn't wait to bask in the limelight himself, emerging from the tunnel on his own and visibly relishing the catcalls that followed his every step.

NO ONE WILL BE DREDGING UP MOURINHO'S MANAGERIAL RECORD AGAINST FERGIE ANY MORE. As the Times put it, 'Call it the end of an aura'.

WHAT WAS BAD?

ALL 4 ENGLISH SIDES THROUGH TO THE QUARTER-FINALS – again.
THE STATE OF SERIE A. It speaks volumes that United didn't have to play that well to see off Inter, the undisputed no. 1 Italian team.

QUOTE OF THE NIGHT

"It was a long European night. I didn't know if it was a game of football or a game of suicide" – *Fergie reflects on careless United's victory.*

VIEWS FROM THE PRESSBOX

"Jose Mourinho embraced Sir Alex Ferguson at the final whistle but it was really the only time that Inter Milan properly got to grips with Manchester United. On another glorious evening for the Premier League, Mourinho and his team tumbled out of Europe with a whimper, not a bang, and Old Trafford serenaded them on their way with chants of "bye, bye Mourinho" and "you're not special any more".

"The real Special Ones are clearly the Premier League clubs, who form half the quarter-final draw. Uefa's president, Michel Platini, may fear the march of the English, he may rail against their indebtedness and failure to develop more home-grown players, but he cannot deny their strength when the whistle sounds." – *The Guardian.*

"Call it the end of an aura. In José Mourinho's dreams, this was going to be the evening when he made an irresistible audition to be Sir Alex Ferguson's eventual successor, but the self-anointed Special One exited the Old Trafford stage to the sound of catcalls, left to ponder an uncertain future as well as the distance that Manchester United have advanced in the 18 months since he departed English football.

"As Sir Alex Ferguson was remarkably eager to point out, United were nowhere near as convincing last night as in the goalless first leg, but these days they do not have to be at their imposing best to win matches, whether in the Barclays Premier League, the Champions League or any other competition that remains within their compass. They have developed an insatiable habit of success and, with headed goals in the fourth minute of each half, from Nemanja Vidic and Cristiano Ronaldo, they were too strong for an Inter Milan team who ultimately lacked the class, composure and perhaps above all the conviction to hold up the United bandwagon." – *The Times*

MATCH FACTS

UNITED: VAN DER SAR, O'SHEA, FERDINAND, VIDIC, EVRA, RONALDO, CARRICK, SCHOLES (ANDERSON 70), GIGGS, ROONEY (PARK 84), BERBATOV BOOKED: ROONEY

INTER MILAN: JULIO CESAR, MAICON, CORDOBA, SAMUEL, SANTON, ZANETTI, CAMBIASSO, VIEIRA (MUNTARI 46), STANKOVIC (ADRIANO 58), IBRAHIMOVIC, BALOTELLI (FIGO 70) [MOURINHO]
BOOKED: SAMUEL, MUNTARI.
ATT: 74,769 REF: WOLFGANG STARK (GER) H-T: 1-0

OTHER SCORES

BARCELONA 5 LYON 2 – BARCA WIN 6-3, ROMA 1 ARSENAL 0 - ARSENAL WIN 7-6 ON PENS, LIVERPOOL 4 REAL MADRID 0 - LIVERPOOL WIN 5-0, JUVENTUS 2 CHELSEA 2 - CHELSEA WIN 3-2.

"I'd like to congratulate Gary on the size of his bulge"

NEWS I

LOVE MOURINHO OR hate him, you just can't ignore him. After making a grand entrance at Old Trafford, he makes an inglorious exit as he slaps a fan who gave him grief as he did a TV interview outside the ground. It's tough to know who comes out of this the worst. Mourinho for not putting up with the usual 'You're not special/chin up/ go home' taunts. Or the 'victim' – who was later described as fat and southern (groan) – for running off and reporting it to the police.

Sounds like the sort of guy who aims for the wet patch at work so he can phone up one of those insurance lines.

MADNESS

United fan Steven Mace, a witness to Mourinho's Cloughie moment, grabs his 60 seconds of fame, telling the Sun:

"Mourinho was giving a TV interview and us lot were giving him a bit of argy-bargy - singing, 'Go home Mourinho'. He finished his interview and just came barging over towards us with this look on his face.

"We thought he was going to give autographs, but he walked straight towards this one fella. He chanted in a sarcastic voice, 'Go home Mourinho'? And the next thing he hit this guy.

"It wasn't a clenched hand - more like a backhand across the face. This other guy was so shocked he didn't react. Then Mourinho calmly walked off. It was a moment of madness from him. I couldn't believe it."

HEADLINE OF THE WEEK

'Punch And Jose' - *The Sun and Mirror*

NEWS II

Surprise, surprise. Arsenal go to Rome, beat Roma on penalties and Arsenal fans get stabbed. In the buttocks. The worst incident sees Italian supporters blocking an Arsenal minibus's progress with a car and hurling stones and bottles at the windows before slinging a burning flare inside. So how do UEFA – who'd already threatened to move the Champions League final elsewhere if any more fans got stabbed – respond? Do they announce a return to Moscow, where no one dared to step out of line because there were more soldiers than fans? How about Wembley? Or the Faroe Islands (the non-Egyptian ones, City fans)? No they announce that the Final's staying put because doing anything else would make things 'less safe'. Gee thanks.

CLOWN OF THE WEEK

'Moving to another place would probably put the arrangements in danger. It would be less safe.' – *UEFA spokesman William Gaillard. Rough translation. We've sorted out all the arrangements in Rome. We can't be arsed changing them. English clubs are getting too good. If their fans respond to the provocation we can dump them out of Europe.*

GOOGLE OF THE WEEK

Fans+buttock+stabbed+Italy = 119,000

PRAVDA.COM

Spot the difference as Rooney's views on Liverpool appear on the United website like this on Thursday lunchtime...

"I'm very excited about the game because I grew up as an Everton fan hating Liverpool and that hasn't changed."

And like this a couple of hours later:

"I'm also very excited about the game because I grew up as an Everton fan."

What's all the fuss about? If it's fine to say you hate marmite why not Scousers too?

WARMING UP FOR THE WEEKEND

"I don't know where it came from and I'm not really interested. I would need to read more of Freud before I could really understand all that" - *Fergie warms up for the visit of Rafa Benitez to Old Trafford.*

"Yes, I read about Freud when I was in school and university. I try to improve my English, so maybe he will understand me if I say something. Sometimes my English is not good enough but I do not understand the Scottish accent" - *Benitez's weirdly withering response.*

SIMON SAYS

The half-dozen subscribers to MUTV receive a shock when a caller to the post-Inter phone-in (fronted by Gordon McQueen's lass, Hayley) sends the discussion veering away from football. As Pally adopts his normal slumped, comatose position, 'Simon from Leicester' pipes up with "I'd like to congratulate Gary on the size of his bulge". While Paul Parker's eyes do their best to pop out of their sockets, and Pally stirs slowly to life (not there), Hayley makes a faux-pas by asking Simon to repeat what he said. Happy to oblige, Simon replies: "Well, it looks like he's got a massive c*ck". After that Hayley bumbles around with comments like "Oh! That's terrible!" and "You are obvious a very jealous man" before really putting her foot in it by suggesting "Perhaps it's the angle"... whilst giving Pally's groin a cheeky once over.

FAPL 14/03/2009

UNITED 1 LIVERPOOL 4

Ronaldo 23(p). Torres 28, Gerrard 44 (p). Aurelio (77), Dossena (90)

So THIS IS what it must feel like to come home and find your red-hot girlfriend doing the bad thing with the sad loser from down the road...

MATCH ACTION
(Let's keep things brief ...)

1-0 (23): Reina brings down Park, Ronaldo scores from the spot. It all looks so straightforward for United but just 5 minutes later...

1-1 (28): Vidic, the defender of the season by a country mile, has an absolute nightmare, allowing the ball to bounce not once but twice and effectively begging Torres to walk through and score.

1-2 (44): Evra, who's just not been his normal self since his injury and farcical ban, trips Gerrard in the box. Gerrard copies Ronaldo.

RED (76): United dominate the second half before Vidic's day goes from disastrous to cataclysmic as he hauls down Gerrard and sees red.

1-3 (77): Aurelio then rubs it in by scoring direct from the free-kick.

1-4 (90): Another suicidal shambles at the back, another goal. No one deals with Reina's long clearance and Dossena chips Van der Sar. So there you have it. United play the better football, Liverpool barely create an outright chance and they end up with their biggest win at Old Trafford since 1936. And that, sadly is a fact...

LIVERPOOL – THE VERBALS

"I thought we were the better team. But the score doesn't reflect that." – *Fergie got a whole pile of grief for this but his point was a sound one. It wasn't Liverpool's good play that killed us. It was our own mistakes.*

"We knew their defence had weaknesses. They are strong in defence but that's because they have plenty of possession elsewhere. They have a lot of quality in attack but that is the main thing that they have. When they don't have the ball and you move the ball quickly and play behind their defenders you know you can beat them." – *Benitez basks in his own tactical wizardry. But if it's so obvious how to beat us how come it took him so long to do it?*

VIEWS FROM THE PRESSBOX

"The souvenir stalls on Sir Matt Busby Way presumably will not be selling any more of those T-shirts mocking Rafael Benítez as 'Deranged! Ludicrous! Insane!'. The front cover of Manchester United's Red News fanzine recently had Liverpool's manager superimposed into a straitjacket but, to borrow a line from The Smiths, that joke isn't funny any more. Benítez's team made sure of that on Saturday when they dismantled the English, European and world champions from A to Z.

"Sir Alex Ferguson's bluff that United had been the "better team" was almost as staggering as seeing a team going for six trophies in one season broken as easily as a dried twig. Fernando Torres single-handedly directed Nemanja Vidic's candidacy as footballer of the year into the nearest dustbin; Rio Ferdinand reverted to the days when he was a danger to his own team; and Patrice Evra had not looked as bad since his first weeks in English football when he used to vomit after matches, describing the experience like "being in a washing machine". It felt like a trick of the mind that this was a team that had gone from 8 November to 21 February without conceding a league goal." – *The Guardian bathes in United's discomfort.*

"Ferguson's claim that United were the better team was ridiculously biased, even by the old grouse's notoriously one-eyed standards. It was too risible for Benitez to bother to gainsay. The stats border on the historic. It was the first time United had conceded four goals at home since 1992, when Queens Park Rangers upset the odds under Gerry Francis, with the unsung Dennis Bailey contributing a hat-trick." – *The Times rips into Fergie. But if Vidic and Evra hadn't had stinkers – like Van der Sar did at Anfield in September – Benitez would almost certainly still have been chasing his first United league victory.*

LOOK AWAY NOW

United have only shipped 4 goals to the Scousers twice at home before, the first time in the first ever match at Old Trafford and the second time in 1936 when (to put things into perspective) we'd just lost 6-2 at Grimsby:

19/02/1910 – United 3 Liverpool 4
Moger, Stacey, Hayes, Duckworth, Roberts, Blott, Meredith, Halse, Homer, S.Turnbull, Wall
21/11/1936 – United 2 Liverpool 5★
John, Griffiths, Roughton, Brown, McLenahan, McKay, Bryant, Mutch, Thompson, Ferrier, Manley

MATCH FACTS

United: Van der Sar, O'Shea, Ferdinand, Vidic, Evra, Ronaldo, Carrick (Giggs 74), Anderson (Scholes 73), Park (Berbatov 74), Rooney, Tévez
Sent Off: Vidic (76)
Booked: Ferdinand, Van der Sar.
Liverpool: Reina, Carragher, Skrtel, Hyypia, Aurelio, Mascherano, Lucas, Kuyt, Gerrard (El Zhar 90), Riera (Dossena 67), Torres (Babel 81) [Benitez]
Booked: Carragher, Mascherano, Skrtel
Att: 75,569 Ref: Alan Wiley h–t: 1–2

OTHER SCORES

Arsenal 4 Blackburn 0; Chelsea 1 City 0

LEAGUE TABLE

1. United 65 (28); 2. Chelsea 61 (29); 3. Liverpool 61 (29); 4. Arsenal 52 (29)

"Why can't he grow normal privet hedges like everyone else?"

IF YOU'RE ANYTHING like me, you went straight home from the match, wedged your head under the pillow, pretended that nothing happened after Ronaldo's penalty and took a vow not to think/read/talk about football until Fulham on Saturday. Or at least the Champions League draw the day before. For a while it was pretty therapeutic too, not finding yourself trapped in front of Sky Sports News watching that Scottish twat with the white hair react to every piece of news as if an H-bomb has just landed in the queen's toilet. But then the lure of Georgie Thompson, Millie Clode and Stan Boardman's lad got too much. And not before time too as a whole pile of news, bad, good and meaningless, hit the yellow ticker...

BIG NEWS

It's Champions League draw time and Bruno Conti (remember him, tight shorts, flowing black hair, cracking left foot) has a belter, pairing Chelsea and Liverpool together for the fifth year straight, placing Barcelona or Bayern in their way to the final and leaving United to fight it out with Porto, Villarreal and Arsenal on the other side of the draw. Arsenal at the Emirates in the semis could be tasty. Villarreal won't be. We haven't scored against them in four games. They haven't scored against us either mind.

Vidic gets a two game ban for his second sending off against Liverpool this season – and his third of the season overall. Has anyone done the red card double before? Has any United player ever been sent off three times in a season before? (Don't look at me – I haven't a clue).

Fergie gets on Benitez's back. Benitez gets his facts wrong. Again (see Worst of enemies).

MEDIUM NEWS

After months of 'will he, won't he' it's nice to finally see one Tévez saga get settled. Unfortunately it's the wrong one. So United won't be paying £25 million to sign Tévez up. Instead West Ham will pay Sheffield United £25 million to make up for the way the ineligible Tévez almost single-handedly sent them down. It all sounds slightly odd to me. If Tévez had scored his goals at the other end of the season and been crap from then on – rather than the other way round – Sheffield would have probably been laughed out of court.

Steve Coppell clocks up 1000 games as manager. And he doesn't look like he's enjoyed a single one of them.

Phil Brown accuses Fabreagas of spitting at his assistant Brian Horton after Arsenal's 2-1 FA Cup quarter-final win against Hull. Fabregas, who appeared on the pitch in his civvies at the final whistle, protests his innocence and does the same when a youtube clip from 2005 appears to show him gobbing on Michael Ballack. Hmmm.

SLIGHTLY LESS IMPORTANT THAN MEDIUM NEWS

Giggsy is awarded the freedom of the city of Salford, following in the footsteps of the likes of Nelson Mandela and LS Lowry. The papers are convinced we're going to buy Valencia – the player, not the, right, you know - in the summer. Four United youngsters - Ravel Morrison, attackers John Cofie and William Keane, and defender Tom Thorpe – get call ups to the England under-16s. Benitez finally gets bored of dragging his contract negotiations out any longer and signs up for 5 more years of grief from Fergie. United fan Usain Bolt is all set to makes his first visit to Old Trafford. I only mention this because my OT neighbour (you know who you are!) asked me if we'd bought a new goalkeeper when she saw him on telly.

GOOD FOR NOTHING NEWS

The Sun reports that Ronaldo's car was gobbed on by a vagrant (The Sun's PC term for a Big Issue seller) in Manchester City centre. A witness said he didn't like it.

And the Telegraph reports that Gary Nev has outraged his neighbours by having some shrubbery outside his gate shaped into the letters MUFC.

One local said: "The design of the property is self indulgence but to have a shrubbery shaped in the letters of his football club is beyond belief. Why can't he grow normal privet hedges like everyone else? This was once a traditional old farming community and now it looks like something out of Beverley Hills."

You've got to feel sorry for them – though if they'd seen Gary's choice of facial shrubbery…

BEST OF ENEMIES

Like watching Ali and Foreman kiss and make up, or Sheringham and Cole going out for dinner together in Alderley Edge, it's strange to see Fergie and Wenger getting on so well. But the entente cordiale is showing no signs of weakening. Here Wenger comes out in support of Fergie's theory – ridiculed by the 'neutrals' in the press - that we were the better team against Liverpool:

"I think it is interesting. I watched a big part of the Manchester United-Liverpool game. For me, United were the dominant team but I could see they were not sharp on the day physically, and Liverpool took advantage of that, because they are very good at doing that."

Good man.

WORST OF ENEMIES.

Fergie reacts to the news that Benitez has signed a new contract by having a nice little dig at how he spends his money and his record with home-grown players:

"You will see Rafa produce an incredible spending spree – that is an absolute certainty now he has signed his new contract. They talk of a recession but there will not be one at Liverpool. There will be a spending splurge at Liverpool, that is his [Benítez's] way. "

"The amazing fact about them is that they have used 60 players in the reserves this season. We have signed 18 players in the last five years but eight of them are young and there is a balance about us. We do things correctly. We like to develop our young players but other clubs are maybe different." *(For the record: Number of Liverpool regulars who've been brought through the ranks by Benitez – 0)*

SPAT OF THE WEEK
(from football365)

"I categorically deny that I spat at anybody after the match. I have never done this in my whole career on the pitch, so why would I do it when I am not even playing?" – *Fabregas, Spain's answer to Roy Hattersley.*

"For Arsenal's club captain to spit at my assistant shows you what this club is all about" - *Phil Brown was the assistant manager of Sam Allardyce for six years. And, it would seem, doesn't like Arsenal too much either.*

"He has no right to be on the pitch dressed like that" - *Brown can't believe Fabregas wasn't wearing tails and swinging a cane as he walked on the Emirates pitch to congratulate his team-mates after the Hull win.*

"He was dressed in jeans and a leather jacket, I thought he looked alright" - *The response of Victoria Derbyshire, the Radio Five Live host whom Brown was talking to.*

"I don't even know who the assistant manager of Hull is or what he looks like" - *And the response of Fabregas to the allegations against him. If it helps, he's the one with your gob on his shoes.*

QUOTES OF THE WEEK

"I was amazed when I saw his claims. I talked to some people in the sports technology department and said: 'check that out'. I am sure I had not spent that much money. I worked out that in the last five years Liverpool had spent £24m more than Manchester United. We don't always succeed – we had our blips a few years ago when we were rebuilding and people told me it was the end of everything and my shelf life was up. But we came through." – *Fergie's not wearing Benitez's money argument.*

"It doesn't matter what Ferguson says, they still have more money than us." – *Benitez clearly thinks if he repeats the same line often enough it will come true.*

"He's a strong boy. He knocks him off...he absolutely rapes him" – *Alan Pardew asks for a shoeing from Middle England with his leftfield summary of Michael Essien's tackle on City's Ched Evans on MOTD.*

FAPL 21/03/2009

FULHAM 2 UNITED 0
Murphy 18(p), Gera 87

As LIVERPOOL PILED on the embarrassment at Old Trafford last week it must have been a toss-up who felt worse – the United players who were on the receiving end, or the Fulham players who knew they had to play us next. But if the home side took to the field fretting about a United backlash that would make the recent 4-0 Cup defeat feel like a victory, it didn't take long for their nerves to settle. United were awful in the first half and Fulham, despite a second half wobble, deservedly held on for their first home win against us since 1964.

So how come it all went so wrong? How come the wounded animal didn't scratch? Well the team tinkering didn't help. In that cup game Rooney and Tévez had taken Fulham to the cleaners almost on their own. This time they started the game on the bench and Ronaldo and Berbatov got the nod up front. Since both of them had one on them, that was asking for trouble. Berbatov fiddled with his hairband and played a handful of half-arsed sideways passes before limping off at half-time. Ronaldo ran around a bit but he was in one of those horrible moods where he dissolves into a hissy fit every time he's touched, tackled or breathed upon.

Then there was Fulham. We've got used to them sitting back and taking it. Our last six matches have gone 5-1, 2-1, 2-0, 3-0, 3-0 and 4-0. But this time they were really up for it, harassing us out of possession and using the ball intelligently. Heck, even Bobby Zamora looked like a player.

But even that wasn't the crucial factor here. It's normally bad form to point the finger at individuals, particularly if they happen to be United legends. But if the Ginger Prince hadn't had one of his occasional blond moments in the first half, getting himself needlessly sent off blocking Zamora's header, it could all have been so different later on. United came close enough to snatching a point or three in the second half with 10 men. If Scholesy had been around to dictate play at the time that Fulham were tightening up like a distressed marathon runner, who knows what could have happened. As it was, Gera finished us off right at the death, Rooney got a ridiculous red card and, instead of a trademark comeback, the press had a United crisis to talk about. And, as every Red knows, there's nothing they like doing more than that...

MATCH ACTION

HANDBALL, RED, GOAL! (18): To get yourself sent off for an unnecessary handball, as Scholesy did in the Super Cup, once in a season is careless. To do it twice is bordering on the barmy. Sure, Scholesy knew that if he hadn't smothered Zamora's header then Fulham would certainly have gone one up. But what was the point of doing it when it was obvious that Fulham were going to get a penalty anyway and that the ref would have no choice but to show him a red? The fact that Danny Murphy – who's got previous against United having scored three winners against us for Liverpool - was around to take the penalty made the whole affair even more absurd. Murphy never looked like missing. Van der Sar never looked like getting in the way. 1-0 to Fulham.

0-2 (87): United struggled to cope with their numerical disadvantage and own bad form for the rest of the first half. But the arrival of Rooney at half-time acted as a catalyst and provoked a 10-man siege of the Fulham goal. Park wastes the best chance United create, allowing Schwarzer to smother from within touching distance of goal, before Fulham finally break in numbers, Van der Sar parries Johnson's sidefoot and Gera hooks the ball in over his shoulder...

RED! (88): And if that wasn't galling enough, Phil Dowd pulls United back for taking a free-kick in the wrong place. Rooney, who'd already been booked, angrily throws the ball back in his direction and Dowd jumps at the chance of giving him a second yellow. The United camp fume that Rooney was only trying to get the game restarted again. The press pack fume about the treatment he dished out to the corner flag on his way down the tunnel. Reading some of the reports you'd have thought he'd just punched a pensioner.

FERGIE – THE VERBALS

"He could have easily not given it. But it's Phil Dowd, so what do you expect?" – *Fergie gets red-eyed in defence of Scholesy.*

"Was it thrown in anger? Yes, because he wanted the game hurried up, he threw with pace to get the game going. The ball was thrown to where the free-kick was being taken - did it hit the referee? No." – *And goes ballistic in defence of Rooney.*

PUB QUIZ QUESTION OF THE DAY

When was the last time United had two players sent off in the same match?★

VIEWS FROM THE PRESSBOX

"When a team of serial winners starts losing as a habit there is clearly something wrong. Manchester United have lost as many leagues games in one week as in the previous 10 months and their supporters would feel a lot more reassured if it were not for the fact that, on both occasions, they have gone down without a great deal of dignity. The damage may still be only superficial but it does, at the very least, inflict upon them the kind of anxieties to which they seemed immune not long ago." – *The Guardian*

"YOU wait an age for one shocking disintegration of poise and invulnerability and suddenly two come along at once. Eight days ago Manchester United were skipping through the forest with seemingly nothing to stop them popping trophies in their basket. Now they are as edgy as Little Red Riding Hoods who have just seen the Big Bad Wolf." – *Anyone else think The Sunday Times report could have been written by a paedophile? (of course we're not suggesting the author was in any shape or form interested in, you know, blah, blah, blah).*

"Fulham had not beaten United at Craven Cottage since 1964. A week earlier Liverpool's 4-1 mauling of the champions was their biggest win at Old Trafford since 1936. Almost inexplicably, United have gone from being trumpeted as possibly the best British side of all time to one that is handing out once-in-a-lifetime results as indiscriminately as someone chucking out breadcrumbs for the pigeons." – *The Guardian again.*

MATCH FACTS

FULHAM: SCHWARZER, PANTSIL, HUGHES, HANGELAND, KONCHESKY, DEMPSEY (GERA 81), MURPHY (DACOURT 67), ETUHU, DAVIES, JOHNSON,

ZAMORA (KAMARA 77) [HODGSON]
BOOKED: PANTSIL, DEMPSEY.
UNITED: VAN DER SAR, O'SHEA (TÉVEZ 70), EVANS, FERDINAND, EVRA, RONALDO, FLETCHER, SCHOLES, PARK, GIGGS, BERBATOV (ROONEY 46).
SENT OFF: SCHOLES (18), ROONEY (89).
BOOKED: EVANS, EVRA, RONALDO, ROONEY.
CRAVEN COTTAGE ATT: 25,652 REF: PHIL DOWD H-T: 0-1

OTHER SCORES

SPURS 1 CHELSEA 0; LIVERPOOL 5 VILLA 0; NEWCASTLE 1 ARSENAL 3

LEAGUE TABLE

1. UNITED 65 (29); 2. LIVERPOOL 64 (30); 3. CHELSEA 61 (30);
4. ARSENAL 55 (30)

> ** Fletcher and Ronaldo were both sent off in the 2-0 win at Villa in May 2004*

"What do you want me to say? He lost his virginity to a man"

STRIKING NEWS

THE PAPERS LINK Diego (our one) with a move to City. It would be great to see him back in town, but only if he still runs around as aimlessly as he did when he was wearing – or trying to put on – a United shirt. They also link Ronaldo with, you'll never guess it, oh give it a try, OK here it is, a move to Madrid. This time they reckon a deal's been agreed at £75 million, which in fairness might not be a bad idea IF the orange one carries on playing like he has been most of this season. This week Tévez is linked with a move to Liverpool which might just be enough for Fergie to fly to the States and beat the Glazer boys to a pulp until they agree to sign him up. And Benzema is apparently coming to Manchester to replace Berbatov. But doesn't he want to play for Madrid?

Oh, and one more thing. Unknown striker Federico Macheda bags a hat-trick in the reserves' 3-3 draw at Newcastle. It didn't seem that big a deal at the time. But give it a few days and boy oh boy...

FACEBOOK ENTRY OF THE WEEK

'Kiko could be on the bench tomoz!'

OTHER NEWS

United are linked with Sporting Lisbon starlet Afonso Taira. Kid keeper Gary Woods goes to Doncaster. And Brad Friedel's red card at Anfield (for bringing down Torres) is rescinded by the FA thus freeing him up to make 25 stunning saves at Old Trafford. As Torres was just about to tap the ball home when Friedel took him out, it looks like a strange decision. Perhaps the FA isn't as United friendly as Benitez's facts make out?

Now that it's too late for anyone to blame him if Newcastle go down, Alan Shearer finally accepts the Newcastle job. Unfortunately he only agrees to stay on till the end of the season which means we won't get the chance to give him a special M16 welcome next year. It also means that he'll probably be back on the Match of the Day sofa in August. So if Shearer's presence in Hansen's shadows makes you want to dropkick your TV into next door's garden, make sure you make the most of the next few weeks.

AIG make themselves the most hated company in the US by paying out massive bonuses to the slimeball executives who brought the company to their knees. Public hostility to the news reaches such a level that AIG employeess are told not to wear the company logo – and the company make plans to change their name to AIU. So much for United's plan to shift all those AIG-sponsored shirts in the US...

NON-UNITED STORY OF THE WEEK

There's only one worth talking about. It's the biggest football shoplifting scandal since Glen Johnson nicked a toilet seat.

From the Sun: "SOCCER hero John Terry's mum and mother-in-law were allegedly caught loading £800-worth of stolen store goods into a car. Sue Terry, 50, and Sue Poole, 54, were nicked and officially cautioned by cops for shoplifting clothes and food from Marks & Spencer and Tesco. By accepting the caution, they formally acknowledged their guilt." *Perhaps she aimed to pay but missed?*

INTERNATIONAL REDS PART I

England win a pointless friendly 4-0 against Slovakia. Rooney batters them – scoring twice - and the media are all over him like a bad tan.

Forgotten new boy Zoltan Tosic plays in the goalless draw between Serbia and Ukraine U21s.

INTERNATIONAL REDS PART II

Rooney and Ferdinand both play as England sneak past Ukraine with a late goal from Sue Terry's boy, John. Rio aggravates a groin injury which means our backline against Villa at the weekend will be wafer thin. Fletcher's Scotland win 2-1 against Iceland. Evra's France beat Lithuania 1-0. Evans's Northern Ireland beat Slovenia. Italy's Pazzini is sent off after 3 minutes for hitting Sheasy but Ireland still need a late equalizer to draw 1-1. Gibson was a second-half sub. Vidic's Serbia win 2-0 in a friendly against Sweden. Park helps South Korea post a 1-0 win in the mother of all derbies against North Korea. Nani and Ronaldo in 2-0 friendly win over South Africa. And, astonishingly, Tévez, Maradona & co. get battered 6-1 in Mars, Bolivia.

PUTDOWN OF THE WEEK/YEAR/DECADE

"What do you want me to say? He lost his virginity to a man" – *Diego Maradona responds to Pele's claims that he's "a negative example" on players such as Robinho.*

BUSINESS QUESTION OF THE WEEK

AIG are the most hated company in the US. Their employees have been warned not to wear the company logo. So it makes sense that they're going to rebrand themselves. But why on earth are they renaming themselves AIU? It's not going to take a genius to work out the link is it?

BIG, BIG CLUB

Hours after the Craven Cottage debacle, the Fulham website announces theyr'e selling a DVD of the match for a tenner:

"Your chance to own a copy of Fulham's sensational 2-0 victory over the Premier League, European and World Club Champions, Manchester United." *Now you can't deny Fulham fans the right to celebrate their first home victory against United for 35 years. But it's a bit depressing when a team in the same division as United act like they can't believe they've beaten them. Especially when they ended the game with TWO extra men.*

QUOTES OF THE WEEK

"You crazy man. You crazy man. What were you doing punching

the flag?" - *Fabio Capello on Rooney's exit from Craven Cottage*

"Paying excessive bonuses to executives with taxpayer funds was unacceptable. It is equally unacceptable for US taxpayer money to go to support an English soccer club." – *Is Democrat representative Ann Kirkpatrick suggesting that AIG break their contract with United? Tut tut.*

"The biggest club in the world against the biggest competition in the world, that is the dilemma." – *Ben Foster on the pros and cons of life at United.*

"His health is fine and he's building a new team. If they win this year then they catch Liverpool in terms of titles won. I can see him doing this year and next — and then that might be it for him." – *Darren Ferguson hints that his dad might do one next year. IF we beat Liverpool's 18.*

HOW DID THAT GO?

APRIL 6, 2006: "We passed up the opportunity to do the world's biggest shirt deal to do the right shirt deal...This deal presents both of us with so many possibilities" - *David Gill, announcing Manchester United's sponsorship deal with AIG.*

MARCH 25 2009: "I think the AIG name is so thoroughly wounded and disgraced that we're probably going to have to change it" - *AIG chief executive Edward M Liddy.*

SINGING THE BLUES
Odd kit stat from Red News:

When Van der Sar wears yellow our record (from 17 league games) is W 12 D 4 L 1 F 25 A 4, an average of 2.35 points a game★.
When Van der Sar wears blue – as he did against Fulham and Liverpool – our record (from 10 league games) is W 6 D 1 L 3 F 20 A 13, an average of 1.9 points a game.
★ *Plus Fozzie wore yellow in the Carling Cup Final.*

DID YOU KNOW?

When it comes to kit colours United leave nothing to chance which is why they employ optometrist Gayle Stephenson. She contacted the club back in the 1995-96 season after United were beaten at Southampton. She has since advised them to wear white socks for night games rather than traditional black so players can pick each other out more easily under lights when they are running with their heads down.

SURPRISE OF THE WEEK

Fergie decides not to move the Villa game forward which gives us 2 days to prepare for Porto. A sign of our priorities?

CHILDISH GIGGLE QUOTE OF THE WEEK

"The problem so far since I became coach is playing away" - *Sven-Goran Eriksson before getting sacked by Mexico (after they lost 3-1 to Honduras)*

RUNNER-UP

"I couldn't see Rooney's tackle from my position – but I assume it was quite dangerous and ruthless" - *Ukraine manager Alexei Mikhailichenko. What would 'Simon' say?*

QUOTE OF THE SEASON

This one from Liverpool's Alvaro Arbeloa really is a belter. Enjoy: "This team is on the way to becoming more famous than The Beatles. There are many weeks of emotion awaiting us in the Champions League and Premier League and this season could end up being historic for us. We are developing a sensational game and now all the pressure is on United. I believe they could fail and we are ready for that moment. Our objective is to win all our league games between now and the end of the season. It is a difficult task but not impossible now our morale's improved so much. That triumph at Old Trafford really increased our desire to be the champions."

FAPL 05/04/2009

UNITED 3 ASTON VILLA 2
Ronaldo 14, Carew 30, Agbonlahor 58, Ronaldo 80, Macheda 90

FERGIE RECKONED THE scrappy Boxing Day win at Stoke was the biggest win of the season. And OK, it got United back on track straight after the Japan trip. But let's face it, it had nothing on this. Think about it. We'd just outplayed Liverpool 1-4, we'd got turned over by Fulham away for the first time since Fergie was 23, Liverpool, who had enjoyed a late show of their own against Fulham the night before, were looking as dangerous as they have for years, half of our record-breaking defence were in the stands and the rest were playing like the specky kid at school who always got picked last. And with 80 minutes on the clock we were losing – completely deservedly - to just about the only team in the league in worst form than us, a team with a deep neurosis of playing against us.

Then came the best 10 minutes of the season so far, and the most unbelievable moment of one young Italian's life. There are lots of things boys of 17 shouldn't be doing. Drinking, watching strippers, fighting for their country, voting, driving HGVs... and scoring goals like this. How do you do justice to it? The touch and turn were outrageous. Then came the shot, the bend and the bedlam. And an in-your-face, soil-your-pants, hug-everyone-in-sight reminder of why we all fell in love with this bloody brilliant game in the first place.

THE MOMENTS THAT MATTERED

1-0 (14): Villa fans haven't had much joy at Old Trafford since Peter Withe and his sweatbands came to town in '83. And they must have had that 'here we go again' feeling again as United were gifted a needless early goal. Milner embarrasses the advancing Friedel with a passback that he has no choice but to handle. Giggs taps the free-kick sideways and Ronaldo arrows his curler superbly into the top corner.

1-1 (30): But it can't have taken the visitors long to realise that United's defensive frailties, vastly weakened line-up (half the team were missing including Ferdinand, Vidic and Rooney) and all-round nervousness offered them their best chance of ending their OT jinx for years. Villa's equaliser was wretchedly simple. Evra allows Barry to cut back onto his left foot and cross from the right, Neville, who had the sort of game the football obituary writers love, loses Carew and he easily steers in his header.

1-2 (58): And if that goal made for disturbing viewing, what about this one? Ronaldo, who'd developed a nasty habit of giving up and sulking every time he's tackled, gives the ball away and then watches as Villa break behind him in numbers. A couple of passes later, Carew crosses from the left and Agbonlahor lunges in bravely to head in at the far post.

INTERESTING... (61): Fergie responds to Villa's second by bringing on the coltish Italian striker Macheda for his debut. It smacks of desperation at the time. Thirty minutes later though...

2-2 (80). At 2-1 the game was undeniably Villa's for the taking but it's United who score next, Ronaldo reminding us of his enduring greatness (have you ever seen a player who's produced so many decisive moments even when they're playing badly?) with a partially scuffed left-footer that sneaks through Davies's legs and past Friedel's left hand.

3-2 (90): The goal changed everything... the atmosphere, the balance of play, the belief in the team. Fergie gambles again, throwing Welbeck up front alongside Macheda. With time running out Welbeck has a great chance but is foiled one-on-one by Friedel. It looks like United are going to have to settle for a good point but then, in the third minute of stoppage time, this happens. Giggs slides a low ball down the inside left channel, Macheda dumps his marker, Young, on his backside with a brilliant drag-back flick and turn and, whilst falling, bends a beautiful curler that starts off outside the right post and ends up inside it. You can tell how big a moment it is. Even Martin Tyler loses it. And he hasn't done that for years

YELLOW (90+): After being wrestled to the floor by his team-mates, Macheda runs to the tunnel to hug his dad who dives out of the crowd. It's got to be one of the all-time great father-son moments, right up there with Derek Redmond's old man helping him to finish at the Olympics. So what does Mike Riley do? Yes, he books Macheda – presumably for inciting the crowd. What a joke. If he'd really wanted to punish him for that he'd have booked him for scoring. If ever there was a crowd that didn't need any more inciting it was this one...

DEPRESSING STAT OF THE DAY

Macheda's dad is 34. How old must that make Giggsy feel?

LITMUS TEST OF THE DAY

Fergie high-fived Fred the Red coming off the pitch. When he does that you know it's been a classic.

VILLA – THE VERBALS

"I'm just grateful to the lad. I think I paid for not having played for a couple of months. But he's shown his quality in a finish that was just unbelievable." – *Gary Nev thanks Macheda for getting him – and the rest of the defence - out of jail.*

"That goal was exactly what you're at this club for. Manchester United is the one club in this world that can guarantee you that almost. There wasn't a soul in that ground who didn't think it was possible. Not a soul." – *Fergie paraphrases the classic Steve McClaren quote (from the days before he became a national joke), 'Manchester United never lose, they just run out of time'.*

VIEWS FROM THE PRESSBOX

"The Premier League champions remained a step ahead by taking a long stride back into their past. This was the Manchester United of old, the side that can improvise in desperate circumstances. Sheer corniness is a rich resource for this club so perhaps we should merely shrug over the remarkable winner in the third minute of stoppage time. The debutant substitute Federico Macheda wheeled to bend a superb shot into the far corner of the net from the left of the penalty area." – *The Guardian*

"He is still four months short of being legally allowed to drink the man of the match champagne presented to him after the game and his Facebook site, complete with pictures alongside numerous glamorous blondes, only highlights his innocence and youthful naivety. Yet Federico Macheda, a seventeen-year-old Italian making his Manchester United debut, might just go down as the boy who struck the telling blow in the 2008-09 Premier League title race with the stunning injury-time goal that enabled the champions to secure a barely deserved victory against Aston Villa that saw them dislodge Liverpool from top spot." – *The Telegraph*

"They wobbled, they teetered and for a time yesterday Manchester United looked like they were in the process of a shocking collapse. As anxiety and excruciating tension filled Old Trafford, along with the grim thought of being beaten to the Barclays Premier League title by their fiercest rivals, it was one of those moments when United's supporters found themselves crying out to someone, anyone, in the hope of salvation.

"United, with at least half a team missing, were desperate, fortunate that two goals from Cristiano Ronaldo had put them on course for the small mercy of a draw against a renascent Aston Villa. But where there is a cavalier spirit and raw enthusiasm, there is hope. And hope, then promise and finally salvation arrived in the unfamiliar shape of Federico Macheda, a 17-year-old Italian forward who was plucked from the Lazio youth team and who had never previously been involved in the first-team squad.

"Whatever he may go on to achieve in the game, at United or anywhere else, Macheda will not forget yesterday. It was the stuff of fairytales, or at very least comic books. Taking a pass from Ryan Giggs, a man twice his age, in the third minute of stoppage time, he had his back to goal but controlled the ball, turned sharply and hit a right-foot shot that curled beyond the grasp of Brad Friedel and into the far corner of the net at the Stretford End, sparking the kind of celebrations that told him he had done more than just win the match." – *The Times*

[RHETORICAL] MACHEDA QUIZ OF THE WEEK

Is Macheda…

The youngest player to score on his debut for United?

The most obscure United scorer since David Wilson against QPR in 1990?

The goalscorer with the highest squad number?

The first ever United player to celebrate with a member of family (Nevilles/Fergusons not included)?

MATCH FACTS

UNITED: VAN DER SAR, NEVILLE, O'SHEA, EVANS, EVRA, NANI (MACHEDA 61), CARRICK, FLETCHER, RONALDO, GIGGS, TÉVEZ (WELBECK 87)
BOOKED: MACHEDA.

ASTON VILLA: FRIEDEL, LUKE YOUNG, CUELLAR, DAVIES, SHOREY, MILNER (REO-COKER 76), PETROV, BARRY, ASHLEY YOUNG, CAREW, AGBONLAHOR [O'NEILL]
BOOKED: MILNER, ASHLEY YOUNG
ATT: 75,409 REF: MIKE RILEY H-T: 1-1

OTHER SCORES

FULHAM 0 LIVERPOOL 1, NEWCASTLE 0 CHELSEA 2, ARSENAL 2 CITY 0.

LEAGUE TABLE

1. UNITED 68 (30) 2. LIVERPOOL 67 (31) 3. CHELSEA 64 (31) 4. ARSENAL 58 (31) 5. VILLA 52 (31)

*'I might be too doting but I can see the
talent of Marco van Basten in him.'*

NEWS (CRAIG DAVID STYLE)

WHAT OTHER NEWS story could compete with this one? On Sunday morning Frederico 'Kiko' Macheda was just another kid with a Ronaldo-style haircut from Sale. By Sunday night he was world news, the most famous young Italian in the country and already the best Italian to have played for United. By Monday morning he had nearly 20,000 new friends on Facebook and every man and his dog had seen that snap of him and four (slightly ropey) blondes in a club. And by Monday evening he was at the centre of an Anglo-Italian spat as Lazio effectively accused 'immoral' United of blackmail and child-snatching. You can understand Lazio's frustration. After all there's something slightly seedy in the way that foreign clubs like United can make off with the best Italian and Spanish kids, just by exploiting the FIFA rule that prevents them signing a pro contract before they're 16. But the moment Pa Macheda opened his mouth, you could sense that Lazio's grip on the moral high ground wasn't going to last...

RED DEVILS
Lazio fume at United's antics:

"Taking Macheda was an act of cowardice and arrogance on the part of Manchester United. In my view they robbed Lazio, just as they robbed Parma for Giuseppe Rossi before. Someone has to do something to change the rules because so many clubs are getting fleeced in this way so that the strongest clubs can just get stronger."
– Ex Lazio sporting director Walter Sabatini.

"We knew Macheda was a great player. We had done everything possible to keep him at Lazio. Nevertheless, Italian laws did not permit that a young lad below 16 years old could sign a contract, so these kids can be stolen by other clubs."

"These clubs do not respect the ethical code and go to the parents of kids, give them money, maybe even find them work so they 'buy' the parents, who then sign on behalf of their kid. These are kids that come from poor families and, to get more money, these families even are willing to go abroad with the hope their kid becomes a great player with a lot of money.

"Manchester United gave Macheda's father 1.5 million euros. The boy only got 80,000 euros of that but they managed to convince the parents by offering a huge figure for a 14-year-old boy.

"I spoke with the parents, making them a great offer — but they had already decided to leave. It's immoral because this is like people behave in the cattle market. In football it should not happen because it's a sport that is based on authentic values like the respect to the rules." – *Lazio president Claudio Lottito.*

FIGHTING BACK

"That Manchester gave us 1.5 million euros is a lie. Ferguson has assured us of a house here in town and that's it. I don't understand why the chairman of Lazio insists on saying things that are not true. I think in our statements, we have always shown gratitude towards the club that launched Federico's career." – *Pasquale Macheda, who had taken on a string of low-paid jobs so he could look after his son's needs, blocks Lottito's allegation...*

"We have decided to go to the most important club in the world. What's wrong with that? If Lottito were offered the presidency of Manchester United what would he do? The former Lazio sporting director understood my situation and we left the club with a handshake. Today, I read these stories that make me sick, because they are not true." ...*And retaliates with an uppercut that Lottito can't defend before Volfango Patarca, the man who discovered Macheda (as well as Di Canio and Nesta), makes the Lazio chairman wear one too...*

"Three times Pasquale asked Lazio for financial help, because it was so tough trying to get Kiko to the training ground every day. It cost money [the Machedas lived 50 miles away, in rundown Ponte Di Nona to the east of Rome] and time away from work. Pasquale asked for the club to fix him up with a job. I believe as little as 500 euros a month could have solved the problem."
And another...

"My understanding is that Lazio only offered to help once they realised that Manchester United were interested in Federico. That was too late because they hadn't seemed to believe in him enough before. So thank God for Manchester United. What would have happened if they hadn't been interested and Kiko's parents had been left with the problem of trying to find the time and money to take the boy such a long way to training every day?

"Without Manchester United, I believe he would have had to stop playing. He would have had to finish with football and would have been lost to the game. Instead, he is in England, where United have helped him to mature far more quickly than he would have done in Italy."

And another...

"You cannot go wrong with Sir Alex Ferguson. Lazio should just be quiet and learn from their mistakes."

ITALIAN HERO

The Italian papers lap up their boy's success - and have a dig at United:

"How many times the Italian, born in just 1991, who has spent two years in the youth team of the world champions, must have dreamed of this scene. But it's all true...On his debut, Macheda leapt like a lion on every ball, straightaway earning the applause of the Old Trafford crowd." - *Tuttosport*.

"Macheda, 17 years-old, the former Lazio youth team player and Manchester, once more made in Italy, king of the Premier League. The Roman touched the ball, controlled it, turned and brought about the 3-2 win which beat Aston Villa, overtook Liverpool and broke the Inter affliction, which had seen United lose two in a row since beating the Italian champions." - *Gazzetta Dello Sport*

"Macheda began his career in the youth teams of Lazio before discovering his El Dorado. Manchester United, in fact, ripped him from the Rome side in the summer of 2007, when he was just 15. The English club offered a professional contract and proposed that the boy move his whole family to England. Sabatini, the Lazio youth coach at the time, could not stop him gambling the life of his parents, his brother, and choosing Ferguson's proposition. At his home today stands a photo of Macheda, his family, and the United coach. No doubt tomorrow it will be joined by his number 41 shirt, worn on an unforgettable debut." - *Corriere Dello Sport:*

"He's not 18 until August 22, this latest talent who left the Lazio youth set up when the club's president, Claudio Lottito, didn't care about it. A trequartista who can adapt to playing upfront, United spotted him in 2007 when they had sent a scout to watch a team-mate, but fell in love with Macheda the footballer. After he turned 16, he made the journey to England, convinced by 80,000 Euros a year and a job for his father." - *La Stampa*

"Sir Alex implored him to attack space. 'They're tired, you're not,' he urged. Kiko received the ball in the area and created a masterpiece. Old Trafford in delirium. And all deserved for little Federico, who for one evening will dine as a star, will feel like a star, will talk with everyone, and will want to go over again and again, for infinity, that wonderful double gesture, turning with his heel, the strike with his right foot, the fruit of the imagination" - *La Repubblica*.

MACHEDA QUOTES OF THE WEEK

"It was hard to pay the bills and we had been worrying about having enough money to get to the end of the month. Then we got that fateful telephone call from someone with an English accent." – *Pasquale Macheda on the moment his son started on the road to Villa.*

"It was like being in a dream. All these people celebrating Federico's goal. I cried. He dedicated the goal to me. He won champagne for being man of the match and gave it to us." – *Macheda senior, living every dad's dream.*

"Macheda is a big talent. It is not easy to leave your home country at 16 and come to a new culture. He signed pro last year but has buckled down and got a professional head on him. We expected him to make progress and he has." – *Ole (talking like a teacher on a school report) praises his protégé.*

QUOTE OF THE WEEK

'I might be too doting but I can see the talent of Marco van Basten in him.' – *Macheda Senior. I still can't believe he's younger than Giggs.*

OH AND ONE LAST THING
Football365 isn't convinced about Claudio Lottito's right to the moral high ground either:

"As students of law and the game will no doubt recall, Lazio were initially relegated from Serie A and deducted seven points (later reduced to no relegation and a three point deduction) for their involvement in the Calciopoli unpleasantness, which centred around the dicey selection of referees in the 2004/5 season. The very moral Lottito took over as Lazio president in 2004."

07/04/2009
CL - QUARTER-FINAL (1ST LEG)
UNITED 2 PORTO 2
Rodriguez 4, Rooney 15, Tévez 85, Mariano Gonzalez 89

OF COURSE YOU can understand why Fergie chose to play the Villa game when he did. The team had been all over the world in midweek. Tévez had – according to Fergie - been to Mars. Our record in Saturday lunchtime kick-offs after international breaks is terrible. And the gap between us and Liverpool was just too small to risk dropping valuable points at home. But as soon as this game kicked off Fergie must have known he was playing Russian roulette with our chances of making it to Rome. Playing two games in two days is a big ask at the best of times. But this was a United team missing two many key men and nursing too many off form players. And our opponents were much better than any of us – Fergie as well? – had expected.

Sure, we all thought Porto would be technically very good but we also thought they'd be timid, wary of their recent run of appalling results in England (Arsenal had battered them 4-0 as recently as September). They were quite the opposite. Instead of sitting back and crossing their fingers, Porto attacked us like no European visitors have since the Galacticos turned it on in 2003. And they kept on attacking us - their front three racing at us, their left-back playing left wing - even when they gifted us an equaliser. They outplayed us before Rooney capitalized on Bruno Alves's desperate back pass, they outplayed us for the rest of the first half and they were a constant danger when both teams started swinging punches at each other in the second. So while Gonzalez's last gasp leveller hurt, no one inside Old Trafford was complaining. Even at 2-2 it felt like we'd got away with it...

GOAL ACTION

0-1 (4): SHOCK... At kick-off, Old Trafford was still intoxicated by the Macheda factor that had left 75,000 people wandering around Stretford in a gurn-faced daze on Sunday night. Four minutes in and we were slapped sober by a hat-trick of defensive crimes. Ronaldo, not for the first or last time, lamely cedes possession and then gives up. Evans, who looks in desperate need of a break after an excellent first season, makes a hash of clearing the resulting centre and then backs off fatally as Rodriguez moves into the box and curls a low left-footer past Van der Sar.

1-1 (15): LIFELINE... Under no pressure, centre-back Bruno Alves knocks a pass-back direct to Rooney, who gratefully lifts the ball over Helton.

2-1 (85): Travesty...United were a different team in the second half from the first but even so they were massively flattered by the lead Tévez nicked them 13 minutes after coming on. Neville throws a Delap-style ball towards Rooney on the by-line, his heel-flicked volley catches Porto by surprise and Tévez pokes the ball into the roof of the net.

2-2 (89): JUSTICE... United's defending since the Liverpool game had been worse than appalling. And this might just have been the worst example of all, Gonzalez being left all alone in the penalty area to finish off Sapunaru's deflected centre at the far post.

WHAT'S GOOD?

AS THINGS STAND WE NEED A GREAT RESULT IN PORTO. We could have needed a miracle.

WHAT'S BAD?

THE DEFENCE: Evans is looking like the Champions League virgin he is, Evra's lost his mojo, Vidic is still getting his head straight after the Torres ordeal and the record clean sheet run seems light years away. How much do we miss Rio?

THE PRIMADONNA: Ronaldo's not chasing back and not caring. It's embarrassing. Rooney and Tévez, who spend far too much of their time doing his running at the best of times, must want to shoot him.

NO ENGLISH SIDE HAS EVER WON AT PORTO IN 11 ATTEMPTS.

PORTO – THE VERBALS

"We are good at firsts at this club. We know what we have to do. We're going to do it." – *Fergie bangs the drum ahead of the must-win game in Oporto.*

"We had a record to defend and when we lost the first goal against

Blackburn [things] started to turn. Since then we've lost really bad goals. We showed tiredness tonight because of the gamble I took [playing on Sunday]." – *Fergie blames it on Santa.*

VIEWS FROM THE PRESSBOX

"For the second time in a little more than 48 hours, a dramatic late goal transformed the mood inside Old Trafford, but this time Manchester United were on the wrong end of it and could have no complaints. Even when it briefly seemed last night that they had papered over the yawning cracks that could be seen during another slipshod display, they looked like a flagging team whose luck was in serious danger of running out." – *The Times*

"An 89th-minute equaliser horrified Old Trafford when it seemed Manchester United had fought back to win. The deeper distress lies in the knowledge that Sir Alex Ferguson's side is wavering at the critical phase of the season. The Champions League holders now face a challenge fit for a club with grand ambitions. Porto have never been beaten at home by an English club in European competition and it looks likely that a win at the Dragao Stadium will be necessary for United. On this evidence they are in no shape to pull off such a feat. Indeed, a draw barely did justice to visitors who were sharper, livelier and superior in all aspects." – *The Guardian. Fair enough.*

"Not for the first time in recent weeks United had been rocked back on their heels. The question is whether they have it in them, physically and mentally, to respond." – *The Times. See p.300 for the answer.*

HEADLINE OF THE NIGHT

'Porto And Lemons' – *High fives for the Daily Mirror.*

WORST HEADLINE OF THE NIGHT

'United Are Port Out' – *Slapped wrists for The Daily Star.*

MATCH FACTS

UNITED: VAN DER SAR, O'SHEA, VIDIC, EVANS (NEVILLE 72), EVRA, FLETCHER, CARRICK, SCHOLES (TÉVEZ 72), RONALDO, ROONEY, PARK (GIGGS 58)

FC PORTO: HELTON, SAPUNARU, ROLANDO, BRUNO ALVES, CISSOKHO, LUCHO GONZALEZ, FERNANDO, RAUL MEIRELES (COSTA 79), LOPEZ, HULK, RODRIGUEZ (MARIANO GONZALEZ 79), COSTA (MADRID 90) [FERREIRA]

BOOKED: BRUNO ALVES, HELTON
ATT: 74,517 REF: KONRAD PLAUTZ (AUSTRIA) H-T: 1-1

OTHER SCORES

CHAMPIONS LEAGUE Q-F: VILLARREAL 1 ARSENAL 1, LIVERPOOL 1
CHELSEA 3, BARCELONA 4 BAYERN MUNICH 0.

*"He can't help it but whinge and moan can he?
He loves it, doesn't he?"*

GOOD NEWS

UNITED'S FINANCIAL RESULTS are out. And they're impressive – a
22% rise in turnover to £256.2m and a 7.5% increase in profits to
£80.4m. Plus the wage costs are still well under 50% of turnover
which is seen as the barometer for a well-run football club. Chelsea
batter Liverpool 3-1 at Anfield in the first leg of their Champions
League quarter-final.

BAD NEWS

If United were a standalone business they'd have more money than
they'd know what to do with. Instead, thanks to the Glazers, our debt
know stands at an eye-watering £649.4m, up £24m in a year. We
wasted £68.8m just paying off the interest on the loans in 2007/8.
And from 2013, when the first major loan needs to be repaid, we'll
have to somehow pay even more. (And to think if it hadn't been for
that bloody horse).

'SHOCK, HORROR' QUOTE OF THE DAY

'United and the Glazer family are not commenting on the latest
accounts.' – *from The Telegraph.*

TALK TALK

*Benitez doesn't talk about other clubs. That's a fact. So who can this be
getting worked up by Fergie's – let's face it – uncontroversial suggestion that
the winner of the Chelsea-Liverpool tie would present more of a domestic
threat?*

"I think it maybe is that he is a little bit scared. If we continue in Big Cup maybe he will think we are tired. If we are not in this competition then he knows that we will be a threat in the Premier League. I would like to be worried about both competitions, it means we will continue to be successful. We just concentrate on our team, while he likes to talk too much about other teams."

REPLY OF THE WEEK

"The interesting thing as far as Rafa Benitez is concerned is that he's got a European tie and he's talking about Alex Ferguson. Fantastic! I didn't know I was that important." – *The Benitez fans in the press would never agree but Fergie's winning this mind battle. Hands down.*

WHAT A DIFFERENCE 2 DAYS (AND GOALS) MAKE
More good sleuthing from football365:

'Liverpool, of course, will plough on. But if there was a day when a team's spirit was going to be broken it was yesterday. For so long it looked as if that team would be United. But if they can get out of the sort of hole they found themselves in yesterday, it's unlikely they will stumble into any more between now and the end of the season' - *Steven Howard, The Sun, April 6.*

'So much for Manchester United being galvanised by the miracle of Federico Macheda 48 hours earlier. So much, according to Alex Ferguson, for United now going into overdrive. More like reverse, downhill, in a steam-roller. It was as if the lessons of Sunday's Great Escape had gone in one ear and out the other' - *Steven Howard, The Sun, April 8.*

QUOTES OF THE WEEK

"He can't help it but whinge and moan can he? He loves it, doesn't he?" - *Fergiephile Sam Allardyce on Benitez*

"What I saw in the first half is, without doubt, the worst football in Bayern's history" - *Franz Beckenbauer after Bayern got battered 4-0 on their first visit to the Nou Camp since you know when.*

"Real Madrid are very talented, but Manchester United have been the most organised team I ever played against" – *Alessandro Del Piero praises United. For the record Del Piero – the one before the injury - might be in the top XI of players I've seen live at Old Trafford*.

OLD BOY OF THE WEEK

"The problem was that there was a field of nettles directly behind the goal. There would be Beckham, Scholes, Yorke, Giggs blasting balls everywhere. The ones that missed would go a mile into these nettles. Then they'd be like, 'Fetch.' I had to put on hats, gloves and tracksuit bottoms and wade into these nettles, getting stung all over. But I wouldn't have swapped it for the world" - *Phil Bardsley recalls his days as the youth-team player in charge of retrieving the balls during the first team's shooting practice.*

*TEAM OF THE WEEK

If you had to name a team made of the best visiting players you've seen at Old Trafford (picked from European sides only) what would it be? Here's mine:

CASILLAS - ZANETTI, HIERRO, SAMMER, ROBERTO CARLOS – MESSI, ZIDANE, REDONDO, NEDVED - DEL PIERO, RONALDO

FAPL 11/04/2009

SUNDERLAND 1 UNITED 2
Scholes 19, Jones 55, Macheda 76

DID HE MEAN IT? Does it matter? The boy's already a legend – and he's only played 50 minutes. When Macheda came on United weren't in the same trouble they had been against Villa, but they were getting sore from banging their heads against the Sunderland defence. Then just 46 seconds later the game was won – and Liverpool's Saturday was ruined. Which begs the question – tongue in cheek of course – which striker has done more damage for United this season... Tévez, Berbatov or Macheda?

THE ANSWER?

Berbatov has copped plenty of stick this season but he has actually scored more decisive goals – 3 - than any other player apart from – here's the next surprise – Darren Fletcher. Here's the list in full (with match-winning goals in bold and point-saving goals in italics).
Berbatov 3 *(6 extra points won)*, Fletcher **1 + 2** *(4)*, Macheda **2** *(4)*, Vidic **2** *(4)*, Rooney **2** *(4)*, Ronaldo **2** *(4)*, Tévez **1** *(2)*, Giggs **1** *(2)*, Park **1** *(1)*.

GOAL ACTION

1-0 (19): One of United's main problems this season has been a lack of goals from central midfield. Anderson has still not opened his duck, Scholes has scored one, Carrick two and Fletcher three. But just when United needed a goal from somewhere, Scholes provided it, ghosting into the area to flick Rooney's floated centre from the left into the top corner.

1-1 (55): Scholes's opener should have settled United's nerves and sent struggling Sunderland into their shells. It didn't. Sunderland were allowed to fire in too many crosses in the direction of the hulking Kenwyne Jones and eventually the tactic paid off. Tainio nutmegs Park, Foster misjudges the flight of the cross – his first genuine mistake for United? – and Jones bundles the ball over the line at the second attempt.

2-1 (76): It was all United from then on but Berbatov and Tévez – who once again didn't look a natural fit – wasted what few clear-cut chances were made. Then Macheda comes on for Berbatov, Carrick fires in a harmless daisycutter of a shot and his first touch takes it into the net. At first glance it looked like a fluke. At second it looks like a brilliant piece of quick thinking. It's too early to say if Kiko will make it of course. But there's no doubt he's got the gift...

INTRO OF THE DAY

"When do miracles become mundane?" – *from The Times.*

WHAT WAS GOOD?

MACHEDA. A legend is born.
SCHOLES – rolling back the years with his late run into the box and goal.

WHAT WAS BAD?

"MACHEDA WOAH, MACHEDA WOAH, HE CAME FROM LAZIO, HE SCORED A WONDERGOAL." *I know there wasn't much time to come up with a Macheda chant up but even so...*

VIEWS FROM THE PRESSBOX

"WHEN do miracles become mundane? The short career of Federico Macheda could be summed up by Sir Alex Ferguson's famous words: 'Football? bloody hell.' The plotting of this sport is haywire but Ferguson has used it to weave winning narratives since he began in management at East Stirlingshire. Call it genius, call it luck, curse it if you are from west London or Liverpool — one thing is certain, it happens too often to be coincidence." — *The Times*.

"For his next trick, Manchester United's new 17-year-old gamebreaker came on and scored the winning goal with a single touch. United might be limping towards the Premier League finish line rather than striding out in front, but as long as they have Federico Macheda they seem capable of staying ahead.

"It will be scant consolation to Liverpool – who must be sick of the young Italian already – that his second Premier League goal in a week was not quite in the same class as the first. They all count and, at this stage of the season, all that matters is the final score. The one thing that was never in doubt was who would claim the goal and those who felt Macheda might struggle to maintain the sensational standard he set on his debut have been answered in less than a week." — *The Observer*.

"In time they may come to call this the Federico Macheda title. For the second consecutive weekend the 17-year-old Italian came off the Manchester United bench not only to score a preposterous match-winning goal but also to re-assert United's leadership of the Premier League...By comparison with last week, the goals were beauty and beast; whereas then Macheda was the author of his story, yesterday he was a bystander as Carrick's drive rattled into his shin and bent away at speed into the far corner. But it was Macheda's goal, Macheda's winner. He has become United's unlikely talisman." — *The Indie*.

SUNDERLAND – THE VERBALS

"Macheda has got something special about him, the boy." — *Fergie states the obvious*.

"It's immaterial whether he meant the goal. Everything he touches turns to gold." — *Ricky Sbragia just sighs*.

MATCH FACTS

SUNDERLAND: GORDON, BARDSLEY, FERDINAND, DAVENPORT (MCSHANE 73), COLLINS, EDWARDS, LEADBITTER, TAINIO (YORKE 85), REID (MURPHY 80), CISSE, JONES [SBRAGIA]
BOOKED: FERDINAND.
UNITED: FOSTER, NEVILLE, EVANS, VIDIC, O'SHEA, PARK (RONALDO 69), CARRICK, SCHOLES, ROONEY, BERBATOV (MACHEDA 75), TÉVEZ (ANDERSON 82).
BOOKED: NEVILLE, ROONEY

Stadium of Light Att: 45,408 Ref: Rob Styles h-t: 1-0

OTHER SCORES

Liverpool 4 Blackburn 0, Chelsea 4 Bolton 3 Wigan 1, Arsenal 4

LEAGUE TABLE

1. United 71 (31) 2. Liverpool 70 (32) 3. Chelsea 67 (32)
4. Arsenal 61 (32)… 17. Sunderland 32 (32)

"There were times I threw up because of the taste, but I kept going because the heart of wanting to become a better footballer was greater than having a good tasting meal every day."

NEWS

Porto coach Jesualdo Ferreira won't be allowed to contact his players before, during or after the United game after UEFA punish him for making an offensive gesture to the referee during Porto's last-16 win against Atletico Madrid. Strangely he then announces that he won't even bother coming to the stadium at all. Advantage United? Chelsea make us all squirm by doing their best to throw away the 3-1 lead they built up against Liverpool at Anfield. Fortunately they come back from 2-0 and 4-3 down to draw 4-4 and win the tie 7-5. *The Mirror* reveals that a favourite pastime of United players is a version of 'scissors, paper, stone' which ends up with Parky being hit on the head with a shoe. While *The Telegraph* gives an insight into the sacrifices the Park family made to turn him into the biggest name in Korean sport…

FROGS 'N' DOGS

From The Telegraph :

"THEY did not tell him what it was, but each night the weakling teenager would be given a bowl of juice, extracted from boiled frogs, by his parents and each night, despite its revolting smell and taste, the lad dutifully tried to keep down as much as he could. 'They said it was good for my health to become stronger and I ate anything that would improve my health,' Ji-Sung Park told his entranced compatriots in a television documentary about his life which recently transfixed a nation.

"'There were times I threw up because of the taste, but I kept going because the heart of wanting to become a better footballer was greater than having a good tasting meal every day. I was willing to do anything to become better."

"His parents made sacrifices. Extraordinarily, Seong-jong gave up his job to run a butchers, just so Park could have the best cuts of meat on hand daily to build him up. Dad would go to frog farms because he had been told 'they're very nutritious and can help people grow'. Mum, Jang Myeong-ja, did not know how to cook them, so boiled them to create the dreaded soup."

STAT OF THE WEEK

In the past 10 years United have sold 380,000 credit and debit cards in the UK. Since their launch in February 2006 – the season that Park arrived from PSV - United have sold 1.2million in South Korea alone.

OLD BOY OF THE WEEK

Gerrard Pique talks pints, pies and people:
"At United there were some incredible things happening. Everyone was allowed to eat what they wanted and one must remember that the English diet is just like people say."

"Every 15 days they would put us on what we dubbed the 'spare-tyre machine' to measure our body fat. You would be amazed at how many top players practically broke the machine because their diet was based on beer and burgers." - *Are you thinking of the same 'top player' that I am?*

"I arrived not being able to speak English and I got lost a little bit in the team-talks. The gaffer speaks a very Scottish kind of English that might as well have been Chinese as far as I was concerned. But I wasn't the worst – there are players in the current squad who still don't understand him."

"The change in Manchester was very hard. But there are no regrets at all because in Manchester they really turned me into a player."

CHILDISH GIGGLE OF THE WEEK

Football365...hang your head in shame:
"He knows the role we want him to play. We want him to penetrate in behind them" - *Alex Ferguson has ideas about what young*

Federico Macheda can do.

QUOTES OF THE WEEK

"Why was he banned? I knew he hadn't attacked me - unlike someone else I know." – *Fergie on Porto coach Ferreira's ban. Who could he be talking about?*

"Asian fans shout at me and chase me; when I go back to Korea maybe I couldn't walk down the streets." – *Parky is almost the invisible man over here. But back in Seoul he's like James Bond - every man wants to be like him, every woman wants to be with him.*

"I have never seen a player as intelligent. I tell him he needs to bring out a video because his movement is such a good example for young players. Park shows it's about the team, not individuals." - *Evra on his pal, Park. Ji-Sung Park.*

15/04/2009
CL QUARTER-FINAL (2ND LEG)

PORTO 0 UNITED 1
(United win 3-2 on aggregate)
Ronaldo 6

BEFORE THE GAME Ramon Calderon was up to his old tricks again, telling everyone who'd listen that he'd already sealed the deal to sign up one of the best players in the world. Everyone added two and two and came up (rightly) with the name Ronaldo. And you know what. I bet there was a bit of you that thought, even then, that we might as well take the Spanish government's millions and run. In fact many Reds would have gone even further and wished we'd done it long ago, even before he ruined last summer. After all, Ronaldo's body language had been terrible for much of the season and his 'only god knows my future' spiel nauseatingly tiresome. He'd given up tracking back. He'd even – let's be honest – been a bit rubbish in some games. And then he does something like this, something so spectacular, brilliant and important that none of it really matters. Who cares if he wants to jump into bed with Madrid? He still scored that goal. Who cares that he doesn't track back? Who else in the team – any team – could have scored that goal? Who cares if he kicks out and throws his toys out of the pram and loves himself more than any player has any right to? He does all that – and worse – and he still scored that goal...

As Ronaldo himself said afterwards it was the best goal he'd ever scored. And it might just be the most important, Moscow apart. Because make no mistake about it United were up against it. Remember the script. Porto had already outplayed us at Old Trafford. They were unbeaten for 24 games and unbeaten against British sides at home forever. And we were playing like idiots, conceding goals and making hard work of beating everyone. Plus it had been ten years since we'd drawn a knock-out game at home and gone through. There was a real danger we were going to suffer a Leverkusen all over again, a frustrating defeat to a team we really should be beating. But then Ronaldo picked up the ball and pulled back his right foot...

GOAL!

1-0 (6): How do you start describing something this special? Ronaldo gets the ball 40 yards from goal and just leathers it. Helton sees it all the way but, as the ball dips and appears to pick up speed, he has as much chance of stopping a bullet. Incredible...

STATS OF THE DAY

39.6 YARDS AND 64 MPH – the measurements for Ronaldo's wondergoal.

LINE OF THE DAY

"Cristiano Ronaldo, how do I love thee? Let me count the ways. They add up to . . . er, well, not very many, actually. But then the oily, smirking, preening little bugger scores a goal like that and, well, what is a chap supposed to do? I need help here." – *Simon Barnes, The Times*

PORTO – THE VERBALS

"Have I seen a better European goal? I think I'd have to go into the memory banks for that. It was fantastic and gave us such a platform to go on to victory." – *Fergie on Ronnie's rocket.*

"I think it's the best goal I've ever scored. I didn't know it was 65mph — wow! When Anderson gave me the ball, I thought I'd just turn and shoot. We haven't played great the last five games but

I hope this will change all that. To play Arsenal is a fantastic tie."
— *Ronaldo. Wow.*

VIEWS FROM THE PRESSBOX

"Not for nothing are Manchester United the champions of England, Europe and the world. Not for nothing is Cristiano Ronaldo the best player on the planet. Team and talisman combined in perfect harmony last night as United came to northern Portugal, saw off Porto and conquered where no British team had done before to reach the semi-finals of the Champions League for a third successive season." — *The Times*

"These are the nights when Cristiano Ronaldo lives up to all the hype, when the World Player of the Year really looks the shining star in the footballing universe. As Manchester United fans twirled their scarves above their heads, as Porto's fortress finally fell to British opposition, Ronaldo's majestic early strike will live long in the memory.

"The advantage gained, United played with great discipline, rarely risking possession, and restricting Porto to few attempts on goal as they progressed to a semi-final with Arsenal, conquerors of Villarreal. Throughout the season, Sir Alex Ferguson has made polite noises about Arsene Wenger, the suspicion being that the United manager did not consider Arsenal a real threat. Real friendship or phoney war? We shall shortly find out." - *The Telegraph*

MATCH FACTS

FC PORTO: HELTON, SAPUNARU (COSTA 80), ROLANDO, BRUNO ALVES, CISSOKHO, LUCHO GONZALEZ (MARIANO GONZALEZ 31), FERNANDO, RAUL MEIRELES, LOPEZ, HULK, RODRIGUEZ (FARIAS 64) [FERREIRA — SITTING AT HOME]
UNITED: VAN DER SAR, O'SHEA, FERDINAND, VIDIC, EVRA, GIGGS, CARRICK, ANDERSON (SCHOLES 78), ROONEY, BERBATOV (NANI 68), RONALDO
BOOKED: VIDIC, EVRA.
ATT: 50,000 REF: MASSIMO BUSACCA (SWITZERLAND) H-T: 1-0

OTHER SCORES

CHAMPIONS LEAGUE QUARTER-FINALS:
ARSENAL 3 VILLARREAL 0, *Arsenal win 4-1,*
CHELSEA 4 LIVERPOOL 4, *Chelsea win 7-5,*
BAYERN 1 BARCELONA 1, *Barcelona win 5-1*

*"He gets all your emotions going, drags you in with the physical, emotional way he plays. When he starts to compete and show that great desire and intensity, you say to yourself, `F****** hell, what is he made of, the boy?"*

NEWS

YOU'LL NEVER GUESS what. Fergie and Benitez are at it again, except this time Fergie's got a friend in tow, Blackburn manager Sam Allardyce. Now I don't know about you but, after the entente cordiale with Wenger and the general chumminess with Mourinho, it's been refreshing to see Fergie taking on his man again. But when a 54 year-old and a 67 year-old get themselves this lathered up about a pretty tame touchline gesture, you've got to wonder if it's all in danger of getting out of hand.

Talking about careless gestures, Liverpool reserve keeper Charles Itandje is in trouble after being spotted laughing and doing dance moves... during the Hillsborough tribute. The papers make mischief by predicting that Rooney will snub Rio's summer wedding because Rio didn't come to his last year. Maybe he just doesn't like owls? United dominate the PFA nominations, taking 6 of the 10 slots. Van der Sar, Ferdinand, Giggs and Vidic compete with Gerrard for the main award while Evans and Rafael fight it out with Young, Agbonlahor, Ireland and Lennon for the young version. Oh and Hamburg knock the world's richest club out of the UEFA Cup. '33 years' anyone?

PINCER MOVEMENT

"It was open arms and then a crossover of the arms. It was as if to suggest that was it." – *Allardyce fumes after copping what he saw as a 'humiliating gesture' from Benitez during Blackburn's 4-0 surrender at the weekend (if you can't remember what Benitez did, think of the move cheeky Paddy Evra made all week when we won the title).*

"Not explaining himself by not turning up in his office really shows what he is like. The only people I saw were Sammy Lee and a few of the staff, but he never showed his face. That was just as disappointing as the gesture, and it typifies the man." – *Sounds like Big Sam's in a big mood.*

"Everton are a big club, not a small one which Benitez arrogantly said. But arrogance is one thing. You cannot forgive contempt, which is what he showed Sam Allardyce last weekend." - *Fergie arrives on the scene...*

"I've never had any of these issues like that (Benitez's 2nd goal celebration against Blackburn). He's never done that to me – never had a chance. I think you should respect a manager. I don't think you'd ever get me doing something like that. You have to have humility." – *And casually forgets the 4-1.*

QUOTES OF THE WEEK

"You're not going to get many players score a goal like that, apart from myself. It was unbelievable!" – *Gazza takes time off from his parrots to rave about Ronaldo's Porto rocket.*

"Nobody has to be told about Kiko's ability. And he's a hard bastard. Strikers need a bit of that." – *Do you think Fergie sees a bit of himself in Macheda?*

"He gets all your emotions going, drags you in with the physical, emotional way he plays. When he starts to compete and show that great desire and intensity, you say to yourself, `F★★★★★★ hell, what is he made of, the boy?' – *Fergie on Rooney.*

MEMORY OF THE WEEK
Everton Captain Dave Watson on the day Rooney was FA Cup Mascot and "helped" warm up Neville Southall:

"The mascot would usually just go out and warm up Big Nev. But Wayne kept chipping him and Nev was getting really p★★★ed off about it. The thing with Nev is that he doesn't really have a polite way of saying things. So it wasn't a case of 'Excuse me son, pack that in', he just told him to f★★★★★g stop that you little so and so!"

PREDICTION OF THE WEEK
(from Fergie's interview with the Sunday Times)

"Danny's a certainty to make it at the highest level. I've told Fabio Capello the boy will be in his World Cup squad next year. Wide left or right or through the middle, he has the intelligence, guts, athleticism and talent to do the job."

"He's going to be a big lad. His height is about 6ft 1in now but the prediction is he'll be 6ft 3in. He's yet to get the conformation in his thighs, so he is still gangly, but he's brave enough to carry that. When he completes his growing, he'll really be something."

NON-UNITED QUOTE OF THE WEEK

"I speak my mind and other chairmen should too. They need to wake up from their coma. They can have lunch with me at Harrods, where I can serve them stags' testicles. We need big balls in this business" – *Fulham fruitcake Mohamed Fayed.*

QUOTE OF THE WEEK

Ian Brown on how it feels to have 'This is the One' played at Old Trafford:

"I wrote that tune in 1986 when I was on the dole, and there was no way I could have known that 20 years later United would be coming on to the pitch to it. It still gets me every time. It's an amazing feeling. I've got three season tickets now in the East Stand, the old K Stand, with my two oldest sons, and they buzz off it. I laugh and say, 'Well, the PRS [Performing Rights Society] is probably paying for the tickets.'

RUNNER-UP

Everyone's favourite Manc monkey on his favourite chant:

"'He plays on the left, he plays on the right, that boy Ronaldo makes England look shite'. That's what I love about United: we're the Republic of Mancunia, no one gives a fuck about England. My next favourite would be 'You can stick yer fucking England up yer arse", which we sing to Chelsea and the London clubs. I love that. When we sing "Argentina" when Tévez comes on, you see the away fans with open mouths. What other club in England would sing "Argentina"? Nobody. I love that."

19/04/2009
FA CUP SEMI-FINAL

EVERTON 0 UNITED 0

(Everton win 4-2 on pens)
Pens: Cahill [missed], Berbatov [missed], Baines, Ferdinand [missed], P.Neville, Vidic, Vaughan, Anderson, Jagielka

LET'S FACE IT. No one knows better than Fergie how to guide a team, and a squad, through the maze of fixtures that closes in on us at this stage each season. And if he thinks his best players need a rest, or that the laughable Wembley surface is going to get them injured, or that picking the Carling Cup team here and leaving the A-team for Portsmouth will put us in pole position to win the league, then who's to argue. Still, it's a shame he left so many stars in their suits for this one. Just remember what we had in front of us. A never-to-be-repeated Quintuple. A second treble. A first double in a decade. A first-ever domestic treble. A first FA Cup for 5 years... And instead we gave an inferior Everton team, a team we still owe for 1995, the chance to enjoy themselves in the Wembley sun.

Mind you, it wasn't all Fergie's fault that we lost this one. Everton's centre-back duo of Lescott and Jagielka did a very passable impersonation of Vidic and Ferdinand to ensure we didn't really fashion a chance. Berbatov did a very passable impersonation of a man who just couldn't be bothered when he missed the crucial penalty kick. And worst of all Mike Riley did a very passable impersonation of a man with no balls when he chose not to see Jagielka's blatant trip on Welbeck. The record books will say we lost this game because Everton scored more penalties than us. In truth, just like last year against Portsmouth, we lost because we were given less penalties than we deserved.

MATCH ACTION (THE CONDENSED VERSION)

GET TO WEMBLEY. Get pink in the sunshine. Laugh at Scousers still wearing shellsuits. Get the team news. Excited by the chance to see Macheda and the kids. Worried that Ronaldo and Rooney aren't even on the bench. Bemused that Nani can't get in the Carling Cup, I mean FA Cup, team. Kick-off. Welbeck and Macheda look the part. Macheda sets up Tévez for the chance of the half. He fluffs it. United are dominant. Everton are just booting it towards Fellaini. Is Moyes fluffing his audition for the United job?

HALF-TIME. All a bit boring so far. See two Reds doing coke off a penknife in the queue for the toilets. Never seen that before. Have to stop mashed–up neighbour falling down the Wembley steps. Have seen that before. United fans go quiet as the booze wears off. Everton fans grow louder as United seem to run out of ideas. But then drama. Welbeck bursts into the box. Jagielka brings him down. Riley bottles it. Fergie goes ballistic, shaking his fists like an OAP who's just watched his bus sail past. Neither side makes a chance. Berbatov replaces Macheda at full time. It seems like a good idea at the time.

EXTRA-TIME is even worse than normal time. 0-0 final score. It's penalties. Yes. Cahill boots his pen into the United crowd. No. Berbatov rolls new Wembley's tamest ever penalty straight at Howard. Several thousand Reds instantly turn nasty. Hardcore Berba-fans think he can't get any more cool and interesting. Baines scores to put Everton one up. Ferdinand misses our second. Advantage Everton. Pip Neville of all people scores. It's 2-0 and almost all over. Where is Foster's ipod? Vidic gets us going. Vaughan scores to make it 3-1. Foster's nowhere. Where is that bloody ipod? Anderson, the surprise spot kick specialist (have you seen him shoot normally?), scores calmly. But it's not enough. Jagielka scores. Everton erupt. Pip Neville makes himself look miserable. A nice touch that. It's Chelsea-Everton in the final. Make a promise not to bother watching it. Break promise...

CUP SEMI WINNERS

Both sets of centre-backs - The only real quality on show all afternoon.

Pip Neville - Showed zero emotion when Everton won. A class act.

The young guns - Macheda didn't score for the first time ever. But he and Welbeck both looked the part.

Moyes - Engineered Everton's first Wembley win since 1995. And won the battle of the mind games by suggesting beforehand that Riley was a closet Red.

Chelsea – will play Everton in the final instead of a full-strength United.

CUP SEMI LOSERS

Tévez - Dropped too deep, never threatened to score and lacked the pace to outrun Jagielka and Lescott. Shouldn't a £35 million player be bossing this sort of game?

United's forwards – failed to score at Wembley for the third time this season.

Nani – not involved at all. Where does he go from here?

Berbatov – Love him or hate him, you can't deny it... that was a truly miserable penalty. And the body language – all bowed head and hairband fiddling - made it worse. It looked an effort for him to walk back to halfway. Actually it looked an effort for him to walk from halfway in the first place.

MIKE RILEY – Made a monkey for his back by giving United a pile of penalties a few years back (the vast majority of them justified, by the way). Now opponents have to commit a criminal offence for us to get one off him.

FERGIE – Lost an FA Cup semi-final for the first time ever (after winning 7 out of 7).

UNITED – lost an FA Cup semi-final for the first time since Leeds in 1970 (after winning 12 out of 12).

WEMBLEY – as if the stadium build wasn't enough of an embarrassment, take a look at the pitch. It looks OK from a distance but it plays like Old Trafford circa 1992.

MOAN OF THE DAY

What's the point of us playing strong teams in earlier rounds, of coming up with magnificent displays like the one that demolished Fulham in the quarters... and then playing the kids in the semi?

UNWANTED ACHIEVEMENT OF THE DAY

United are the only team to have played at Wembley three times in a season – and failed to score in any game.

PLUS:

United are also the only team to have taken part in three Wembley penalty shoot-outs in the same season. They're the only side to have played 4 games at Wembley in the same season (1993-94). And they're the only side to have played 3 games at Wembley in the same season on more than one occasion (see below):

UNITED – 1982-83: 1-2 v LIVERPOOL (MILK CUP) 2-2, 4-0 v BRIGHTON (FA CUP).

UNITED – 1993-94: 1-1 v ARSENAL (CHARITY SHIELD), 1-1 v OLDHAM (FA CUP SEMI), 1-3 v ASTON VILLA (LEAGUE CUP), 4-0 v CHELSEA (FA CUP).

UNITED – 2008-09: 0-1 v PORTSMOUTH (CHARITY SHIELD), 0-0 v SPURS (LEAGUE CUP), 0-0 v EVERTON (FA CUP SEMI).

PUB QUIZ QUESTION OF THE DAY

Who are the only other teams to have played at Wembley three times in the same season?★

EVERTON – THE VERBALS

Fergie on the 'penalty' and Moyes's pre-match dig about Riley being a Red:

"I think it might have been (a factor in the game). I'm not saying that for certain. I've no idea if it affected the decision but you never know. It may have. It can prey on a referee's mind. Why would he [Welbeck] go down when he had the goalkeeper stranded out of his goal? It was a major decision and unfortunately it has gone against us. When he [Riley] sees it he'll probably realise he's made a mistake but I can't say that's the reason for us losing."

Phil Neville thanks his missus:

"We played Middlesbrough three weeks ago and when I got home that night my wife said I needed to practise penalties. She had a feeling that was how the semi-final was going to be settled so, for the last three weeks, I have been practising. I was 11 when I last took one and I missed. But I knew, as captain, against my old club, I needed to show my leadership qualities."

Fergie pays tribute to a favourite Fledgling:

"Phil is one of the special people in the game so I hope he is picking up that cup. Everyone knows his connection to Manchester United. He was here so long as a kid. I know he was captaining Everton in a semi-final but don't tell me there was not one small part in him that was saying, 'Christ I am going to knock Manchester United out of the cup here'. It goes to show you the integrity of the man. He is a fantastic person and no-one in the game deserves it more than he does."

And finally Fergie joins the growing chorus of managers who've complained about the state of the pitch at new Wembley:

"It looked spongy and dead and difficult to move the ball quickly around it. We should have won it but that's the issue with Wembley there's very few games where there's a lot of goals"

VIEWS FROM THE PRESSBOX

"There is a world of difference between wanting victory, as United's players did, and yearning for it, like their opponents, and, as Phil Jagielka banged the decisive penalty past Ben Foster, sparking euphoric celebrations among the hordes of Everton fans, it was impossible to escape the feeling that justice had been done.

"Sir Alex Ferguson will take issue with that, arguing the toss over the penalty that his team appeared to have been wrongly denied when Jagielka tripped Danny Welbeck midway through the second half, but the United manager ceded the right to too much sympathy when he chose to field a weaker lineup than he had sent out in most of the Carling Cup matches this season. With Edwin van der Sar, Michael Carrick, Cristiano Ronaldo and Wayne Rooney left in Manchester and Patrice Evra and Dimitar Berbatov only substitutes, Ferguson left the distinct impression that he and United had bigger fish to fry." – *The Times seems to think that justice was done because Everton – a team with far fewer distractions than United – picked a stronger team. Huh?*

"Manchester United have distracted themselves to defeat at last. On this rare occasion, they could not keep one tournament under control while preserving players for the two others that are still open to them. The line-up was fractionally unequal to the task against David Moyes' well-drilled team." – *The Guardian*

MATCH FACTS

UNITED: FOSTER, RAFAEL DA SILVA, FERDINAND, VIDIC, FABIO DA SILVA (EVRA 63), WELBECK, GIBSON, ANDERSON, PARK (SCHOLES 67), TÉVEZ, MACHEDA (BERBATOV 91)
BOOKED: RAFAEL DA SILVA, TÉVEZ, SCHOLES.
EVERTON: HOWARD, HIBBERT, JAGIELKA, LESCOTT, BAINES, OSMAN, NEVILLE, FELLAINI (VAUGHAN 102), PIENAAR, CAHILL, SAHA (RODWELL 70) [MOYES]
BOOKED: FELLAINI, CAHILL.
WEMBLEY ATT: 88,141 REF: MIKE RILEY H-T: 0-0

OTHER SCORES

FA CUP SEMI-FINAL: CHELSEA 2 ARSENAL 1
Arsenal and Sheffield Wednesday –
1992-93 2-1 (League Cup), 1-1, 2-1 (FA Cup)

"Berbatov has a Brazilian mentality.
Someone should always kick his a*@!"

NEWS

MUST WIN THEIR first battle in the war against United's ticket pricing as the Office of Fair Trading forces the club to make their season ticket policies fairer to fans. From now on United must provide more information on when, where and why season tickets are relocated for cup games, more information on the potential cost of long cup runs and a clearer appeal process for disputes over season-ticket cancellations because of non-payment of cup games. But – and this is the crucial bit – the OFT won't be making United do anything about the hated Automatic Cup Scheme any time soon. Apparently it would be too expensive for them to launch a full probe into the rights and wrongs of the case. So while the government saves money, we're all forced to spend more...

Possebon chooses to play for Italy rather than Brazil at international level. Which seems like a smart move. With his quietly sophisticated rather than carnival style he's always looked more like a European Latin than a South American one. As the Benitez-Fergie feud is put on the back burner for a couple of days, the Calderon-Fergie feud resumes. And (watch out alliteration fans) Andrei Arshavin's four goals in Arsenal's epic draw at Anfield give United vital breathing space in the title race...

OUTLANDISH INTRO OF THE WEEK
From The Daily Telegraph:
'How did Andrei Arshavin score four goals against Liverpool? Well, judging by the history books, we shouldn't discount the possibility that the Russian may have injected himself with monkey testicles.'

So what's the link? Actually it's a pretty interesting story. The last visiting player to score four league goals at Anfield was Wolves's Dennis Westcott in 1946. And like the rest of his team-mates, Westcott had been put on a systemic doping programme by Wolves boss Major Frank Buckley that included injecting players with – that's right - small slices of monkey testicles. It can't have done Westcott any harm. That season he scored 38 goals in 35 games. And left home to live in a tree.

'HISTORY IN THE MAKING'

"This team is on the way to becoming more famous than The Beatles. There are many weeks of emotion awaiting us in the Champions League and Premier League and this season could end up being historic for us." – *Alvaro Arbeloa, 25 March 2009.*

"A point was insufficient. It is going to be terribly difficult for us to win the league after failing to beat Arsenal." - *Alvaro Arbeloa after Liverpool's 4-4 draw, 21 April 2009.*

STILL BITCHIN'

"All the talk about Cristiano was coming from Calderon. He is a dinosaur. He has been buried" – *After all the Benitez drivel it's almost a relief to hear Fergie turn his attention back to his other favourite Spaniard.*

"He must have had some tremendous problems in his life as he seems to be a tormented man. He only opens his mouth to attack other Premier League managers, but above all, Real Madrid." – *Ramon Calderon, El Dinosaurio.*

NEWS II

Fulham defender John Pantsil reveals that Roy Hodgson gave him a cash gift of £10,000 for successfully man-marking Ronaldo out of the Fulham game. Given the mood Ronaldo was in that day Hodgson may think he overpaid. Liverpool are linked with a cheeky bid for Tévez. And the debate that's simmered among United fans since August reaches the boil in the wake of his awful penalty miss at Wembley. So what do you think. Is Berbatov good for us? Or is he a lazy, unprofessional and disinterested waste of money who's too laidback to fit in with United's high-tempo game?

BERBATOV THE DEFENCE

I've got to declare an interest here. I can't get enough of the man. He's intriguing, he's different, he's classy and if his first touch was any sweeter he'd be using it to pull angels out of the sky. There's no point pretending he's had a great season but he did give us a glimpse of what he could do for us with his October goal spurt, the damage he did at the turn of the year and best of all that moment of genius against West Ham. He's always going to suffer from comparisons with a workaholic like Tévez but since when has ability to chase lost causes and bother centre-backs like a rabid Jack Russell been the hallmark of a truly great centre-forward? Watch out for him when he gets a close season under his belt and he gets properly settled in. Those people who are slagging him off now are going to feel very stupid worshipping him in a year's time.

Mind you if the case had to be settled today...

BERBATOV THE PROSECUTION

Let's ignore the lack of running, the refusal to get into the box to get on the end of crosses, the endless fiddling with his hairband, the half-arsed body language, all those easy balls back to the centre-backs and the worst penalty ever, let's get the stats to do the talking. Berbatov might have been responsible for setting up 9 of United's 54 league goals (only Lampard, Van Persie and Malbranque can match that). And 4 of his 13 goals in all competitions might have been winners. But only one of them has come against a team in the top six (Chelsea in January), he hasn't scored for 9 matches and hasn't scored in the Champions League since October 21. And he's set up just one goal for Rooney all season – and that was against punchbags West Brom. The new Veron? On what we've seen so far, it's hard to disagree...

QUOTES OF THE WEEK

"People told me it's a big thing here. I think Manchester United is the biggest thing in Manchester and then after that it is Coronation Street." – *Ronaldo's been here since 2003 and not seen the Street? Madness.*

"I don't see any evidence of Berbatov's season tailing off. He has missed a few games and overall on Sunday, I thought he did really well. He will get criticism because when you pay £30million for a player everyone thinks he should be able to score with a penalty kick. He was upset and disappointed, as we all were." – *Fergie just stops short of shouting 'Youse are all idiots' as he defends his man.*

"Ideally we wanted three points, so we see it as two points dropped but this point could be big." – *Gerrard clutches straws after the Liverpool-Arsenal 4-4.*

REGRET OF THE WEEK

"It was impossible thinking we could do that [the quintuple]. In the last few weeks we've had a lot of injuries to defenders and we have been patching things up. If all the players had been fit, you never know, we might have gone for it. But realistically it was always difficult." – *Fergie's not crying about the end of the 'impossible' Quintuple dream. But hold on, if we'd beaten Everton on Sunday our patched up team would have had to play just one extra game – the Cup Final - after everything else had been settled. It still feels like a wasted opportunity to me.*

NO SH★T COMMENT OF THE WEEK

"Berbatov has a Brazilian mentality. Someone should always kick his a★@!" - *Klaus Augenthaler, Berbatov's coach at Leverkusen.*

RUNNER-UP
From football365:
   "You have to say the move has worked out well for him" -
*European Champion and two-time Premier League winner Wayne Rooney
will be relieved that his uncle Richie thinks signing for Manchester United
was a good option.*

FAPL 22/04/2009
UNITED 2 PORTSMOUTH 0
Rooney 9, Carrick 82

I DON'T KNOW how Scholesy celebrated becoming only the fourth man
to play 600 games for United. Though you get the feeling it wouldn't
have involved anything more dramatic than a 12" meat feast from
Asda and a rerun of Britain's Got Talent on Sky-plus. But as usual
the world's least starry footballer was demanding attention with his
play out on the pitch. It wasn't his most spectacular performance
of course – in fact the truly spectacular Scholesy days are bound to
come around less and less often now he spends most of his time out of
the box (or on the bench). But it was a performance crammed with
classic Scholes moments, one minute pulling an impossible ball out
of the air, the next sweeping a 50 yard pass onto Ronaldo's beloved
pecs, the next threatening to kick an opponent's testicles into Hulme.
And it was absolutely fitting that it was his killer pass for Carrick
that finally finished the game off and made sure that United took
full advantage of Liverpool's car-crash defending against Arsenal the
night before. 3 points clear with a game in hand and fixtures running
out fast. Now that, Rafa, really is a 'fact' worth bringing up...

GOAL ACTION

1-0 (9): As Fergie said, United played some of the best football of
the season in the first half and should have made a major dent in
Liverpool's goal difference advantage. Instead they missed chance
after chance and only had Rooney's classy opener to show for their
dominance. Anderson, starting to show last season's form at last,
lands a superb reverse pass onto Giggs's chest, he controls it expertly

on the run and rolls across the sort of ball that forwards get giddy over. Rooney's sidefoot does the rest.

2-0 (82): But if you don't finish teams off, you're asking for trouble. And that's what happened here. After an hour of almost constant pummeling, Portsmouth suddenly twig they're still in a game they should have lost ages ago. Three half-chances follow as they come of the ropes swinging like a poor man's Ali. But then Scholes picks out the run of Carrick with the second best pass of the night and he fires low right to left past James.

WHAT WAS GOOD?

EVERYTHING OUTSIDE THE BOX (in the first half at least).
WE'RE BACK ON TRACK.

WHAT WAS BAD?

THE FINISHING INSIDE THE BOX.

BERBATOV BEING BOOED following his Wembley penalty miss. When will the G-stand grumblers learn – you just don't boo one of your own (not unless he's Scottish and bandy-legged anyway). Like I said earlier, let's hope Berbatov shoves the boos down their throat when he settles in properly.

ANDERSON'S SHOOTING. What happens to that boy when he sees the goal?

THE FEELING THAT WE COULD HAVE PLAYED A PROPER TEAM AT WEMBLEY ON SUNDAY – and still won comfortably tonight.

POMPEY – THE VERBALS

"We're in a better position tonight than we were on Monday, but having seen that second-half and how we got so casual, I'm not taking anything for granted and we've got to put the foot down all the time. Six games seems like a short time but it can be a long time and the players had a little warning today. If you don't take your chances you do make it hard for yourself, and in first half some of our play was stunning." – *Fergie's not getting carried away.*

"It is not difficult for me to appreciate Paul Scholes. I use him as an example to all the kids I work with at Portsmouth and have done for many years. Whatever anyone says about Paul Scholes, I have said it as well. He is a shining example of someone who doesn't take liberties with the ball. He controls everything stone dead. It all looks perfect." – *Pompey manager Paul Hart lavishes praise on the Ginger Prince.*

VIEWS FROM THE PRESSBOX

"The contest for the Premier League title appears to be coming to a serene end. There are more awkward occasions than this to come for Manchester United and an improving Tottenham Hotspur are here on Saturday but it was hard not to feel that the reigning champions have re-established complete control. They have a three-point lead over Liverpool with a game in hand." – *The Guardian calls the end to squeaky bum season – prematurely.*

"These should be the sweetest of times for Manchester United, back on top of the Barclays Premier League and looking forward to a Champions League semi-final against Arsenal, but Sir Alex Ferguson's expression at the final whistle betrayed a nagging sense of unease.

"Beating Liverpool to the title was supposed to be fun — and no doubt it will be when the time comes — but this, not for the first time, had the feel of a difficult slog that carries some worrying portents for the forthcoming battles on the European front.

"No victory in the Premier League should be sniffed at — particularly not when Liverpool received so many plaudits for an error-strewn performance 24 hours earlier in what is likely to prove a costly 4-4 draw with Arsenal — but United are toiling and finding the going tougher than Ferguson would have hoped." – *The Times is less impressed.*

THE FOUR TOPS
United's top 4 appearance makers at the final whistle
GIGGS – 693 (106) – 799
CHARLTON – 756 (2) – 758
FOULKES 685 (3) – 688
SCHOLES 495 (105) – 600

'THE BEST'
It's amazing how many of the tributes Scholesy has received – from the great and good of the game – over the years have contained the same four-letter word:

"Scholes is the best English player. Intelligence, technique, strength... all the attributes are there. At Manchester United I saw what he could do on the training field. Phew!" - *Laurent Blanc.*

"Scholes is undoubtedly the best midfielder of his generation." - *Zinedine Zidane.*

"I'm not the best, Paul Scholes is. Every one of us (midfielders) is just trying to become as good as him. Everyone can learn from Paul Scholes." - *Edgar Davids.*

"Paul Scholes would have been one of my first choices for putting together a great team - that goes to show how highly I have always rated him. He would have been one of the first players I'd have bought, given the chance." - *Marcello Lippi.*

"You've missed Paul Scholes - and he's my best player." - *What Fergie said to a barrister (when he was giving evidence on behalf of a former trainee) when she reeled out a list of United's top players.*

"No celebrity bullshit... just an amazingly gifted player who has remained an unaffected human being." - *Roy Keane.*

"People say he is a great player, but you have to define what a great player is. For me, it is a player who has a bottom level that means his worst performance is not noticed. If he is having a bad game, a team-mate might feel Paul Scholes is not quite on his game, but a spectator wouldn't notice. Scholes, of all the players I have played with, has the highest bottom level. His reading of the game is unsurpassed. He has an eye for a pass, for what the play or the game needs at that precise moment, that I have never seen anyone else have. He controls and distributes the play and the game better than anyone I have ever seen." - *Peter Schmeichel.*

"For me, it's Paul Scholes. He'll do ridiculous things in training like say, "You see that tree over there?" - it'll be 40 yards away - "I'm going to hit it". And he'll do it. Everyone at the club considers him the best." - *Rio Ferdinand.*

"I wouldn't swap Paul Scholes for anybody. He is quite simply the most complete footballer I have ever played with. He is the best." - *Gary Neville.*

MATCH FACTS

UNITED: VAN DER SAR, NEVILLE (O'SHEA 13), VIDIC, EVANS, EVRA, FLETCHER, SCHOLES, ANDERSON (CARRICK 76), GIGGS, RONALDO, ROONEY, O'SHEA (RAFAEL DA SILVA 52)
BOOKED: VIDIC.
PORTSMOUTH: JAMES, JOHNSON, CAMPBELL, DISTIN, HREIDARSSON, DAVIS, MULLINS, HUGHES, BELHADJ, NUGENT (PENNANT 46), CROUCH [HART]
ATT: 74,895 REF: PETER WALTON H-T: 1-0

OTHER SCORES

CHELSEA 0 EVERTON 0, LIVERPOOL 4 ARSENAL 4.

LEAGUE TABLE

1. UNITED 74 (32) 2. LIVERPOOL 71 (33) 3. CHELSEA 68 (33)
4. ARSENAL 62 (33)... 14. PORTSMOUTH 37 (33)

*"What is wrong with this fat spanish waiteress,
does he have nothing to do?"*

NEWS

WE'RE IN THE middle of the worst recession in living memory. Inflation is going down, unemployment is going up, interest rates are at a record low and football clubs the length of the country are freezing or lowering their ticket prices in a desperate bid to keep their turnstiles busy. So what do United do? They put prices up by an average of 5% and opt not to pass on the 2.5% saving they gained in last year's cut in VAT. What's that old saying about death, taxes and United ticket rises?

L

"We are still on average turning away nearly 5,000 people per game and more for bigger games like City, Arsenal and Liverpool, and we believe it represents good value for money." – *A United spokesperson massages the figures (the empty seats at games like Wigan told a different story)*

U

"It has been said in the past that the owners of the club will squeeze United supporters until the pips squeak and this is clearly the case. Earlier in the year, the government gave a 2.5% reduction on the price of VAT on tickets. The Glazers have absorbed this benefit and added more increases on top." – *MUST's superbly named Sean Bones.*

H

"People who claim that with constant success most Manchester United supporters have ceased to mind the fact that their club is massively in debt and is owned by cuckoos are dead wrong. Tens of thousands of fans are still seething at the regime change. They understand all too well that the Glazers have the power to do as

they please. What they also know is that they do not have the right."
– *The Mirror of all people sum up the Red mood.*

G

£29 – *what the most expensive ticket in Old Trafford cost in 2004 before the Glazer coup.*
£49 – *what the most expensive ticket costs today (and they'll cost even more for Champions League knockout games).*

NEWS II

Bad news if you've got seats right at the back of Tier One – or don't fancy hearing some chump in a suit who's had too much pop sharing his wisdom about our team. United are turning 8 boxes into 'super suites' complete with an outdoor balcony. Each box holder will also get, on top of the free booze and dining for 16 people, a visit of a former player each match, a visit to Carrington to watch the team train, four guests sitting in the Directors Box once a season and "allocation of match tickets for home and away games on request". And the price? £215,000, which is presumably 'good value'. Tévez drops the biggest hint yet he's leaving. And Keano returns to football as manager of Ipswich and immediately comes out swinging against Tony Cascarino, one of the many who'd gleefully penned his managerial obituary back in December...

SHOVE IT UP YOUR BOLLOX (AGAIN)

"I am happy to comment on people's opinion in football I respect, but Tony Cascarino is a man I certainly do not respect, for a lot of reasons, and if I told you, you would be shocked. So the day I worry about Tony Cascarino will be a very sad day of my life." – *You know who.*

CARLOSS

"I need a regular place in the team to offer my best level and if that cannot happen at Manchester (United) I believe it will be my last year (at the club). Out of respect to the fans and the history of Manchester United I do not want to leave the club in a bad way. But in my situation an exit will be the best solution." – *It's a shame but Tévez is probably right.*

'KEEPING SCHTUM' (AGAIN)

"I'm not having a battle of words with Alex Ferguson. But I believe that he can see that we are the better side and that we're very close to United. He has been playing these kind of mind games for many years. Nobody has ever said anything against him or stood up to him. It seems like he has a licence to do these sort of things. I try not to talk too much, but all I can do when I speak is to defend my own team. I did not say that he seems frightened, but I said that he looks nervous as he can see that we are very close to his team." - *Benitez really has got cocky since the 4-1 accident.*

RIPOSTE OF THE DAY
(from the Times's comments section)
    Aziz in NAIROBI KENYA Said, April 23rd, 2009 @16:31
    "What is wrong with this fat spanish waiteress, does he have nothing to do? bastard"

RUNNER-UP

"He is definitely saying a lot. But I am happy for him to carry on with it. I have to trust my players. I know they are good enough. I have trusted them for years now. That is why I have picked them. They are a good bunch of lads and we will just carry on the way we always have." – *Fergie paraphrases Aziz.*

QUOTES OF THE WEEK

"What's left to say about them? They're just unbelievable professionals with fantastic talent and ability who are great people to learn from and the perfect example of what it is to be a winner at this club. They're an inspiration to us all. To keep producing over such a long period at the highest level is frightening. Not many people can do that and it speaks volumes for the kind of players and people they are." – *Carrick on Scholes the 600 man, and Giggs who'll hit 800 the next time he plays.*

    "Our record against the top four is impeccable." – *On the eve of Spurs's visit to Old Trafford, Jonathan Woodgate is just asking for trouble*

    "You know why we've had no inquiry? Because they all know. They all know he would never leave. He has maybe had private approaches, people begging him to join them. He could have played in any league in Europe – no problem. But they all know he wouldn't want to leave here." – *Fergie on the Red legend, the Ginger Prince.*

QUOTE OF THE WEEK

"Many great players have worn the shirt of Manchester United.

SPURS (H)

Players I worshipped, then lost with my youth in Munich. Players like Denis Law and George Best who I enjoyed so much as teammates and now, finally, players I have watched closely in the Ferguson era. And in so many ways Scholes is my favourite. I love his nous and conviction that he'll find a way to win, to make the killer pass or produce a decisive volley. When a game reaches a vital phase, these qualities seem to come out of his every pore. He's always on the ball. He's always looking to bring other people into the action and if he loses possession you think he must be ill." - *Sir Bob gives Scholes perhaps his biggest compliment yet.*

25/04/2009 - FAPL
UNITED 5 SPURS 2
Bent 29, Modric 32, Ronaldo 57 p, Rooney 67, Ronaldo 68, Rooney 71, Berbatov 79

I'VE ALREADY SAID that Macheda's goal against Villa was the best, biggest and most important moment of the season. And I'm sticking to that. But I could never have envisaged something like this happening so soon afterwards. Consider the scenario at half-time. Tottenham had just scored twice at Old Trafford for the first time since 1986 and were flying. Robbie Keane was licking his lips at the idea of becoming the first Spurs player since 1961 to win the league. And every United defender apart from Vidic was having a game to forget – Evra was being skinned by Lennon, Rafael couldn't cope with the movement of Modric, Rio just didn't look right. Things couldn't have looked gloomier.

But then United came out and reminded us of the truth behind the old cliché: that there's no better sight in football than a United side, blood dripping off their fangs, every player primed to attack, chasing a game. Tottenham claimed, understandably enough, that United's opener, a dodgy penalty courtesy of Howard Webb, made all the difference. But, watching the awesome foursome combine spectacularly for the first time all season, it was hard to see how Spurs could possibly have survived much longer anyway. The 22 minutes it took United to go from 2-0 down to 5-2 up were extraordinary, a surreal symphony of power and panache. And as Old Trafford wiped itself down afterwards, the stunned Spurs fans, their bottom lips flapping limply against their chins, must have been asking themselves the same question. What the hell have we done to deserve another beating like this?

THE MOMENTS THAT MATTERED

0-1 (29): It sounds strange to think now but the first 29 minutes were a bit of a letdown. United dominated the ball without creating much. Lennon looked in the mood but his team-mates looked inhibited and increasingly nervous. But then loose defending gifts Spurs the lead. Corluka swings in a run-of-the-mill centre from the right, Ferdinand heads the ball against the back of Vidic and Bent hammers in from point-blank range.

0-2 (32): Spurs are used to being a goal up at Old Trafford. After all, they've done it two years in a row in the fourth round of the cup. But they haven't been two up for donkey's years. In fact they haven't scored twice in any game here since the 3-3 in 1986 (I was only a kid but I think Gary Mabbutt scored a diving header). So what the hell are they thinking scoring twice in 3 minutes? If anything United's defending for this goal was even worse than for the first. Evra makes sure Lennon doesn't beat him by not going anywhere near him, Lennon chips to the far post, Ferdinand and Bent wipe each other out and, with Rafael on walkabout, Modric has no problem killing the ball and poking it on the volley past Van der Sar.

HALF-TIME: It's champagne time for Liverpool fans who've just watched their team stroll to a 3-1 win at Hull. Is it hairdryer time for the United players? According to Rooney afterwards, no. Instead Fergie orders them to ramp up the tempo and throws a tracksuit in the direction of Nani, who's replaced by Tévez. If we're going to go down here, we're going to go down with all guns blazing.

PENALTY! (56): Denis Wise could start a fight in an empty room. Tévez could inject life into a roomful of Mormons. His arrival immediately gives United the extra aggression and purpose Fergie was looking for. Even so, Spurs were just about hanging on to their two goal lead when Webb, who's having a season to forget, makes another high-profile slip. At first glance it looks like Gomes might just have taken out Carrick as he runs on to Rooney's cute defence-splitter. At second glance there's no doubt about it. Gomes gets a good glove on the ball. It shouldn't be a penalty. But Redknapp can rant, rave and turn red all he likes, there's no way Webb can do anything about it now...

GOAL! (57): And it's game on, Ronaldo slamming his penalty right down the middle.

GOAL! (66): United are flying now and draw level with a goal of absolutely stunning quality. Ronaldo, under pressure from two Spurs players near halfway, fires the ball at Tévez who immediately fires the ball at Berbatov. His control is excellent and as two more Spurs players arrive on the scene (like hapless extras in a Bond finale) he coolly flicks the ball back to Tévez. Tévez bursts deep into Spurs territory, draws his man and feeds Rooney. He cuts in from the left and drills a low shot through Corluka's legs that beats the unsighted Gomes at his near post.

GOAL! (67): I like to call it the Nou Camp pause, the split second of silence when fans who are still buzzing off one goal immediately get another one to celebrate. It happened in '99, it happened in the Roma 7-1 and now it happens here. Rooney swings in a sumptuous cross from the left. King can't get near it and Ronaldo scores with a diving nod back across goal. You'd have to be strapped to your seat not to be bouncing around after this one. Certainly Fergie's on the move, doing his best granddad at a wedding jig down the touchline.

GOAL! (72): And he's only just off the dance-floor when he's hopping around again as United piece together a virtual rerun of Modric's goal. Ronaldo plays the Lennon role, minus the chavvy tramlines. Rooney plays the Modric role, cushioning the ball and then scoring with a firm side-foot that trickles over the line via touches off Gomes and the sliding Woodgate.

GOAL! (79): And just when Spurs fans thought things couldn't get any worse, their favourite ex-player, Berbatov, scores. Rooney, who ran the left flank on his own in the second half, crosses pinpoint style, Berbatov slams his header straight at Gomes but then, almost apologetically, pokes in the rebound. It's funny. Berbatov has more skill than perhaps any player in the league, he's capable of amazing goals, but this season he's specialised in scruffy ones. His goal against Spurs in the Cup was perhaps the only one that scored more than 4.0 for style.

OFF (87): Keane, who's hardly had a kick, is dragged off and replaced by Huddlestone. I don't want to tempt fate. But it doesn't look like you're getting that league medal this year old boy.

QUOTE OF THE DAY

"I think that was a prime example of a referee crumbling under pressure at Old Trafford" – *Jermaine Jenas conveniently forgets that Howard Webb wasn't the only one who crumbled under the pressure today (even after the penalty, Spurs were 2-1 up with little more than 30 minutes to play).*

SPURS – THE VERBALS

"The referee made a terrible mistake. The players can't believe it because it changed the face of the game. United were not going to win unless something like that happened." – *Like Jenas, Redknapp forgets that a penalty only counts as one goal.*

"He's supposed to be our best referee; if he's the best, I'd like to see our worst." – *Redknapp keeps ranting.*

"We were a bit fortunate with the penalty. Last season Harry Redknapp came here with Portsmouth and got a penalty that shouldn't have been given. Maybe this was one to pay us back. Last week we were knocked out of the Cup by a penalty not being given. Football is funny that way." – *Fergie makes a good point. Redknapp can hardly complain about bad penalty decisions after the Portsmouth cup game last season (mind you, it wasn't the penalty that Portsmouth got that day that was the problem, it was the penalties that United didn't).*

VIEWS FROM THE PRESSBOX

"Before yesterday, Manchester United's supporters might have wondered whether the defining moment of their season might be Federico Macheda's stoppage-time heroics against Aston Villa. But then Tottenham Hotspur had the temerity to take a two-goal lead at Old Trafford and, once again, Sir Alex Ferguson's men demonstrated their ability to pull off the most astounding feats of escapology.

"In the end, we were left to contemplate whether it was here, in a match of unrelenting and enthralling drama, that the title race had its most significant moment to date. United deserve all the superlatives for the determination, drive and sheer guts of their fightback, even if Tottenham were possibly entitled to be aggrieved about the penalty that precipitated the cloudburst of five goals in 22 minutes. It was a demonstration of attacking, penetrative football at its highest level, with two each for Wayne Rooney and Cristiano Ronaldo and the fifth for Dimitar Berbatov, playing as though affronted by the criticisms of his recent performances." – *The Observer*

"NO MATTER how often Manchester United write the script their supporters will never tire of it. You wouldn't pay to watch the same movie repeatedly or continually buy the same book but the entertainment business of football is unique.

"United down and out before springing off the canvas to knock out their opponent with a quick flurry of blows: how often have we heard it? They even keep using the same fall-guys. For Spurs, leading 2-0 at 6.46pm, trailing 5-2 by 7.08pm, this was almost as bad as their collapse in 2001-02 when they lost 5-3 to United, having been 3-0 ahead at the interval." – *The Sunday Times*

"Manchester United failed to keep a clean sheet for the seventh time in eight Premier League matches, showed specific vulnerability in the full-back areas and needed the aid of Howard Webb's mistaken award of a penalty to spark the comeback. All in all, however, it turned out to be a very heartening occasion for the victors. Out of necessity, they learned that their energy levels are uncannily high as they enter the key weeks of a long campaign." – *The man from the Guardian walks away with the award for the dourest report. Is he a Liverpool fancier by any chance?*

THE GREAT ESCAPES

There's no better feeling than winning a game from 2-0 down. And us Reds have now been lucky enough to enjoy the feeling five times in the Fergie years. Here are the previous four. Enjoy the memories...

07/11/93 – CITY 2 (QUINN 2) UNITED 3 (CANTONA 2, KEANE)
21/04/99 – CL SEMI FINAL JUVENTUS 2 (INZAGHI 2) UNITED 3 (KEANE, YORKE, COLE)
29/09/01 – SPURS 3 (RICHARDS, FERDINAND, ZIEGE) UNITED 5 (BECKHAM, BLANC, COLE, VAN NISTELROOY, VERON)
06/01/02 – FA CUP VILLA 2 (TAYLOR, P.NEVILLE OG) UNITED 3 (VAN NISTELROOY 2, SOLSKJAER)

MATCH FACTS

UNITED: VAN DER SAR, RAFAEL (O'SHEA 70), FERDINAND, VIDIC, EVRA, RONALDO, CARRICK, FLETCHER (SCHOLES 61), NANI (TÉVEZ 46), BERBATOV, ROONEY
BOOKED: TÉVEZ, SCHOLES, RONALDO
TOTTENHAM: GOMES, CORLUKA, WOODGATE, KING, ASSOU-EKOTTO, LENNON, PALACIOS, JENAS, MODRIC (BALE 86), KEANE (HUDDLESTONE 87), BENT [REDKNAPP]
BOOKED: WOODGATE, JENAS, GOMES.

ATT: 75,458 REF: HOWARD WEBB H-T: 0-2
OTHER SCORES
HULL 1 LIVERPOOL 3; WEST HAM 0 CHELSEA 1; ARSENAL 2 BORO 0
LEAGUE TABLE
1. UNITED 77 (33); 2. LIVERPOOL 74 (34); 3. CHELSEA 71 (34);

"You could have one match of Ryan Giggs which could be worth 40 of another player, so sometimes you don't just drink the best wine in the world every night of the week but it can have a long-lasting effect"

LIFETIME ACHIEVEMENT AWARD

GIGGSY WINS THE PFA player of the year award, the first time he's won any individual award since he took home the Young Player version twice in the early 90s. He was obviously the sentimental choice – Vidic was the player of the year by a mile. Even so, there was no need for the endless debate that it provoked. Even less for the sniping about the lack of minutes Giggs had spent on the pitch (though there was an amusing stat doing the rounds that Sicknote Anderton made more starts than him this season. And he retired in December). The thing to remember was this. Giggs may only have started a handful of games but he'd played three different positions – left-wing, centre mid, support striker – and he'd nailed every one of them. The goal against West Ham from the left wing made everyone who saw it yearn for the days when he gave full-backs the slalom treatment every week. The way he ran the game at Goodison with a mix of sharp dribbling and subtle passing was a lesson for every midfielder in the land – Gerrard included. And his merciless destruction of Ballack at Old Trafford in January was one of the highlights of the season. The question the Gerrard fans and other snipers should have been asking wasn't why Giggs won the award this time. But why his fellow pros – all of whom will queue up to praise him when he retires - hadn't voted for him in larger numbers before.

TEAM OF THE WEEK

THE **PFA XI:** Van der Sar, Johnson, Ferdinand, Vidic, Evra, Ronaldo, Gerrard, Giggs, Young, Anelka, Torres*
**who'd scored a total of five league goals by the time the votes were cast*

THE 8TH RED

PFA winners since the award came into being in 1974:
Hunter, Todd, Jennings, Gray*, Shilton, Brady, McDermott, Wark, Keegan, Dalglish, Rush, Reid, Lineker, Allen, Hughes, Platt, Hughes, Pallister, McGrath, Cantona, Shearer, Ferdinand, Shearer, Bergkamp, Ginola, Keane, Sheringham, Van Nistelrooy, Henry, Henry, Terry, Gerrard, Ronaldo*, Ronaldo, Giggs
* *The only 2 players to win the senior and junior versions of the award in the same year*

'SURPRISE' QUOTE OF THE WEEK

"The PFA Awards were handed out this week and I was surprised to see that Ryan Giggs had won the Player of the Year award...In reality Steven has been the best player in the Premier League this season and deserved the award." – *Who did John Barnes used to play for again?*

RUNNER-UP

More wisdom from Tony Cascarino:

"The fact that Ryan Giggs has won the PFA Player of the Year award is absolute nonsense in my opinion. I've nothing against Ryan who has been a fantastic advocate for the game and his club but he has won purely on a sentiment vote. Giggs has made less Premier League starts than in any of his previous seasons barring his debut season and scored just once in the league yet wins the award. How does that make sense?

"Let's be brutally honest, Steven Gerrard has been 10 times better than Giggs this season. Apart from one poor game against Chelsea in the Champions League he has been great this season. *Someone hit him. Keano?*

QUESTION OF THE WEEK

Why is everyone griping about Gerrard missing out and not bothered about Vidic? He's been the best defender in the country by a mile, the rock around which United's record-breaking defensive exploits have been built. Plus he's scored two winning goals. So why is everyone reading so much into the fact he let a couple of balls get away from him in one game?

NEWS

United are linked with a £50m move for Kaka. Rafael gets a two-year contract extension. Howard Webb holds his hands up over the United penalty against Spurs. How come these referees never feel the need to scream mea culpa when they give United a rough time? (we're still waiting Mike Riley). The City council announce that preparations are being made for a homecoming parade should United win the European Cup. That'll be just a year too late then. And Chelsea, who had just 29% of possession, bore everyone silly en route to a 0-0 draw in the Nou Camp in the first leg. Us Reds can't give them too much grief though. We did the same sort of job on Barca at the same stage last year.

QUOTES OF THE WEEK

"For me, the Dutchman can't kick a ball properly and tends to shank it all over the place. He is certainly not in the same class as the likes of Peter Schmeichel and David Seaman. If you had to pick a keeper I'd have gone for Aston Villa's Brad Friedel or Liverpool's Jose Reina who have both performed really well." – *Cascarino shows just how on the ball he is by arguing against Van der Sar's inclusion in the PFA team. Yes, that's the same Van der Sar who didn't let in a goal for half the season and who could easily be the best footballing keeper English football's ever seen.*

"It's all about convenience and practicality. Sometimes there are a rush of commitments at the end of the season." – *Gordon Taylor's dubious explanation for the PFA award being voted for in February.*

'I can only tell you the situation as it is and if you are not happy then if you consider yourself such an expert on ballots perhaps you had better go to Zimbabwe or Russia the next time they have elections and tell everybody how they should vote as they put their votes in the ballot box!" – *Gordon Taylor with an even more dubious reply to a City fan who emailed him to ask why Giggsy won the award (he probably thought Stephen Ireland should have got it).*

QUOTE OF THE WEEK

"You could have one match of Ryan Giggs which could be worth 40 of another player, so sometimes you don't just drink the best wine in the world every night of the week but it can have a long-lasting effect" - *Gordon Taylor puts Ryan Giggs' lifetime achievement award into perspective. Well if you're earning as much as Taylor you should at least be able to come up with a good one-liner...*

29/04/2009
CL SEMI-FINAL (1ST LEG)

UNITED 1 ARSENAL 0
O'Shea 18

IN THE PRESS conference he'd given that afternoon, just hours before the biggest United-Arsenal game ever, Fergie had said that a 1-0 score-line would be a 'fantastic' result. At the end of an evening in which United did everything but pin Arsenal's weaklings down and give them a wedgie, he must have thought it was a travesty. United have given Arsenal some famous beatings over the years, most notably the 4-0 cup win last year, the Sharpie-inspired 6-2 in 1990 and the 6-1 drubbing of the Arsenal of Luzhniki and Stepanovs in 2001. But it's no exaggeration to say that if it hadn't been for a mix of dodgy linesmanship, brilliant keeping from Almunia and the woodwork, the winning margin here could have been even more comprehensive. And United wouldn't just be favourites to reach Rome, the Red Army would already be snapping up stab-proof tangers, filling Rome's hotels and mentally sipping Limoncello in the sun...

THE BIG SEMI - THE MOMENTS THAT MATTERED
PREAMBLE OF THE NIGHT *(from the Guardian):* "This is the first time Manchester United and Arsenal have met in European competition, although the loud splat of pizza on Sir Alex Ferguson after Manchester United ended Arsenal's 49-match unbeaten run at Old Trafford in 2004 did lend the game a slightly continental feel." I like it...
ROONEY! SAVE! (1): As against Barcelona last year BELIEVE is spelt out in giant mosaics at the Stretford End as the teams take to the field. But unlike last year, when we were all terrified of what Messi and Eto'o were going to do to us, there's no real need for the message of encouragement. Against an Arsenal side that's shown a soft centre all season there's no lack of belief inside the stadium. And that feeling intensifies into mild cockiness as United rip into Arsenal and almost score from their first attack, Almunia scrambling across his line to make a brilliant save from Rooney's looping header.

OOPS (2): A slip by rookie full-back Kieran Gibbs momentarily allows Ronaldo to get in behind the Arsenal defence. He really should get those studs checked out before the second leg...

BRILLIANT! (17): What a move. What a save. Anderson feeds Ronaldo, he flicks it to Tévez who, despite being taken out from behind, feeds O'Shea overlapping on the right. O'Shea centres and Tévez, who'd jumped straight back to his feet and attacked the space at the near post, looks certain to score until Almunia produces a stunning point-blank save low to his left.

GOAL! (18): Unluckily for Almunia, the save doesn't count for much as moments later United finally break through. Carrick does excellently to rescue a corner at the far post and trick his way to the byeline. His low left-footed centre deflects off Silvestre, making his second appearance against United in the Champions League, and right into the path of O'Shea who shows great technique to leather the ball into the roof of the net. The celebration is the same as every Sheasy celebration – i.e. crap.

ARSENALS'S FIRST DECENT TRY (26): Walcott, widely (and wrongly) backed to do to Evra what Lennon had done at the weekend, finally gets a yard of space to run into before rolling the ball back to Fabregas whose low drive is comfortably smothered by Van der Sar.

RONALDO! SAVE! (29): This is getting ridiculous. Almunia has always come across as a clown keeper but he's just made another incredible save, his third of the night. This time Tévez picks out Ronaldo with a wonderful cross from the right and Almunia somehow blocks his header from point-blank range.

BAR! (68): What. A. Goal (almost). Ronaldo latches on to a loose pass, gallops into space and thumps a dipping shot that fizzes over the motionless Almunia and dips down to almost break the crossbar. It wouldn't have been as good as his goal against Porto, but it wouldn't have been far off.

ROBBED! (78): Carrick threads the ball of the night from wide on the right to send Giggs – making a landmark 800th appearance – clear one-on-one. Giggs beats Almunia with ease but is denied the goal he and United deserved by a badly-timed flag. On the sidelines the fourth official gets an earful from Sir Alex.

BENDTNER! MISS! (84): United have one lucky break and it's this, Bendtner getting just too much head on Fabregas's dinked free-kick. It's not all good news for United, though. As the ball was in the air Van der Sar accidentally kung-fued Ferdinand in the ribs and for the umpteenth time in this injury-hit season, Rio has to go off.

LUCKY ARSENAL (92): It's game over. And the Gunners will be wondering how the hell they're still in the Cup (here's a clue – he's got a dodgy dye job and he plays in goal).

WHAT WAS GOOD?

Almunia – What a performance, the best from a visiting keeper for years. Had no right to make the 3 saves he pulled off against Rooney, Tévez and Ronaldo in the first half.

The power - pressing and passing of the midfield trio Carrick, Fletcher and Anderson – Arsenal just couldn't live with them.

Rooney – United's new left winger gave Sagna a nightmarish evening. It's not Rooney's best position if he's forced to defend. But if he's allowed to attack, boy, what a player he looks there...

The atmosphere – OK it had nothing on Barca last year but in a low-key season it was right up there with the very best.

United have never won at the Emirates – but Arsenal have never managed a scoreline there that would be good enough to knock us out.

WHAT WAS BAD?

We've got one foot in the final... we should have both.

We've got an important league game at Boro at the weekend. Arsenal have got an end-of-season kickaround at Portsmouth. As Fergie said, "He [Wenger] could pick Pat Rice at right back and Arsène can play centre forward. The Portsmouth game doesn't matter to them."

ARSENAL – THE VERBALS

"I'm pleased with our performance level and maybe we should have scored four. Before the game I wanted to win without losing a goal. The game's not over because we can go there and score. This team can make chances again – maybe I'll pick a different team with different tactics but we'll have a goal threat. We reached a high level against a very good team. We know the tie's not over, but we can score there." – *Fergie's feeling bittersweet...*

"It is advantage to Manchester United after they played well. But I am confident because I believe we will be on top next time. We will see a different Arsenal team. I believe we can do it at home. It is an opportunity for us to show character and mental strength and I am confident we will do it." – *Wenger's feeling like he's just been hit by a truck, and survived...*

"He is one of the great professionals of our time. He never complains and is happy to play anywhere. He is so versatile. If I had to pick a team for the final now, then he would be in it." – *Fergie pays tribute to match-winner Sheasy, who dedicated his goal to his ill father Jim.*

"Congratulations to Manuel Almunia because, if he was not there, we could have won 4-0. Let's hope he doesn't have the same performance in the next game" – *Evra pays tribute to the man of the match, Almunia.*

VIEWS FROM THE PRESSBOX

"Manchester United overwhelmed Arsenal, yet neglected to leave the full evidence in the result. That could be termed carelessness, but it is the habit of this side, with its emphasis on control, to show circumspection. In consequence the visitors will have left Old Trafford in good heart, but that is simply because they avoided devastation in the first leg of this Champions League semi-final." – *The Guardian*

MATCH FACTS

UNITED: VAN DER SAR, O'SHEA, FERDINAND (EVANS 87), VIDIC, EVRA, FLETCHER, CARRICK, ANDERSON (GIGGS 66), RONALDO, TÉVEZ (BERBATOV 66), ROONEY
BOOKED: TÉVEZ.
ARSENAL: ALMUNIA, SAGNA, TOURE, SILVESTRE, GIBBS, SONG, DIABY, WALCOTT (BENDTNER 70), FABREGAS, NASRI, ADEBAYOR (EDUARDO 82) [WENGER]
ATT: 74,733 REF: CLAUS BO LARSEN (DENMARK) H-T: 1-0

OTHER SCORE

CHAMPIONS LEAGUE SEMI-FINAL: BARCELONA 0 CHELSEA YAWN

"We have to take care that this sort of child trafficking is stopped."

NEWS

AFTER HIS OLD TRAFFORD heroics, a strange bandwagon starts rolling in support of Manuel Almunia playing for England. I don't want to give away too much but the bandwagon hits the buffers not long into the rematch... Two good games against an out-of-form Paddy Evra and the papers reckon Aaron Lennon is worth twenty million of our Mancunian pounds. Fergie calls for a new FA law to regulate the size of dressing rooms. It sounds silly but so must the sight of 20 or 30 highly-paid professionals squeezing themselves into a room that a gimp would get claustrophic in. And an online campaign for Giggsy to get a knighthood gets the backing of a handful of local MPs. Crikey. Don't tell people that. There'll be hell to pay if Gerrard doesn't get one too...

OUTBURST OF THE WEEK
From The Sun:

BAYERN MUNICH chairman Karl-Heinz Rummenigge has amazingly likened Arsene Wenger's transfer policy to "child trafficking."

"We have to take care that this sort of child trafficking is stopped. This has taken on a different scale in the meantime — the word kidnapping is not too far off anymore."

QUOTES OF THE WEEK

"He said I had beautiful eyes and I was like 'Wow, thanks', but he's so tiny" – *Ronaldo's ex, and silicone fan, Gemma Atkinson on the time she met Diego Maradona. Beautiful eyes you say?*

"My brother is far too serious. He's always worrying about things that are going to happen. Things that he shouldn't worry about. I don't. But professionally, he is skilful. A killer. I mean he scores loads of goals. If he is near the area and the ball falls to him, he will score a goal." – *Rafael leaves us salivating about Fabio.*

"Everton's are so narrow it is unbelievable. Portsmouth's away dressing room is not great and the one at Craven Cottage is smaller than my office. You have requirements for stadiums to be eligible for certain divisions, so the quality of the dressing room should be part of that. There is plenty of room in the dressing rooms at Old Trafford and, of the away grounds, Arsenal's are the best by far." – *Fergie's guide to the nation's changing rooms.*

"Ryan Giggs, as well as an outstanding record on the pitch, has a proud record of voluntary work off the pitch, including with young players in Salford. He is a positive role model in so many ways that he deserves the recognition of a knighthood." – *Salford MP Hazel Blears backs Giggsy to be the 4th (United) Knight.*

RETRO QUOTE OF THE WEEK

"At Man United, when Dave Sexton went there he was trying all sorts of corner kicks and bits and bobs. Gordon McQueen said: 'Why don't we do that one we've been using for years when Steve Coppell just puts it in the box and I head it in the back of the net? That has always been a good one.'" - *Gordon Strachan reveals the tactical wizardry behind United's late-70s glory days.*

BIG TIME CHARLIE

"He changed a lot of things, although not so much tactically. He moved the bar psychologically and opened the club to the outside world. Thanks to his network we brought in Brazilian, Portuguese and Angolan players. He changed the culture of the club and made us understand that we could no longer hope to field a team made up of young homebred players, like the Beckham, Giggs, Scholes era... You now have to think 'world'." – *Fergie pays tribute to the impact Carlos Queiroz had at Old Trafford. It sounds strange to think -given how much grief we used to give him – but Quieroz could go down as one of the most important figures in United's modern history (though I've got my doubts if many of his Angolan discoveries will make the grade).*

PREDICTION OF THE WEEK

NICKLAS BENDTNER: "I am 100 per cent sure that we will pass through to the final. Of course you never feel good after a defeat but we look positive at the return game. I am confident that we will play in the final. Can we manage to score three goals? Yes, we have those qualities."

FAPL 02/05/2009
MIDDLESBROUGH 0 UNITED 2
Giggs 25, Park 51

FIVE GAMES LEFT and ten points needed to make sure we nail another league title... and just as importantly stop the Scousers getting their grubby mitts on our trophy. So pretty much the last thing we needed was a trip to Middlesbrough sandwiched in between a massive Champions league double-header.

We all know what normally happens at the Riverside. Fergie fiddles with the team, the defence goes AWOL, the weather turns biblical, Boro play like millionaire footballers always should do and Manchester echoes to the sounds of bums squeaking. So when Fergie picked a team with Macheda at centre-forward and old wrinklies Giggs and Scholes in central midfield, there was a definite feeling that this could be Liverpool's day.

But as things turned out there was absolutely nothing to be worried about. Boro, who had only won twice since November, were so short of class, confidence, muscle and goal threat that not even the visit of United could rouse them into something resembling a genuine problem. Admittedly, they were fairly competitive for the 20 minutes or so it took us to warm up but as soon as Giggs banged in the first they collapsed. And the second half was as one-sided on the pitch as it was on the stands where the best the locals could muster was the old "We support our local team" bull. To which United fans retorted. "You support a load of crap." Harsh? Not at all. Boro really do deserve to go down this year. And if that happens let's see how many Smoggies support their local team... down in the Championship.

GOAL ACTION

1-0 (25): So Giggsy's not a worthy winner of the Player of the year award? Try telling that to the Middlesbrough midfielders who spent their Saturday lunchtime watching him obliterate what was left of their confidence. The darting dribbles, the change of pace, the sharp passing, you name it, it was all there. His goal wasn't bad either, a virtual rerun of the arrow that made absolutely sure we won the league at the Riverside in 1996. Vidic plays the ball inside, Macheda muscles his man out of the way and Giggs finds the bottom right corner from the edge of the box.

2-0 (51): Considering we didn't give Boro a kick we should have scored at least a couple more in the second half. But even if we had, we'd have struggled to produce a better team goal than this one. Giggs, Scholes and Rooney work space midway in Boro's half, Rooney picks out Park's run from right to left and while the Middlesbrough backline, particularly the lumbering, granite-faced

Wheater, stagger around like dizzy drunks, Park fires low and left-footed across Brad Jones and into the net.

WHAT WAS GOOD?

THE RESULT - Giggs and the almost certain knowledge that 'Mad Dog' Pogatetz is going down.

WHAT WAS BAD?

ARSENAL'S WIN AT PORTSMOUTH - guarantees that the Top Four will finish in the top 4... again. Yawn.

VIEWS FROM THE PRESSBOX

"Ryan Giggs no longer starts enough games to be an obvious choice for PFA player of the year, but as Sir Alex Ferguson has just said, you won't find many professional footballers who begrudge him the honour. Manchester United's captain for the day could easily win next year's award at this rate. Only the fact that he will not be allowed to play Middlesbrough every week appears to be preventing him ending up like a more decorated version of Sir Stanley Matthews." – *The Observer*

"There was no turbulence, no bravura comeback and there were no heroics from Federico Macheda, who looked just a boy rather than a boy wonder when asked to start rather than come off the bench. But, for Manchester United, there were three more points and Ryan Giggs, their man of the match, can contemplate a quite ridiculous 11th Premier League winners' medal." – *The Sunday Times*

BORO – THE VERBALS

"Liverpool won't give up, so we just keep concentrating on the games still to come. It's been a memorable week for me, but I just go from game to game too. Playing central midfield isn't too much of a problem when you've got young legs around you." – *Giggsy, Player of the Year*

"We were beaten by a better team, none of our players would get in their side." – *Southgate sounds depressed.*

MATCH FACTS

MIDDLESBROUGH: JONES, MCMAHON (DIGARD 55), WHEATER, HUTH, HOYTE, O'NEIL (EMNES 70), SANLI, BATES, DOWNING, KING (ALVES 55), ALIADIERE [SOUTHGATE]
BOOKED: HUTH.

UNITED: FOSTER, O'SHEA, VIDIC, EVANS, EVRA (RAFAEL DA SILVA 78), PARK (NANI 74), SCHOLES, GIGGS, ROONEY, BERBATOV, MACHEDA (TÉVEZ 55)
BOOKED: MACHEDA
THE RIVERSIDE ATT: 33,767 REF: MARK HALSEY H-T: 1-0

OTHER SCORES

CHELSEA 3 FULHAM 1, PORTSMOUTH 0 ARSENAL 3,
LIVERPOOL 3 NEWCASTLE 0.

"He can only work with the tools he's been given"

NEWS

THE KAKA RUMOURS that were doing the rounds a few weeks ago sounded outlandish enough. But nothing like as weird as the rumour that United have bid £63 million for Frank Ribery. Zidane raves about him – and I'm guessing he knows a thing or two about football – but he's always looked like a slightly better Poborsky to me. Ronaldo says he wants to buy a red London bus for his family. Susan Boyle devotee and new Gooner Piers Morgan manages to make himself look even more of a tw1t with an attempt at football satire that even Paul Hince would have condemned to the Recycle Bin. And that's about it as far as United news goes. Manchester United that is...

BARTON STINK

APRIL 24: "I've had no problems with him whatsoever. Whatever we've asked of him, he's done" - *Alan Shearer, the Messiah, becomes the latest manager to convince himself Joey Barton is worth the hassle.*
MAY 3: "Shit manager" with "Shit tactics" and "you're a prick" – *What Barton said to Shearer after the Messiah slagged him off for getting himself stupidly sent off during Newcastle's 3-0 surrender at Anfield.*
MAY 5: "Newcastle United can confirm that Joey Barton has been suspended from the club until further notice. The club will be making no further comment at this time." – *A Newcastle club statement confirms that Barton has wasted his last 'last chance'. Until he gets another one.*

APT SUMMARY OF THE WEEK
Nice one, football365:

"He can only work with the tools he's been given" - *Chris Waddle discusses Alan Shearer's job at Newcastle. Quite so.*

WORST HEADLINE OF THE WEEK

'So Nero...Yet So Far' - *The Sun looks ahead to the Champions League final in Rome....and stinks the place out.*

SWINE OF THE WEEK
Piers Morgan shoots for a United-themed piss-take that satirises the swine flu scare. And ends up with this:

"There's no doubt about it. I've got Manchester United Swine Influenza. Or Red Swine Flu as it's better known. A potentially lethal affliction that emanates from pig-like creatures wallowing together in a muddy, rain-infested sty in the Trafford borough of Manchester. So here is my 10- point guide to surviving Red Swine Flu...

"When swine are distressed they oink, a persistent moaning sound. United are world-class at this, led by oinker-in-chief Ferdinand. With the oinking comes indiscipline. And the best way to start them oinking is to score an early goal.

"Swine are greedy and they don't come greedier than Cristiano Ronaldo. To nullify his undoubted threat every Arsenal supporter must toss a £50 note into the air each time he step-overs his way down the wing and watch his pockmarked little snout go crazy.

"Perhaps the most dangerous of all swine is the Rooney. More compact than normal, with a larger head and shorter legs, it's a very strong, feral beast with limited cerebral mass but extremely dangerous if left to roam.

"Swine are sometimes known as hogs, which is particularly appropriate in the case of the Carrick. This lanky, gormless-looking crossbreed (he used to reside in the East End of London) hogged the damn ball all flaming night last Wednesday and must be deprived of such possession again..."

Oh dear.

RUNNER-UP
Meet Guadalajara defender Hector Reynoso who fired a nasal torpedo with a difference during his side's Libertadores Cup game at Everton of Chile:

"Reynoso, following an incident in the game, reacted by spitting at Everton player Sebastian Penco and then releasing nasal secretions at the face of the player," said the CSF (South America's version of UEFA) in a statement. "This situation, lamentable in its own right, was aggravated by the risk of a possible infection of the disease AH1N1 [swine flu]."

Here's hoping John Terry doesn't catch the disease...

05/05/2009
CL SEMI-FINAL (2ND LEG)

ARSENAL 1 UNITED 3
(United win 4-1 on agg)
Park 6, Ronaldo 10, 60, Fabregas (P) 74.

As ARSENAL LIMPED onto their coach after the first game, Wenger did his best to rally the troops, filling the Stretford air with sound bites like "we still have a good chance to reverse the result", "we have the quality to do it" and "I'm confident because I know we will be on top on Tuesday". When Tuesday came, though, his tub-thumping was exposed for what it was, an exercise in wishful thinking. United were a class above Arsenal in the first leg but forgot to turn their dominance into a big score. They didn't make the same mistake at the Emirates. Some dubbed it the 10-minute massacre. Paddy Evra tagged it men against boys. Personally I'd call it the best night of the season by a country mile.

But whatever you want to call it, enjoy...

ARSENAL-BEATING – A MINUTE-BY-MINUTE GUIDE

PREAMBLE: There's one change each from the sides that met in the first leg mismatch a week ago. Park comes in for United as Tévez joins Berbatov on a star-studded bench while Djorou comes in for Mickey Silvestre for Arsenal. As the teams come into view, Tyldesley rattles off one of his trademark speeches: "For the fifth year in succession there will be an English team in the Champions League final. But who and how many we will soon know. The longest yard on the road to Rome starts here."

2: Arsenal start the yard the quickest, Gibbs getting round the back before dinking in a cross that's mopped up by Ferdinand before

Fabregas almost initiates a rerun of Lampard's equaliser in Moscow, his mistimed shot deflecting off both Vidic and Ferdinand before rolling just wide.

5: United reply, Van der Sar punting a long ball over Toure for Ronaldo who juggles the ball between his chest, shoulder and thigh before laying it back to Rooney who immediately looks to slide in Anderson. Only a decent interception from Toure prevents Anderson from missing another opportunity to break his United duck.

AWAY GOAL! PARK! 6: And then comes the moment all Arsenal fans had been dreading; 63 seconds of possession football, 16 passes, 1 crucial slip and the vital away goal that means their side will have to score three. Evra clears a poor cross from Sagna to Ronaldo on halfway. He rolls it back to O'Shea who then slides a ball down the line for Park. Park backtracks and returns the ball to O'Shea who pops it off to Ronaldo, who's having a breather on halfway. Possession moves from Ronaldo to Carrick to Vidic to Van der Sar and back to Vidic again. Rooney beats Sagna to Vidic's chip down the line and nods down to Anderson. Anderson releases Ronaldo down the inside-left channel, Gibbs slips trying to cut out his instant low centre and Park takes a touch before lifting the ball over Almunia. "Away goal for Manchester United," screams Tyldesley. "A goal that could be worth twice its weight in gold". Which might make it very valuable indeed, depending on how much a goal weighs. More sensibly, Tyldesley points out that it's Park's first ever goal in Europe for United.

7: "Park, Park, wherever you may be, you eat dogs in your own country…" echoes around a stunned Emirates. "But it could be worse you could be Scouse, eating rats in your council house."

9: Gibbs was Arsenal's best outfield player in the first leg but his slip for the goal has clearly upset him and he makes another error here, playing Fabregas into trouble and allowing Fletcher to nick possession. The ball rolls to Ronaldo who is fouled clumsily by Van Persie…

UNBELIEVABLE! 10: Ronaldo rubs his thigh for a moment, then picks himself up and does the valve thing with the ball. He's six grass stripes away from goal – about 40 yards – and he's only 5 or so yards from the touchline. Most managers would go apoplectic if one of their players went for goal from there. Most players wouldn't even consider it, particularly not on a night like this. But not Ronaldo. As he runs up, Tyldesley prophetically mutters "Not too far for Ronaldo to think about it". A second later, as the ball is bouncing out of Arsenal's net, he explodes into "AAAAAH. Absolutely sensational. It went through Almunia, beaten for pace. And Cristiano Ronaldo has matched the scorcher he scored in Porto to leave Arsenal all but beaten already." He's right too. As the camera pans round the Emirates every expression is locked in stunned resignation and disbelief. One dark-haired girl in a leather jacket looks like she's just been told her boyfriend has run off with her dad. Only Pat Rice, sitting next to Wenger, looks the same as he did a minute ago. Then again Pat Rice changes expressions as often as Fergie changes hairstyles (actually, make that Wilf McGuinness).

11: As ITV show the replay of Ronaldo's wonder-goal, Jim Beglin picks away at Almunia for diving under it and then tries to argue it wasn't a free-kick in the first place (Van Persie only trod on Ronaldo's foot and kicked his thigh). Get hold of yourself man, Almunia shouldn't have been beaten from that distance but that was still one of the all-time great Champions League moments. You've got to be a very special player* to score a goal like that even once in your career. But to do it twice in consecutive Champions League away games...
(*And you've got to be a very bitter ex-Scouser not to enjoy the moment)

11: It's 7.56 at night. It's still light and this one's all over. See you in Rome mio amico!

12: Blimey. Evra's ball over the top sends Ronaldo clear again but his shin-pads get in the way of his attempts to kill the ball and it rolls tamely through to Almunia, the man formerly known as England's future no.1.

15: Everywhere you look there's a red-faced Arsenal fan with one or both their hands covering their eyes, face or mouth. Pat Rice is the only exception. What a poker player he'd make.

ROONEY! SAVE! RONALDO! MISS! 16: Ooh, almost three. Fletcher rolls the ball back to Rooney and his low curler brings a brilliant save from Almunia, who would have only seen the ball when it was almost past him. From the resulting corner Ronaldo heads just over the angle of post and bar. As the only player marking him was Vidic he might have done better with that one. Not that anyone's going to be nitpicking at him after what he's going to do to Arsenal tonight.

18: 'Keep the Faith' reads a banner in the Arsenal end. It's a nice enough sentiment but it'll take some doing. Arsenal are all over the place here. They can't defend, can't attack and can't hold on to possession. Other than that, and the 3 goal deficit, they're doing just fine.

25: Wenger has his head in his hands. Pat Rice still isn't moving.

31: Ronaldo sends in another dipping bullet from 30 yards. Almunia deals with it pretty well but if there'd been as much horizontal movement on the ball as there was vertical he'd have been picking another one out of his net.

44: Arsenal must have had worst nights than this one, but I can't think of one, certainly not against United. Fabregas, Van Persie and Adebayor are missing in action, the rest of the team hasn't created a single chance while United are cutting them apart at the back almost at will. This time Fletcher opens his legs on the left and cuts the ball back to Ronaldo who slightly mistimes a left-footer straight at Almunia.

HALF-TIME: As ITV heads for adverts, Steve Ryder makes the most ludicrous statement of the night: "Wretched luck for Arsenal who really do deserve better." Sure, Gibbs was unlucky with his slip but Arsenal deserve better? They should have lost by three or four at Old Trafford and they're lucky not to be three goals down here. Wretched Arsenal might have made sense. But wretched luck? No chance.

The half-time input of Jens Lehmann is just as baffling. Now you may remember that Mad Jens was never much of a fan of Almunia when they were both at Arsenal. In fact Almunia freely admits that Lehmann despised him. So most viewers were expecting the German to go to town on Almunia's failure to lay a glove on Ronaldo's 40-yarder. Instead Lehmann gets out his goalkeepers' union card and points a finger at the new balls which, according to him, pick up speed after they've been hit. Nice try Jens, but I'm not sure you'll find many physicists agreeing with you over that.

46: As Arsenal saunter almost apologetically back onto the pitch, the cameras pick up Becks taking his seat amongst the VIPs. He looks pretty damn pleased with himself. His neighbour, Milan team-mate, and ex-Gunner, Flamini, does not.

47: A large section of the Arsenal crowd hasn't come out for the second half. Are they drinking the bars dry? Throwing up in the loos? On the way home on the tube? In fact there's been a suspicious package spotted and they're waiting for the sniffer dogs to give them the all clear. Unfortunately for the locals it turns out to be a false alarm. Which means they're back in their seats in plenty of time to watch an excruciating evening turn even worse...

48: Sometimes Ronaldo doesn't look a good fit at centre-forward. He doesn't see enough of the ball, he gets isolated and he gets shepherded down blind alleys. But at times like this he's just about unplayable, a jinking, high-speed wrecking machine. You get the feeling he could play Gallas, Djorou, Sagna and Clichy on his own and still have time to shape his eyebrows. This time he cuts inside Djorou and lashes in a low left-footer that Almunia – who's actually having another fine game here - does well to palm round the post.

59: Arsenal finally make an attempt to up the pace, winning a couple of corners and sending in three or four dangerous crosses. But by exposing their chin they merely leave themselves open for a classic sucker punch...

BRILLIANT! JUST BRILLIANT! 60: Vidic rises imperiously to head clear from inside his own six yard box, Ronaldo drops back deep inside his own half to pick up possession and, without slowing down, back-heels the ball to Park. While Ronaldo is turning and getting on his bike, Park is sliding a pass through to Rooney who's storming free down the left. He could have gone on his own but, seeing two defenders coming towards him, he squares the ball for the galloping Ronaldo to smash into the roof of the net. "How about that? HOW ABOUT THAT?" yelps Tyldesley. How about that indeed. What a breakaway. From Vidic heading the ball to Ronaldo scoring it took three players three passes and eleven seconds. Breathtaking.

60: The sight of Ronaldo doing his peacock celebration is too much for the many Arsenal fans who'd stopped 'keeping the faith' about an hour before. In scenes reminiscent of the United-Chelsea game in 2001 – the day of the infamous 'missing 30,000' – thousands head for the exits. This was billed as one of the biggest ever night at the Emirates. Instead it's turned into a disaster.

62: Giggs comes on for the excellent Anderson and Bendtner comes on for Walcott, who's hardly touched the ball in both games. So much for the predictions that he was going to 'do a Lennon' to Evra. He's spent most of the time watching the flying Frenchman disappear into the Arsenal half.

63: Arsenal finally have a shot of note, a thumper from Van Persie that the other van, der Sar, parries comfortably.

64: The second biggest worry before this game was that the left flank of Evra and Rooney would pick up the yellow cards that would rule them out of Rome. No one could have imagined that Fergie would have the luxury of protecting them this early. Rafael comes on for Evra. Berbatov comes on for Rooney.

70: ITV shows a replay of Beckham rubbing his hands when Ronaldo thumped in the second. Once a Red, always a Red.

OH CRAP 74: So far the night had been almost too good to be true. Here comes the evil twist. Fabregas runs onto Van Persie's dink over the top and looks certain to score until Fletcher snakes out a leg and nudges the ball to the side. "A wonderful recovery from Fletcher," Tyldesley remarks before spotting that Italian referee Rosetti has pointed to the spot and – even worse – sent Fletch off. It's OK, though, the video evidence is on our side. UEFA won't allow this travesty to stand. He'll be there in Rome, right?

[NO] CONSOLATION 76: Van Persie smashes the penalty that never was high into the right corner.

81: Adebayor, who was only marginally less anonymous than Walcott, finally makes an impression on the tie, getting booked for a terrible, over-the-ball stamp on Carrick. So an ankle-breaker of a challenge gets a yellow card and a perfectly timed tackle gets a red. Spot the justice there. And the news gets even worse for Fletch. According to touchline man Gabriel Clarke, UEFA rules state that red cards can only be overturned for mistaken identity. It's ridiculous. If the Premier League can retrospectively overturn bad decisions, surely UEFA can find a way to do the same, particularly when the penalty is as steep as this.

83: Wenger has his head in his hands again. Pat Rice is still not – you know the rest. .

FULL TIME: ARSENAL 1-3 MANCHESTER UNITED. And that's that. The non-contest is over. Arsenals' unbeaten European record at the Emirates lies in tatters (they're now the only English team to have lost home Champions league ties at three venues). United are just one game away from becoming the first team to retain the European Cup since Milan kept hold of it in 1990. Evra and Rooney will be in Rome. But unless there's an unexpected outbreak of common sense at UEFA HQ, Fletcher, the big-name hunter, won't be. And, with Hargreaves still holed up in Colorado, that would prove more costly than anyone could have imagined at the time.

VIEWS FROM THE PRESSBOX

"This was men against boys, United not so much beating Arsenal as teaching them and their manager a harsh lesson about the realities from which they have hidden for too long.

"While Wenger waits for his young players to gain the experience vital to any team with serious aspirations, United live for the here and now, with Cristiano Ronaldo, the World Player of the Year, propelling them to a second successive Champions League final with two goals, the first a stupendous long-range free kick and the second the result of a magnificent counter-attack." - *The Times*

"When the final whistle sounded the Last Post on Arsenal's season, there were as many embarrassing gaps on the terraces as there had been in the hosts' defence. Manchester United did not just defeat Arsenal, they destroyed them and the Emirates began emptying early and quickly.

"It was time for the road home for Arsenal fans, while United's supporters danced merrily down the road to Rome.

"In reaching the Champions League final in the Eternal City, the European champions did to Arsenal what Manny Pacquaio had done to Ricky Hatton, devastating combinations smashing through naïve defending, bringing an early knock-down. Arsenal were out cold, out of the competition that so obsesses Arsene Wenger.

"This was not men against boys, this was skilled professors against callow pupils, a mismatch that the referee, the appalling Roberto Rosetti, must have been tempted to step in to spare Wenger's young charges further punishment. Arsenal's suffering was that bad. United were that good." – *The Telegraph*

THE EMIRATES – THE VERBALS

"It was 11 men against 11 boys. They're just too young to compete. Chelsea and Barcelona are on another level compared to Arsenal. The difference wasn't just experience, it was quality, too. It's not just about playing pretty. We're pretty too, but we also score goals and we also defend well." – *One delighted Frenchman (Paddy Evra)*

"The fans were up for a big night and to disappoint people, it hurts really. The game was over before it started and that's the most difficult thing to swallow. We can only look at ourselves. It's very disappointing to fight such a long way and then to give the game away like we did tonight." – *One dejected Frenchman (Wenger)*

MATCH FACTS

ARSENAL: ALMUNIA, SAGNA, TOURE, DJOUROU, GIBBS (EBOUE 45), WALCOTT (BENDTNER 63), FABREGAS, SONG BILLONG, NASRI, VAN PERSIE (VELA 79), ADEBAYOR [WENGER]
BOOKED: NASRI, ADEBAYOR, EBOUE.

GOALS: VAN PERSIE 76 PEN.
UNITED: VAN DER SAR, O'SHEA, FERDINAND, VIDIC, EVRA (RAFAEL DA SILVA 65), FLETCHER, CARRICK, ANDERSON (GIGGS 63), PARK, RONALDO, ROONEY (BERBATOV 66)
SENT OFF: FLETCHER (75). GOALS: PARK 8, RONALDO 11, 61

THE EMIRATES ATT: 59,867 REF: ROBERTO ROSETTI (ITALY) H-T: 2-0

"I'm not a man, I am Cantona"

NEWS

FOR 90 MINUTES at Stamford Bridge it looked like Rome was going to host a rerun of last year's final. But Iniesta's injury-time screamer means we've got the final the whole world wanted. United v Barcelona for the biggest prize in football. It doesn't get any better than that....

HUMBLE PIE

Piers Morgan suffers for his swine flu nonsense. From the Mail:
    "The first 'oink, oink, oink' email arrived about three seconds after the final whistle on Tuesday night.
    "Manchester United fans were rather keen to remind me that my red swine flu had just proved fatal. And who can blame them? In over 40 years of being an Arsenal fan, I don't think I have ever felt so sickened as I was by the embarrassing, humiliating, degrading farrago at the Emirates Stadium.
    "No, it was something far worse – a sudden horrifying awareness that Manchester United were now simply on a different planet from us. The gulf in class between the two teams was so big even Cherie Blair's grin and the Grand Canyon would struggle to compete.
    "I've spent all season poking and prodding at Sir Alex and his men, trying to convince myself that they were a busted flush, an empire in terminal decline.
    "But the reality – the harsh, bitter, hurtful reality – is that the side I saw destroy my club on Tuesday is the best United team I've ever seen. And in Cristiano Ronaldo, on the basis of his stunning performance, they have indisputably the best player in the world. And probably the best player they've ever had."

NEWS II

Chelsea get themselves into trouble with their behaviour at the end of the Barcelona game. Fair enough, Norwegian referee Tom Ovrebo did turn down no fewer than three strong penalty appeals. But that's no excuse for Drogba to wrestle with security and scream 'f**king disgrace' at the cameras, for Bosingwa to call Ovrebo a thief or for Ballack to get in his face and effectively beat him up without using his arms (imagine an irate torso swinging punches and you'll get the gist).

UEFA announce that United and Barcelona – who pulled in a total of 169,733 punters for their home semis – will get just 19,500 tickets each for the 67,000 capacity Olympic Stadium. That's a couple of thousand down on last year even. The MEN goes undercover and reveals that tickets are going for 10 times face value. Look out next week for their exposé on where bears do their business.

Fletch looks doomed to sit out the final as the UEFA jobsworths have their say on his red card. Both Barcelona's full-backs, Alves and Abidal, will also miss the game through suspension. It's a toss-up who will be missed more. Fletcher, for his engine and undeniable big game presence, or Alves for his free-kick benders and driving runs down the right. Darren Fergusons's estranged wife Nadine and their son Charlie suffer nasty injuries in a car crash in Chesire. Fortunately both are expected to make a full recovery. Ken Loach's 'Looking for Eric', starring you know who, opens in Cannes. And it doesn't take long for the Big Final scare-mongering to start in the press. Last year it was all about how the Russian police were going to nick your passports and roubles and dump you in AIDS-infested prisons. This year it was all about what the knife-wielding locals were going to do to your legs and buttocks. Though if the past is any guide the local Carabinieri won't be rolling out the welcome mat either...

THERE WILL BE BLOOD

From The People:

"Cops have cracked a hooligan plot to ambush Manchester United supporters in Rome and turn the European Champions League final into a bloodbath.

"Knife-wielding AS Roma thugs plan to attack fans as they arrive in the Italian capital for the showdown against Barcelona on May 27. Police are tracking troublemakers via informers and monitoring web messages promising bloodshed.

"Up to 10,000 officers will be on duty for the final – twice the number present when 11 British fans were hospitalized★ after riots at a Roma– United game in Italy two years ago."
★*(that's the worry. If 5,000 officers can put 11 Reds in hospital, what are 10,000 going to do?)*

QUOTES OF THE WEEK I

"It is the right final. The two teams deserve to be there and it's the game that everyone wanted to see. Manchester United and Barcelona play the best football in Europe – they are brilliant, strong sides. While Barça are a great side to watch, United are solid as well as full of talented individuals." – *Looks like Kaka's planning to crack open a few tinnies and enjoy the show on May 27th.*

"I do not know if he is a referee or a thief. There are no words to describe the person that was on the pitch here." – *Chelsea full-back Bosingwa on bungling referee Ovrebo.*

"At times it was a bit like men against boys. Does the club need to take a step up? Of course. To be first in the world, to be first in Europe, you must have a much stronger bench. Look at United on Tuesday night. They had at least £100million in talent sitting on the bench." – *Arsenal shareholder Alisher Usmanov on the Emirates massacre.*

QUESTION OF THE WEEK

All season long there have been whispers about Abramovich. Has he fallen out of love with Chelsea? Does he want to sign any more big cheques after watching his fortune decline 40% to 'just' £7 billion in 12 months? Has he been fazed by the fact he's not the richest kid on the block any more? Can he take Chelsea losing any more big Champions League games? Well here's a couple of interesting pointers...

IN THE SUMMER OF 2006: Chelsea splashed out more than £80m on Shevchenko, Kalou, Mikel, Cole and Boulahrouz and Ashley Cole were recruited in deals worth £50m. In the 5 transfer windows since Chelsea's net spend has been less than West Brom's: £5m.

IN JANUARY 2007: in a briefing after they bought Liverpool, Tom Hicks and George Gillett claimed to have seen a leaked document detailing Abramovich's plans for Chelsea and predicted that the spending would stop once Abramovich's personal outlay went significantly over £500m. His total net spend on Chelsea today? £578m.

IN THE CANNES

"He was a lovely bloke, Cantona, just one of the lads, and he was happy to take the piss out of himself - there's a line where I tease him about his proverbs and the bloody seagulls, which I just improvised. I was worried I'd upset Eric with it but he thought it was very funny and Ken's kept it in the film." - *Steve Evets, Eric's postman co-star in Looking for Eric.*

"I am not a man, I am Cantona." – *the line that launched 100,000 Youtube hits.*

QUOTES OF THE WEEK II

"Me? I have not been treated as a member of the family. I do not feel wanted. I feel bad over my situation, I do, but it's very, very difficult to stay any longer. I guess what I'm saying is goodbye." – *Tévez is lucky so many of us have got the blinkers on about him. Otherwise we'd be asking why he's making noises like this in the* News of the World *on the morning of a vital derby.*

"We deserve to be on top of the league." – *Gerrard succumbs to Benitez disease.*

"It's a derby and if they make a mistake they will be feeling the pressure. Manchester City are a difficult team to play against. Clearly our position is very good, we have to keep pushing and wait - hopefully we can be top of the league next weekend." – *Benitez's fat fingers can't get enough of those straws. Hmmmm.*

"Carlos' final destination will be made solely on what's best for Carlos and his family." – *Kia Joorabchian suggests that Tévez's owners, the same people who stand to make a fortune out of his next move, are only interested in his own well-being. (If that was the case wouldn't they have accepted United's lower offer months ago?)*

CONSPIRACY THEORY OF THE WEEK
From The Sun:

'CHELSEA fans blasted UEFA after discovering the final score of 1-1 was posted on its website HOURS before kick-off' blarts the paper.

'Blues supporters were stunned that the governing body of European football correctly predicted the outcome of the explosive Champions League semi-final with Barcelona.'

THE PARTY LINE

"It opens Pandora's box if you can challenge every decision. And if you rule that it is not a red card, then you are also saying it is not a penalty, and therefore not a goal, and what do you do then - start changing the results of matches afterwards?"- *A 'UEFA source' rules out the possibility of Fletch's ban being overturned — even though everyone who's seen the replay knows it should be. It's a strange argument, especially as no one suggested that the penalty should have been wiped out of the record books too.*

YOU WERE SAYING?

ARSENE WENGER, MAY 4: "I am very confident the team will produce a magnificent performance and that we will manage it."

NICKLAS BENDTNER, MAY 4: "I am 100 per cent sure we will pass through to the final."

FAPL 10/05/2009

UNITED 2 CITY 0
Ronaldo 18, Tévez 45

COME ON, ADMIT IT, you had a sneaking suspicion there was going to be another twist in the title race. That City were going to play party-pooper again, like they did last year. That Robinho was going to clamber out of Rafael's pocket and do something memorable for all the wrong reasons. But it wasn't like that. The only moment of genuine drama came when Ronaldo threw a hissy fit – and his trackie top – when he was substituted in the second half. As for the rest of the afternoon, it was as low-key as you could get, with Munich-chanting Blues only getting animated when an inflatable City player scored a penalty during the half-time, er, entertainment. Fergie called the match horrible, and from an aesthetic point of view he had a point, particularly in the second half when we basically stopped attacking. But with three games left and just four points needed - and with a pack of gormless Blues to welcome to work in the morning - who cares about the quality? Just enjoy the result.

THE MOMENTS THAT MATTERED

1-0 (18): Before the game Hughesie warned Ronaldo that he could risk long-term damage from the unique way he takes free-kicks. He might be proved right (in fact, given his size, and the grief his Achilles gets from defenders, would anyone be shocked if Ronaldo was still turning it on in his thirties?). But right now his technique is serving him just fine. This effort wasn't in the same league as the Emirates miracle – in fact it needed a deflection off the wall to beat Given - but what did that matter. United had the crucial opener. And when the second came on the stroke of half-time this year's Old Trafford derby was as good as over...

2-0 (45): It was no ordinary goal either. Berbatov, playing arguably his best game at Old Trafford, kills Fletcher's long ball over his shoulder with almost unnerving ease and laconically lays it off to Tévez. Tévez had already lashed one screamer against the corner of post and bar. This time he adjusts his sights by an inch or so and scores with a beauty in off the same post before racing off to celebrate, pointedly, in front of Fergie and the money men. The cupped ears – drawing attention to the love messages from the Stretford End and the chants of 'Fergie sign him up' – said it all...

TANTRUM (58): The whole season had been marred by the rumour circus surrounding Tévez and Ronaldo. So it was perhaps fitting that on the same afternoon that Tévez sent out a very public message of discontent, that Ronaldo followed suit, launching into a childish hissy fit when he was subbed off. Fergie, who did his best to downplay the incident later, pretended not to notice Ronaldo snatching angrily at a trackie top and then giving the wobbly bottom lip act on the bench. Which in a weird way was probably the biggest compliment he could pay him. If any other player had thrown a tantrum like that he'd have left the ground with a boot wedged in his eye.

VIEWS FROM THE PRESSBOX

"Only in a city synonymous with rain could clouds threaten to obscure the silver lining that will embellish a gilded season for Manchester United. A third successive Premier League title is within touching distance and could be secured against Arsenal at Old Trafford on Saturday lunchtime, but the overriding feeling after a comfortable win over the local rivals was a strange one, as if glory is not enough for some of these players.

"There was a time when scoring in a derby match would

effectively give you the freedom of half the city, at least until the next game, but Cristiano Ronaldo and Carlos Tévez seemed more interested yesterday afternoon in airing grievances than in celebrating the United victory that their goals secured.

"Tévez marked his goal by sprinting towards the directors' box and cupping his ears — as if he had not said enough about the deafening silence from the boardroom about his future — while Ronaldo's pathetic hissy-fit, as he was replaced by Paul Scholes with the match already won, was an embarrassing act that caused awkward looks among the team-mates who were watching from the stands."
– *The Times goes big on the Ronaldo-Tévez subplot.*

CITY – THE VERBALS

"We didn't play well today. I think derby games can be like that, they can be horrible games and I think we got a horrible game today. A win is a win at this time of the season, I congratulate the players, it's been a great week but a hard week and well done to the lads." – *Fergie on the 'horrible' derby.*

"We felt hard done by as it was not a fair reflection on the game." – *Come again Sparky?*

"We did not ask enough questions of them. We did not have that presence needed. We had a lot of possession but there was not much of an end product." – *Sparky defeats his own argument.*

"He had an incredible performance at Arsenal in midweek, he ran his socks off. We have to think about how we get through our games and keeping him fresh. He wanted to stay on. He is in great form. But I've got to look at the big picture. I've got to think about keeping our players as fresh as we can for the games ahead." – *Fergie tries his best to diffuse the Ronaldo bomb...*

"I didn't read any of it, you hear things, he's a Manchester United player. They [the Old Trafford crowd] want triers, that's the great thing about football, a lad who tries all the time can be forgiven many things." – *... and leaves Tévez in no doubt what he really thinks about him (i.e. he's a great trier rather than a great player).*

WHAT WAS GOOD?

"ISTANBUL, ISTANBUL, YOU'RE NOT GOING..." – Like all the best p★ss-takes, it's childish, fun and annoying.

RAFAEL PUTTING ROBINHO IN HIS POCKET... again.

VIDIC AND FLETCHER – the men of the season again showed their class. Vidic won everything to once again make mockery of the obituaries handed out to his season after his Torres. Fletcher bossed the midfield. Has a player ever come on so much so late in his career?

BERBATOV'S FIRST TOUCH – I forgot who wrote this but they're right, his right foot really could pull a swallow out of the sky without hurting it.

BERBATOV'S PERFORMANCE. All season he's shown the touch of an angel and the work ethic of a Scouser. Against City he showed what he could do when he can be bothered to turn and start running at people rather than playing simple balls backwards. At times he was untouchable. Should Fergie have dropped him earlier?

TÉVEZ – gave his best performance of the season too. If he'd played like this all year, and scored goals like this (this was still only his 4th in the league), he wouldn't need to be acting up to the crowd. He'd have a 5-year contract in his pocket, presumably where his daughter's dummy used to be.

IT'S ONLY 5 WEEKS TILL ERIC'S FILM IS OUT.

THE ROMAN LEGIONNAIRE'S HATS IN THE STANDS – so bad they're good.

ANOTHER DERBY DOUBLE – surprisingly only the 5th in the Fergie era.

WHAT WAS BAD?

RONALDO'S TANTRUM. Pathetic doesn't cover it.

RONALDO AND TÉVEZ DOING THEIR BEST TO SOIL WHAT WAS REALLY A GREAT DAY - after all, it doesn't get much better than beating City and all but sealing the title on the same day.

"SAME OLD MUNICHS, ALWAYS CHEATING…" – Witty banter from the City end. See above.

THOSE REDS WHO WOLF-WHISTLED THE GROUP OF GYMNASTS AT HALF-TIME. They were about 8. Shame on you.

MICAH RICHARDS – fat and past it at 20?

THE NEW SONGS DEVOTED TO ROME AND CHAMPIONS LEAGUE FINAL. Whoever wrote the lyrics to the Que Sera Sera (we're going to Italy) song deserves to be stabbed. In the backside.

INTRO OF THE DAY

From the Guardian's minute-by-minute guide:

"The greatest-ever derby between Manchester United and Manchester City was played at Old Trafford nearly 41 years ago. At the Old Trafford cricket ground, that is. In front of a crowd of 15,000 in July 1968, the reigning league champions took on the holders of the European Cup. City were all out for a paltry 168, but still won as United could only rack up a frankly pathetic 79. The pitch was then invaded by a load of bottle-throwing kids, which really wasn't cricket, and 'five youths aged between 13 and 16 were charged with various offences including carrying offensive weapons, causing a breach of the peace, and assaulting a policeman'. Now then, we'll have none of that today."

WORST INTRO OF THE DAY

'THE winker has apologised for being a snatcher after being branded a plonker" - *The Sun after Cristiano Ronaldo's apologises to assistant kitman Alec Wyllie for snatching a tracksuit top out of his hand and throwing it to the floor during his derby day sulkathon.*

QUESTION OF THE DAY

Why does the automated PA safety announcer at Old Trafford have a lisp? *(and why does 'she' say words beginning in an 's' so often?)*

MATCH FACTS

UNITED: VAN DER SAR, RAFAEL DA SILVA, VIDIC, EVANS (O'SHEA 71), EVRA, RONALDO (SCHOLES 58), FLETCHER, GIGGS, PARK (ROONEY 58), BERBATOV, TÉVEZ
BOOKED: FLETCHER.
CITY: GIVEN, RICHARDS, ONUOHA, DUNNE, BRIDGE, ELANO, IRELAND, KOMPANY, DE JONG (PETROV 73), ROBINHO (EVANS 89), CAICEDO (BOJINOV 63) [HUGHES]
BOOKED: IRELAND.
ATT: 75,464 REF: CHRIS FOY H-T: 2-0

OTHER SCORES

ARSENAL 1 CHELSEA 4, WEST HAM 0 LIVERPOOL 3

LEAGUE TABLE

1. UNITED 83 (35) 2. LIVERPOOL 80 (36) 3. CHELSEA 77 (36)
4. ARSENAL 68 (36)... 10. CITY 47 (36)

"The lads can take care of that. I am focused on winning the Premier League"

NEWS

REMEMBER BACK IN 1999 when Ginola won the PFA player of the year because the United vote had been split? Well, it's happened again, as Gerrard takes advantage of a split vote between Giggs, Vidic and Rooney to claim the writers' award. Now don't get me wrong, Gerrard's a fine player who's had a fine season (though all those pundits who blabber on about the number of goals he gets 'for a midfielder' forget that he takes penalties and free-kicks and actually plays up front these days). But he's failed to win anything. Again. And, as Gerrard sportingly pointed out afterwards, no one, I mean no one, has done more to single-handedly shape this season than Vidic. Amazingly, memories of that one nightmare moment against Torres mean he doesn't even feature in the writers' top 3.

Elsewhere Stevie Coppell resigns from Reading after they lose to Burnley in the Championship play-off semi-finals. And FC United, who recently missed out on a fourth successive promotion (remaining in the Northern Premier League Premier Division, 3 tiers beneath the Football League), do a Radiohead by launching a 'pay what you like' season ticket scheme.

MAN OF THE WEEK

"The lads can take care of that. I am focused on winning the Premier League." – *Fletch, making the jump from Scottish Player to Red Hero in just 9 months.*

RUNNER-UP

"Vidic and Rio Ferdinand have been superb and they have saved United so many points this season and, for me, United owe those two big time. I voted for Vidic in the PFA awards and, if I'd had a Football Writers' vote, I would have voted for him again, because he has had a magnificent season. Possibly, he's been judged because of the incident against us at Old Trafford when he didn't deal with the ball and Fernando [Torres] scored. Maybe that's gone against him for both awards. He's still had a great season and it's just unfortunate –

but maybe I have to thank Fernando for this award!" – *Any else think that Gerrard is an annoyingly decent guy?*

LEAKY ARGUMENT OF THE WEEK

The Mayor of Rome, Gianni Alemanno, gets all shirty about the abuse the city has received for the behaviour of its football fans, and particularly the unofficial campaign to get the final moved to a place where English fans don't get stabbed:

"The campaign against us is quite simply ungenerous and insulting. This is not the first time that Rome has hosted the Champions League final. I should also like to point out, by way of an answer to the statements in the article, that a Google search with the words 'London' and 'stabbed' brings up 2,670,000 pages, 10 times those that appear for Rome. That alone should prove beyond reasonable doubt how mistaken the affirmations in that article really are."

Quite so sir. How could we have been so wrong?

RUNNER-UP

"He wasn't [protesting about United]. Before the game he [Tévez] said: 'Someone told me there was an article in the newspaper about me last week' and I said, 'Yes, there was and they were saying you were not a prolific goalscorer.' So he said: 'I want to know where the pressbox is because I want to go and show them my ears if they wrote that." *Kia Joorabchian does his best to pretend that, after 2 years at the club, Tévez hasn't worked out where the press boys sit… and where the men in suits do.*

QUOTES OF THE WEEK

"Rome has now become a defacto neutral venue for the final which should make life easier. We are confident we will have everything in place to ensure a safe final for all fans." - *UEFA spokesman William Gaillard inadvertently admits they were wetting themselves about another all-English final.*

"We live in a league now where the divers are rewarded. It is not right, but it is like that."- *Arsene Wenger's quite right. Which is presumably why he's spent all those years clamping down on it…*

DEFENCE OF THE WEEK

You may be interested to know that if you use the Google defence, like the Mayor of Rome, you'll come up with the following results*:

HITLER BAD – 1,530,000, HITLER GOOD – 6,670,000.
BEARDSLEY UGLY - 35,500, BEARDSLEY BEAUTIFUL – 504,000
SCOUSERS UNEMPLOYED – 8,020, SCOUSERS EMPLOYED – 10,700
So there you have it. Peter Beardsley is god's gift to women, Scousers aren't work-shy and Hitler was just plain misunderstood.
(Mind you, the Google defence isn't always flawed. 'Manchester City small' beats 'Manchester City massive' by 7,620,000 to 637,000).
*as of August 2009

FAPL 13/05/2009

WIGAN 1 UNITED 2
Rodallega 28, Tévez 61, Carrick 86

LAST MAY WE won the league in a torrent at Wigan. A year on history as good as repeated itself. And as Carrick swept in his imperious winner and Evra took the mickey out of Benitez (mimicking his 'it's all over' gesture that so upset Fergie), one thing became clear... United can be right bastards at times. We could have put Liverpool out of their misery at Old Trafford back in March. Instead we allowed the Scousers to think they had a real chance in the title race. We gifted them the 4-1. We played hari kari football at Fulham. We allowed them to get within a handful of points. And just when the best fans in the world™ were daring to believe, when the Fat Waiter had convinced himself he'd assembled the best team since Jan Molby could still fit into shorts, we simply put our foot down and left them behind. It was almost cruel, like enticing a stray dog in from the road with a juicy steak... and then devouring it in front of it.

OK, maybe it wasn't planned like that. No Red would ever want to see us lose any match to Liverpool, never mind by the sort of score they'll still be banging on about in 2050. But there's no getting around it, that nightmare afternoon in March turned a successful season into a memorable one. If we'd cleared Liverpool out that day what memories would we have of the league season? Little more than an epic run of clean sheets, that's what. But because Vidic let that ball bounce, we'd been treated to a month of thrilling tension. Two Roy of the Rovers afternoons at Old Trafford didn't make this a great season★ of course but no one who saw Macheda's moment, or the Fab Four turn it on against Spurs, are going to forget the finale in a hurry.

MATCH ACTION

0-1 (28): Do you remember Charlton under Curbishley? They'd always overperform till Christmas, get themselves safe and then switch off for the season. Wigan had been suffering with the same problem ever since we pinched the points against them at Old Trafford in January, winning just 11 points out of the last 42. But you wouldn't have guessed it from the way they went at us here. Valencia should have given them an instant lead when he burst through from halfway. Rooney and Carrick then missed great opportunities at the other end before Wigan went ahead with a strange goal from new £4.5m Colombian Hugo Rodallega. Vidic and Rodallega compete for a long ball into the area, both lose their bearings but only Rodallega keeps his feet. An instinctive half-volley takes the ball past Van der Sar from close range.

1-1 (61): Apparently Fergie has a theory that we play better when the rain's banging down. Watching United zip the ball around the slippery pitch in response to the Rodallega setback, it was hard to disagree. Even so, it took a wonder moment from supersub Tévez to finally break Wigan down. Carrick's low centre from the right looks to be too far behind him to be genuinely threatening but Tévez somehow adjusts and turns his body and heel-flicks the ball into the net.

2-1 (86): After the Tévez moment we needed 3 points from 210 minutes of football to make certain of the league. After Carrick's ubersweet left-footer into the top corner we needed 1 point from 180 minutes. We weren't over the finishing line yet but as Rooney did a Steve Morrow over Carrick's shoulders, and Evra did his Benitez act, you had the feeling it would take an act of God to stop us.

WHAT WAS GOOD?

WE NEED ONE POINT TO MAKE IT 18.

WATCHING THE FAB FOUR TURN IT ON IN THE LAST 30 MINUTES.

ROONEY'S SELFLESSNESS. Compare and contrast the way he's got stuck into his unfavoured new role on the left (the key positional change that makes the Fab Four work) to Ronaldo's toy-throwing reaction when he was subbed in one game.

WHAT WAS BAD?

THE FACT THAT IT'S TAKEN UNTIL MAY for us to work out a way of playing Ronaldo, Rooney, Tévez and Berbatov in the same team.

IT LOOKS AS UNLIKELY AS EVER THAT TÉVEZ WILL STILL BE PART OF THE FAB FOUR NEXT SEASON (see 'Dashed' below).

ROONEY'S SELFLESSNESS. Remember Fergie's pledge from last summer? "We have to define Wayne's role a bit better for us, because I think he sacrificed himself for the team last season. He has sacrificed himself and never complained about it, which says a lot for the lad. It's fair to say that, if the player moans, you would have to review the situation because it does happen that some players know what their best position is and they don't want to challenge themselves in another position." If Rooney is going to develop into the world great we all think he can, is it about time he started moaning more and sacrificing himself less?

DASHED

"He is a fantastic player. He knows I want him to stay. I had a chat with him today and David Gill has had meetings with him. I think Carlos himself is okay. I think the terms he has been offered are good." – *Fergie skips out of the JJB dressing-rooms (the ones at the ground obviously) to raise one last hope of a deal being struck for Tévez.*

"We actually have not had any offer for Carlos, no offers for personal terms for Carlos. I had a chat with David Gill, we had a meeting but no offer was made to Carlos." – *Almost as soon as Fergie finishes speaking, Kia Joorabchian pops up on Sky Sports News to deny that any real progress has been made...*

"It is true David Gill came to see Mr Joorabchian and they had a cordial meeting. It is categorically untrue that Manchester United made an offer to try to persuade Carlos Tévez to stay at the club. In 2007 Manchester United agreed a two-year loan deal for Carlos Tévez and at the same time agreed the terms that would make the transfer permanent. They have not taken up that option." ... *and just in case there's any room left for doubt Joorabchian's spokesman removes it.*

FORUM ENTRY OF THE NIGHT
From 'Jeff' on football365:

"18......I can finally feel it in my bones. Never in my life time did I believe this would or could happen. I can remember 1992 and 18-7 like it was yesterday. All those teenage years in the 80's watching that lot draw further and further away !!! How fitting that this year, they've been our closest challengers.

"In 1994 there was a banner at Anfield saying "come back and sing Ooohh Ahh Cantona when you've won 18". We'll be there next season to sing it for you !!!!"

THE JJB – THE VERBALS

"We had to show the resolve of champions against a very determined Wigan side. This was a really tough hurdle, but we got there with a fantastic second-half performance. We were determined, we never gave in, kept going and got a little bit of luck in the second half, but we were fantastic." – *You're not so bad yourself, Fergie.*

"I thought this was going to be the night, but I'm still trying. They've [Wigan] shown everyone the quality and integrity of the Premier League. There's no question they were rattled, but we needed to go another ten minutes. We did everything we possibly could." – *Brucie just doesn't know what he's got to do to get one over his old gaffer.*

VIEWS FROM THE PRESSBOX

"The chants of "sign him up" are getting louder by the week and Carlos Tévez is clearly determined to ensure that wherever he ends up next season, be it with Manchester United or in the employment of another club, his final act of the Premier League season will be to dictate the destination of the trophy.

"When Tévez was summoned from the bench and brought into a night of high tension and, ultimately, euphoric celebrations, the team that now stand on the brink of an 18th league title were running the risk of being embarrassed by a side that had not won since 22 March and of offering Liverpool hope of a late twist to the title race. Within minutes Tévez had scored a goal of audacious nerve and class. After that there was a sense of inevitability about the proceedings." – *The Guardian on the moment of the night.*

*TEN OF THE BEST

What order would you put Fergie's title-winning seasons? Anything like this?

1. 1993-4 (Cantona at his best, Kanchelskis and Giggs on the wings, Ince and Keane dominating the midfield. And a first double to boot.)
2. 1998-9 (Everything about this season felt magical).
3. 1992-3 (No. 1 in terms of importance, but loses points because of

the lack of quality in the autumn).

4. 1995-6 (So you don't win anything with kids eh? Reeling in Newcastle with the Class of '92 was perhaps Fergie's biggest achievement).

5. 2006-7 (Vital. The first title win after Chelsea's money changed the face of football).

6. 2007-8 (Ronaldo's gift to us all).

7. 2002-3 (Still don't know how we managed to win this one. Epic night at Highbury).

8. 1999-2000 (The year of Taibi, Brazil and the FA Cup farce. Too easy and overshadowed by Euro disappointment).

9. 1996-7 (Ole arrives. The first league season to be overshadowed by a Champions League campaign).

10. 2000-01 (We beat Arsenal 6-1. Too easy and overshadowed by Euro disappointment).

MATCH FACTS

Wigan: Kingson, Melchiot, Boyce, Bramble, Figueroa, Valencia, Cattermole, Scharner, Brown, N'Zogbia (Mido 82), Rodallega [Brucie]

United: Van der Sar, O'Shea, Vidic, Evans, Evra, Carrick, Scholes (Giggs 75), Anderson (Tévez 58), Ronaldo, Berbatov (Park 89), Rooney.

Subs Not Used: Kuszczak, Neville, Nani, Rafael Da Silva.

JJB Stadium Att: 21,286 **Ref:** Rob Styles **h-t:** 0-1

"We lose against Man United who have 10 times more resources, it's not a shame. They are the best in the world."

NEWS

Zlatan Ibrahimovic's agent links him with a move to United. Would there be a more moody strike-force than him and Berbatov together? Great news for tabloid headline writers. United sign another young Brazilian, Corinthians' 17 year-old centre-back Dodo. Red as a Dodo anyone? Fergie pinches yet another foreign kid, 16 year-old Le Havre midfielder Paul Pogba, from under the nose of Wenger (not that that narrows the field down that much – boom boom).

Wenger then cops a load of flak from Arsenal fans – one of whom has the cheek to brand Silvestre a geriatric - at a stormy meeting with shareholders. It seems like Wenger's relationship with the fans is showing the same sort of strain that Fergie's did back in 2005.

Barcelona are one step away from their own treble after swamping Bilbao 4-1 in the Spanish Cup Final. The City council announce that live football will never be shown in Manchester again after the UEFA Cup aggro last year. I wouldn't mind so much if it had been Mancs who'd gone on the rampage.. And Benitez reacts to United's imminent title success with all the charm and grace you'd expect... from a spoilt 5 year-old.

NO CLUE, NO CLASS

"It just means they have more points." – *Benitez when asked if the best team always wins the league.*

"There are a lot of good teams in the Premier League. Without putting them in any order, I'd say Chelsea, United, Liverpool and Arsenal are the best. United have more points, it only means they have more points, that's all, nothing else." – *Benitez really hasn't got the idea of how this 'most points wins' rule works.*

"United are a strong team. They have a good squad which is important because when you are talking about the league you are talking about nine months. But you cannot imagine if Steven Gerrard and Fernando Torres had been fit all season where we would be now." - *Now he claims Liverpool would have won the title if their front two had played every game. It's a decent argument in a sense. But imagine what would have happened if Ronaldo had been properly fit in the autumn, or if Hargreaves had been around, or if United hadn't had to traipse around the Far East at Christmas, or if we hadn't played 5 more cup games, or if we hadn't had to play catch-up all season...*

BEGGING FOR IT

Des Kelly in the Mail gives Benitez the shoeing he was asking for:

"Rather than ask what might have happened if Gerrard and Torres were fit, Benitez would have been better served addressing other questions, although I suspect he might not like the answers.

Questions like: What if he'd been braver and played more positive football when Liverpool had a lead at the top of the table and United were away in Japan? What if he hadn't drawn 11 games and allowed United to seize back control? What if he'd actually used Robbie Keane properly during Torres's absence, instead of shunting him out the door? What if he'd kept his counsel instead of launching that distracting attack on Ferguson? What if he had played key players more often instead of leaving them on the bench? What if he had bought more wisely and gathered together a squad better equipped for the challenges of a long season? Why is Benitez blaming a lack of 'financial power' when he spent £7million on a third-choice left back and £40m last summer?"

INTRO OF THE WEEK

From The Telegraph's report on the Wigan game:

"At the end of a day when Liverpool's captain, Steven Gerrard, was inexplicably voted Footballer of the Year, Manchester United showed why they are the team of the year, why they will again be champions this year, and why they are brim full of stars blessed with an astonishing work ethic, players who deserve to carve up the individual honours of the year."

DASHED

"He is a fantastic player. He knows I want him to stay. I had a chat with him today and David Gill has had meetings with him. I think Carlos himself is okay. I think the terms he has been offered are good." – *Fergie raises hope of a deal being struck after Tévez's wonder-flick at Wigan.*

"We actually have not had any offer for Carlos, no offers for personal terms for Carlos. I had a chat with David Gill, we had a meeting but no offer was made to Carlos." - *Kia Joorabchian immediately dashes it.*

FLAT TRACK BULLIES

The Guardian notes how we've all but won the league by feasting on the small fry:

"Of 69 points available against those 12 sides – in descending order, West Ham United, Manchester City, Wigan Athletic, Stoke City, Bolton Wanderers, Blackburn Rovers, Portsmouth, Sunderland, Newcastle United, Hull City, Middlesbrough and West Bromwich Albion – United have taken 67, the one blemish being a 1-1 draw at home to Newcastle on the opening weekend of the league season.

"United, however, have not recorded a single victory in their away games against the seven teams directly behind them, taking four points out of 21 and scoring only four goals in the process. They have also taken 10 points fewer than Liverpool in terms of matches between the top four clubs,

"Liverpool's advantage has been lost, however, by their inferior record against the bottom 12 teams, dropping 13 points against Middlesbrough, Hull, Stoke (twice), Wigan and Manchester City."

QUOTES OF THE WEEK

"A very good goalkeeper, probably the best defence in the world, and a perfect attacking line with Rooney, Berbatov and particularly Ronaldo." – *Apart from that, Andrei Arshavin doesn't really rate us.*

"I'd love to see a player of Ryan Giggs' quality and stature playing for Cardiff City. But I haven't got a crystal ball, so I don't know whether it will happen, or when." – *Dear old Peter Ridsdale. Still as deluded as ever.*

"It is a bit far-fetched really .We could all break our contracts. You could leave The Sun... and go to the Beano tomorrow!" – *Fergie has a nice dig at Neil Custis of* The Sun *after a rumour goes around that Tévez could join United on a Bosman free.*

QUOTE OF THE WEEK

"We lose against Man United who have 10 times more resources, it's not a shame. They are the best in the world. Congratulations to them. If you play tennis tomorrow and you lose against [Rafael] Nadal, you can still say you are a good player." – *Wenger sets the Arsenal shareholders straight on where their club stands these days.*

RUNNER-UP

"I saw them [United] against Aston Villa and you felt nearly sorry for them. They won the game in the end but they were closer to lose 3–1 or 4–1 than to make 2–2 and then win 3–2. They gained the momentum at the right time. We miss something, I don't deny that, because we were 1–0 up against Chelsea in the FA Cup semi-final and we lost so there is that and, secondly, there is to say 'OK, Man United was the better team'. That is the beauty of sport. We have not to be scared to say someone is better." – *Since when has Wenger been speaking so much sense?*

FAPL 16/05/2009

CHAMPIONS 0 ARSENAL 0

OK, so IT wasn't done the United way. In fact it's hard to think of a home game that United, who left first Tévez and then Ronaldo hopelessly isolated on their own up front, have approached more negatively. But frankly who cares. We'd done it. A hat-trick of league titles for the second time – a stunningly unique achievement. 18 league titles in total to bring us level with Liverpool – and give us a new song to taunt El Waiter with. A Carling Cup and league double for the first time ever. And the promise of a new, if plastic-coated, version of the Treble to come in Rome. And to think that Fergie was doing a jig round the Millennium Stadium when we only won the Carling Cup against Wigan only 3 years ago...

Mind you, if anyone tells you this was an epic Old Trafford party, they'd either spent the day pouring rocket fuel down their necks, or they've never been here when the old place is really rocking. The Spurs win in 1999, the only previous time we'd clinched the Premier League title at home, was like a mashed-up rave, a Roman orgy and VE Day rolled into one. This was more like your Nan's eightieth down the Legion (complete with roller-disco tunes and all-round Keegan-esque cheesiness of course) – in other words, you wouldn't want to miss it but it's not something you'll bore your kids about. The game played a part in that. Let's not mince words, it was utter crap – one-paced and indifferent, a real Veron of a game. So did the fact (get that Rafa) that Rome was on most people's minds and we've had two decades of unprecedented success so we're now right spoilt gits. But the real party-pooper was something different. You've got to be some sort of player and personality to overshadow a title win AND inadvertently wreck the annual Fergie address. But that's what the prospect of losing Tévez did. Now some people in the press have taken to making snide comments about the Stretford End's love affair with Tévez, as if we don't recognize class and are fooled by hard work. But they miss the point. Tévez might not be a Messi or a Rooney. In fact he might not be a great player at all. He's certainly not a great goalscorer or worth £35 million. But he scores more crucial late goals than anyone else at the club. And he plays like United mean everything to him. In many ways he's the nearest thing to Ole we've got, a baby-scaring assassin if you like. And that's why no one wants to see him go. And we'll miss him badly when he does…

(Mind you, looking back it was all a bit embarrassing that we drowned out Fergie for a guy who'd end up doing one to City.)

WRAPPING UP THE LEAGUE
(THE CONDENSED VERSION)

Van Persie puts a free header over. Rooney puts a free header wide. North Stand lower runs out of pies (again). Old Trafford echoes with boos and then rich applause as Tévez is pulled off. Tévez waves to all corners of the ground. Sky spot tears as he reaches the bench. Andy Gray is convinced he's saying goodbye. So is everyone else. Park's Ronaldo engineered tap-in is wrongly ruled out for offside. Fabregas hits the post. The uber-tw*t in the seat behind screams for Giggs, Carrick and Ronaldo to be taken off (we've already used two subs). Chris Foy blows up. Old Trafford goes mental (sort of). 'Are you watching Merseyside?', 'Que Sera Sera' (Italy version), '18 times and that's a fact', '19 years and that's a fact'. Keegan pumps out cheese. An army of groundstaff build a podium. Cathedrals have been built quicker. 3 army boys bring out the Cup. One of them is marching with a crutch. It's probably harder than it looks. The players return. Fred the Red braces himself for a kicking. It doesn't come. Mickey P and co come up first. Maybe Quieroz wasn't such a miss after all? Bit-part players get a cheer but no medal. Macheda deserves one as much as anyone. Giggs turns down the chance to lift the trophy. Unknown Barclays woman with perm hands it over. Gary Nev disappears under a mass of Reds and streamers. We'll keep the trophy for winning three. Champagne fights start. 'We are the champions', 'Are you watching Merseyside?' (I have my doubts),Anderson mimics the squaddies as they march off. Ronaldo picks up his mum. Fergie's speech is interrupted by the crowd. 'Fergie, Fergie sign him up'. "We'll bring that cup back from Rome". Lap of honour with the kids. Fletch carts his twins around. Berbatov doesn't make the whole lap (too far?). Tévez brings along the whole family. Potty Paddy E does his Benitez celebration. 'Giggs will tear you apart', 'Only one Darren Fletcher'. Gravy and chips. Text Liverpool fan from work. Drink…

QUOTE OF THE DAY

`Does it get better then this? Now we look forward to a nice trip to Rome. And we're gonnae bring that Cup back.' – *Fergie's championship address.*

CHAMPIONS – THE VERBALS

"It makes you want to go on for ever." – *Fergie's feeling immortal.*

"I never thought we could get 11 titles - *never in a million years.*" – *Fergie again.*

"It is an exceptional achievement and congratulations to Sir Alex Ferguson. It is fantastic what his team have done this year. The overall achievement is remarkable. United are worthy champions. They did well in every single competition and that is very difficult." – *Wenger gives Benitez a lesson in humility.*

"The thing about us this season is you can't name our best side. It has been about our squad, and everybody has contributed - whether they have played enough games to win a medal or not." – *Gary Nev on the Year of the Squad.*

"This team are better than any we've ever had. Some of the football they play is fantastic. It is in the best Manchester United traditions. It has been hard playing three games a week at times, but we deserve to be champions" – *Sir Bobby.*

"I like Manchester. I like the fans. It is very difficult to leave Manchester," he said. Asked whether he had been waving goodbye he replied: "Maybe, maybe." – *There's no maybe to it. Tévez is saying goodbye.*

VIEWS FROM THE PRESSBOX

"United are living in a sunny spell and possess just about everything they need. With the Old Trafford club about to equal Liverpool's total of 18 League titles, it was easy to see why Rafael Benítez chose to play to the Anfield gallery last week with his suggestion that United are not necessarily the best team. That was the Spaniard's way of reminding everyone that Liverpool had beaten them home and away. In their league fixtures with the rest of the top four Ferguson's team have had only one victory, against a Chelsea line-up whose manager Luiz Felipe Scolari was soon to be dismissed . In the different context of the Champions League, United would show their superiority with the harrowing of Arsenal.

"Benítez's line of argument is, intrinsically, ridiculous. What procedure could be more rigorous than 20 sides meeting one another home and away over 10 months? The Liverpool manager can fault United, but he has explaining to do for his own side's wavering in January, when they drew three consecutive matches, allowing late equalisers against Everton and Wigan. At a critical phase when they could have consolidated, Liverpool faltered.

"Progress has been made at Anfield and they are a little nearer to supplanting Ferguson's team. Even so, the reigning champions are adept at working to slender margins. United have often won by a hair's breadth in their melodramatic history, but the difference in modern times is that they virtually do it on purpose. This is an outstanding line-up and, with few members approaching the end of their careers, these footballers may well go down as the greatest in the club's history. The case might be unanswerable nine days from now if the Champions League is retained against Barcelona." – *The Guardian puts Benitez in his place.*

CHANT OF THE WEEK

"18 years. AND THAT'S A FACT" – *Predictable but who cares, it's true.*

STAT OF THE WEEK

7-16 – the score (between United and Liverpool) in league titles when Fergie arrived in Manchester.
18-18 – the score now.

MATCH FACTS

UNITED: VAN DER SAR, O'SHEA, VIDIC, EVANS, EVRA, RONALDO, FLETCHER, CARRICK, GIGGS, ROONEY (ANDERSON 90), TÉVEZ (PARK 67)
ARSENAL: FABIANSKI, SAGNA, TOURE, SONG BILLONG, GIBBS (EBOUE 76), NASRI (BENDTNER 69), DENILSON, DIABY, FABREGAS, ARSHAVIN (WALCOTT 69), VAN PERSIE [WENGER]
BOOKED: VAN PERSIE, ARSHAVIN, FABREGAS, NASRI, SONG BILLONG.
ATT: 75,468 REF: MIKE DEAN H-T: 0-0

OTHER SCORES

WEST BROM 0 LIVERPOOL 3; CHELSEA 2 BLACKBURN 0

LEAGUE TABLE

1. UNITED 87 (37); 2. LIVERPOOL 83 (37); 3. CHELSEA 80 (37);

*"Being part of Manchester United
is the greatest ride in the world"*

NEWS

VIDIC SHOULD HAVE cleaned up at the PFA and FWA bashes. Instead he has to make do with being awarded the Fans' Player of the Year and Players' Player of the Year at the club's end of season do. Other awards go to Ronaldo (for his goal of a lifetime at Porto) and James Chester (Reserve Player of the Year gong) while the Academy prize goes to a young Italian they think might make a name for himself (that's Macheda if you've just tuned in). Not for the first time, the papers try and make a drama about us fielding a weakened team at Hull on the final day. The story dies an instant death when Newcastle, Sunderland and Boro all agree that Fergie has earned the right to pick the team that he wants. United fans get the go ahead to unveil a massive mural before the European Cup Final paying tribute to Sir Matt. And Liverpool, stunned by losing their status as English football's most successful club, make an amusing stab at rewriting history...

GETTING DESPERATE
From the official Liverpool website:
    'Ask any Kopite how many League titles Liverpool Football Club have won and 99 times out of 100 they'll tell you it's 18. It's widely regarded as the record number of championship triumphs in England, but in actual fact, we've won 20. We won one in the First World War (1916) and another one in the Second World War (1943).'
    Only two problems with that theory chaps. The wartime leagues weren't a proper competition because teams basically fielded whichever soldiers happened to be on leave nearby. And in 1943 Blackpool won the northern title, Arsenal the southern title, Lovell's Athletic the western regional gong. And the Scousers won nothing.

EEERIE SEQUENCE OF THE WEEK
The Telegraph picks up on a strange pattern of league wins that United and Liverpool have followed over the years:
    "Liverpool won two titles before United had drawn blood. Then

United won two without Liverpool interruption. Then Liverpool won three, before United picked up three. Then Liverpool took one, United one, Liverpool one and United one. Then Liverpool won 11 without Mancunian intervention, before United completed the same number this season."

QUOTE OF THE WEEK I

"The tribalism [in English football] forces you to do well in the Premier League but the real excitement comes in Europe. The Wednesday night atmosphere when you, maybe, go to Madrid and Barcelona. You can smell the cigars and there's perfume wafting down from the stands. It's wonderful, it's different. I love it. You go to Milan and everyone's so stylish. Every woman who passes you by is Miss World. The whole atmosphere at these places is unreal." – *Fergie the Europhile.*

QUOTES OF THE WEEK I

"I am honoured. It is amazing to win these awards, especially when I consider the quality of the players I play alongside every day. I would like to say thank you to the fans and to my team-mates. I enjoy being here every day and playing with these players and working with the coaches. I'm very happy here at United." – *Vidic, the undisputed player of the year.*

"On Saturday I was thinking that no other team has won the title four times on the trot and that is the challenge for next season." – *Giggsy even sounds like Fergie these days.*

"He was a sentimental man and he would be absolutely delighted that the fans still remember him with such affection and still sing songs in his honour. But this is something else - he will be the proudest man in heaven." – *Sandy Busby on the planned tribute to his dad in Rome.*

BITTER LOSER OF THE WEEK

"I prefer just to say well done to the club, a big club, a good club. Normally you have to be polite and respect the other manager but during the season we have seen a lot of things that I didn't like, so that's it. I say congratulations to United because they have won. And that's it." – *Benitez. Sigh.*

"We may well break our transfer record, but certainly not Manchester United's. But it does not matter about the prices, it is doing the right thing and finding the right players. The next step is to overcome Manchester United, and that is the hardest. It does all come down to the money they have been able to spend, that is the difference." – *For once Rafa, look at the damn facts, the real ones, the ones that show we've both spent about the same.*

QUOTES OF THE WEEK II

"That's a nonsense. Analysis was done that shows we're broadly in line with them over the last few years in terms of net spend on players. – *Gill rips into Benitez's money moan.*

"We are confident all our players will be here next season. Things will develop during the close season like they always do at such a big club. But the manager will deal with those situations" – *What did the FA say about Mickey Phelan being an unreliable witness?*

"I will try to persuade Carlos to stay, We need him and the fans love him. I speak with him every day. He won't go anywhere because I will keep him in my house." – *Evra on his fellow Three Amigo, Tévez. It's too late though. He's all but gone.*

QUOTE OF THE WEEK II

"Being part of Manchester United is the greatest ride in the world" – *Sir Bobby*

FAPL 24/05/2009

HULL 0 UNITED 1
Gibson 24

IF THIS HAD been any other day all the attention would have been on Gibson's screamer, the raw but exciting talent of Danny Welbeck and the scary sight – for the rest of the league anyway – of us dominating a pumped-up Premiership team on their own turf with a team featuring Gary Neville and half-a-dozen players who could be his kids. But of course the big story wasn't at KC Stadium, where United's third team were making their debut. It came 100 miles away at Villa Park where Newcastle – farcical, ludicrous Newcastle – were fighting for their Premiership lives. They needed to better what Hull did here. In the end they were just as bad. And the sight of Barcodes getting their moobs out in midwinter will be restricted to Championship grounds next season. You shouldn't laugh, you shouldn't laugh, but what the hell. All together now, "Cheer up Alan Shearer, oh what can it mean..."

GOAL!

1-0 (24): When he did next to nothing on loan to Wolves even Darron Gibson must have doubted his ability to make it at United. A year on you just wonder how he managed to struggle in the Championship (though the fact Mick McCarthy was there might have something to do with it). He's not a certainty to make it at Old Trafford, not with all the other midfield talent on the books, but he's certainly got the class and style. If Carrick is the most technically gifted passer of the ball at the club, Gibson isn't far behind. And, as he showed here, he's got bullets in his boots. His first league goal was sensational, a dipping, curling, thumping drive from the left angle of the box.

WHAT WAS GOOD?

WELBECK – another Henry? OK, he spends chunks of each game running up blind alleys, tripping over the ball and getting the blinkers on. But Fergie wouldn't have said the things he said about him if he wasn't special. And when he was running round, past and through Hull's defence you could see what he meant. His turn of pace is unbelievable. He's strong and he's skilful. And he's from Manchester.

WHAT MORE COULD YOU WANT?

HULL SURVIVED - OK, they stunk the place out here, as they have done pretty much since Phil Brown lost the plot and gave his half-time team talk on the pitch at Eastlands. But in a defence-minded league they deserve to survive just for the spirit and ambition they brought to their game in the autumn. No other team in the bottom half gave it such a go at Old Trafford as they did.

SHEARER – the 'Messiah' takes Newcastle down. How brilliantly was this season scripted?

WHAT WAS BAD?

PHIL BROWN'S POST-MATCH SINGING – the most embarrassing on-pitch incident since Delia Smith grabbed the mic and started screaming 'Let's be havin' you' in 2005. It's weird. At the start of the season Phil Brown was possibly the nation's favourite manager, urbane, funny, open. Now he's like David O'Leary without the piggy nose... cringeworthy, perma-tanned, self-publicising and annoying.

NEWCASTLE, MIDDLESBROUGH, WEST BROM: going down while Bolton, Stoke and the rest stay up – No matter how amusing it is to see the Toon Army in the Championship, and how much of a relief it is for us to lose one of our bogey grounds (The Riverside), at least the relegated teams could be counted on to play some football. How many of the other sides who finished in the bottom half of the table can say that?

VIEWS FROM THE PRESSBOX

"The sudden release of tension can do funny things to people. After the final whistle, Phil Brown grabbed the microphone for a performance that proved he was right to go into coaching rather than crooning. He belted out a verse of Sloop John B, by The Beach Boys, the lyric given a more positive slant: "I don't wanna go home/ this is the best trip I've ever been on". – *The Times picks up on the most cringe-worthy sight/noise of the day.*

FACT OF THE DAY

Liverpool are the first team ever to not win the league having lost only two matches.

STAT OF THE DAY

261 – What United's squad numbers against Hull added up to. An unofficial record.

UNITED STORY OF THE DAY

RITCHIE DE LAET : Before his debut here, the Belgian's most recent first-team outing had been in November for Wrexham in front of 2,403 fans at Kidderminster in the Vauxhall Conference. He was replaced after just 39 minutes.

MATCH FACTS

HULL: MYHILL, RICKETTS, TURNER, KILBANE, DAWSON, GARCIA (COUSIN 81), MARNEY, BOATENG, BARMBY (MENDY 68), GEOVANNI (FOLAN 54), FAGAN [BROWN] BOOKED: BARMBY, MARNEY
UNITED: KUSZCZAK, RAFAEL DA SILVA (ECKERSLEY 60), NEVILLE, BROWN, DE LAET (POSSEBON 79), NANI, FLETCHER, GIBSON, WELBECK (TOSIC 87), MARTIN, MACHEDA. BOOKED: GIBSON.
KC STADIUM ATT: 24,945 REF: ALAN WILEY H-T: 0-1

OTHER SCORES

LIVERPOOL 3 SPURS 1, ASTON VILLA 1 NEWCASTLE 0,
SUNDERLAND 2 CHELSEA 3, WEST HAM 2 MIDDLESBROUGH 1

FINAL LEAGUE TABLE:

1.	MANCHESTER UNITED	38	28	6	4	68	24	+44	90
2.	LIVERPOOL	38	25	11	2	77	27	+50	86
3.	CHELSEA	38	25	8	5	68	24	+44	83
4.	ARSENAL	38	20	12	6	68	37	+31	72
5.	EVERTON	38	17	12	9	55	37	+18	63
6.	ASTON VILLA	38	17	11	10	54	48	+6	62
7.	FULHAM	38	14	11	13	39	34	+5	53
8.	TOTTENHAM HOTSPUR	38	14	9	15	45	45	0	51
9	WEST HAM UNITED	38	14	9	15	42	45	−3	51
10.	MANCHESTER CITY	38	15	5	18	58	50	+8	50
11.	WIGAN ATHLETIC	38	12	9	17	34	45	−11	45
12.	STOKE CITY	38	12	9	17	38	55	−17	45
13.	BOLTON WANDERERS	38	11	8	19	41	53	−12	41
14.	PORTSMOUTH	38	10	11	17	38	57	−19	41
15.	BLACKBURN ROVERS	38	10	11	17	40	60	−20	41
16.	SUNDERLAND	38	9	9	20	34	54	−20	36
17.	HULL CITY	38	8	11	19	39	64	−25	35
18.	NEWCASTLE UNITED	38	7	13	18	40	59	−19	34
19.	MIDDLESBROUGH	38	7	11	20	28	57	−29	32
20.	WEST BROMWICH ALBION	38	8	8	22	36	67	−31	32

*"I'm going to strip myself butt-naked
and run round the stadium if I score."*

NEWS

BURNLEY ARE BACK in the big league for the first time since 1976
after beating Sheffield United 1-0 in the play-off final. They join
Wolves and Birmingham in the Premier League while Newcastle,
Boro and West Brom go the other way. Cheer up Geordies, at least
you'll have a trip to Blackpool to look forward to. Gary Nev earns
a surprise recall to the England team for the summer double-header
against Kazakhstan and Andorra. If he plays one more game he'll
equal Kenny Sansom's record for a full-back of 86 caps.

The *News of the World* links us with a swoop for Stephen Ireland.
He's got more chance of looking like Barry Gibb. *The Mirror* says that
Ronaldo warmed up for Rome by 'scoring' (see what they've done
there?) with a blonde in an Italian restaurant. Rome-bound Reds are
left dismayed as the authorities announce a ban on the sale of alcohol
on the day of the final... then relieved as it turns out that the ban
only affects areas around the Stadio Olimpico. And the 26th sees us
celebrate the 10th anniversary of the Barcelona miracle... and the

100th birthday of the man who made it all happen, Sir Matt.

NOU CAMP MEMORIES OF THE WEEK

"This was a great shock. We could have won the Champions League title for the first time in 23 years. It was the hardest, toughest, most dramatic defeat I remember. We needed over a year to handle the loss." – *Bayern's Aryan stereotype Oliver Kahn*

"Some players went to bed, some players went to the party - I was with my parents, staring at the table." – *But while depression was setting in at the Kahn table…*

"I've never celebrated on a pitch for so long, I think we must have done three or four laps of honour. We really milked the moment. We were not just celebrating the Champions League, we were celebrating the previous 11 days, winning the Premier League and the FA Cup. We chilled out in the bath after that for a while but we made up for it that night, we were still partying at seven in the morning. Without a doubt it was the most enthusiastic celebrations of my career – we were celebrating winning the Treble, so we made it one hell of a party in Barcelona" – *Teddy Sheringham was getting ready for the night of all nights.*

EBAY SELLER OF THE WEEK

A Scouser tries to flog a replica Liverpool away shirt on ebay. And earns himself a verbal seeing-to from football365:

'This is Liverpool FC unique embroided away shirt shirt,this beautiful shirt has been embroided professionally as you can see in the pictures, it has the match details and result from the Manchester Massacare, the day we hammered the so called world champions on thier own theatre of nightmares, this shirt would be a great addition to any shirt collector either of Liverpool FC or just a collector of shirts in general, shirt is in near new mint condition and is xlarge in size (spelling mistake),,from pet and smoke free home,,selling at a very low price.' *Well if it comes from a 'PET AND SMOKE FREE HOME', it's well worth the £25 asking price. One question though…what's a massacare?*

QUOTES OF THE WEEK

"Alan Shearer has been brilliant for eight weeks. If there is one man to get us back up into the Premier League, it is him." – *Damien Duff does a fine job of ignoring the facts, particularly the one that says that Shearer won just five points from the eight games he was in charge.*

"We have to be proud because when you talk about 86 points, it's massive. But still it's not enough to win the title. Clearly we have to improve and be almost perfect if we want to win the title." – *Has Benitez inadvertently just called us 'almost perfect'?*

QUOTE OF THE WEEK

"I don't know in how many years' time, but my name is already written on the Manchester United bench." – *Eric the Red wants to be United manager...*

"I'm not saying Ferguson will go. I hope with all my heart that he has eternal life with the Reds." – *Eric finishes off."* ... *but only when Fergie says it's time to go.*

RUNNER-UP

"Honestly, nothing is like Manchester United... When you play for Manchester United it's something else. When you play in Old Trafford you don't need sunshine. Every day I just say 'Thank God I play for United'." – *The legendary Paddy E.*

UNLIKELY FORFEIT OF THE WEEK

"I'm going to strip myself butt-naked and run round the stadium if I score." – *Anderson (75 United games, 0 goals)*

CHAMPIONS LEAGUE FINAL
27/05/2009

BARCELONA 2 UNITED 0
Eto'o 10, Messi 70

WHAT A DIFFERENCE 81 minutes make. For the opening nine minutes in Rome United were strutting around the pitch like legends in the making. We were too quick and slick for Barcelona who just couldn't get a foot on the ball. Ronaldo fired in three shots before Messi had a meaningful touch. Only a brilliant block from Pique stopped Park sidefooting United in front. And then Iniesta slides in Eto'o on the right, he cuts inside Vidic and, bang...

The rest of the night was a horrible blur. We waited for United to react. We waited for Barcelona to give the ball away. We waited for our midfield to get in the same frame as the peerless Xavi and Iniesta. And for Rooney and Ronaldo to do something magical. And we waited. And we waited. And waited. And all we got in return was as painful and embarrassing lesson in cerebral football, the likes of which I can only remember us suffering twice. In the San Siro in 1997 and the Nou Camp in 1994.

So instead of watching United make history as the first team to retain the Champions League, we watched a great Barcelona side celebrate their own historic treble. But not even those pressbox ABUs who queued up afterwards to slag us off and – bizarrely – write the team's obituary could dispute the facts. The 2008-9 season didn't make for a great drama. The football had been just too dull for that, there had been too many annoying distractions (Japan, Ronaldo and Tévez) and too few goals, while this final reel should definitely have been left to collect dust on the cutting room floor. But try telling any United fan that the blip against Barcelona meant this season was one to forget. For the last five months we'd been able to sing that we were the Champions of England, Champions of Europe and Champions of the World. And how many of us, back when Kenny Dalglish was guiding Liverpool to their last league title – 19 long Scouse years ago – would ever have thought we'd be able to do that...

MATCH FACTS

BARCELONA: VALDES, PUYOL, TOURE YAYA, PIQUE, SYLVINHO, XAVI, BUSQUETS, INIESTA (PEDRITO 90), MESSI, ETO'O, HENRY (KEITA 72) [GUARDIOLA]
SUBS NOT USED: PINTO, CACERES, MUNIESA, GUDJOHNSEN, BOJAN
BOOKED: PIQUE
UNITED: VAN DER SAR, O'SHEA, FERDINAND, VIDIC, EVRA, ANDERSON (TÉVEZ 46), CARRICK, GIGGS (SCHOLES 75), PARK (BERBATOV 66), RONALDO, ROONEY
SUBS NOT USED: KUSZCZAK, RAFAEL, EVANS, NANI
BOOKED: RONALDO, SCHOLES, VIDIC
STADIO OLIMPICO ATT: 72,700 REF: MASSIMO BUSACCA (SWITZERLAND)
H-T: 0-I

EPILOGUE

It's 10 o'clock in the morning of 11th June 2009...

As THE RED Republik settles down to work, we receive the news many of us had been dreading – and Red hardliners had been waiting for - for over a year. Ronaldo has got his wish. Fergie, who'd vowed never to sell that Spanish mob a virus, never mind the best United player since Best, has given his blessing to an £80 million move to Madrid.

It marked the end of an era for United, and a giant step into the unknown. Inevitably we're going to miss him. How could any team not miss their chief weapon, the guy who's scored 91 goals in his last 143 appearances, a player who can play every forward position brilliantly (often at the same time), who can head the ball like Tommy Taylor, who takes free-kicks like no other player ever has and who can score from 40 yards and produce miracles on tap?

But just how much will we miss him? Will United flatter to deceive as they did in the wake of Eric's departure in '97? Will we continue to be a force in England but struggle without the Ronnie factor in Europe? Or will we be a better team now there's no Ronaldo there to rely on?

A quite bizarre summer of transfer dealing only served to muddy the waters. Tévez, as expected, joined the big-name castoffs lured to Eastlands. Fergie's prime target - the sulky Frenchman Benzema - joined Ronaldo, Kaka and the rest at Madrid. Links with David Villa, David Silva, Sergio Aguero and the ludicrously overpriced Ribery sadly came to nothing. Manucho followed Ronaldo to Spain. And who came in? Gabriel Obertan, a young Frenchman with reported pyscholigical problems who'd struggled to get a game for Bordeaux. Antonia Valencia, an unproven speed merchant from Wigan. And, most bizarre of all, Michael Owen, whose career had plumbed such depths that his agents had felt the need to issue a brochure reminding people of his past glories, on a free from Newcastle.

As the new season loomed into view, we'd lost the best player on the planet and last season's terrace hero. And we'd replaced them with the next David Bellion, a winger with 7 goals to his name in 3 seasons and a jowly shadow of the Scouse tyro we'd spent the best part of a decade despising. In the circumstances it was hard not to be a little concerned about our prospects.

But there is hope, plenty of it. United's title success was based on our defence. And they're all there again, Vidic, Evra, Rio and the rest. Berbatov, who suffered as much as anyone from the Ronaldo dependency last year, is just too talented not to shove the boos down the idiots' throats this time aroud.

But best of all, the real heart of soul of United remains. Rooney allowed himself to get sucked into Ronaldo's shadow over the last 3 years. Now he's the undisputed main man, it's time for him to make the leap into greatness we've been waiting for ever since that hat-trick against Fenerbahce. And if 2009/10 turns out to be Rooney's year, I'll bet anything it will be United's too.

And if Owen, the man we used to despise and harangue like no other, can pop in a Derby day winner, all will be forgiven on that score too...

MANCHESTER UNITED 2008-09

Sun 10 Aug	PORTSMOUTH	N	CS	0-0		84,8

after extra time, Manchester United won 3-1 on penalties; played at Wembley

Sun 17 Aug	NEWCASTLE UTD	H	L	1-1	*Fletcher 24*	75,5
Mon 25 Aug	PORTSMOUTH	A	L	1-0	*Fletcher 32*	20,5
Fri 29 Aug	ZENIT	N	SC	1-2	*Vidic 73*	

played at Stade Louis II, Monaco

Sat 13 Sep	LIVERPOOL	A	L	1-2	*Tevez 3*	44,1
Wed 17 Sep	VILLARREAL	H	CL	0-0		74,9
Sun 21 Sep	CHELSEA	A	L	1-1	*Park 18*	41,7(
Tue 23 Sep	MIDDLESBROUGH	H	LC	3-1	*Ronaldo 25; Giggs 79; Nani 90*	53,7
Sat 27 Sep	BOLTON W	H	L	2-0	*Ronaldo 60p; Rooney 77*	75,4
Tue 30 Sep	AAB AALBORG	A	CL	3-0	*Rooney 22; Berbatov 55,79*	10,3
Sat 04 Oct	BLACKBURN R	A	L	2-0	*Brown 31; Rooney 64*	27,3
Sat 18 Oct	WBA	H	L	4-0	*Rooney 56; Ronaldo 69;*	
					Berbatov 72; Nani 90	75,4
Tue 21 Oct	CELTIC	H	CL	3-0	*Berbatov 29,51; Rooney 76*	74,6
Sat 25 Oct	EVERTON	A	L	1-1	*Fletcher 22*	36,0
Wed 29 Oct	WEST HAM	H	L	2-0	*Ronaldo 14,30*	75,3
Sat 01 Nov	HULL CITY	H	L	4-3	*Ronaldo 3,44; Carrick 29; Vidic 57*	75,3
Wed 05 Nov	CELTIC	A	CL	1-1	*Giggs 84*	58,9
Sat 08 Nov	ARSENAL	A	L	1-2	*Rafael 90*	60,1
Tue 11 Nov	QPR	H	LC	1-0	*Tevez 76p*	62,5
Sat 15 Nov	STOKE CITY	H	L	5-0	*Ronaldo 3,89; Carrick 45;*	
					Berbatov 49; Welbeck 84	75,3
Sat 22 Nov	ASTON VILLA	A	L	0-0		42,5
Tue 25 Nov	VILLARREAL	A	CL	0-0		26,0
Sun 30 Nov	MANCHESTER CITY	A	L	1-0	*Rooney 42*	47,3
Wed 03 Dec	BLACKBURN R	H	LC	5-3	*Tevez 36,51p,54,90; Nani 40*	53,9
Sat 06 Dec	SUNDERLAND	H	L	1-0	*Vidic 90*	75,4
Wed 10 Dec	AAB AALBORG	H	CL	2-2	*Tevez 3; Rooney 52*	74,3
Sat 13 Dec	TOTTENHAM H	A	L	0-0		35,8
Fri 26 Dec	STOKE CITY	A	L	1-0	*Tevez 83*	27,5
Mon 29 Dec	MIDDLESBROUGH	H	L	1-0	*Berbatov 69*	75,2
Sun 04 Jan	SOUTHAMPTON	A	FAC	3-0	*Welbeck 20; Nani 48p; Gibson 81*	31,9
Wed 07 Jan	DERBY COUNTY	A	LC	0-1		30,1
Sun 11 Jan	CHELSEA	H	L	3-0	*Vidic 45; Rooney 63; Berbatov 87*	75,4
Wed 14 Jan	WIGAN ATHLETIC	H	L	1-0	*Rooney 1*	73,9
Sat 17 Jan	BOLTON W	A	L	1-0	*Berbatov 90*	26,0